S0-AUA-349

TV TIE-INS

A BIBLIOGRAPHY OF
AMERICAN TV TIE-IN PAPERBACKS

KURT PEER

NEPTUNE PUBLISHING
Tucson, Arizona
1997

TV Tie-Ins: A Bibliography of American TV Tie-In Paperbacks

Copyright © 1997 by Kurt Peer. All rights reserved. Printed in the United States of America. No part of this book may be used or reproduced in any manner without prior written permission, except in the case of brief quotations embodied in critical articles or reviews. For information, contact:

Neptune Publishing
P.O. Box 32066
Tucson, Arizona 85751

FIRST EDITION

ISBN 0-9654536-3-4 (softcover)
ISBN 0-9654536-4-2 (hardcover)

Library of Congress Catalog Card Number: 96-92907

Additional copies of this book may be purchased through Neptune Publishing at the above address for $24.95 softcover or $55.00 hardcover. Add $4.00 postage and handling for the first book and $2.50 for each additional book. Arizona residents please add 7% sales tax.

Neptune Books are available at quantity discounts with bulk purchases for educational, entertainment, or sales promotional uses. For more information, contact the publisher at 1-800-992-1093; Fax 1-800-968-5675; E-mail kpeer@mindspring.com. Also, check out our Website at http://www.mindspring.com/~tvtieins.

All photos are used for illustration purposes only and are not meant to infringe on the rights of any party. This is a scholarly work intending to explore the evolution of TV tie-ins through 1990.

TABLE OF CONTENTS

To Fred
and TV fans everywhere

ACKNOWLEDGEMENTS

This work would not have been possible without the generous assistance of many individuals. I would like to thank Lance Casebeer of Portland, Oregon, with whose encouragement this work took shape initially. The kingpin of paperback book collecting, and holder of one of the largest collections in the world, Casebeer's home is a museum of paperbacks and the site of the annual "Lance-Con" conventions held each August.

Special thanks also to Bill Ewald of Argus Books in Sacramento, for providing essential information in the early stages of this work, and for his continued support throughout.

Many special thanks to friend Fred Delich, computer programmer extraordinaire, for creating the magnificent TV tie-in database using the FilePro software. Without his diligence and true expertise, this work would also not have been possible.

Special thanks also to Jeff Thompson, for his expertise on *Dark Shadows* and related subjects, and for putting me in touch with "Marilyn" Ross.

Special thanks to Derek Tague, TV buff, for his research assistance, which helped get me through a number of situations.

Special thanks also to the following individuals, for contributing information or assistance: Diane Albert; Burl Barer; Peter Barkley; Victor Berch; Daniel Bodenheimer; Terry S. Bowers; Joe Brockowski; Kevin Burns; Phyllis Butters; Ned Cumstock; Scott Cupp; Bruce Edwards; Mark Garvey; Judy Lee Goldenberg; Bridget Hanley; Steve Holland; Rose Idlet; Ken Johnson; Cherie Kendall; Kathy Lewis; the research staffs at the City of Phoenix, City of Tempe, and City of Scottsdale Libraries; Larry Lowery; Nina Martin; Scott McAdam; Jeff Michael; Michael and Patrick and Gerald; Lynn Munroe; Will Murray; Robert Newnham; Gil O'Gara; Paul Payne; Karen Plunkett-Powell;

Barbara Pazmino; Gail Reese; Jeff Roadknight; Steve Santi; Jack Santore; Kathy Simmons; David Spencer; Robert Speray; James Tate; Linda Terpstra; Shanny and Colette; Albert Tonik; Raymond J. Torrence; Karen Valentine; Gordon Van Gelder; Fred Velez; Helen Weber; and Rhonda Wharnke.

Special thanks also to my Mother and Father and the rest of my family, and to Willie Turner and Michael and Joel and Martin for their support, and to Jim Grossmann, for his editorial assistance.

Finally, many special thanks to the TV tie-in authors and editors themselves, for lending their support and sharing their stories in the making of this work: Angelica Aimes; Richard Anobile; Michael Avallone; Jay Barbree; Donald Bensen; Lee Bergman; Joe Blades; James A. Bryans; Lou Cameron; Bruce Cassiday; Louis Chunovic; Joel Cohen; Norman Daniels; Kate Duffy; Harlan Ellison; Rolf Erikson; Skip and Gloria Fickling; Leonore Fleischer; Alan Dean Foster; Dudley Frasier; Richard Gallagher; Ron Goulart; Jerry Gross; Lee Hays; Evan Heyman; Michael Jahn; Paul Kupperberg; Alan Landsburg; Elizabeth Levy; Rob MacGregor; Kathleen Malley; Jack Matcha; Doris Meredith; Tom Miller; Victor Miller; Evan Morley; Patrick O'Connor; Talmage Powell; Thom Racina; Ron Renauld; Dan Ross; William Rotsler; Rosemarie Santini; Mrs. Con Sellers; Jane Seskin; Gordon Shirreffs; Henry Slesar; Dorothea Snow; Wayne Sotona; Madeline Tabler; Robert Tralins; David Vowell; Walter Wager; Howard Weinstein; Robert Weverka; Collin Wilcox; Richard Woodley; and Patrick Macnee.

INTRODUCTION

Television and TV Tie-Ins: A Brief History

Television: The transmission and reception of sound and visual images by electronic means; a set for receiving such broadcasts.

Paperback: A book with a flexible paper binding and covers.

Tie-In: An arrangement whereby related products are marketed or sold together; a book that inspired or was inspired by a movie or television program.

* * *

Television as a widespread mass medium has been around since the middle of the 20th Century, but its early history goes back much further than that. It wasn't invented by any one person nor developed overnight, but evolved over decades through the efforts of numerous individuals building on the work of their predecessors. TV's earliest beginnings are traced back to 1873, when it was accidentally discovered that the element selenium was a strong conductor of electricity when exposed to light, and that its electrical resistance varied with the amount of light shining on it ... and the idea of sending pictures by wire (converting light variances into electrical signals) was born. Excited by the possibilities, several schemes were quickly set into motion, and for the next 40 years a handful of inventors developed some of the basic components of the TV set. The ground had been broken and the stage was set, but it was all brought to a halt by World War I.

Following the war the work resumed, with a number of large corporations becoming involved. In 1923 Vladimir Zworkyin invented

1

the iconoscope (the basic eye of the TV set), and came to be known as the "Father of Television" for it. In 1927 the first public demonstration of a TV set was made; in 1928 the first public broadcast was transmitted. During the 1930's, RCA, General Electric, AT&T, and other companies worked to improve the quality of the TV set, and while a limited number of shows were broadcast during this period, it wasn't until 1939 (with the opening of the World's Fair in New York) that regular public programming was first launched. For the next two years, New York City's NBC and CBS stations broadcasted shows to a local audience which grew to some 50,000 viewers. The medium was beginning to pick up steam, but it was brought to a halt by World War II.

With the end of that war in 1945 the work was resumed again with renewed vigor, and television as it is today truly began. TV stations sprung up around the country, regional networks were formed, and the number of sets in use jumped from 6,000 in 1946 to nearly 10 million in 1950. In 1949 the East Coast and Midwest were linked; in 1951 the link was completed to the West Coast. The medium as it then came to be known--the big three networks with a nationwide affiliation and viewing audience--took firm hold in the early 1950's. Throughout that decade (which saw the sale of some 70 million sets, and which also saw movie theater attendance drop by nearly 75 percent), television quickly and irreversibly wove itself into the American cultural landscape.

It was during the 1950's that another cultural phenomenon was also taking hold, that of the paperback book. While paperbacks had been published sporadically in the 19th Century, it wasn't until the 1930's that they were first introduced on a large scale, by England's Penguin Books in 1936 and America's Pocket Books in 1939. This new form of book signaled a new chapter in the publishing industry. During World War II the demand for books soared, and led to the publishing and distribution to the armed forces of some 125 million paperbacks in a government-sponsored effort. Following the war paperbacks flourished, and by the early 1950's the paperback revolution was firmly underway. During that decade, thanks to their cheapness, wide range of literature covered, and ease of distribution, paperbacks became a dominant force in the publishing industry and spread throughout the world, coincident with the rise of TV.

Concerning TV, by 1960 most American households had at least one set, as that medium too was spreading its influence throughout society (and indeed shaping society). The influence that television has had is profound. Other significant inventions like the telephone, automobile, airplane, and computer have contributed their parts in altering the course of history and furthering the advancement of humanity, but the TV set stands out in its cultural influence and immediacy.

TV's influence, which has gone largely unchecked, has taken place in manners which are easy to identify (it has made news and information readily available, provided entertainment and an escape from our daily lives, given us heroes and role models to identify with, created marketing trends, shaped politics, etc.) and in manners which can only be guessed at. It is currently estimated that 98 percent of American households have at least one TV set, and that the average household watches TV for more than five hours a day. Americans traveling abroad note how little TV is watched in foreign countries by comparison (noted one foreigner: "The problem with America is the TV set"), and many people feel there's a direct link between television and how value-depleted and violence-prone our own culture has become.

TV's early years--from the mid-1950's to the mid-1960's--are often referred to as the "Golden Age of Television," for it was during that time that the medium retained its youthful innocence and charm, and shows like *I Love Lucy* and *Bewitched*, *Gunsmoke* and *Bonanza*, *Lost in Space* and *Star Trek* were being shown for the first times in our living rooms.

Nowadays the popularity of such shows is on the rise, just as the good old days the shows represent drift further into the past. A popular culture phenomenon of the 1990's is in fact the renewed popularity of these classic shows. Television became a forum for artistic expression and cultural snapshot, and by watching these shows nowadays one is reminded of one's past and of the styles, products, and ideals of the times. Thanks to cable networks, VCR's, the Information Superhighway, and dedicated fans, the shows are becoming more and more assessable. Many are being resurrected through a slew of such recent movies as *The Fugitive*, *The Brady Bunch Movie*, *Maverick*, and *Mission: Impossible*, movies which are giving renewed life to the original shows, and helping preserve TV's heritage.

TV's heritage is being preserved through another means as well, for it was during these early years that paperback book publishers were issuing hundreds of books--TV tie-ins--about the shows. First published in the mid-1950's, during the paperback revolution, TV tie-ins became commonplace by the early 1960's, and then the floodgates opened! The period from the early 1960's to the early 1970's is clearly the heyday of TV tie-ins, for it was during that time that the majority were issued. They began to decline in the late 1970's, however, and since the early 1980's far fewer have been published. TV tie-ins thus have a distinct place on the American cultural landscape, as paperback representatives of TV's earlier years. The books are almost like snapshots from an imaginary past, for the covers of most TV tie-ins bear photographs taken from the shows.

While TV tie-ins were published to be read and discarded, they were also being collected, and the decade of the 1980's saw their popularity among book collectors rise. Just as the old TV shows were becoming more popular, so too were the TV tie-ins about them. Their connection to the hit shows of the time, and their sequential natures (most TV tie-ins were issued in numbered series) helped drive their collectability. Today, TV tie-ins are among the hottest collectible categories of paperback books.

TV Tie-Ins Defined

In its most basic sense, a TV tie-in is taken to mean a paperback book that was based on or issued in conjunction with a TV show. However, every definition of TV tie-ins will have at least a few exceptions and be subject to some interpretation. Broadly speaking, any merchandise originally intended to promote a television show could be called a TV tie-in, and as such, there have been TV tie-in lunch boxes, toys, games, trading cards, etc., in addition to books. TV shows have been promoted in a variety of book formats as well, the most common of which is the mass market or regular-size paperback. Other, less common forms of books TV shows have been promoted in include trade or oversize paperbacks, hardbacks, coloring books, activity books, digests, annuals, etc. However, space does not permit a catalog of every TV tie-in book ever published, and as such this bibliography only covers mass market paperbacks (the term TV tie-in is often associated with the term mass market paperback anyway), a few oversize (generally, 7-1/2 inch tall) paperbacks (such as those published by Scholastic Book Services), and the Whitman line of children's hardbacks. The Whitmans include the 100-plus standard-size TV books plus the handful of Whitman "Big Little" TV books, but not the Whitman "Tell-A-Tale" books (the thin, 6-inch tall books). The Whitmans, which are the only hardbacks included, comprise a prominent subset of TV tie-ins, and are of interest to many. For a complete list of the Whitmans, please see that publisher in the section TV Tie-Ins Indexed by Publisher.

In addition to the United States, TV tie-ins have been published in such countries Great Britain, Australia, France, Japan, and Germany. However, the scope of this work is with the American TV tie-ins published through 1990. (Books about post-1990 shows, like *Beverly Hills 90210, Quantum Leap, Star Trek: Deep Space Nine,* and *The X Files,* are thus excluded.)

Concerning British TV tie-ins (whether British versions of American tie-ins, or separate British tie-ins altogether), while they're not included in this work in the sense that there are no entries for them, they are sometimes mentioned in the notes or narrative commentary section for a show. A British tie-in might be mentioned if it's a British version of an American tie-in but has a different title, byline, or series number from the American version, or when a British series has more titles than an American series (like *Alias Smith and Jones,* with two American and six British titles). It should also be noted that for the purposes of this work the country of a show's origin doesn't matter, so long as the books were published in America. Shows of British, Canadian, and Australian origin have all engendered American TV tie-ins.

TV Tie-Ins Described

The vast majority of TV tie-ins are novels, either original novels (original works by the author based on the characters and concepts from a show) or novelizations (books adapted from an episode or episodes of a show). However, TV tie-ins also include a wide assortment of cookbooks, humor books, joke books, cartoon books, puzzle books, anthologies (collections of short stories by different authors assembled by a single editor), short story collections (collections of stories by the same author), compilations (as with collections of fan mail), star biographies, books about the "making of" the shows, etc. The entries in this work cover the gamut from the above examples.

Most TV tie-ins bear a clear connection to the show they're about, which typically includes a reference to the TV show on the cover ("show-mention") and a photo of the star or stars. For instance, the book *The Man From U.N.C.L.E.* includes a photo of Robert Vaughn as Napoleon Solo on the cover, along with the blurb: "Based on the exciting MGM-ARENA TV series *The Man From U.N.C.L.E.*" The book *The Fugitive* includes a photo of David Janssen on the cover, along with the blurb: "Dr. Richard Kimble, the hunted innocent of ABC-TV's *The Fugitive*."

Some TV tie-ins are connected to a show more subtly, however. The book *This Man Dawson* makes no reference to the TV show on the cover nor pictures the star, and only mentions the show on the first page in the statement: "*This Man Dawson* is based on the popular television series produced by ZIV-United Artists, Inc. and starring Keith Andes." The book *Mr. Lucky* makes no reference to the show at all (on the covers or inside the book), but includes an illustration of star John Vivyan on the cover.

Finally, there are some books that make no reference to the TV shows they're about nor include any photos of the stars; only their titles, contents, and issue dates reveal a connection to the show. These are "inferred TV tie-ins," and an example is the book *Wanted: Dead or Alive*. This book makes no reference to the TV show and doesn't picture star Steve McQueen, but has the same title as the show, features the same character in Josh Randall, and was issued at the same time as the show, all of which infer its connection.

Other inferred TV tie-ins are found in certain series of books (a series being all of the books about a show by the same publisher), wherein one or two of the books in the series bears a connection to the show while the others do not. For instance, only the first book in the 13-book *Saint* Macfadden series includes a Roger Moore photo and mentions the show; the 12 sequels do not, but are included as inferred TV tie-ins. A similar situation is found in the Pocket *Peyton Place* series.

Which Came First?

TV tie-ins generally fall into two broad categories, depending on whether the show inspired the book or the book inspired the show. That is, which came first (the show or the book) and led to the other? In most cases it was the show that came first (the show aired, and the books quickly followed), but in some cases it was the book that came first (the book, which had been published previously, inspired the TV show, and was re-issued as a TV tie-in with the airing of the show). An example is with the TV show and book series *The Saint*. Published extensively since the 1930's, the Leslie Charteris mysteries inspired the TV show

The Saint in the 1960's, and with the airing of the show a number of the books were re-issued as TV tie-ins with Roger Moore covers.

Oftentimes, such show-inspiring books inspired a movie or series of movies prior to the show. For example, The Saint had been seen in a series of movies in the 1940's and 50's prior to the TV show. Other examples of such books include the *Dr. Kildare* books by Max Brand (first published in the 1930's, they inspired a series of movies in the 1930's and 40's prior to the 1961-66 show), the 1952 book *Executive Suite* (it inspired that 1954 movie prior to the 1976-77 show) and the book *Guestward Ho!* (first published in 1956, it inspired the 1960-61 TV show, but no movies). The point is that when such books, once having inspired a show, are re-issued as TV tie-ins with the airing of the show, the re-issues are included in the scope of this work.

The prior printings of such books, if they were issued by the same publisher that issued the TV tie-in reprints, are sometimes called "pre-TV tie-ins." That is, a pre-TV tie-in is a book that becomes a TV tie-in upon a subsequent printing, and while they're not included in this work, examples include the first printings of the books *The Asphalt Jungle, Anna and the King,* and the *Honey West* books.

An Important Disclaimer

Any pre-1990 mass market paperback or Whitman hardback by an American publisher that was issued in conjunction with and during the original run of a TV show is included within the scope of this work. Examples of books not included are books about mini-series, books about TV-specials, books about made-for-TV movies (unless the movie served as a show's pilot episode), books about cartoon shows (as opposed to cartoon books about regular shows, like Signet's *Batman* books), books published after a show was canceled (the idea being that books not only based on shows but consistent with their original time periods are sought), books about more than one show, and certain biographies. Finally, while recognizing that some subjectivity is necessarily involved in the defining of the scope of a work on this somewhat nebulous subject (no two people would draw the same exact boundaries), every attempt has been made to be as consistent and logical as possible in doing so.

This bibliography of mass market TV tie-ins is intended to be as thorough as possible, but by its nature it cannot be exhaustive. The kinds of books listed here were distributed on over 350 shows, over a period of 35 years, by some 50 different publishers that kept poor records, and include many obscure and scarce titles. Nevertheless, this work represents over 20 years of collecting and part-time research, and is quite probably the most complete bibliography of its kind available. Naturally, the author would appreciate any information on possible new entries.

Publishers and Studios

As television and paperbacks were emerging simultaneously as new social phenomena, the two mediums soon formed a common bond. The fast and furious world of paperback publishing and the mass entertainment world of TV found that by cross-pollinating or working together, their mutual interests could be enhanced. For the publishers TV tie-ins were a potentially profitable revenue source (notes author Michael Avallone, "Publishers wanted to make money, and TV hits were rather a guarantee of sales success"), for the studios the books were an effective means of advertising the shows - and a means they were most anxious to exploit.

The rights to the TV shows and characters were held by the studios, and the publishing of TV tie-ins involved first the licensing of a show's book rights to the publishers. The publishers had contacts at the studios, either through the studios' own Licensing Departments (which handled all subsidiary rights, including merchandising rights, theatrical rights, etc.) or through separate licensing companies, such as Licensing Corporation of America. The publishers would buy the name of the show and the right to use the characters. In cases where the publishers were subsidiaries of the studios (such as the Berkley Publishing division of MCA/Universal), the studios simply fed the books through to the publishers.

The rights for a single book, or for a single book plus an option for additional books, or for a set number of books that were packaged at a discount, would be purchased. Financial arrangements included an up front fee paid to the studio plus typically a royalties arrangement that took effect once a predetermined sales level was met. Ace paid $6,000 for the rights to the first *Man From U.N.C.L.E.* book; Popular Library paid $30,000 for the rights to the seven *I Spy* books. At an extreme, Popular Library paid $100,000 for the rights to *The Wit and Wisdom of Archie Bunker*, a book which sold over 1,000,000 copies and was a gamble that paid off for Editor-in-Chief James A. Bryans, one of the first people to recognize the potential of TV tie-ins.

The publishers would be risking a fair amount of money on a book (that paid to the studio, the writer, and the costs of production and distribution) but the financial rewards could be great. If a publisher guessed right and the show became a hit, the paperbacks could generate substantial immediate or long-term income. On the other hand, a show could be canceled before the books even hit the stands, causing at times heavy losses for the publishers. (Sometimes when a show was canceled early, books written and perhaps typeset and perhaps even printed but not yet distributed were simply written off at that point in an attempt to cut losses, and never made it to the public ... or into this bibliography.) And to further complicate things, since many publishers were doing TV tie-ins at the time there was often heavy competition among them for the rights to the books in the first place. (In any case, the shelf life of a TV tie-in was short; the book had very little time in which to perform - to either be purchased or returned to the publisher to make way for subsequent titles.)

Patrick O'Connor (Editor-in-Chief at Curtis, Popular Library, and Pinnacle) recalls: "At the beginning of each season we'd pack a lunch and go to the various networks and watch pilots all day. It was a fun day. And then afterwards we'd have some very serious decisions to make. We'd pick the shows we liked, and then negotiate, sometimes in competition, sometimes not ... Some shows worked and others didn't ... We'd pass the books out to our friends, who needed the money or were working on other projects ... The important thing was fast. The writers were always up against the deadline. Once the decision was made the books had to go into production fast. So, first we were interested in fast, and second we were interested in good, and very few people were able to do that. Walter Wager was one of the best."

Jerry Gross (Senior Editor at Ace, Editorial Director at Paperback Library): "You really took a gamble, because you didn't know if a show would hit a nerve with the public or not. And it was incredibly competitive, you had to move fast ... TV tie-ins were very important to the industry from a financial standpoint. *Dark Shadows* and *The Man From U.N.C.L.E.* just went on and on ... They declined because they became old hat and also I think the level of taste rose. There's a fierce competition for rack space, and people started to want a better quality book ... TV tie-ins are probably the earliest example of the power of TV on popular culture. Remember, TV was not as common then as it is now. What we take for granted now as an everyday part of our lives still had a lot of freshness and vitality to it. People literally watched the shows and went out and bought the books. They really helped sell each other ... Today if an author is on Oprah Winfrey or Rosie O'Donnell we know they'll sell a lot of books, but long before Oprah there were these TV tie-ins that showed the power of television to sell books."

Evan Heyman (Editor at Lancer, author): "TV tie-ins were a thriving sub-genre ... Paperback companies that didn't have a lot of money to buy the rights from hardcover publishers could acquire the rights for TV tie-ins from the studios relatively cheaply. For small companies it was a big plus."

TV Tie-In Authors

Once the deal was made with the studios, the next step was to hire an author to write the book, and work-for-hire or "contract writing" arrangements were the standard. As such, the writers were paid an advance or flat fee to write the books, and retained no interest in them; the copyrights were almost always held by the studios. Advances typically ranged from $1,500 to $3,000 per book in the 1960's and 70's. Agents were sometimes involved, and served as the go-between with the publisher and writer, negotiating the advance on behalf of the writer. A few books paid the authors royalties in addition to advances (the *Dark Shadows* and *Partridge Family* books most notably) but they were in the minority. If a book did well it was the publisher alone that typically reaped the benefits. But then again, it was the publisher that was taking the gamble originally, and the show more so than the author that was generally responsible for a book's success.

The authors ranged from upstarts, to established writers, to award-winning writers well-respected in their genres. Certain authors came to write a number of TV tie-ins and are often associated with them: Michael Avallone, Norman Daniels, Richard Deming, Chris Stratton, and of course, William Johnston, who wrote more than 65 TV tie-ins over a 15 year period (some he may have farmed out as outlines to ghostwriters) and is the most prolific author of TV tie-ins by far. TV tie-in authors better known for their work in other areas include Ron Goulart, Keith Laumer, Thomas Disch, Jim Thompson, and Beverly Cleary.

The authors were generally given fairly broad latitude in the writing of the stories in the 1960's and 70's. As long as the stories adhered to the tone of the show, weren't libelous or scandalous, and were delivered on time (most within a two to four week period), few restrictions were imposed. Notes William Rotsler: "You know what Spock looks like and talks like, and as long as you don't violate that, you're okay."

The writers sometimes embellished the stories, by adding detailed back-history for the lead characters (as Walter Wager did in the *I Spy* series), by creating new series characters of their own (as Wager and others did), or even by modifying the concepts from the show (as Keith Laumer did in *The Invaders* series). This all changed in the 1970's and 80's, however, when the studios exercised much greater control and imposed stricter guidelines on the writing of the stories.

While TV tie-ins were often denigrated as a writing form, and recognized as a matter of economic necessity rather than an artistic outlet, the authors generally seemed to enjoy writing them. Comments by Michael Avallone ("I always gave it my best shot"), Ron Goulart ("I tried to give the readers what they got from the show"), Norman Daniels ("potboilers ... written for fast money"), Lou Cameron ("these are not high art"), Michael Jahn ("writing TV tie-ins got me started as a science fiction and mystery novelist"), William Rotsler ("having your name on TV tie-ins was a good way of getting exposure for your other work"), Thom Racina ("I'd write a *Baretta* or a *Quincy* in a weekend when I needed some extra cash"), Victor Miller ("I enjoyed taking on the Telly Savalas persona"), Dan Ross ("writing *Dark Shadows* was a happy experience"), and Walter Wager ("I had a marvelous time") show a range of sentiments felt.

A Note on Novelizations

Through the 1960's most TV tie-ins were original stories, with a trend toward novelizations (stories adapted from episodes) taking place in the 1970's. In some cases a single episode was novelized to form a full-length story. In other cases two or more episodes were novelized to form a single full-length story, with the authors often finding a common thread between the episodes. Still other books are collections of "short story novelizations," with the episodes being individually adapted in the books through a series of short stories.

The trend toward novelizations was facilitated by the collective bargaining agreement reached by the Hollywood Writer's Guild in 1966. Prior to it, the writers of teleplays retained all rights to the stories, meaning that a publisher had to negotiate with the writer directly for the novelization rights. The 1966 agreement allowed the writer to sell the rights to the studios, making it possible for the publisher to negotiate with the studios for the novelization rights, a much simpler process.

The 1966 agreement gave a scriptwriter three basic options: to retain all rights to the teleplays, to agree up front to sell the rights "at minimum" on demand, or to sell the rights outright. Few writers chose the first option, while about equal numbers chose the second and third.

Once the deal was made, the studio would send the script or scripts to be novelized to the publisher. Pilot episodes (which could be either the first episode in the weekly series, or a made-for-TV movie that aired prior to the weekly series) were often novelized.

The amount of control the studios exercised over the writing of the novelizations varied, but was almost always greater than the amount of control they had exercised over the writing of the original stories in the 1960's. In some cases the writers were required to adhere strictly to the scripts and even use every word from them, while in other cases the writers were given broader latitude. In any case, the studios retained final control and had the right to demand any changes they saw fit.

Novelizations--which were sometimes written first person, and which often contained dialog that was cut during the editing process and didn't make it to the screen--represent a unique writing form. Alan Dean Foster, who novelized the *Star Trek Animated Series* as well as several hit science fiction movies, sums up the novelizer's requirements as threefold: "expand on the characterizations, develop the plots, fix the mistakes." William Rotsler notes: "When you novelize a TV-script you have about half a book [which is why more than one episode, or the longer pilot episodes, are often novelized], so you have to find ways to extend it." The author must come up with additional material, by extending the main plot, adding subplots of his own (Ron Goulart added a touring Shakespeare company to one of his *Kung Fu* novelizations), developing the characters, adding scenes that are too difficult or expensive to shoot, etc., all while maintaining the overall consistency and continuity of the main plot. Rotsler and others have described the writing of novelizations as a "craft."

Lou Cameron notes: "You may not have to think up the basic concept and a lot of plotting is done for you. But then you have to explain why on earth anyone would be behaving so strangely. A reader and viewer are not on the same wavelength. When you're <u>watching</u> David Carradine get belted and keep coming back for more whilst quoting kindly Oriental sages, you accept it because you see it going down. But a reader is perforce taking an active part in imagining what the writer is trying to sell him, and it's a lot tougher to <u>imagine</u> a guy going head first through a window and bouncing back up with a weary smile..."

Victor Miller, who novelized the *Kojak* series, notes that writing novelizations based on scripts, and in turn writing scripts based on novels ("taking a scene from *Casablanca* and turning it into a chapter in a Hemingway novel"), is a good way of learning about both writing forms.

Finally, a common complaint among novelizers is script revisions, and the extra work they entail. Basically, novelizations can be written either after the episode has aired (in which case there wouldn't be script revisions) or simultaneously with the script, with both the novelization and the episode being targeted for similar release dates. Since scripts are notoriously revised up to and during production, the novelizer is forced to follow suit. Laments one: "The money doesn't change, the deadline doesn't change, the script changes."

By the mid to late 1970's most TV tie-ins were novelizations, as that's where the trend had taken them. And they were beginning to glut the market, causing at times heavy losses for the publishers. It was becoming evident that the public was no longer interested in a quick rehashing of an episode, but wanted a fresher and more in depth look at a show. Moreover, the studios, having seen how profitable TV tie-ins could be in the 1960's, were demanding higher up front moneys for rights to the books. TV tie-ins by the early 1980's thus fell into decline, and only a handful of series and a few miscellaneous titles were published that decade. Notable 1980's tie-ins include those in the *A-Team, Miami Vice,* and *Murder, She Wrote* series, plus the Soaps & Serials books by Pioneer Communications Network, and the original *Star Trek* books by Pocket.

What Lies Ahead?

The 1990's has seen a resurgence in TV tie-ins, which may be signalling a new era in them. Following the lead of Pocket Books, whose original *Star Trek* books (borne in 1979 following the first *Star Trek* movie) were highly successful throughout the 1980's, TV tie-ins of the 1990's are mostly original novels rather than novelizations, between 220-260 pages in length rather than 120-160 pages as they typically were in the 1960's and 70's, and of a generally more consistent and better writing quality. Only proven shows are now being pursued, rather than the publishers "rolling the dice" at the beginning of the new seasons as they often did in the past. Author advances are now ranging from about $7,000 to $12,000 per book (sometimes much higher), and royalties are generally included. The authors are competing strongly for the assignments, often submitting detailed book proposals that go through rigid reviews as part of the process. Science fiction and fantasy series have taken the lead in this new wave of TV tie-ins, beginning with the 1989-90 *Beauty and the Beast* series, and continuing with such early 90's entrants as *Quantum Leap, Alien Nation,* and *The X Files*.

A Note on Multiple Printings and Cover Variations

Multiple printings (copies of the same book issued in different press runs, as indicated on the copyright pages) are common among TV tie-ins, and paperbacks in general. Publishers often issue books in conservative amounts originally to test the market, and re-issue them as subsequent printings if demand warrants. Multiple printings can be "identical" or "cover-variation."

Identical multiple printings all have the same cover. For instance, the book *Get Smart* has some ten identical printings, as while the copyright pages change to reflect the different printings (they say "first printing," "second printing," etc.), the covers never do (they all feature the same Don Adams photo). Both the front covers and back must match among the printings, it should be noted, in order for the printings to be considered identical (some printings differ by virtue of the back covers only).

Cover-variation multiple printings have different covers depending on the printing. For example, the book *Gunsmoke* has a full-body photo of James Arness as Matt Dillon on the cover of the first printing, and a close-up photo on the cover of the third printing.

With identical multiple printings, this work's Master List includes the book's first appearance only, which is usually the first printing. Book collectors generally seek out first printings, with identical subsequent printings having less collectible value. Thus, the Master List includes the first printing only of the book *Get Smart*.

With cover-variation multiple printings, the Master List includes the first appearance of each variation, with the subsequent printing identified as the cover-variation. Thus, the Master List includes the first and third printings of the book *Gunsmoke*, with the third printing identified as the cover-variation.

Sometimes a book goes into numerous printings, with the first few printings having one cover and the next few a different cover. The book *Dark Shadows* has one cover for its first three printings, and a different cover from its fourth printing on. The Master List includes the first and fourth printings of this book (the first, because it's the first printing, the fourth, because it's the first one with the new cover).

Most cover-variations, like *Gunsmoke's*, are obvious. Some books have covers that differ only slightly, however, and in some cases barely at all. For them, the one variation is considered to be the main or regular version, and the other a "variant version" that's not included on the Master List. Examples of variant versions include special editions, special book club editions, books with covers lacking certain features like book numbers or logos, subsequent printings identical to first printings except for a subsequent printing stamp on the cover (*The Nurses*), etc. Special book club editions represent overstock issued by the publisher for a tax write-off, and are widely regarded as having little collectible value. It's important not to confuse cover-variations with variant versions: cover-variations are sought, variant versions are not.

Many books note their printing status on the copyright page, and those books that do are sometimes referred to as "stated printings." Printing statuses are usually indicated by the simple statement "first printing," "second printing," or whatever the case may be. Some books indicate their printing status by a series of consecutive numbers on the copyright page, with the lowest number in the series representing the printing.

Some books fail to note their printing statuses, and for them the printings statuses are assigned. If such a book appears to be its first or only appearance, it's assumed to be a first printing. If such a book appears to be a subsequent printing, the term unspecified subsequent printing ("unsp" on the Master List) is used.

Most books also note their issue dates (which may or may not be the same as their copyright dates) on the copyright page. For books which fail to note their issue dates, the issue dates are assigned. For most such books, the issue date is assumed to be the same as the copyright date, if such an assumption appears reasonable. The book *Nanny and the Professor* only notes its 1970 copyright date, no issue date. Since the show *Nanny and the Professor* ran from 1970-71, and since the book's cover price and book number are consistent with books then issued, an issue date of 1970--the copyright date's--is assumed.

With some books that fail to note their issue dates, the assigning of an issue date is more difficult, as some books have copyright dates that could not coincide with their issue dates. In assigning the issue dates for them, one must look to the book's copyright date, book number, and cover price, and to the show's run dates, for assistance. The book *Blind Man's Bluff*, in the *Longstreet* series, only notes its 1943 copyright date, no issue date. Since the show *Longstreet* ran from 1971-72, and since the book's cover price and book number are consistent with books then issued, an issue date of 1971 is assumed.

How the TV Tie-Ins are Indexed

The Master List

In the main index or Master List, the books are listed alphabetically by TV show. The show is noted first, along with the run dates and network, and the individual book entries follow. For each show, the books are sorted by publisher and listed chronologically by their order of publication within the series (a series again being all the books about a show by the same publisher). For numbered books (*Mannix #1, Mannix #2,* etc.), the order of the book entries is obvious. For non-numbered books (like Pocket's three *Dragnet* books), the order of the book entries is still based on their publishing chronology, but rather than having the series numbers as reference points one must look to the books' issue dates, book numbers, and cover prices for assistance.

A numbered book is a book which includes any reference to a series number. References range from clear (the book *Cannon #2: The Stewardess Strangler*, for instance, clearly displays the "#2" on the cover and spine) to subtle (the *Dark Shadows* book *The Curse of Collinwood's* only reference to a series number is in the back cover blurb "*The Curse of Collinwood* is the fifth in a series of thrilling novels based on ABC-TV's popular suspense drama, *Dark Shadows*").

Any series number reference leads to a book's being so titled on the Master List (the book entry includes the series number). On the other hand, the lack of a series number reference causes the book to be listed without a series number, even if the order of the book within the series is obvious. Many series (*The Brady Bunch* and *Mission: Impossible* among them) begin with un-numbered first books, with the numbered books in the series beginning with the second book. Either at the time of the first book other books were not planned (a publisher would often issue a single book to test the market, and follow with numbered sequels if it sold well), or the publisher simply chose not to number the book. While it's obvious in such cases that the un-numbered book is book number one in the series, since the book itself lacks a series number, that is how it is listed in this work.

Series numbers are assigned by the publisher in the order the books are issued, and subtitles are also usually given to the numbered sequels. Thus, while the first *Brady Bunch* book is simply titled *The Brady Bunch* the second is titled *The Brady Bunch #2: Showdown at the P.T.A. Corral*. Series numbers provide convenience to the publishers, and to the collectors as well, who glean over time the relative scarcity of the different titles in a series. Seasoned buffs know, for instance, that the first few *Man From U.N.C.L.E.* books are very easy to find while the last few are impossible, and likewise for *The Avengers #8* (spit and you'll hit one) vs. *#9* (hardly anywhere to be found).

In the Master List, the book entries begin with the name of the TV show the book is based on, even if the name of the show is not found in the title of the book itself. For example, all that is found on the title page of the book *The Defenders: Eve of Judgment* is the subtitle "Eve of Judgment." The title page makes no reference to the TV show the book is based on, and to simply list the book as "Eve of Judgment" would be incomplete (incomplete not so much in the Master List, where the show has already been given, as in the Author and Publisher Lists, where the book stands apart from the show). With certain books, like *Beaver and Wally*, where the TV show is obvious from the book's title in the Master List context, the book is listed without the show title in the Master List and with it in the Author and Publisher Lists. Thus, the above book is listed as *"Beaver and Wally"* in the Master List and as *"Leave it to Beaver: Beaver and Wally"* in the Author and Publisher Lists.

The features of the books are listed in the following order on the Master List:

1)   Book Title

2)   Author or Co-Authors. The byline or author attributed on the book is always given. If the byline is a pseudonym and the identity of the author is known, the author's identity is given in brackets next to the byline.

3)   Publisher

4)   Book number

5)   Copyright date. If a book indicates two copyright dates, both dates are given on the Master List. If a book indicates more than two copyright dates, the first date is given followed by a " + ".

6)   Printing (in parentheses following the copyright date)

7)   Issue date. If the issue date is different from the copyright date, the issue date is given in parentheses next to the printing. If the issue date is the same as the copyright date, no separate issue date is given, with the one date given in such instances representing both the copyright date and issue date.

The preceding features are listed for all of the books. In addition, the following information is listed for certain books, as the cases warrant:

8)   Cover price. Nearly all of the books include cover prices. For books lacking them, such as certain Scholastic Book Services titles and most Whitmans, no cover price indication is made.

9)   All oversize books are so noted (there are only a few). <u>On the Master List, a book is a mass market paperback unless the entry notes "oversize," in which case the book is an oversize paperback, or unless the publisher is Whitman, in which case the book is a Whitman hardback.</u>

10)   All novelizations are so noted, along with the name of the episode
       or episodes novelized. Most books that are novelizations indicate
       somewhere on the cover or inside the book which episode has been
       adapted, and give credit to the scriptwriter. For books known to
       be novelizations but which fail to indicate the adapted episode, the
       determination of the episode is accomplished through research.
       Original stories are only so noted on the Master List if they're
       within a series of books (like *Police Woman*) that also includes
       novelizations.

       If the novelized episode is a regular episode as opposed to a pilot
       episode, the entry notes "novelization of the episode _____."
       If the novelized episode is the pilot episode, and the pilot episode
       is in the form of the first episode in the weekly series, the entry
       notes "novelization of the pilot episode _____." If the
       novelized episode is the pilot episode, and the pilot episode is in
       the form of a made-for-TV movie that aired prior to the weekly
       series, the entry notes "novelization of the TV-movie pilot
       _____" and in this case also gives the air-date. This is the only
       time an episode's air-date is given in the Master List (it's given as
       it falls prior to the run dates of the show). For a complete list of
       air-dates of all the novelized episodes, please see the Episodes
       Novelized List.

       The prior examples are for books that novelize a single episode,
       but as noted earlier many books novelize more than a single
       episode. If the resulting book is a single full-length story and the
       novelized episodes are easily determinable, the entry notes
       "novelization of the episodes _____." If the resulting book is
       a single full-length story and the novelized episodes are either not
       easily determinable or many in number, the entry simply notes
       "novelization of several episodes." If the resulting book is a
       collection of short stories, each based on one episode, the episodes
       are listed either in the book entries themselves (as "includes the
       novelizations _____") or in the narrative commentary section
       following the book entries.

11)   Any actors pictured on the front and back covers of the TV tie-ins
       are noted next, with the initials "FC" and "BC" used to denote the
       front and back covers. Actors are listed in left to right and/or top

to bottom order as they appear on the covers, and explanatory comments regarding their placement on the covers are included if necessary. The notation indicates whether the actor is pictured in a photo or illustration, and actors are only noted if there is a clear resemblance (many illustrated covers, for instance, include only vague likenesses of the actors). Only the regular stars in the TV show are noted, no guest stars, professional models, or extras which might be pictured, and none of a book's interior photos are noted. Back cover photos are only noted if they include actors not already pictured on the front covers. For books with entries lacking Actors Pictured notations, no actors are pictured.

TV Tie-Ins Indexed By Author

In the Author List, the books are sorted alphabetically by the byline or author attributed on the book. The author is noted, and the individual book entries follow, in alphabetical or Master List order. For books with cover-variations, only the first variation is noted. The book entries include the following features in the Author List:

1)   Title
2)   Publisher
3)   Book number
4)   Issue date

The byline can be the author's real name or a pseudonym. Pseudonyms can be regular pseudonyms (when a book is written by a single person under a different name), joint pseudonyms (when a book is written by two or more people under a single different name), or house pseudonyms or "house names" (when a publisher uses the same pseudonym for a series of books written by different authors, such as was the case with the *A-Team, Gunsmoke,* and *Kung Fu* series).

The identity of the person behind the pseudonym is often not easy to ascertain, as the publishing industry has notoriously been haunted by "ghosts." Pseudonyms are used for several reasons, one being to hide the identity of the author. An author may wish to have his identity hidden because of the nature of the work (TV tie-ins have been written under pseudonyms for this reason) or because of his or her gender. Men have written romance novels under female names, and women have written action and adventure novels under male names, because such works sell better under such bylines. The use of either-sex first names, or initials instead of first names, are other means of obscuring an author's gender.

Pseudonyms are used for other reasons too. Authors can easily become typecast, and pseudonyms allow them to write under genres different from the ones to which they have become associated. They also allow prolific authors to continue to produce output without having their names on too many covers (which might lead one to suspect the quality of their work), and they allow writers to choose a pleasing name (as a book's byline often has a bearing on its success). Pseudonyms are also used for convenience, with an author writing for one publisher under one name and a different publisher under a different name.

In the Author List, if the byline is the author's real name, the author's life dates and name portions not included in the byline are noted, if known. For authors known to be real but for whom no life dates or additional name portions are known, a brief biographical notation is given to indicate that the byline is not a pseudonym.

If the byline is a pseudonym, the author's identity is noted if known, and given its own separate entry. The books are always listed under the byline attributed to them, and in the case of pseudonymous bylines are sometimes listed under the author's real name as well.

If the author wrote TV tie-ins primarily under the pseudonym (as Richard Hubbard wrote as Chris Stratton, and W.T. Ballard wrote as Brian Fox) the books are listed under the pseudonym only, with the entry for the real name simply referring back to the pseudonym. Thus, the *Alias Smith and Jones* books W.T. Ballard wrote as Brian Fox are listed under Brian Fox only. The Brian Fox entry lists the books and notes Fox to be a pseudonym of W.T. Ballard. The Ballard entry notes Ballard's full name and life dates and refers back to Brian Fox, without listing the books itself.

If the byline is a joint pseudonym, both authors are given their own entries, with the book listed under both the joint pseudonym plus the separate entries. The book *The Man From U.N.C.L.E. #12: The Mind-Twisters Affair*, co-written by Gene DeWeese and Robert Coulson as "Thomas Stratton," is listed under both Thomas Stratton plus DeWeese and Coulson. The Stratton entry notes that that is a joint pseudonym for the two authors. The DeWeese and Coulson entries indicate that the book was co-written with the other author, "as Thomas Stratton."

Books co-written by two authors, with both authors credited in the byline, are listed under both authors, with both entries indicating the book was co-written with the other author. The book *V: East Coast Crisis*, by A.C. Crispin and Howard Weinstein, is such a book.

For authors that wrote certain TV tie-ins under their own names and certain TV tie-ins under pseudonyms, those written under the pseudonyms are listed under both the pseudonym plus the author's real name. *The Partridge Family* books written by Michael Avallone under the Vance Stanton byline are listed under both Michael Avallone and Vance Stanton. The Stanton entry notes that Stanton is a pseudonym of Michael Avallone. The Avallone entry separates those books written "as Michael Avallone" from those written "as Vance Stanton."

Books written under house names are listed under both the house name plus the names of the authors that wrote them. The *Gunsmoke* books, written by Gordon Shirreffs and Donald Bensen under the Jackson Flynn house name, are listed under both Jackson Flynn plus either Shirreffs or Bensen, as the case may be. The Jackson Flynn entry notes that that is a house name for the other authors, and indicates which books were written by which authors. The entries for Shirreffs and Bensen note that the books were written "as Jackson Flynn."

Despite much research, the identities of the authors behind certain bylines remains unknown. Information regarding author identities is encouraged by users of this work, with contributors acknowledged in future editions or supplements to this work.

TV Tie-Ins Indexed By Publisher

In the Publisher List, the books are sorted by publisher. The publisher is noted first, and the individual book entries follow, listed according to each publisher's own numbering system. The book entries include the following features in the Publisher List:

1)   Book number
2)   Title
3)   Byline
4)   Issue date

The book number, which is usually found on the book's cover and spine, is the identification number the publisher has given the book, and each publisher had its own system of doing so.

In the 1950's and 60's many publishers included letters with the book numbers, with the letters indicating the cover price. For instance, the "B" in the "B156" book number of Dell's *Have Gun, Will Travel* indicates the book's 35 cent cover price.

Beginning in the late 1960's many publishers instituted prefixes and suffixes with the book numbers. Some books had prefixes only, with the prefixes indicating the cover price. For instance, the "60" prefix in the "60-8049" book number of Popular Library's *Love Letters to the Monkees* indicates the book's 60 cent cover price. Other books were given prefixes and suffixes, with the suffixes indicating the cover price and the prefixes identifying the publisher. The "075" suffix in the "441-51939-075" book number of Ace's *Marcus Welby, M.D. #2: The Acid Test* indicates the book's 75 cent cover price; the "441" prefix identifies the publisher, Ace Books. The balance or core number-- 51939--is specific to the book itself, and only it is noted in the various lists of this work.

The Actors Pictured List

The Actors Pictured List provides an alphabetical listing of all the actors pictured on the front and back covers of the TV tie-ins. The actor is noted along with life dates, if known, and name of the TV show and character played. If the same actor appeared on the covers of books about more than one show--such as George Peppard, with three--each show and character is noted.

The Episodes Novelized List

The Episodes Novelized List provides a list of all the TV episodes novelized in the books. The episodes are sorted by TV show and listed either alphabetically, or in air-date order if indicated. The episodes' original air-dates are also given. Often, the name of the episode novelized in a book provides the book's subtitle. For instance, the *Starsky and Hutch* episode "Death Ride" was novelized in the book *Starsky and Hutch #3: Death Ride*.

The Selected Index

The Selected Index references the page numbers all those items not already indexed in the Master List, Author List, Publisher List, Actors Pictured List, or Episodes Novelized List.

Thus, if one is seeking all references to *Dark Shadows* in this work, to avoid extreme repetitiveness the Selected Index doesn't reference the *Dark Shadows* entries in the Master List, Author List, Publisher List, etc., for those entries have already been so indexed. However, the Selected Index does note all additional references to *Dark Shadows* in this work, such as in the Introduction section and in the *Partridge Family* and *Strange Paradise* sections of the Master List.

A Final Note

With over 1,400 books included in this work, a broad and colorful canvas of TV shows and characters is painted. From Samantha Stephens to Emma Peel, *The Munsters* to *The Mod Squad*, from the Chief on *Get Smart* to *The Brady Bunch's* Alice, the Ewings to *The Waltons*, they're here. And while many of the more noteworthy shows do include TV tie-ins, there are exceptions: Why there are 23 *Man From U.N.C.L.E.* books but no *Streets of San Franciscos,* six *McClouds* and six *Columbos* but no *McMillan and Wifes*; why books about shows like *The Ugliest Girl in Town* and *Captain Nice* and *The New People*, but none about *Hogan's Heroes* or *Green Acres*, are some of the interesting aspects of TV tie-ins.

Of interest too is the varying scarcity of the books: why so many *That Girls* and *The Partridge Family #2's*, but so few *Addams Family Strikes Backs* and *Flying Nun #5's*; why *Gunsmoke #2, The Mod Squad #4,* and *The Avengers #8* are so much easier to find than the other books in those series. And why is it you can never find a first printing of *Gomer Pyle?* The answer of course is that the books were issued in different amounts - and often no records were kept.

In hand with scarcity is desirability (certain books are inherently more desirable than others - a *Land of the Giants* is inherently more desirable than an *Eight is Enough*), and both factors--scarcity and desirability--lead to value. With coins, scarcity alone determines value. With books, which cover a broad array of topics, are written by a broad array of authors, and are published by a broad array of publishers, the factor of desirability comes into play, and combines with scarcity in determining value. That is, assuming equal scarcity between *Land of the Giants* and *Eight is Enough*, the former is the more valuable book because it's more desirable (it was based on a more noteworthy show, was written by a more noteworthy author, has a more interesting cover, etc.). On the other hand, *The Avengers #8* is surely just as desirable a book as *The Avengers #9* (both were based on the same show, issued by the same publisher, written by the same author, and are even further equal in featuring Tara King over Emma Peel). However, *The Avengers #9* is the more valuable book in this case because it's scarcer. Needless to say, the value of TV tie-ins varies widely, and while the purpose of this work is to simply list the books, a future edition may include values.

(The final factor in determining value is of course condition, which is perhaps the most important factor of all - see "Grading the Condition of TV Tie-Ins" in the Addenda for details.)

Finally, readers are once again encouraged to notify the author of possible new entries to this work, within its defined scope, and to provide additional information or corrections on existing entries. Despite first hand verification of information when possible and double-checking, errors are inevitable in such a work as this. Contributors will be acknowledged in future editions or supplements to this work.

TV TIE-IN MASTER LIST

A FOR ANDROMEDA
1961 - 1962; Syndicated

_____ A For Andromeda; by Fred Hoyle and John Elliot; Crest d773; c 1962 (1st: 1964); $.50

_____ Andromeda Breakthrough; by Fred Hoyle and John Elliot; Crest R1080; c 1964 (1st: 1967); $.60

British series *A For Andromeda* and its sequel *Andromeda Breakthrough* inspired the above books, whose co-authors worked for the shows, as producer (Elliot) and writer (Hoyle).

THE A-TEAM
January 23, 1983 - June 14, 1987; NBC

Dells

_____ The A-Team; by Charles Heath [Ron Renauld]; Dell 10009; c 1984 (1st); $2.50 [novelization of the pilot episode "The A-Team"] [FC Illus: George Peppard, Dirk Benedict, Melinda Culea, Dwight Schultz, Mr. T]

_____ The A-Team 2: Small But Deadly Wars; by Charles Heath [Ron Renauld]; Dell 10020; c 1984 (1st); $2.50 [novelization of the episodes "A Small and Deadly War" and "Black Day at Bad Rock"] [FC Photos: Mr. T, Peppard]

_____ The A-Team 3: When You Comin' Back, Range Rider?; by Charles Heath [Ron Renauld]; Dell 10027; c 1984 (1st); $2.50 [novelization of the episode "When You Comin' Back, Range Rider?"] [FC Photos: Mr. T, Peppard, (inset) Schultz]

_____ The A-Team 4: Old Scores to Settle; by Charles Heath [Ron Renauld]; Dell 10034; c 1984 (1st); $2.50 [novelization of the episodes "The Only Church in Town" and "Recipe for Heavy Bread"] [FC Photos: Mr. T, Peppard, (inset) Culea, Schultz]

_____ The A-Team 5: Ten Percent of Trouble; by Charles Heath [Ron Renauld]; Dell 10037; c 1984 (1st); $2.50 [novelization of the episodes "Steel" and "Maltese Cow"] [FC Photos: Mr. T, Peppard]

_____ The A-Team 6: Operation Desert Sun: The Untold Story; by Charles Heath [Louis Chunovic]; Dell 10039; c 1984 (1st); $2.50 [original story] [FC Photos: Mr. T, Peppard]

Wanderers

_____ The A-Team #1: Defense Against Terror [Plot-It-Yourself]; by William Rotsler; Wanderer 49608; c 1983 (1st); $3.95 [oversize] [FC Photos: (top) Mr. T, Peppard, (bottom) Benedict, Culea, Schultz]

_____ The A-Team #2: The Danger Maze [Plot-It-Yourself]; by William Rotsler; Wanderer 52761; c 1984 (1st); $3.95 [oversize] [FC Photos: (top) Mr. T, Peppard, (bottom) Benedict, Schultz]

Miscellaneous

_____ Mr. T: The Man With the Gold; by Mr. T; St. Martin's Press 90274; c 1984 (1st); $3.95 [FC Photo: Mr. T]

   A-Team Dells, issued under the Charles Heath house name by the noted authors, were also published (under the Heath byline) in Britain by Target, which issued four additional titles not released here: *#7: Bullets, Bikinis and Bells* (by Ron Renauld as Renauld), *#8: Backwoods Menace* (by Renauld as Renauld), *#9: Bend in the River* (by David George Deutsch), and *#10: Death Vows* (by Max Hart).

ADAM-12
September 21, 1968 - August 26, 1975; NBC

Awards

_____ Adam-12: The Runaway; by Chris Stratton [Richard Hubbard]; Award AN1002; c 1972 (1st); $.95 [FC Photo: Martin Milner, Kent McCord]

_____ Adam-12: Dead On Arrival; by Chris Stratton [Richard Hubbard]; Award AN1027; c 1972 (1st); $.95 [FC Photo: Milner, McCord]

_____ Adam-12: The Hostages; by Chris Stratton [Richard Hubbard]; Award AN1174; c 1974 (1st); $.95 [FC Photo: McCord, Milner]

_____ Adam-12 #4: The Sniper; by Michael Stratford [Bruce Cassiday]; Award AN1266; c 1974 (1st); $.95 [FC Photo: Milner, McCord]

   Police show inspired four Award tie-ins. Richard Hubbard wrote the first three, as Chris Stratton, and had started the fourth at the time of his 1974 death. Bruce Cassiday was brought in to complete it (he started it from scratch), as Michael Stratford.

THE ADDAMS FAMILY
September 18, 1964 - September 2, 1966; ABC

Pocket Books

_____ The Addams Family: Drawn and Quartered; by Chas Addams; Pocket 50058; c 1941,42 (1st: 1964); $.50

_____ The Addams Family: Black Maria; by Chas Addams; Pocket 50059; c 1960 (1st: 1964); $.50

_____ The Addams Family: Nightcrawlers; by Chas Addams; Pocket 50060; c 1957 (1st: 1964); $.50

_____ The Addams Family: Monster Rally; by Chas Addams; Pocket 50061; c 1950 (1st: 1965); $.50

_____ The Addams Family: Homebodies; by Chas Addams; Pocket 50062; c 1954 (1st: 1965); $.50

_____ The Addams Family: Addams and Evil; by Chas Addams; Pocket 50063; c 1940+ (1st: 1965); $.50

Berkley

_____ The Addams Family: Dear Dead Days: A Family Album; by Chas Addams; Berkley F1175; c 1959 (1st: 1966); $.50 [compilation of photos and clippings from the "private world" of Charles Addams]

Pyramids

_____ The Addams Family; by Jack Sharkey; Pyramid R-1229; c 1965 (1st); $.50 [FC Photo: (clockwise from left) John Astin, Jackie Coogan, Ted Cassidy, Rock Blossom, Ken Weatherwax, Carolyn Jones, Lisa Loring]

_____ The Addams Family Strikes Back; by W.F. Miksch; Pyramid R-1257; c 1965 (1st); $.50 [FC Photo: (clockwise from top left) Jones, Cassidy, Weatherwax, Blossom, Loring, Astin, Coogan]

The show was based on the drawings by macabre cartoonist Charles Addams, which had been featured in *The New Yorker Magazine* since the 1930's. First appearing in paperback in 1946's *Drawn and Quartered* (Bantam 37), a series Simon & Shuster cartoon hardbacks followed, beginning with 1950's *Monster Rally*. With the airing of the show in 1964 the books were re-issued by Cardinal, two--*Monster Rally* and *Homebodies*--with front cover show-mention (the others are considered inferred TV tie-ins). The show also inspired two original Pyramids, including the scarce *Addams Family Strikes Back*.

THE ADVENTURES OF JIM BOWIE
See JIM BOWIE

ALFRED HITCHCOCK PRESENTS
October 2, 1955 - September 6, 1965; CBS/NBC

Dells

_____ Alfred Hitchcock Presents: 12 Stories They Wouldn't Let Me Do On TV; by Alfred Hitchcock, ed.; Dell D231; c 1957 (1st: 1958); $.35 [FC Photo: Alfred Hitchcock]

_____ Alfred Hitchcock Presents: 13 More Stories They Wouldn't Let Me Do On TV; by Alfred Hitchcock, ed.; Dell D281; c 1957 (1st: 1959); $.35 [FC Photo: Hitchcock]

Avons

_____ Alfred Hitchcock Presents Clean Crimes and Neat Murders; by Henry Slesar; Avon T-485; c 1960 (1st); $.35 [BC Photo: Hitchcock]

_____ Alfred Hitchcock Introduces A Crime For Mothers and Others; by Henry Slesar; Avon F-121; c 1962 (1st); $.40

Alfred Hitchcock, who'd been directing films with much success since the 1920's, moved to the small-screen in 1955 as host of the suspense anthology show *Alfred Hitchcock Presents*, renamed *The Alfred Hitchcock Hour* when it expanded to 60 minutes in 1962. Hitchcock directed a number of episodes over the course of the show and oversaw the selection of the stories, among the sources for which were the recently-launched *Alfred Hitchcock Mystery Magazine*, and the Hitchcock mystery anthologies which Dell had been publishing since the 1940's. Dell continued to publish them throughout the run of the show (the above two, which mention the show in the titles, are included here) and beyond.

Stories in *12 Stories...* are: "Being a Murderer Myself" (Arthur Williams); "Lukundoo" (Edward Lucas White); "A Woman Seldom Found" (William Sansom); "The Perfectionist" (Margaret St. Clair); "The Price of the Head" (John Russell); "Love Comes to Miss Lucy" (Q. Patrick); "Sredni Vashtar" (H.H. Munro aka "Saki"); "Love Lies Bleeding" (Philip MacDonald); "The Dancing Partner" (Jerome K. Jerome); "Casting the Runes" (M.R. James); "The Voice in the Night" (William Hope Hodgson); and "How Love Came to Professor Guildea" (Robert S. Hichens).

Stories in *13 More Stories...* are: "The Moment of Decision" (Stanley Ellin); "A Jungle Graduate" (James Francis Dwyer); "Recipe for Murder" (C.P. Donnel, Jr.); "Nunc Dimittis" (Roald Dahl); "The Most Dangerous Game" (Richard Connell); "The Lady on the Grey" (John Collier); "The Waxwork" (A.M. Burrage); "The Dumb Wife" (Thomas Burke); "Couching at the Door" (D.K. Broster); "The October Game" (Ray Bradbury); "Water's Edge" (Robert Bloch); "The Jokester" (Robert Arthur); and "The Abyss" (Leonid Andreyev).

Contrary to the books' titles, at least three of the stories they featured did appear as episodes: "The Jokester" (Oct-19-1958), "The Waxwork" (Apr-12-1959), and "Water's Edge" (Oct-19-1964).

Avon in addition published two collections of short stories by Henry Slesar, who began his prolific TV-scriptwriting career with the show. (He'd written a number of stories for the *Alfred Hitchcock Mystery Magazine*, had attracted the attention of the TV people--"the stories were in the non-violent, ironic, often droll vein the (almost) all-British staff preferred"--and had been given the chance to write for the show.) Slesar, who wrote over 60 episodes in all with the Avon anthologies developing from them, later commented: "The show seemed almost antediluvian in its attitude toward writers. They actually let writers write. They didn't change their scripts or have them re-written behind their backs. I went to work on a dozen other primetime shows but never recaptured that happy experience."

Stories in *Clean Crimes and Neat Murders* are: "Not the Running Type," "A Fist Full of Money," "Pen Pal," "'Trust Me, Mr. Paschetti'," "One Grave Too Many," "40 Detectives Later," "The Morning After," "The Deadly Telephone," "Something Short of Murder," "The Right Kind of House," "M is for the Many," "The Last Escape," "The Man With Two Faces," "Case of the Kind Waitress," "Make Me an Offer," "Sleep is for the Innocent," and "The Day of the Execution."

Stories in *A Crime for Mothers and Others* are: "A Crime For Mothers," "The Man in the Next Cell," "And Beauty The Prize," "A Woman's Help," "Father Amion's Long Shot," "Servant Problem," "Keep Me Company," "Cop For a Day," "Welcome Home," "Murder Out of a Hat," "First-Class Honeymoon," "The Right Kind of Medicine," "The Last Remains," "Thicker Than Water," "Won't You Be My Valentine?" and "Burglar Proof."

ALIAS SMITH AND JONES
January 21, 1971 - January 13, 1973; ABC

Awards

_____ Alias Smith and Jones: Dead Ringer; by Brian Fox [W.T. Ballard]; Award A896S; c 1971 (1st); $.75 [FC Photo: Ben Murphy, Pete Duel]

_____ Alias Smith and Jones: The Outlaw Trail; by Brian Fox [W.T. Ballard]; Award AS1006; c 1972 (1st); $.75 [FC Photo: Murphy, Roger Davis] [Book opens: "They were an unlikely pair to be crouching chest deep in an icy mountain stream..."]

The above books, by award-winning Western writer W.T. Ballard as Brian Fox, picture Ben Murphy as Jed Curry on both covers. Curry's partner Hannibal Heyes was played by Pete Duel, pictured on the first book with Murphy, until Duel's suicide in late 1971. Show-narrator Roger Davis replaced Duel in the cast, and is pictured on the second book with Murphy. It was said the talented, principled, high-sighted Duel--despondent perhaps at seeing in *Alias Smith and Jones* a deepening rut and the demise of his stage career--shot himself in his home after watching an episode of *Alias Smith and Jones*, which would have been the Dec-30-1971 episode "Miracle at Santa Marta." The show was a takeoff of the 1969 hit movie *Butch Cassidy and the Sundance Kid*.

Note: Ballard used the Brian Fox pseudonym for these and all his Award movie and TV tie-ins. The above *Alias Smith and Jones* books were also published in Britain by Tandem, which issued four additional Ballard as Fox titles not released here: *Cabin Fever, Apache Gold, Dragooned,* and *Trick Shot. Apache Gold* and *Dragooned* were apparently commissioned by Award (along with a Ballard *Bearcats!* TV tie-in) but not published.

ALL IN THE FAMILY
January 12, 1971 - September 21, 1983; CBS

Popular Librarys

_____ The Wit and Wisdom of Archie Bunker; by Eugene Boe, ed.; Popular Library 08194; c 1971 (1st); $.95 [quotes and photos excerpted from episodes] [FC Photo: Carroll O'Connor]

_____ Edith Bunker's All in the Family Cookbook; by Eugene Boe; Popular Library 08195; c 1971 (1st); $.95 [recipes by June Roth, text by Eugene Boe] [FC Photo: O'Connor, Jean Stapleton]

_____ Archie Bunker's Family Album; Popular Library 08216; c 1973 (1st); $.95 [FC Photo: (clockwise from top) Rob Reiner, Sally Struthers, O'Connor, Stapleton]

Bantams

_____ All in the Family; by Burton Wohl; Bantam Q2566; c 1976 (1st); $1.25 [FC Photo: (from left) Reiner, Struthers, Stapleton, O'Connor]

[6 short story novelizations: "Women's Lib," "Archie's Aching Back," "The Games Bunkers Play," "Archie is Jealous," "Cousin Maude's Visit" (from the Dec-11-1971 episode that led to the spinoff series *Maude*), and "Second Honeymoon"]

_____ God, Man and Archie Bunker; by Spencer Marsh; Bantam T7913; c 1975 (1st: 1976); $1.50 [FC Photo: O'Connor] [*]

Miscellaneous

_____ Edith the Good; by Spencer Marsh; Harper & Row RD 214; c 1977 (1st); $2.95 [oversize] [FC Photo: Stapleton] [*]

_____ TV's First Family; by Louis Solomon; Scholastic Book Services TK2297; c 1973 (1st) [FC Photo: (clockwise from top left) Reiner, Stapleton, O'Connor, Struthers]

[*] Through excerpts and stills, the Reverend Spencer Marsh shows that Archie is "a cigar-smoking Adam who weekly creates God, man, and everything in his own image" and that "no one need [as Edith did] feel stifled."

ALL MY CHILDREN
January 5, 1970 -; ABC

Joves

____ Agnes Nixon's All My Children Book I: Tara & Philip; by Rosemarie Santini; Jove B4892; c 1980 (1st); $2.25 [novelization of several episodes]

____ Agnes Nixon's All My Children Book II: Erica; by Rosemarie Santini; Jove B4895; c 1980 (1st); $2.25 [novelization of several episodes]

____ Agnes Nixon's All My Children Book III: The Lovers; by Rosemarie Santini; Jove K4896; c 1981 (1st); $2.50 [novelization of several episodes]

Pioneer Communications Network

____ All My Children #1/#2 [combined]: Once and Always, Book One and Two; by Marcia Lawrence (#1) and Teresa Ward (#2); Pioneer 350; c 1987 (1st); $2.50 [novelization of several episodes]

AMAZING STORIES
September 29, 1985 - May 15, 1987; NBC

TSR's

____ Amazing Stories Book 1: The 4-D Funhouse; by Clayton Emery and Earl Wajenberg; TSR 74176; c 1985 (1st); $2.95

____ Amazing Stories Book 2: Jaguar!; by Morris Simon; TSR 74177; c 1985 (1st); $2.95

____ Amazing Stories Book 3: Portrait in Blood; by Mary Kirchoff; TSR 74186; c 1985 (1st); $2.95

____ Amazing Stories Book 4: Nightmare Universe; by Gene DeWeese and Robert Coulson; TSR 74817; c 1975,85 (1st: 1985); $2.95

____ Amazing Stories Book 5: Starskimmer; by John Gregory Betancourt; TSR 74353; c 1986 (1st); $2.95

____ Amazing Stories Book 6: Day of the Mayfly; by Lee Enderlin; TSR 74352; c 1986 (1st); $2.95

Charters

____ Steven Spielberg's Amazing Stories; by Steven Bauer; Charter 01906; c 1986 (1st); $3.50

____ Steven Spielberg's Amazing Stories Volume II; by Steven Bauer; Charter 01912; c 1986 (1st); $3.50

Anthology series created by Stephen Spielberg inspired tie-ins by TSR (six plot-it-yourself-type adventures) and Charter (two collections of short story novelizations).

Stories in the first Charter are: "The Mission," "Vanessa in the Garden," "Guilt Trip," "Mr. Magic," "The Main Attraction," "Ghost Train," "The Sitter," "Santa '85," "One for the Road," "Hell Toupee," and "No Day at the Beach."

Stories in the second Charter are: "The Amazing Falsworth," "Mirror, Mirror," "Fine Tuning," "Remote Control Man," "Boo," "Grandpa's Ghost," "Mummy Daddy," "Alamo Jobe," "The Secret Cinema," "Gather Ye Acorns," and "Dorothy and Ben."

AMERICAN BANDSTAND
August 5, 1957 - October 7, 1989; ABC/Syndicated/USA

_____ American Bandstand: Your Happiest Years; by Dick Clark; Cardinal GC-96; c 1959 (1st: 1961); $.50 [FC Photo: Dick Clark]

This "frank and friendly book for and about young adults" is by *American Bandstand* host Dick Clark.

THE AMERICANS
January 23, 1961 - September 11, 1961; NBC

_____ The Americans; by Donald Honig; Popular Library PC1006; c 1961 (1st); $.35 [FC Illus: Darryl Hickman, Dick Davalos]

ANDY BURNETT
See WALT DISNEY

ANNA AND THE KING
September 17, 1972 - December 31, 1972; CBS

_____ Anna and the King of Siam; by Margaret Landon; Pocket 77653; c 1943,44 (19th: 1972); $.95

_____ Anna and the King of Siam [cover-variation]; by Margaret Landon; Pocket 77653; c 1943,44 (20th: 1972); $.95 [FC Photo: Samantha Eggar, Yul Brynner]

The show was based on the 1943 book *Anna and the King of Siam* by Margaret Landon. The book inspired the 1946 movie of the same name and the Rodgers and Hammerstein musical play *The King and I* (the play was in turn adapted into the 1956 screen musical of that name). The book was issued extensively by Pocket starting in 1949 (#576) and continuing beyond the run of the show. The show is first mentioned on the 19th printing (a cover-variation from the 18th), and again on the cover-variation 20th.

ANNETTE
See THE MICKEY MOUSE CLUB

ANNIE OAKLEY
1953 - 1956; Syndicated

Whitmans

_____ Annie Oakley in Danger at Diablo; by Doris Schroeder; Whitman 1540; c 1955 (1st) [FC Photo: Gail Davis]

_____ Annie Oakley in the Ghost Town Secret; by Doris Schroeder; Whitman 1538; c 1957 (1st) [FC Illus: Davis]

_____ Annie Oakley in Double Trouble; by Doris Schroeder; Whitman 1538; c 1958 (1st) [FC Illus: Davis]

TV's first Western to star a woman, this *Gene Autry* spinoff inspired the above books. The book *Double Trouble* includes, and the other two books lack, the "TV" logos found on most Whitman TV tie-ins.

ANOTHER WORLD
May 4, 1964 -; NBC

Ballantines

_____ Another World; by Kate Lowe Kerrigan [Frances Rickett]; Ballantine 25859; c 1978 (1st); $1.95 [FC Illus: Victoria Wyndham (top), Jacqueline Courtney, George Reinholt]

_____ Another World II; by Kate Lowe Kerrigan [Frances Rickett]; Ballantine 25860; c 1978 (1st); $1.95 [FC Illus: Wyndham (top), Courtney, Reinholt] [says "First Edition: June 1978"]

_____ Another World II [cover-variation]; by Kate Lowe Kerrigan [Frances Rickett]; Ballantine 28127; c 1978 (unsp: 1978); $1.95 [says "First edition: September 1978"]

Pioneer Communications Networks

_____ Another World #1: Let's Love Again; by Edwina Franklin; Pioneer 31; c 1986 (1st); $2.50 [novelization of several episodes]

_____ Another World #2: Love's Destiny; by Martha Winslow [Frances Rickett]; Pioneer 32; c 1986 (1st); $2.50 [novelization of several episodes]

_____ Another World #3: Affairs of the Moment; by Martha Winslow [Frances Rickett]; Pioneer 33; c 1986 (1st); $2.50 [novelization of several episodes]

_____ Another World #4: Love's Encore; by Martha Winslow [Frances Rickett]; Pioneer 34; c 1986 (1st); $2.50 [novelization of several episodes]

_____ Another World #5: Caress From the Past; by Martha Winslow [Frances Rickett]; Pioneer 35; c 1986 (1st); $2.50 [novelization of several episodes]

_____ Another World #6: Forgive and Forget; by Virginia Grace; Pioneer 36; c 1986 (1st); $2.50 [novelization of several episodes]

_____ Another World #7: Tangled Web; by Marlene Creed; Pioneer 37; c 1986 (1st); $2.50 [novelization of several episodes]

_____ Another World #8: Haunted by the Past; by Cordelia Burke; Pioneer 38; c 1986 (1st); $2.50 [novelization of several episodes]

_____ Another World #9: Suspicions; by Dylan Malloy; Pioneer 39; c 1986 (1st); $2.50 [novelization of several episodes]

_____ Another World #10: Deceptions; by Martha Winslow [Frances Rickett]; Pioneer 40; c 1987 (1st); $2.50 [novelization of several episodes]

_____ Another World #11: Whispers From the Past; by Chloe Seid; Pioneer 050; c 1987 (1st); $2.50 [novelization of several episodes]

_____ Another World #12: Love Play; by Amanda Perkins; Pioneer 051; c 1987 (1st); $2.50 [novelization of several episodes]

_____ Another World #13: Schemes and Dreams; by Cordelia Burke; Pioneer 052; c 1987 (1st); $2.50 [novelization of several episodes]

_____ Another World #14: The Art of Love; by Amanda Perkins; Pioneer 053; c 1987 (1st); $2.50 [novelization of several episodes]

APPLE'S WAY
February 10, 1974 - January 12, 1975; CBS

_____ Apple's Way; by Robert Weverka; Bantam 9848; c 1975 (1st) [novelization of unspecified episode]

_____ Apple's Way [cover-variation]; by Robert Weverka; Bantam N6316; c 1975 (2nd); $.95 [BC Photos: Ronny Cox, Frances Lee McCain, Malcolm Atterbury, Eric Olson, Patti Cohoon, Vincent Van Patten, Kristy McNichol]

   Book includes a "Special Book Club Edition" first printing (without cast member photos on the back cover) and a regular edition second printing (with cast member photos on the back cover). Most Bantam Special Editions are subsequent printings and identical to the first printing regular editions; this book is an exception.

THE AQUANAUTS
September 14, 1960 - February 22, 1961; CBS

_____ The Aquanauts; by Daniel Bard; Popular Library G516; c 1961 (1st); $.35 [FC Illus: Keith Larsen]

ARREST AND TRIAL
September 15, 1963 - September 6, 1964; ABC

   Lancers

_____ Arrest and Trial; by Norman Daniels; Lancer 72-696; c 1963 (1st); $.50 [FC Photos: Ben Gazzara, Chuck Connors]

_____ Arrest and Trial: The Missing Witness; by Norman Daniels; Lancer 72-723; c 1964 (1st); $.50 [FC Photos: Connors, Gazzara]

ART LINKLETTER'S HOUSE PARTY
September 1, 1952 - September 5, 1969; CBS

Cardinals

_____ Kids Say the Darndest Things!; by Art Linkletter; Cardinal C-330; c 1957 (1st: 1959); $.35 [FC Photo: Art Linkletter]

_____ The Secret World of Kids; by Art Linkletter; Cardinal GC-92; c 1959 (1st: 1960); $.50 [FC Photo: Linkletter]

_____ Confessions of a Happy Man; by Art Linkletter with Dean Jennings; Cardinal GC-124; c 1960 (1st: 1962); $.50 [FC Photo: Linkletter]

_____ Kids Still Say the Darndest Things!; by Art Linkletter; Cardinal GC-157; c 1961 (1st: 1962); $.50 [FC Photo: Linkletter]

Crests

_____ Kids Sure Rite Funny! [logo top center]; by Art Linkletter; Crest k646; c 1962 (1st: 1963); $.40 [*]

_____ Kids Sure Rite Funny! [logo upper left]; by Art Linkletter; Crest k997; c 1962 (unsp: 1965); $.40 [*]

> [*] This book, subtitled "A Child's Garden of Misinformation," shouldn't be confused with the separate book of that name.

_____ A Child's Garden of Misinformation; by Art Linkletter; Crest d949; c 1965 (1st: 1966); $.50 [FC Photo: Linkletter]

Pockets

_____ Oops! Or, Life's Awful Moments; by Art Linkletter; Pocket 75179; c 1967 (1st: 1968); $.75 [FC Photo: Linkletter]

_____ Kids Say the Darndest Things!; by Art Linkletter; Pocket 75278; c 1957 (25th: 1968); $.75 [cover-variation reprint of #C-330 may have earlier printing than 25th as #75278; 1961, 22nd printing as C-330 has been seen]

_____ I Wish I'd Said That!; by Art Linkletter; Pocket 75412; c 1968 (1st: 1969); $.75 [FC Photo: Linkletter]

_____ Kids Still Say the Darndest Things!; by Art Linkletter; Pocket 75430; c 1961 (3rd: 1968); $.75 [FC Photo: Linkletter] [cover-variation reprint of GC-157]

The long-running daytime variety show, renamed *The Linkletter Show* in 1968, included the famous segment in which host Art Linkletter interviewed a group of children, whose unrehearsed answers inspired the above series of books.

THE ARTHUR MURRAY PARTY
1950 - 1960; ABC/DUMONT/CBS/NBC

_____   My Husband, Arthur Murray; by Kathryn Murray with Betty Hannah Hoffman;
Avon T510; c 1959,60 (1st: 1960); $.35 [FC Photo: Kathryn and Arthur
Murray]

       This biography of dancing schools founder Arthur Murray was co-written
by his wife Kathryn, hostess of the 1950's summer replacement dancing
programs that bore his name.

AS THE WORLD TURNS
April 2, 1956 - ; CBS

Pioneer Communications Networks

_____   As the World Turns #1: Magic of Love; by Bob Bancroft; Pioneer 41; c 1986
(1st); $2.50 [novelization of several episodes]

_____   As the World Turns #2: Ruling Passions; by Cathy Cunningham [Chet
Cunningham]; Pioneer 42; c 1986 (1st); $2.50 [novelization of several episodes]

_____   As the World Turns #3: Lovers Who Dare; by Johanna Boyd; Pioneer 43; c
1986 (1st); $2.50 [novelization of several episodes]

_____   As the World Turns #4: Horizons of the Heart; by John Boyd; Pioneer 44; c
1986 (1st); $2.50 [novelization of several episodes]

_____   As the World Turns #5: Forbidden Passions; by Sonni Cooper; Pioneer 45; c
1986 (1st); $2.50 [novelization of several episodes]

_____   As the World Turns #6: Love Trap; by Sonni Cooper; Pioneer 46; c 1986 (1st);
$2.50 [novelization of several episodes]

_____   As the World Turns #7: Now and Forever; by Angelica Aimes; Pioneer 47; c
1986 (1st); $2.50 [novelization of several episodes]

_____   As the World Turns #8: Shared Moments; by Angelica Aimes; Pioneer 48; c
1986 (1st); $2.50 [novelization of several episodes]

_____   As the World Turns #9: In the Name of Love; by Kacia Bennett; Pioneer 49;
c 1987 (1st); $2.50 [novelization of several episodes]

_____   As the World Turns #10: This Precious Moment; by Kacia Bennett; Pioneer 50;
c 1987 (1st); $2.50 [novelization of several episodes]

_____   As the World Turns #11: Full Circle; by Margaret Brownley; Pioneer 000; c
1987 (1st); $2.50 [novelization of several episodes]

_____   As the World Turns #12: Storm Warnings; by Margaret Brownley; Pioneer 001;
c 1987 (1st); $2.50 [novelization of several episodes]

_____   As the World Turns #13: The Second Time Around; by Angelica Aimes;
Pioneer 002; c 1987 (1st); $2.50 [novelization of several episodes]

_____ As the World Turns #14: Always and Forever; by Kacia Bennett; Pioneer 003; c 1987 (1st); $2.50 [novelization of several episodes]

THE ASPHALT JUNGLE
April 2, 1961 - September 4, 1961; ABC

_____ The Asphalt Jungle; by W.R. Burnett; Pocket 6078; c 1949 (3rd: 1961); $.35 [FC Photo: Arch Johnson, Jack Warden, Bill Smith]

  The show was based on the 1950 movie, which in turn was based on the 1949 book by W.R. Burnett. First published by Pocket in 1949 (#714), the book was re-issued as a TV tie-in with the show.

THE ASSOCIATES
September 23, 1979 - April 17, 1980; ABC

_____ The Associates; by John Jay Osborn, Jr.; Popular Library 04530; c 1979 (1st); $2.25 [FC Photo: (men) Martin Short, Wilfred Hyde-White, Joe Regalbuto, Tim Thomerson, (women) Alley Mills, Shelley Smith]

THE AVENGERS
March 28, 1966 - September 15, 1969; ABC

  Berkleys

_____ The Avengers #1: "The Floating Game"; by John Garforth; Berkley F1410; c 1967 (1st); $.50 [FC Photo: Diana Rigg, Patrick Macnee]

_____ The Avengers #1: "The Floating Game" [cover-variation]; by John Garforth; Berkley X1666; c 1967 (2nd: 1969); $.60 [FC Photos: (top) Macnee, Rigg, (bottom) Linda Thorson, Macnee]

_____ The Avengers #2: "The Laugh Was On Lazarus"; by John Garforth; Berkley F1411; c 1967 (1st); $.50 [FC Photos: Macnee, Rigg]

_____ The Avengers #2: "The Laugh Was On Lazarus" [cover-variation]; by John Garforth; Berkley X1667; c 1967 (2nd: 1969); $.60 [FC Photos: (top) Macnee, Rigg, (bottom) Thorson, Macnee]

_____ The Avengers #3: "The Passing of Gloria Munday"; by John Garforth; Berkley F1431; c 1967 (1st); $.50 [FC Photo: Rigg, Macnee]

_____ The Avengers #3: "The Passing of Gloria Munday" [cover-variation]; by John Garforth; Berkley X1668; c 1967 (2nd: 1969); $.60 [FC Photos: (top) Macnee, Thorson, (bottom) Macnee, Rigg]

_____ The Avengers #4: "Heil Harris!"; by John Garforth; Berkley F1445; c 1967 (1st); $.50 [FC Photo: Rigg, Macnee]

_____ The Avengers #4: "Heil Harris!" [cover-variation]; by John Garforth; Berkley X1669; c 1967 (2nd: 1969); $.60 [FC Photos: (top) Rigg, Macnee, (bottom) Thorson]

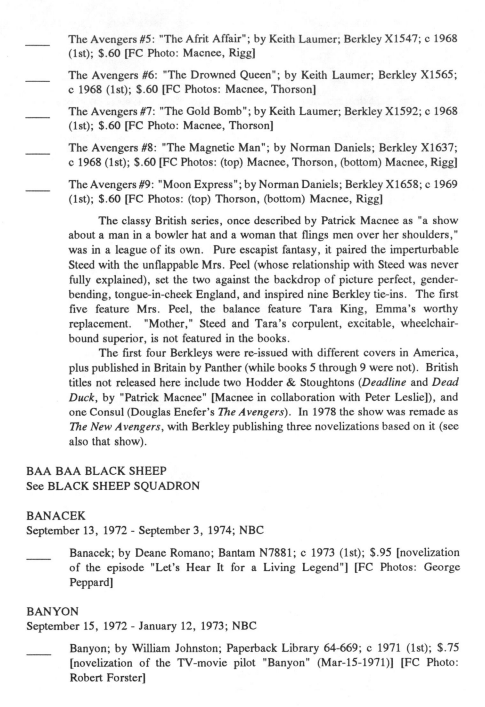

_____ The Avengers #5: "The Afrit Affair"; by Keith Laumer; Berkley X1547; c 1968 (1st); $.60 [FC Photo: Macnee, Rigg]

_____ The Avengers #6: "The Drowned Queen"; by Keith Laumer; Berkley X1565; c 1968 (1st); $.60 [FC Photos: Macnee, Thorson]

_____ The Avengers #7: "The Gold Bomb"; by Keith Laumer; Berkley X1592; c 1968 (1st); $.60 [FC Photo: Macnee, Thorson]

_____ The Avengers #8: "The Magnetic Man"; by Norman Daniels; Berkley X1637; c 1968 (1st); $.60 [FC Photos: (top) Macnee, Thorson, (bottom) Macnee, Rigg]

_____ The Avengers #9: "Moon Express"; by Norman Daniels; Berkley X1658; c 1969 (1st); $.60 [FC Photos: (top) Thorson, (bottom) Macnee, Rigg]

The classy British series, once described by Patrick Macnee as "a show about a man in a bowler hat and a woman that flings men over her shoulders," was in a league of its own. Pure escapist fantasy, it paired the imperturbable Steed with the unflappable Mrs. Peel (whose relationship with Steed was never fully explained), set the two against the backdrop of picture perfect, gender-bending, tongue-in-cheek England, and inspired nine Berkley tie-ins. The first five feature Mrs. Peel, the balance feature Tara King, Emma's worthy replacement. "Mother," Steed and Tara's corpulent, excitable, wheelchair-bound superior, is not featured in the books.

The first four Berkleys were re-issued with different covers in America, plus published in Britain by Panther (while books 5 through 9 were not). British titles not released here include two Hodder & Stoughtons (_Deadline_ and _Dead Duck_, by "Patrick Macnee" [Macnee in collaboration with Peter Leslie]), and one Consul (Douglas Enefer's _The Avengers_). In 1978 the show was remade as _The New Avengers_, with Berkley publishing three novelizations based on it (see also that show).

BAA BAA BLACK SHEEP
See **BLACK SHEEP SQUADRON**

BANACEK
September 13, 1972 - September 3, 1974; NBC

_____ Banacek; by Deane Romano; Bantam N7881; c 1973 (1st); $.95 [novelization of the episode "Let's Hear It for a Living Legend"] [FC Photos: George Peppard]

BANYON
September 15, 1972 - January 12, 1973; NBC

_____ Banyon; by William Johnston; Paperback Library 64-669; c 1971 (1st); $.75 [novelization of the TV-movie pilot "Banyon" (Mar-15-1971)] [FC Photo: Robert Forster]

_____ Banyon [cover-variation]; by William Johnston; Warner 74-285; c 1971 (2nd: 1972); $.75 [FC Photo: Forster]

This book includes a 1971 Paperback Library first printing and a 1972 Warner second printing. Warner Books bought Paperback Library (which had grown in leaps and bounds thanks largely to the success of the *Dark Shadows* series) in 1972. The first few Warners, including this one, were issued as "Warner Paperback Library" editions.

BARETTA
January 17, 1975 - June 1, 1978; ABC

Berkleys

_____ Baretta: Beyond the Law; by Andrew Patrick; Berkley 03515; c 1977 (1st); $1.50 [FC Photo: Robert Blake]

_____ Baretta: Sweet Revenge; by Thom Racina; Berkley 03559; c 1977 (1st); $1.50 [FC Photo: Blake]

BAT MASTERSON
October 8, 1958 - September 21, 1961; NBC

_____ Bat Masterson; by Richard O'Connor; Bantam A1888; c 1957 (1st: 1958); $.35 [FC Illus: Gene Barry]

_____ Bat Masterson; by Wayne C. Lee; Whitman 1550; c 1960 (1st) [FC Illus: Barry]

The show was based on the adventures of the famous frontier sheriff, whose 1957 biography Bantam re-issued with the show.

BATMAN
January 12, 1966 - March 14, 1968; ABC

Signets

_____ Batman; by Bob Kane; Signet D2939; c 1940+ (1st: 1966); $.50 [cartoon book]

_____ Batman vs. Three Villains of Doom; by Winston Lyon [William Woolfolk]; Signet D2940; c 1966 (1st); $.50 [original story, featuring The Penguin, Catwoman, and The Joker] [FC Photo: Adam West]

_____ Batman vs. The Joker; by Bob Kane; Signet D2969; c 1951+ (1st: 1966); $.50 [cartoon book]

_____ Batman vs. The Penguin; by Bob Kane; Signet D2970; c 1952+ (1st: 1966); $.50 [cartoon book]

_____ Funniest Fan Letters to Batman; by Bill Adler, ed.; Signet D2980; c 1966 (1st); $.50

_____ Batman vs. The Fearsome Foursome; by Winston Lyon [William Woolfolk]; Signet D2995; c 1966 (1st); $.50 [novelization of the 1966 companion film *Batman*] [FC Photos: West, Burt Ward; BC Photo: Burgess Meredith, Frank Gorshin, Lee Meriwether, Cesar Romero]

Whitman

_____ Batman and Robin in the Cheetah Caper; by George S. Elrick; Whitman Big Little Book 2031; c 1969 (1st)

The show was based the cartoon character created by Bob Kane for *Detective Comics* in 1939, in the story "The Case of the Chemical Syndicate." Appearing in comic books continually since, the caped crusader was featured in two movie serials--1943's *Batman* and 1948's *Batman and Robin*--and a syndicated newspaper strip long before the show. With the 1966 airing of the show Signet released the above *Batman* paperbacks, the cartoon books featuring original Batman comics reprinted by Signet.

Cartoons in *Batman* are "The Legend of the Batman," "Fan-Mail of Danger!" "The Crazy Crime Clown!" "The Crime Predictor," "The Man Who Could Change Fingerprints!" and "The Testing of Batman!"

Cartoons in *Batman vs. The Joker* (all feature The Joker) are "The Challenge of the Joker," "The Joker's Winning Team!" "The Joker's Millions!" "The Joker's Journal!" and "Batman - Clown of Crime!"

Cartoons in *Batman vs. The Penguin* (the first four feature The Penguin, the fifth features The Catwoman) are "The Parasols of Plunder," "The Golden Eggs!" "The Penguin's Fabulous Fowls!" "The Return of the Penguin," and "The Sleeping Beauties of Gotham City!"

The 1966 film *Batman*, upon which *Batman vs. the Fearsome Foursome* was based, was released after the show had aired and as a companion to it. In 1989 Warner Bros. released the top-grossing movie *Batman*, and has followed with several very successful sequels.

BATTLESTAR GALACTICA
September 17, 1978 - August 4, 1979; ABC
January 27, 1980 - May 4, 1980; ABC

Berkleys

_____ Battlestar Galactica; by Glen A. Larson and Robert Thurston; Berkley 03958; c 1978 (1st); $1.95 [novelization of the pilot episode "Saga of a Starworld"] [BC Photos: (middle) Herbert Jefferson, Jr., (right, top) Richard Hatch, Lorne Greene, (right, bottom) Dirk Benedict, (left, bottom) Noah Hathaway]

_____ Battlestar Galactica: The Photostory; by Richard J. Anobile; Berkley 04139; c 1979 (1st); $2.50 [photo-novelization of the pilot episode "Saga of a Starworld"] [FC Photo: Hatch; BC Photos: Greene]

_____ Battlestar Galactica 2: The Cylon Death Machine; by Glen A. Larson and Robert Thurston; Berkley 04080; c 1979 (1st); $1.95 [novelization of the episode "The Gun on Ice Planet Zero"]

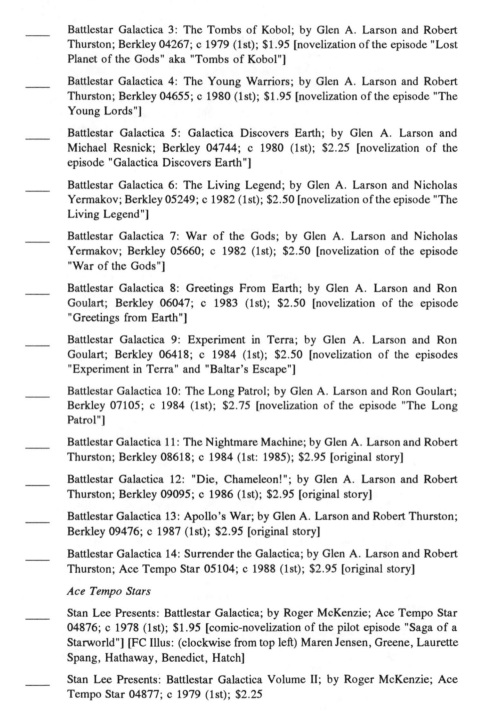

____ Battlestar Galactica 3: The Tombs of Kobol; by Glen A. Larson and Robert Thurston; Berkley 04267; c 1979 (1st); $1.95 [novelization of the episode "Lost Planet of the Gods" aka "Tombs of Kobol"]

____ Battlestar Galactica 4: The Young Warriors; by Glen A. Larson and Robert Thurston; Berkley 04655; c 1980 (1st); $1.95 [novelization of the episode "The Young Lords"]

____ Battlestar Galactica 5: Galactica Discovers Earth; by Glen A. Larson and Michael Resnick; Berkley 04744; c 1980 (1st); $2.25 [novelization of the episode "Galactica Discovers Earth"]

____ Battlestar Galactica 6: The Living Legend; by Glen A. Larson and Nicholas Yermakov; Berkley 05249; c 1982 (1st); $2.50 [novelization of the episode "The Living Legend"]

____ Battlestar Galactica 7: War of the Gods; by Glen A. Larson and Nicholas Yermakov; Berkley 05660; c 1982 (1st); $2.50 [novelization of the episode "War of the Gods"]

____ Battlestar Galactica 8: Greetings From Earth; by Glen A. Larson and Ron Goulart; Berkley 06047; c 1983 (1st); $2.50 [novelization of the episode "Greetings from Earth"]

____ Battlestar Galactica 9: Experiment in Terra; by Glen A. Larson and Ron Goulart; Berkley 06418; c 1984 (1st); $2.50 [novelization of the episodes "Experiment in Terra" and "Baltar's Escape"]

____ Battlestar Galactica 10: The Long Patrol; by Glen A. Larson and Ron Goulart; Berkley 07105; c 1984 (1st); $2.75 [novelization of the episode "The Long Patrol"]

____ Battlestar Galactica 11: The Nightmare Machine; by Glen A. Larson and Robert Thurston; Berkley 08618; c 1984 (1st: 1985); $2.95 [original story]

____ Battlestar Galactica 12: "Die, Chameleon!"; by Glen A. Larson and Robert Thurston; Berkley 09095; c 1986 (1st); $2.95 [original story]

____ Battlestar Galactica 13: Apollo's War; by Glen A. Larson and Robert Thurston; Berkley 09476; c 1987 (1st); $2.95 [original story]

____ Battlestar Galactica 14: Surrender the Galactica; by Glen A. Larson and Robert Thurston; Ace Tempo Star 05104; c 1988 (1st); $2.95 [original story]

Ace Tempo Stars

____ Stan Lee Presents: Battlestar Galactica; by Roger McKenzie; Ace Tempo Star 04876; c 1978 (1st); $1.95 [comic-novelization of the pilot episode "Saga of a Starworld"] [FC Illus: (clockwise from top left) Maren Jensen, Greene, Laurette Spang, Hathaway, Benedict, Hatch]

____ Stan Lee Presents: Battlestar Galactica Volume II; by Roger McKenzie; Ace Tempo Star 04877; c 1979 (1st); $2.25

The unsuccessful *Star Wars* takeoff inspired the extensive series of Berkley tie-ins, which were issued and sold well long after the show was canceled. The series includes novelizations through book 10, and original stories for books 11-14. Show-creator/executive producer Glen A. Larson is given co-author credit for the books, but wasn't involved in the writing. The show was revived as *Galactica 1980* for a second season (the episode "Galactica Discovers Earth," which piloted it, is novelized in the fifth book), but lasted only a few months under its new format.

In 1978 *Marvel Comics* bought the rights to do a series of comic books on the show, and in turn sold the reprint rights to them to Ace Tempo, which reissued the comics in book form.

BEACON HILL
August 25, 1975 - November 4, 1975; CBS

Popular Librarys

_____ Beacon Hill; by Henry Clement [Edward Fenton]; Popular Library 08397; c 1975 (1st); $1.50 [novelization of the pilot episode "Part I"] [FC Photo: (standing) David Dukes, Kathryn Walker, Stephen Elliott, Kitty Winn, Deann Mears, Maeve McGuire, (seated) Nancy Marchand]

_____ Beacon Hill #2: The Colonel and Fawn; by Henry Clement [Edward Fenton]; Popular Library 08427; c 1975 (1st); $1.50 [novelization of several episodes] [FC Photo: Walker]

The lavish and disastrous *Upstairs, Downstairs* takeoff flopped after 13 episodes, but not before Popular Library issued two books on the show, "total failures on every level" per Senior Editor Patrick O'Connor, "historical inaccuracies, endless script revisions, unyielding producers" per Dudley Frasier, who oversaw them.

BEAUTY AND THE BEAST
September 25, 1987 - August 4, 1990; CBS

Avons

_____ Beauty and the Beast; by Barbara Hambly; Avon 75795; c 1989 (1st); $3.95 [novelization of several episodes] [FC Illus: Linda Hamilton, Ron Perlman]

_____ Beauty and the Beast: Song of Orpheus; by Barbara Hambly; Avon 75798; c 1990 (1st); $3.95 [novelization of several episodes] [FC Illus: Perlman, Hamilton]

_____ Beauty and the Beast: Masques; by Ru Emerson; Avon 76194; c 1990 (1st); $3.95 [novelization of several episodes] [FC Illus: Hamilton, Perlman]

BEN CASEY
October 2, 1961 - March 21, 1966; ABC

Lancers [*]

____   Ben Casey; by William Johnston; Lancer 70-006; c 1962 (1st); $.40 [FC Photo: Vince Edwards]

____   Ben Casey: A Rage for Justice; by Norman Daniels; Lancer 70-011; c 1962 (1st); $.40 [autographed pin-up of Edwards inside] [FC Photo: Edwards]

____   Ben Casey: The Strength of his Hands; by Sam Elkin; Lancer 70-037; c 1963 (1st); $.40 [FC Photo: Edwards]

____   Ben Casey: The Fire Within; by Norman Daniels; Lancer 70-045; c 1963 (1st); $.40 [FC Illus: Edwards; BC Photo: Edwards (wallet-size cut-out)]

Belmont

____   Vince Edwards: A Biography of Television's "Dr. Ben Casey"; by George Carpozi, Jr.; Belmont L92-556; c 1962 (1st); $.50 [FC Photo: Sam Jaffe, Harry Landers, Edwards]

      [*] Original novels are counterparts to Lancer's *Dr. Kildare* series, then also being issued.   The two medical shows were rivals throughout their simultaneous runs, this show the less popular of the two.

THE BEVERLY HILLBILLIES
September 26, 1962 - September 7, 1971; CBS

Avons

____   The Clampetts of Beverly Hills; by Jerry Fay; Avon G1203; c 1964 (1st); $.50 [FC Photo: (clockwise from left) Donna Douglas, Max Baer, Jr., Buddy Ebsen, Irene Ryan]

____   The Beverly Hillbillies Live it Up!; by Jerry Fay; Avon G1250; c 1965 (1st); $.50 [FC Photo: Baer, Douglas, Ryan, Ebsen] [*]

Whitman

____   The Beverly Hillbillies: The Saga of Wildcat Creek; by Doris Schroeder; Whitman 1572; c 1963 (1st) [FC Photo: (clockwise from top) Baer, Douglas, Ryan, Ebsen]

Miscellaneous

____   The Beverly Hillbillies Book of Country Humor; by Lewis R. Benton, Ph.D., ed.; Dell 0553; c 1964 (1st); $.45 [FC Illus: (clockwise from top left) Douglas, Ryan, Baer, Ebsen] [illustrations by Jack Davis]

____   Jim Owen's Hillbilly Humor; by Jim M. Owen; Pocket 75623; c 1970 (1st); $.75 [BC Photo: (clockwise from top left) Douglas, Jim Owen, Ryan, Baer, Ebsen] [**]

[*] Back cover says "GRANNY takes to doctorin' the neighborhood with lizard eggs an' dried beetles; JED aims to get him a wealthy widow lady for a bride; JETHRO takes a high dive for a splashy gal; and ELLY MAY almost finishes off a girls' finishing school."

[**] Foreword by show-creator Paul Henning, who used many of Jim Owen's Hillbilly expressions (originally told by Owen to tourists on his Ozark Mountain fishing trips) in the show.

BEWITCHED
September 17, 1964 - July 1, 1972; ABC

_____ Bewitched; by Al Hine; Dell 0551; c 1965 (1st); $.45 [FC Illus: Dick York, Elizabeth Montgomery]

_____ Bewitched: The Opposite Uncle; by William Johnston; Whitman 1572; c 1970 (1st) [FC Illus: Agnes Moorehead, Montgomery, Dick Sargent]

The supernatural sitcom remains one of the medium's most memorable shows, and spawned a generation of fans who fantasized about having magical powers of their own. Al Hine's *Bewitched* is a delightful and at times hilarious account of Darrin and Samantha that begins with their first encounter and weaves novelizations of seven of the first eight episodes (see the Episodes Novelized List for details) together with an original through line and climax. With visits from the bumbling Aunt Clara, intrusions from Gladys Kravitz, advertising accounts nearly lost to witchcraft, and the always-within-earshot Endora, this scarce TV tie-in is a must-read for fans. (In the book, Samantha's maiden name is given as Dobson.)

Note: The uncle featured in William Johnston's *Bewitched: The Opposite Uncle* is not Uncle Arthur from the TV show but the original character in Uncle Kindly ... whose problem is worse than Arthur's. This book was released during the Dick Sargent years (he's pictured on the cover) and features the inept Esmerelda.

THE BIG VALLEY
September 15, 1965 - May 19, 1969; ABC

_____ The Big Valley; by Charles Heckelmann; Whitman 1569; c 1966 (1st) [FC Photos: (top) Barbara Stanwyck, (bottom) Lee Majors, Richard Long, Linda Evans, Peter Breck]

THE BIONIC WOMAN
January 21, 1976 - September 2, 1978; ABC/NBC

Berkleys

_____ The Bionic Woman: Welcome Home, Jaime; by Eileen Lottman; Berkley Z3230; c 1976 (1st); $1.25 [novelization of the pilot episode "Welcome Home, Jaime"] [FC Photo: Lindsay Wagner] [issued in UK by Star as "Double Identity," under Lottman's pseudonym of Maud Willis]

_____ The Bionic Woman: Extracurricular Activities; by Eileen Lottman; Berkley 03326; c 1977 (1st); $1.25 [novelization of the episodes "Claws" and "Canyon of Death"] [FC Photo: Wagner] [issued in UK by Star as "A Question of Life," as by Willis]

Miscellaneous

_____ Lindsay Wagner: Superstar of The Bionic Woman; by David Houston; Belmont Tower 50979; c 1976 (1st); $.95 [FC Photo: Wagner]

_____ The Bionic Woman's Brain Teasers; by Rose Paul; Tempo 12528; c 1975,76 (1st: 1976); $.95 [oversize] [FC Photo: Wagner]

The two-part pilot episode "Welcome Home, Jaime" began as a *Six Million Dollar Man* episode Jan-11-1976 and concluded as a *Bionic Woman* episode Jan-21-1976. The Bionic Woman had been a semi-regular on *The Six Million Dollar Man* since March of 1975, as Steve Austin's love interest.

BLACK SHEEP SQUADRON
September 21, 1976 - September 1, 1978; NBC

Bantams

_____ Baa Baa Black Sheep; by Col. Gregory "Pappy" Boyington; Bantam 10790; c 1958 (1st: 1977); $1.75

_____ The Black Sheep Squadron: Devil in the Slot; by Mike Jahn; Bantam 11938; c 1978 (1st); $1.95 [novelization of the episodes "Devil in the Slot" and "The Fastest Gun"]

_____ The Black Sheep Squadron: The Hawk Flies on Sunday; by Michael Jahn; Bantam 13645; c 1980 (1st); $2.25 [novelization of the episodes "Divine Wind," "The Hawk Flies on Sunday," and "Hotshot"]

Golden Apple

_____ The Black Sheep Squadron: The Hawk Flies on Sunday [cover-variation]; by Michael Jahn; Golden Apple 19746; c 1980 (1st: 1984); $2.50

The show (originally entitled *Baa Baa Black Sheep*) was based on Colonel Gregory "Pappy" Boyington's 1958 book *Baa Baa Black Sheep*, about his adventures as a World War II flying ace and leader of a misfit squadron called "The Black Sheep." With the release of the show in 1976 the book was re-issued by Bantam, along with two Mike Jahn novelizations. Later describing him as a "crusty maverick barely contained by U.S. military regulations," Jahn particularly enjoyed writing *The Hawk Flies on Sunday*, in which Boyington duels a top Japanese flying ace over the Solomon Islands in 1943. The adventure ends when the two men shoot each other down, parachute to safety on the same island, and share an American chocolate and a Japanese cigarette.

BLAKE'S 7
January 2, 1978 - December 21, 1981; BBC

_____ Terry Nation's Blake's 7: Their First Adventure; by Trevor Hoyle; Citadel Press
1103; c 1977 (1st: 1988); $3.95 [novelization]

_____ Terry Nation's Blake's 7: Scorpio Attack; by Trevor Hoyle; Citadel Press 1082;
c 1981 (1st: 1988); $3.50 [novelization]

_____ Terry Nation's Blake's 7: Project Avalon; by Trevor Hoyle; Citadel Press 1102;
c 1979 (1st: 1988); $3.95 [novelization] [FC Illus: Gareth Thomas]

BLONDIE
September 26, 1968 - January 9, 1969; CBS

Signets

_____ Blondie #1; by Chic Young; Signet P3710; c 1968 (1st); $.60 [BC Photo:
(clockwise from top left) Henny Backus, Jim Backus, Will Hutchins, Patricia
Harty, Pamelyn Ferdin, Peter Robbins]

_____ Blondie #2; by Chic Young; Signet P3711; c 1968 (1st); $.60 [BC Photo: same
as Blondie #1]

Show was based on the popular comic strip created by Chic Young in
1930. Still appearing in newspaper columns on a wide basis, Blondie Bumstead
inspired a series of movies in the 1930's and 40's and a brief 1957 NBC show
before CBS's 1968 remake. With the latter, Signet released the above cartoon
books, featuring comics reprinted from the *King Features* strip.

THE BOLD ONES
September 14, 1969 - January 16, 1973; NBC

Manor Books

_____ The Bold Ones: The Surrogate Womb; by Bruce Cassiday; Manor 95260; c
1973 (1st); $.95 [novelization of the episode "A Substitute Womb"] [FC Photo:
David Hartman, E.G. Marshall]

_____ The Bold Ones #2: A Quality of Fear; by Bruce Cassiday; Manor 95296; c 1973
(1st); $.95 [novelization of the episode "A Quality of Fear"] [FC Photo: John
Saxon, Hartman, Marshall]

_____ The Bold Ones #3: To Get Along With the Beautiful Girls; by Bruce Cassiday;
Manor 12215; c 1974 (1st); $1.25 [novelization of the episode "A Standard for
Manhood"] [FC Photo: Marshall, Hartman]

The show featured four rotating segments--"The Doctors," "The
Lawyers," "The Law Enforcers" (aka "The Protectors"), and "The Senator"--
during its first three seasons, before going strictly to "The Doctors" in the fourth
season, for which Manor Books issued the above Bruce Cassiday novelizations.

BONANZA
September 12, 1959 - January 16, 1973; NBC

Popular Library

____ Bonanza; by Noel Loomis; Popular Library PC1000; c 1960 (1st); $.35 [FC Illus: Pernell Roberts, Lorne Greene, Michael Landon, Dan Blocker]

Media Books

____ Bonanza: One Man with Courage; by Thomas Thompson; Media M101; c 1966 (1st); $.75 [FC Photos: Blocker, Landon, Greene]

____ Bonanza #2: Black Silver; by William R. Cox; Media M102; c 1967 (1st); $.75 [FC Photos: Greene, Landon, Blocker]

Paperback Librarys

____ Bonanza #1: Winter Grass; by Dean Owen [Dudley Dean McGaughy]; Paperback Library 52-726; c 1968 (1st); $.50 [FC Photo: Greene; BC Photo: Blocker, Greene, Landon]

____ Bonanza #2: Ponderosa Kill; by Dean Owen [Dudley Dean McGaughy]; Paperback Library 52-757; c 1968 (1st); $.50 [FC Photo: Landon; BC Photo: Blocker, Landon, Greene]

Whitmans

____ Bonanza: Killer Lion; by Steve Frazee; Whitman 1568; c 1966 (1st) [FC Photo: Landon, Blocker]

____ Bonanza: Heroes of the Wild West; by B.L. Bonham, ed.; Whitman 1569; c 1970 (1st) [FC Illus: Blocker, Landon, Greene]

> [9 stories of Western heroes "selected by the Cartwright Family": "Gold Stage to Plum Creek" (by William F. "Buffalo Bill" Cody), "Biscuits or Bullets" (Hank Wilson), "Mountain Ordeal" (Thomas Fitzpatrick), "The Price of Law and Order" (James Butler "Wild Bill" Hickok), "Little Black Bull" (Nat Love), "The Long Walk" (Christopher "Kit" Carson), "Treachery on the River" (William H. Ashley), "Up to Beaver" (Jedediah Strong Smith), and "A Funeral for the Princess" (Henry Maynadier).]

____ Bonanza: Treachery Trail; by Harry Whittington; Whitman 1571; c 1968 (1st) [FC Illus: Blocker, Greene, Roberts]

____ Bonanza: The Bubble Gum Kid; by George S. Elrick; Whitman Big Little Book 2002; c 1967 (1st) [FC Illus: Greene, Blocker, Landon]

The landmark Western inspired tie-ins by Thomas Thompson (an associate producer and writer for the show, his *One Man With Courage* "frames the background of Ben Cartwright and his sons on the legendary Ponderosa ... against a much broader canvas of history than could possibly be reproduced within the limits of the television screen"), William R. Cox (who also wrote for the show), Noel Loomis (twice-winner of the Western Writers of America Spur Award), Dean Owen, and others.

BOOTS AND SADDLES
1957 - 1959; Syndicated

_____   Boots and Saddles; by Edgar Jean Bracco; Berkley G-180; c 1958 (1st); $.35

Book includes 6 stories ("The Gift," "The Gatling Gun," "The Indian Scout," "The Marquis of Donnybrook," "The Court Martial," and "The Proud Condemned") "based on the California National Productions Television Series BOOTS AND SADDLES, The Story of the Fifth Cavalry."

BRACKEN'S WORLD
September 19, 1969 - December 25, 1970; NBC

Paperback Librarys

_____   Bracken's World #1; by Daoma Winston; Paperback Library 64-237; c 1969 (1st); $.75 [FC/BC Photos: Eleanor Parker, Elizabeth Allen, Peter Haskell, Linda Harrison, Laraine Stephens, Karen Jensen, Parker, Stephen Oliver]

_____   Bracken's World #2: The High Country; by Daoma Winston; Paperback Library 64-279; c 1970 (1st); $.75 [FC Photos: (top) Parker, Allen, Haskell, Harrison, Stephens, Jensen, Parker, Oliver, (bottom) Dennis Cole]

_____   Bracken's World #3: Sound Stage; by Daoma Winston; Paperback Library 64-364; c 1970 (1st); $.75 [FC Photos: (top) Cole, Allen, Haskell, Harrison, Stephens, Jensen, Cole, Oliver, (bottom) Harrison, Cole]

THE BRADY BUNCH
September 26, 1969 - August 30, 1974; ABC

Lancers

_____   The Brady Bunch; by William Johnston; Lancer 73-849; c 1969 (1st); $.60 [FC Photos: (clockwise, men first) Robert Reed, Barry Williams, Christopher Knight, Michael Lookinland, Maureen McCormick, Eve Plumb, Susan Olsen, Florence Henderson] [First page says: "Oh, Those Bradys!"]

_____   The Brady Bunch #2: Showdown at the P.T.A. Corral; by William Johnston; Lancer 73-864; c 1969 (1st); $.60 [FC "Lollipop" Photo: (top) Reed, (middle) Plumb, Williams, McCormick, Olsen, Henderson, (bottom) Lookinland, Knight]

_____   The Brady Bunch #3: Count Up to Blast-Down!; by William Johnston; Lancer 73872; c 1970 (1st); $.60 [FC Photo: (clockwise from top) Reed, Plumb, McCormick, Olsen, Henderson, Lookinland, Knight, Williams] [various copies were issued with two different logos - either will do]

_____   The Brady Bunch #4: The Bumbler Strikes Again; by William Johnston; Lancer 73891; c 1970 (1st); $.60 [FC Photo: (top) Williams, Henderson, Plumb, Reed, (bottom) Knight, Olsen, McCormick, Lookinland]

_____ The Brady Bunch #5: The Quarterback Who Came to Dinner; by William Johnston; Lancer 73206; c 1970 (1st); $.60 [FC Photo, from the same shoot as #3: (clockwise from top) Reed, Plumb, McCormick, Olsen, Henderson, Lookinland, Knight, Williams - Peter looks better in #3]

Tiger Beats

_____ The Brady Bunch in "The Treasure of Mystery Island"; by Jack Matcha; Tiger Beat XQ2011; c 1972 (1st); $.95 [FC Photo: McCormick, Knight, Lookinland, Plumb, Olsen, Williams]

_____ The Brady Bunch in the New York Mystery; by Jack Matcha; Tiger Beat XQ2014; c 1972 (1st); $.95 [FC Photo: McCormick, Williams, Knight]

_____ The Brady Bunch in Adventure on the High Seas; by Jack Matcha; Tiger Beat XQ2017; c 1973 (1st); $.95 [FC Photos: all the kids but Jan]

Here's eight stories of a lovely lady ... *The Brady Bunch* inspired tie-ins by Lancer and Tiger Beat. The Lancers are lighthearted adventures, while in the Tiger Beats the Bradys become involved in mysteries during family outings. Ann B. Davis as housekeeper Alice isn't pictured on any of the books.

Tiger Beat author Jack Matcha received "literally hundreds" of letters from fans, many of whom felt a kinship with the Brady kids in the stories. Matcha answered a few of the letters but unfortunately later discarded them. In the first two Lancers, Cindy Brady speaks with a lisp; by the third book the lisp (and irritation to the reader) is gone. Alas, poor Cindy is really the geek in these.

THE BRIAN KEITH SHOW
See THE LITTLE PEOPLE

BRIDGET LOVES BERNIE
September 16, 1972 - September 8, 1973; CBS

_____ Bridget Loves Bernie; by Paul Fairman; Lancer 74795; c 1972 (1st); $.75 [FC Photo: David Birney, Meredith Baxter-Birney]

THE BROTHERS BRANNAGAN
1960; Syndicated

_____ The Brothers Brannagan; by Henry E. Helseth; Signet S1973; c 1961 (1st); $.35

THE BUCCANEERS
September 22, 1956 - September 14, 1957; CBS

_____ The Buccaneers; by Alice Sankey; Whitman Big Little Book 1646; c 1958 (1st) [FC Illus: Robert Shaw]

BUCK ROGERS IN THE 25TH CENTURY
September 20, 1979 - April 16, 1981; NBC

Dells

_____ Buck Rogers in the 25th Century; by Addison E. Steele [Richard A. Lupoff]; Dell 10843; c 1978 (1st); $1.95 [novelization of the pilot episode "The Awakening"] [FC Illus: Gil Gerard, Erin Gray]

_____ Buck Rogers #2: That Man on Beta; by Addison E. Steele [Richard A. Lupoff]; Dell 10948; c 1979 (1st); $1.95 [FC Illus: Gerard, Gray] [FC says "Based on a story and teleplay by Bob Shayne"]

Fotonovel

_____ Buck Rogers in the 25th Century Fotonovel; Fotonovel Vol. 12; c 1979 (1st); $2.75 [photo-novelization of the pilot episode "The Awakening"] [FC Illus: (center) Gerard, Gray, (left) Pamela Hensley]

Pilot episode "The Awakening," novelized in the first Dell and the Fotonovel, was first seen as the 1979 feature film *Buck Rogers in the 25th Century*.

THE BUGALOOS
September 12, 1970 - September 2, 1972; NBC

Curtis'

_____ The Bugaloos and the Vile Vibes; by Chris Stratton [Richard Hubbard]; Curtis 07131; c 1971 (1st); $.75 [FC Photo: John Philpott, Carolyn Ellis, Wayne Laryea, John McIndoe]

_____ The Bugaloos #2: Rock City Rebels; by Chris Stratton [Richard Hubbard]; Curtis 07132; c 1971 (1st); $.75 [FC Photos: (clockwise from top left) McIndoe, Ellis, Laryea, Philpott]

_____ The Bugaloos #3: Benita's Platter Pollution; by Chris Stratton [Richard Hubbard]; Curtis 07136; c 1971 (1st); $.75 [FC Photo: McIndoe, Ellis, Laryea, Philpott]

Saturday morning children's show is pronounced "BUG-a-lews." On the spines, covers, and title pages of the three Curtis books they call it "Bugaloos" eight times and "The Bugaloos" four times.

BURKE'S LAW
September 20, 1963 - May 5, 1965; ABC

Perma/Pocket

_____ Burke's Law: Who Killed Beau Sparrow?; by Roger Fuller [Don Tracy]; Perma M-4310; c 1964 (1st); $.35 [novelization of the episode "Who Killed Beau Sparrow?"] [BC Photo: Gene Barry] [issued in UK by Fontana as "Burke's Law"]

_____ Burke's Law: Who Killed Madcap Millicent?; by Roger Fuller [Don Tracy]; Pocket 50030; c 1964 (1st); $.50 [original story?] [FC Photo: Barry] [issued in UK by Fontana as "The Martini Murders"]

CHiPS
September 15, 1977 - July 17, 1983; NBC

_____ CHiPs: The Erik Estrada Scrapbook; by Susan Katz; Tempo 17209; c 1980 (1st); $1.95 [FC Photo: Erik Estrada]

CADE'S COUNTY
September 19, 1971 - September 4, 1972; CBS

_____ Cade's County; by Alfred Lawrence; Popular Library 08184; c 1972 (1st); $.75 [FC Photo: (from left) Edgar Buchanan, Glenn Ford, Taylor Lacher, Victor Campos]

CAGNEY & LACEY
March 25, 1982 - August 25, 1988; CBS

_____ Cagney & Lacey; by Serita Deborah Stevens; Dell 11050; c 1985 (1st); $2.95 [novelization of the TV-movie pilot "Cagney & Lacey (Oct-08-1981)] [FC Photo: Sharon Gless, Tyne Daly]

CAIN'S HUNDRED
September 19, 1961 - September 11, 1962; NBC

_____ Cain's Hundred; by Evan Lee Heyman; Popular Library PC1010; c 1961 (1st); $.35 [FC Photo: Peter Mark Richman]

CAN YOU TOP THIS?
1970-1971; Syndicated

_____ Can You Top This?; by Panelists and Guest Stars; Tempo 05365; c 1971 (1st); $.75 [FC Illus: Wink Martindale, with panelists]

CANNON
September 14, 1971 - September 19, 1976; CBS

_____ Cannon #1: Murder By Gemini; by Richard Gallagher; Lancer 74783; c 1971 (1st); $.75 [FC Photo: William Conrad]

_____ Cannon: Murder By Gemini [cover-variation]; by Richard Gallagher; Magnum 74783; c 1971 (unsp: 1976); $1.50 [FC Photo: Conrad]

_____ Cannon #2: The Stewardess Strangler; by Richard Gallagher; Lancer 75260; c 1971 (1st); $.95 [FC Photo: Conrad]

The show with the opening credits that featured a series of round balls making patterns to tuba music as it introduced heavyweight private eye Frank Cannon (he could throw his weight around with the best of them--in some of the most hilarious action sequences on TV--but he also had a soft side) inspired two Lancer tie-ins. The first, *Murder By Gemini*, was re-issued by Magnum; the re-issue is identical to the first printing but lacks the "#1" in the title, causing its front cover to vary. Author Richard Gallagher based the story on an actual event in which two identical twins were acquitted of the murder one of them committed, because it was impossible to prove which one did it.

Murder By Gemini was also issued in Britain by Triphammer, which issued three additional titles not released here: *The Golden Bullet, The Deadly Chance,* and *I've Got You Covered*, all by Paul Denver.

CAPITOL
March 29, 1982 - March 20, 1987; CBS

Pioneer Communications Networks

____ Capitol #1: Unspoken Desires; by Mae Miner; Pioneer 91; c 1986 (1st); $2.50 [novelization of several episodes]

____ Capitol #2: Intimate Glimpses; by Madeline Tabler; Pioneer 92; c 1986 (1st); $2.50 [novelization of several episodes]

____ Capitol #3: Forbidden Tomorrows; by Cathy Cunningham [Chet Cunningham]; Pioneer 93; c 1986 (1st); $2.50 [novelization of several episodes]

____ Capitol #4: Passion's Masterpiece; by Cathy Cunningham [Chet Cunningham]; Pioneer 94; c 1986 (1st); $2.50 [novelization of several episodes]

Additional titles by the above authors were written but apparently not published, due to the cancellation of the show.

CAPTAIN DAVID GRIEF
1956; Syndicated

____ Adventures of Captain David Grief; by Jack London; Popular Library PC300; c 1911+ (1st: 1957); $.25

The show was based on the Jack London adventure stories featured in the 1911 book *A Son of the Sun*. Later renamed *Adventures of Captain David Grief*, the book was re-issued by Popular Library as a TV tie-in in 1957. Its stories are: "The Proud Goat of Aloysius Pankburn," "The Devils of Fautino," "The Jokers of New Gibbon," "A Little Account With Swithin Hall," "A Goboto Night," "The Feathers of the Sun," and "The Pearls of Parlay."

CAPTAIN NICE
January 9, 1967 - August 28, 1967; NBC

____ Captain Nice; by William Johnston; Tempo T-155; c 1967 (1st); $.60 [FC Photo: William Daniels]

CHARLES IN CHARGE
October 3, 1984 - July 24, 1985; CBS
1987 - 1990; Syndicated

Scholastic Book Services

_____ Charles in Charge; by Elizabeth Faucher; Scholastic Book Services 33550; c 1984 (1st); $2.25 [novelization of the pilot episode "Charles in Charge"] [FC Photo: Scott Baio; BC Photo: (clockwise from top left) James Widdoes, Julie Cobb, Willie Aames, Baio, Michael Pearlman, Jonathan Ward, April Lerman] [re-issued as #42024]

_____ Charles in Charge, Again; by Elizabeth Faucher; Scholastic Book Services 41008; c 1987 (1st); $2.50 [novelization of the episode "Amityville"] [FC Photo: Baio; BC Photo: (clockwise from top left) Willie Aames, James Callahan, Sandra Kerns, Josie Davis, Nicole Eggert, Baio, Alexander Polinsky]

First *Charles in Charge* book is from the show's 1984-85 CBS run, when Charles was in charge of the Pembroke family. Second book is from the show's late-80's syndicated run, when Charles was in charge of the Powell family. The books' back covers picture the respective families.

CHARLIE'S ANGELS
September 22, 1976 - August 19, 1981; ABC

Ballantines

_____ Charlie's Angels; by Max Franklin [Richard Deming]; Ballantine 25665; c 1977 (1st); $1.50 [novelization of the TV-movie pilot "Charlie's Angels" (Mar-21-1976)] [FC Photo: Jaclyn Smith, Farrah Fawcett-Majors, Kate Jackson]

_____ Charlie's Angels #2: The Killing Kind; by Max Franklin [Richard Deming]; Ballantine 25707; c 1977 (1st); $1.50 [novelization of the episode "The Killing Kind"] [FC Photo: Fawcett-Majors, Jackson, Smith]

_____ Charlie's Angels #3: Angels on a String; by Max Franklin [Richard Deming]; Ballantine 25691; c 1977 (1st); $1.50 [novelization of the episode "Angels on a String"] [FC Photo: Jackson, Fawcett-Majors, Smith]

_____ Charlie's Angels #4: Angels in Chains; by Max Franklin [Richard Deming]; Ballantine 27182; c 1977 (1st); $1.50 [novelization of the episode "Angels in Chains"] [FC Photo: Jackson, Smith, Fawcett-Majors] [*]

[*] The episode "Angels in Chains," in which the women go undercover in a women's prison, remains a popular favorite among fans.

_____ Charlie's Angels #5: Angels on Ice; by Max Franklin [Richard Deming]; Ballantine 27342; c 1978 (1st); $1.75 [novelization of the episode "Angels on Ice"] [FC Photo: Smith, Jackson, Cheryl Ladd]

Biographies

_____ Farrah: An Unauthorized Biography of Farrah Fawcett-Majors; by Patricia Burstein; Signet W7723; c 1977 (1st); $1.50 [FC Photo: Fawcett-Majors]

_____ Farrah's World; by Claire Susans; Dell 12922; c 1977 (1st); $1.50 [FC Photo: Fawcett-Majors]

_____ Farrah & Lee; by Connie Berman; Tempo 14275; c 1977 (1st); $1.25 [FC Photo: Fawcett-Majors, Lee Majors]

_____ Peter Travers' Favorite TV Angels; by Peter Travers; Xerox N 104; c 1978 (1st) [FC Photos: (clockwise from top) Fawcett-Majors, Jackson, Smith, Ladd]

Aaron Spelling's biggest hit inspired the above books. The first four Ballantines novelize episodes from the show's first season, and picture Kate Jackson, Jaclyn Smith, and Farrah Fawcett-Majors (*Angels* Sabrina, Kelly, and Jill) on the covers. The fifth book novelizes a second season episode, and pictures Jackson, Smith, and Cheryl Ladd on the cover. The delectable Fawcett-Majors, whose braless jiggle was a national sensation, left the show after the first season to pursue a movie career, and was replaced Cheryl Ladd (Ladd's character Kris being the younger sister of Fawcett-Major's Jill).

CHASE
September 11, 1973 - August 28, 1974; NBC

_____ Chase; by Norman Daniels; Berkley 02553; c 1974 (1st); $.95 [novelization of the TV-movie pilot "Chase" (Mar-24-1973)]

Two additional *Chase* books were planned, and had been assigned to Norman Daniels, but were dropped when the show was canceled.

CHEERS
September 30, 1982 - August 19, 1993; NBC

_____ The Cheers Bartending Guide; by Marcia Rosen and Gerry Hunt; Avon 70189; c 1983 + (1st: 1986); $3.95 [FC Photo: (top) George Wendt, Shelley Long, Kelsey Grammer, Ted Danson, John Ratzenberger, (bottom) Woody Harrelson, Rhea Perlman]

With Norm's Guide to Beers of the World, Carla's Hangover Helpers, Cliff's Bar Toasts For Any Occasion, and more.

CHEYENNE
September 20, 1955 - September 13, 1963; ABC

_____ Cheyenne and the Lost Gold of Lion Park; by Steve Frazee; Whitman 1587; c 1958 (1st) [FC Illus: Clint Walker]

CHICO AND THE MAN
September 13, 1974 - July 21, 1978; NBC

_____ Chico and the Man: The Freddie Prinze Story; by Maria Pruetzel and John A. Barbour; Master's Press 89251; c 1978 (1st); $2.25 [FC Photo: Freddie Prinze; BC Photos: Jack Albertson, Prinze]

This biography of suicide-victim *Chico and the Man* star Freddie Prinze was co-authored by his mother, Maria Pruetzel.

CIMMARON STRIP
September 7, 1967 - September 19, 1968; CBS

_____ Cimmaron Strip; by Richard Meade [Ben Haas]; Popular Library 60-2245; c 1967 (1st); $.60 [FC Photos: (top) Stuart Whitman, (bottom) Randy Boone, Percy Herbert, Jill Townsend]

CIRCUS BOY
September 23, 1956 - September 11, 1958; NBC/ABC

Whitmans

_____ Circus Boy: Under the Big Top; by Dorothea J. Snow; Whitman 1549; c 1957 (1st) [FC Illus: Mickey Dolenz]

_____ Circus Boy: War on Wheels; by Dorothea J. Snow; Whitman 1578; c 1958 (1st) [FC Illus: Dolenz]

Then-child star and future Monkee Mickey Dolenz used the stage name Mickey Braddock for his starring role in *Circus Boy*, in which he played a 12-year old orphan adopted by members of a traveling circus. With *The Monkees* TV show several years later Dolenz achieved much greater fame, but his former role was not forgotten, for in the Feb-13-1967 *Monkees* episode "The Monkees and the Circus" Dolenz is heard singing the *Circus Boy* theme song.

COLUMBO
September 15, 1971 - June 23, 1978; NBC

Popular Librarys

_____ Columbo; by Alfred Lawrence; Popular Library 01524; c 1972 (1st); $.75 [original story] [issued in UK by Star as "The Christmas Killing"] [FC Photo: Peter Falk] [*]

_____ Columbo #1 [cover-variation]; by Alfred Lawrence; Popular Library 08382; c 1972 (unsp: 1975); $1.25 [FC Photo: Falk] [*]

[*] Issued as "Columbo" in 1972 and as "Columbo #1" in 1975.

_____ Columbo #2: The Dean's Death; by Alfred Lawrence; Popular Library 00265; c 1975 (1st); $1.25 [original story] [FC Photo: Falk]

_____ Columbo #3: Any Old Port in a Storm; by Henry Clement [Edward Fenton]; Popular Library 00317; c 1975 (1st); $1.25 [novelization of the episode "Any Old Port in a Storm"] [FC Photo: Falk]

_____ Columbo #4: By Dawn's Early Light; by Henry Clement [Edward Fenton]; Popular Library 00326; c 1975 (1st); $1.25 [novelization of the episode "By Dawn's Early Light"] [FC Photo: Falk]

_____   Columbo #5: Murder by the Book; by Lee Hays; Popular Library 03109; c 1976 (1st); $1.50 [novelization of the pilot episode "Murder by the Book"] [FC Photo: Falk]

_____   Columbo #6: A Deadly State of Mind; by Lee Hays; Popular Library 03118; c 1976 (1st); $1.50 [novelization of the episode "A Deadly State of Mind"] [FC Photo: Falk]

One of TV's most popular crimefighters, the wily Columbo inspired six very successful Popular Library tie-ins, including two by distinguished children's book author Edward Fenton as Henry Clement (the pseudonym was derived from his father, Henry Clemence Fenton). Among the episodes novelized in the series was "Murder by the Book," directed by a young Steven Spielberg and a favorite episode among fans. While the episode aired Sep-15-1971 as the first in the regular series, Peter Falk had played the character in two prior TV-movies: "Prescription: Murder" (Feb-20-1968) and "Ransom for a Dead Man" (Mar-01-1971). The show, canceled in 1978, was resurrected eleven years later, with Falk returning to the legendary role in a series of TV-movies.

COMBAT
October 2, 1962 - August 29, 1967; ABC

Lancers

_____   Combat; by Harold Calin; Lancer 70-042; c 1963 (1st); $.40 [FC Photo: Rick Jason; BC Photo: Vic Morrow]

_____   Combat: Men, Not Heroes; by Harold Calin; Lancer 70-060; c 1963 (1st); $.40 [FC Photo: Jason]

_____   Combat: No Rest for Heroes; by Harold Calin; Lancer 72-910; c 1965 (1st); $.50 [BC Photo: Jason, Morrow]

Whitman

_____   Combat: The Counterattack; by Franklin M. Davis, Jr.; Whitman 1520; c 1964 (1st)

Popular World War II drama inspired the above scarce Lancer tie-ins. Noted for its realism and human interest stories, the show was about a U.S. Army platoon making its way across Europe after D-Day. The books picture star Vic Morrow, killed in 1982 when a helicopter crashed in a freak accident during the filming of the movie *The Twilight Zone*.

DAKTARI
January 11, 1966 - January 15, 1969; CBS

_____   Daktari; by Jess Shelton; Ace G-604; c 1966 (1st); $.50 [FC Photo: Marshall Thompson; BC Photo: (L-R, middle actor unkn) Cheryl Miller, Yale Summers, Hedley Mattingly, Hari Rhodes] [*]

_____ Daktari: Night of Terror; by George S. Elrick; Whitman Big Little Book 2018; c 1968 (1st)

[*] Book was also published (as *#1: Mystery at Wameru*) in Britain by Souvenir Press/Four Square, which issued three additional titles not released here: *#2: The Pintu Dogs* (by Frank Denver), *#3: The Happy Hippo* (Denver), and *#4: The Frighteners* (Peter Leslie).

DALLAS
April 2, 1978 - May 3, 1991; CBS

Dells

_____ Dallas [white cover]; by Lee Raintree [Con Sellers]; Dell 11752; c 1978 (1st); $2.25 [FC Illus: (top) Barbara Bel Geddes, Jim Davis, Patrick Duffy, Charlene Tilton, (bottom) Larry Hagman]

_____ Dallas [red cover]; by Lee Raintree [Con Sellers]; Dell 11752; c 1978 (1st new Dell: 1980); $2.50 [FC Photo: (clockwise from top left) Hagman, Linda Gray, Victoria Principal, Duffy, Bel Geddes, Tilton, Davis]

Bantams

_____ The Ewings of Dallas; by Burt Hirschfeld; Bantam 14439; c 1980 (1st); $2.75 [novelization of several episodes] [FC Illus: Gray, Hagman; BC Illus: Bel Geddes, Duffy, Principal, Davis, Tilton]

_____ Dallas: The Quotations of J. R. Ewing; by Diane J. Perlberg & Joelle Delbourgo, eds.; Bantam 14440; c 1980 (1st); $1.50 [48-page book with stapled spine, has photos and quotes excerpted from the show] [FC Photo: Hagman]

_____ The Women of Dallas; by Burt Hirschfeld; Bantam 14497; c 1981 (1st); $2.75 [novelization of several episodes] [FC Illus: (standing) Tilton, Mary Crosby, Hagman, Gray, Principal, (seated) Bel Geddes]

_____ The Men of Dallas; by Burt Hirschfeld; Bantam 20390; c 1981 (1st); $2.95 [novelization of several episodes] [FC Illus: Steve Kanaly, Duffy, Hagman, Davis, Ken Kercheval]

Miscellaneous

_____ The Official Dallas Trivia Book; by Jason Bonderoff; Signet AE3504; c 1984 (1st: 1985); $2.95 [FC Photos: Principal, Kercheval, Tilton, Gray, Hagman, Donna Reed, Kanaly, Susan Howard, Duffy]

Pioneer Communications Networks

_____ Dallas #1: Love Conquers Fear; by Paul Mantell & Avery Hart; Pioneer 81; c 1986 (1st); $2.50 [novelization of several episodes]

_____ Dallas #2: Ardent Memories; by Paul Mantell & Avery Hart; Pioneer 82; c 1986 (1st); $2.50 [novelization of several episodes]

_____ Dallas #3: Love's Challenge; by Paul Mantell & Avery Hart; Pioneer 83; c 1986 (1st); $2.50 [novelization of several episodes]

_____ Dallas #4: The Power of Passion; by Paul Mantell & Avery Hart; Pioneer 84; c 1986 (1st); $2.50 [novelization of several episodes]

_____ Dallas #5: Dangerous Desire; by Paul Mantell & Avery Hart; Pioneer 85; c 1986 (1st); $2.50 [novelization of several episodes]

_____ Dallas #6: Double Dealing; by Paul Mantell & Avery Hart; Pioneer 86; c 1986 (1st); $2.50 [novelization of several episodes] [FC Photos: Kanaly, Tilton, Kercheval]

_____ Dallas #7: Hostage Heart; by Paul Mantell & Avery Hart; Pioneer 87; c 1986 (1st); $2.50 [novelization of several episodes] [FC Photos: Principal, Duffy]

_____ Dallas #8: This Cherished Land; by Paul Mantell & Avery Hart; Pioneer 88; c 1986 (1st); $2.50 [novelization of several episodes] [FC Photo: Bel Geddes]

_____ Dallas #9: Power Play; by Paul Mantell & Avery Hart; Pioneer 89; c 1987 (1st); $2.50 [novelization of several episodes] [FC Photos: Gray, Kercheval]

_____ Dallas #10: Winner Take All; by Paul Mantell & Avery Hart; Pioneer 90; c 1987 (1st); $2.50 [novelization of several episodes] [FC Photos: Gray, Duffy]

_____ Dallas #11: Reality Strikes; by Mary Clare Kersten; Pioneer 100; c 1987 (1st); $2.50 [novelization of several episodes] [FC Photo: Tilton]

_____ Dallas #12: Shattered Dreams; by Laura Taylor; Pioneer 101; c 1987 (1st); $2.50 [novelization of several episodes]

_____ Dallas #13: A Cry in the Night; by Monica Dean; Pioneer 102; c 1987 (1st); $2.50 [novelization of several episodes]

_____ Dallas #14: Family Secrets; by Mary Clare Kersten; Pioneer 103; c 1987 (1st); $2.50 [novelization of several episodes] [FC Photo: Principal]

Evening soap about lust and greed in the oil business inspired the above books. The book *Dallas*, by Con Sellers as Lee Raintree, began as an unfilmed *Dallas* script the producers asked Sellers to rewrite. Sellers suggested turning it into a novel instead, and in so doing much of his original work pertaining to the Ewing family background provided the framework for the TV show (it was still in its first season). Immensely successful--and profitable to Sellers--the book went into numerous printings and several foreign editions. Additional *Dallas* titles were by Bantam (a series of very successful Burt Hirschfeld novelizations) and Pioneer Communications Network.

DANGER MAN
April 5, 1961 - September 13, 1961; CBS

_____ Danger Man: Target for Tonight; by Richard Telfair [Richard Jessup]; Dell First Edition K111; c 1962 (1st); $.40

Patrick McGoohan introduced the character of John Drake in this 1961 show, and resumed the role in the 1965-66 show *Secret Agent* (see also it). Both shows were produced in England; the first version was 30-minutes and had Drake working for NATO, the second was 60-minutes and had him working for the British Intelligence. The above book's only reference to the show is in the front cover blurb "an exciting novel of international intrigue and suspense, featuring Danger Man John Drake."

DARK SHADOWS
June 27, 1966 - April 2, 1971; ABC

Paperback Library Numbered Series

_____ Dark Shadows #1; by Marilyn Ross; Paperback Library 52-386; c 1966 (1st); $.50 [illustrated cover]

_____ Dark Shadows #1; by Marilyn Ross; Paperback Library 52-386; c 1966 (4th: 1968); $.50 [Photo cover: Jonathan Frid, Alexandra Moltke]

_____ Dark Shadows #2: Victoria Winters; by Marilyn Ross; Paperback Library 52-421; c 1967 (1st); $.50 [illustrated cover]

_____ Dark Shadows #2: Victoria Winters; by Marilyn Ross; Paperback Library 52-421; c 1967 (2nd: 1968); $.50 [Photo cover: Moltke, Frid]

_____ Dark Shadows #3: Strangers at Collins House; by Marilyn Ross; Paperback Library 52-543; c 1967 (1st); $.50 [illustrated cover]

_____ Dark Shadows #3: Strangers at Collins House; by Marilyn Ross; Paperback Library 52-543; c 1967 (2nd: 1968); $.50 [Photo cover: Moltke, Frid]

_____ Dark Shadows #4: The Mystery of Collinwood; by Marilyn Ross; Paperback Library 52-610; c 1968 (1st); $.50 [illustrated cover]

_____ Dark Shadows #4: The Mystery of Collinwood; by Marilyn Ross; Paperback Library 52-610; c 1968 (3rd: 1968); $.50 [Photo cover: Frid, Moltke]

_____ Dark Shadows #5: The Curse of Collinwood; by Marilyn Ross; Paperback Library 52-608; c 1968 (1st); $.50 [FC illus: Frid]

_____ Dark Shadows #6: Barnabas Collins; by Marilyn Ross; Paperback Library 62-001; c 1968 (1st); $.50 [FC Photo: Frid]

_____ Dark Shadows #7: The Secret of Barnabas Collins; by Marilyn Ross; Paperback Library 62-039; c 1969 (1st); $.50 [FC Photo: Frid]

_____ Dark Shadows #8: The Demon of Barnabas Collins; by Marilyn Ross; Paperback Library 62-084; c 1969 (1st); $.50 [FC Photo: Frid]

_____ Dark Shadows #9: The Foe of Barnabas Collins; by Marilyn Ross; Paperback Library 62-135; c 1969 (1st); $.50 [FC Photo: Frid]

_____ Dark Shadows #10: The Phantom and Barnabas Collins; by Marilyn Ross; Paperback Library 62-195; c 1969 (1st); $.50 [FC Photo: Frid]

_____ Dark Shadows #11: Barnabas Collins versus the Warlock; by Marilyn Ross; Paperback Library 62-212; c 1969 (1st); $.50 [FC Photo: Frid]

_____ Dark Shadows #12: The Peril of Barnabas Collins; by Marilyn Ross; Paperback Library 62-244; c 1969 (1st); $.50 [FC Photo: Frid, Roger Davis, Louis Edmonds, David Selby]

_____ Dark Shadows #13: Barnabas Collins and the Mysterious Ghost; by Marilyn Ross; Paperback Library 63-258; c 1970 (1st); $.60 [FC Photo: Frid, Selby]

_____ Dark Shadows #14: Barnabas Collins and Quentin's Demon; by Marilyn Ross; Paperback Library 63-275; c 1970 (1st); $.60 [FC Photo: (clockwise from left) Selby, Edmonds, Frid, Nancy Barrett]

_____ Dark Shadows #15: Barnabas Collins and the Gypsy Witch; by Marilyn Ross; Paperback Library 63-296; c 1970 (1st); $.60 [FC Photo: Frid]

_____ Dark Shadows #16: Barnabas, Quentin and the Mummy's Curse; by Marilyn Ross; Paperback Library 63-318; c 1970 (1st); $.60 [FC Photo: Frid, Selby]

_____ Dark Shadows #17: Barnabas, Quentin and the Avenging Ghost; by Marilyn Ross; Paperback Library 63-338; c 1970 (1st); $.60 [FC Photo: Frid, Selby]

_____ Dark Shadows #18: Barnabas, Quentin and the Nightmare Assassin; by Marilyn Ross; Paperback Library 63-363; c 1970 (1st); $.60 [FC Photo: Frid, Edmonds, Selby]

_____ Dark Shadows #19: Barnabas, Quentin and the Crystal Coffin; by Marilyn Ross; Paperback Library 63-385; c 1970 (1st); $.60 [FC Photo: Frid, Selby]

_____ Dark Shadows #20: Barnabas, Quentin and the Witch's Curse; by Marilyn Ross; Paperback Library 63-402; c 1970 (1st); $.60 [FC Photo: Selby, Frid]

_____ Dark Shadows #21: Barnabas, Quentin and the Haunted Cave; by Marilyn Ross; Paperback Library 63-427; c 1970 (1st); $.60 [FC Photo: Selby, Frid]

_____ Dark Shadows #22: Barnabas, Quentin and the Frightened Bride; by Marilyn Ross; Paperback Library 63-446; c 1970 (1st); $.60 [FC Photo: Frid, David Henesy, Selby]

_____ Dark Shadows #23: Barnabas, Quentin and the Scorpio Curse; by Marilyn Ross; Paperback Library 63-468; c 1970 (1st); $.60 [FC Photo: Barrett, Selby]

_____ Dark Shadows #24: Barnabas, Quentin and the Serpent; by Marilyn Ross; Paperback Library 63-491; c 1970 (1st); $.60 [FC Photo: Davis, Frid, Edmonds]

_____ Dark Shadows #25: Barnabas, Quentin and the Magic Potion; by Marilyn Ross; Paperback Library 63-515; c 1970 (1st: 1971); $.60 [FC Photo: Frid]

_____ Dark Shadows #26: Barnabas, Quentin and the Body Snatchers; by Marilyn Ross; Paperback Library 63-534; c 1971 (1st); $.60 [FC Photo: Frid]

Dark Shadows #27: Barnabas, Quentin and Dr. Jekyll's Son; by Marilyn Ross; Paperback Library 63-554; c 1971 (1st); $.60 [FC Photo: Henesy, Frid]

Dark Shadows #28: Barnabas, Quentin and the Grave Robbers; by Marilyn Ross; Paperback Library 63-585; c 1971 (1st); $.60 [FC Photo: Selby, Frid]

Dark Shadows #29: Barnabas, Quentin and the Sea Ghost; by Marilyn Ross; Paperback Library 64-663; c 1971 (1st); $.75 [FC Photo: Frid]

Dark Shadows #30: Barnabas, Quentin and the Mad Magician; by Marilyn Ross; Paperback Library 64-714; c 1971 (1st); $.75 [FC Photo: Selby]

Dark Shadows #31: Barnabas, Quentin and the Hidden Tomb; by Marilyn Ross; Paperback Library 64-772; c 1971 (1st); $.75 [FC Photo: Frid]

Dark Shadows #32: Barnabas, Quentin and the Vampire Beauty; by Marilyn Ross; Paperback Library 64-824; c 1972 (1st); $.75 [FC Photo: Frid, Barrett]

Paperback Library Miscellaneous Titles

Barnabas Collins in a Funny Vein; Paperback Library 62-062; c 1969 (1st); $.50 [FC Photo: Frid]

Barnabas Collins: A Personal Picture Album; by Jonathan Frid, ed.; Paperback Library 62-210; c 1969 (1st); $.50 [FC Photo: Frid]

The Dark Shadows Book of Vampires and Werewolves; by Barnabas and Quentin Collins, eds.; Paperback Library 63-419; c 1970 (1st); $.60 [FC Photo: Selby, Frid]

> [9 stories: "The Vampyre" (by John Polidori), "Mrs. Amworth" (E.F. Benson), "Wolves Don't Cry" (Bruce Elliott), "The Vampire of Croglin Grange" (Augustus Hare), "Men-Wolves" (From the Polish), "For the Blood is the Life" (F. Marion Crawford), "Count Magnus" (M.R. James), "The Vampire Legend: Its Origin and Nature" (Lewis Spence), and "The Vampire Nemesis" ("Dolly").]

House of Dark Shadows; by Marilyn Ross; Paperback Library 64-537; c 1970 (1st); $.75 [novelization of the movie] [FC Photo: (5 in foreground) Grayson Hall, Frid, Kathryn Leigh Scott, Joan Bennett, Edmonds, (3 in background) Henesy, Barrett, Thayer David]

Ace Cookbook

The Dark Shadows Cookbook; by Jody Cameron Malis; Ace 13810; c 1970 (1st); $.75 [FC Photo: Frid; BC Photo: Selby]

After a lackluster first season, the Gothic soap *Dark Shadows* took an eerie turn by adding the vampire Barnabas Collins to its roster. Former stage actor Jonathan Frid stepped into the part with ease, and the show's popularity soared! Unlike other screen vampires which preceded him, Barnabas was played as brooding, guilt-prone, and serene, and the audience loved it. The show quickly gained a cult following, and enjoyed four very successful subsequent seasons. Its popularity continues, through such means as the annual *Dark*

Shadows conventions, and an important part of the picture is the numerous *Dark Shadows* TV tie-ins.

Canadian novelist Dan Ross had written a number of successful Gothics for Paperback Library when the publisher bought the rights to do the *Dark Shadows* books and asked him to write them. Although not a fan of the show and unable to watch it in his New Brunswick hometown, he liked the idea, and recounts: "I read material put out on the show and excerpts from the various half-hours, which gave me an idea of its tone ... I formed my own opinion of its world and didn't deviate from it ... I was given free reign, and felt privileged to do the books." In *Barnabas Collins*, the sixth book and his favorite, he introduced the character of Barnabas as he saw him and set the tone for the balance of the series. Ross took a compassionate view of the vampire character and maintained it throughout.

Ross also wrote the movie tie-in *House of Dark Shadows*, based on the 1970 companion film (its cover pictures Lyndhurst Mansion in Tarrytown, New York, which is often visited by *Dark Shadows* conventions), but no books were written about the 1971 sequel *Night of Dark Shadows*. The series also includes *The Dark Shadows Book of Vampires and Werewolves* (an anthology of horror stories with an "Introduction by Barnabas and Quentin Collins"), *Barnabas Collins in a Funny Vein* (a book of vampire-jokes), and *Barnabas Collins: A Personal Picture Album* (with "more than 100 photos of Jonathan Frid at work and at play"). The 32 novels in the series are self-contained and can be read in any order. A 33rd novel, *Barnabas, Quentin, and the Mad Ghoul*, was outlined by Ross but never written. A scarce boxed set includes latter printings of the first eight novels. The books have no foreign editions.

The first five books in the series have illustrated covers, with photo covers used for the sixth book on and for subsequent printings of the first four books. Paperback Library's Art Director Rolf Erikson oversaw the illustrated covers, after having rendered the Gothic concept visually in the first place ("the ominous mansion in the background with one light in the window and the concerned woman hurrying away in the foreground ... blues were the best colors and oils were used"). For the photo covers, Erikson and crew went to the studio to shoot Frid and cast between morning dress rehearsals and afternoon takes.

Ross wrote some 350 novels and 600 short stories in all, under more than a dozen pseudonyms (that of Marilyn Ross came from his wife Marilyn), and in addition to Gothics contributed fine works to the mystery, romance, historical fiction, and Western genres. The *Dark Shadows* books, which earned him substantial royalties, were his only novels based on the central characters created by someone else. Ross died in 1995 at age 82.

Editorial Director Jerry Gross adds: "Before there was Anne Rice there was *Dark Shadows*, and in a sense Barnabas Collins was a big sex symbol. Many women were intrigued by the idea of being attacked by a vampire, and remember, Barnabas was a vampire in spite of himself. He was sensitive and caring, like a 90's man, but you know how these urges come over you..."

Gross had not only the highly successful *Dark Shadows* books to his credit but the entire Gothic line. He was an editor at Ace Books in 1959 when he discovered a dog-eared copy of *Rebecca* by Daphne du Maurier at his mother's home. It turned out his mother knew every word by heart because "they didn't publish those kinds of books any more," so he set out to change that. He compiled a list of hundreds of Gothic/Romance titles back to 1938 (the year *Rebecca* was published) and started to buy the paperback rights to those books: "We couldn't keep them on the shelves! So we started to commission originals. We took the basic formula from the hardcovers and handed it out to writers to write original variations. Soon every paperback house in America was doing five, six, seven of these books a month, and I couldn't tell my books from my competitors. There were literally walls of these books in the stores ... What genre readers want is the same thing only slightly different, which is the essence of a category. The basic plot is that a young woman inherits an old mansion or goes there to be a governess or secretary, meets one or two mysterious men, and finds her life in danger ... I created one of the most enduring categories in American paperback."

DAVY CROCKETT
See WALT DISNEY

DAYS OF OUR LIVES
November 8, 1965 -; NBC

Popular Library

____ Days of Our Lives; by Frances Forbes; Popular Library 60-2397; c 1969 (1st); $.60

Pioneer Communications Networks

____ Days of Our Lives #1: Love's Shattered Dreams; by Gilian Gorham; Pioneer 51; c 1986 (1st); $2.50 [novelization of several episodes]

____ Days of Our Lives #2: Hearts Past Reason; by Gilian Gorham; Pioneer 52; c 1986 (1st); $2.50 [novelization of several episodes]

____ Days of Our Lives #3: Search for Love; by Gilian Gorham; Pioneer 53; c 1986 (1st); $2.50 [novelization of several episodes]

____ Days of Our Lives #4: Sentimental Longings; by Gilian Gorham; Pioneer 54; c 1986 (1st); $2.50 [novelization of several episodes]

____ Days of Our Lives #5: Passion's Lure; by Serita Deborah Stevens; Pioneer 55; c 1986 (1st); $2.50 [novelization of several episodes]

____ Days of Our Lives #6: Forsaken Dreams; by Tara Lee; Pioneer 56; c 1986 (1st); $2.50 [novelization of several episodes]

____ Days of Our Lives #7: Red Sky at Dawn; by Stella Flint; Pioneer 57; c 1986 (1st); $2.50 [novelization of several episodes]

____ Days of Our Lives #8: The Summer Wind; by Nicole Brooks; Pioneer 58; c 1986 (1st); $2.50 [novelization of several episodes]

_____ Days of Our Lives #9: Friends and Lovers; by Nicole Brooks; Pioneer 59; c 1987 (1st); $2.50 [novelization of several episodes]

_____ Days of Our Lives #10: Promises and Lies; by Marcia Lawrence; Pioneer 60; c 1987 (1st); $2.50 [novelization of several episodes]

_____ Days of Our Lives #11: Fantasies; by Deidre Duncan; Pioneer 150; c 1987 (1st); $2.50 [novelization of several episodes]

_____ Days of Our Lives #12: Past Loves and Lies; by Marcia Lawrence; Pioneer 151; c 1987 (1st); $2.50 [novelization of several episodes]

_____ Days of Our Lives #13: Crimes of the Heart; by Nicole Brooks; Pioneer 152; c 1987 (1st); $2.50 [novelization of several episodes]

_____ Days of Our Lives #14: Obsessions; by Marcia Lawrence; Pioneer 153; c 1987 (1st); $2.50 [novelization of several episodes]

THE DEFENDERS
September 16, 1961 - September 9, 1965; CBS

Gold Medal

_____ The Defenders; by Edward S. Aarons; Gold Medal s1164; c 1961 (1st); $.35

Pockets

_____ The Defenders: All the Silent Voices; by Roger Fuller [Don Tracy]; Pocket 50056; c 1964 (1st); $.50 [novelization of the episode "All the Silent Voices"] [FC Photo: E.G. Marshall, Robert Reed]

_____ The Defenders: Ordeal; by Roger Fuller [Don Tracy]; Pocket 50107; c 1965 (1st: 1964); $.50 [novelization of the episode "Ordeal"] [FC Photo: Reed, Marshall]

_____ The Defenders: Eve of Judgment; by Roger Fuller [Don Tracy]; Pocket 50190; c 1965 (1st); $.50 [novelization of the episode "Judgment Eve"] [FC Illus: Marshall, Reed]

Robert Reed of subsequent Mike Brady fame is pictured, as lawyer Kenneth Preston, on the covers of the Pocket *Defenders* tie-ins.

THE DEPUTY
September 12, 1959 - September 16, 1961; NBC

_____ The Deputy; by Roe Richmond; Dell First Edition B172; c 1960 (1st); $.35 [FC Illus: Henry Fonda, Allen Case]

THE DETECTIVES
October 16, 1959 - September 21, 1962; ABC/NBC

_____ The Detectives; by Norman Daniels; Lancer 71-316; c 1962 (1st); $.35 [FC Photo: Robert Taylor; BC Illus: Taylor, Tige Andrews, Lee Farr, Adam West]

DIVORCE COURT
1957 - 1969; NBC

Pocket Books

_____ Divorce Court #1: Gilchrist vs. Gilchrist: A Question of Adultery; by Jack Pearl; Pocket 75667; c 1971 (1st); $.75 [FC Photo: Voltaire Perkins]

_____ Divorce Court #2: Lazer vs. Lazer: The Black Widow; by Jack Pearl; Pocket 75668; c 1971 (1st); $.75 [FC Photo: Perkins]

The trials and tribulations of everyday adults trying to end bad marriages, duking it out in no-holds-barred smearfests overseen by stern Judge Perkins.

DR. I.Q.
1953 - 1954, 1958 - 1959; ABC

_____ The Dr. I.Q. Quiz Book; by Lee Segall; Ace 15700; c 1971 (1st); $.75

DR. KILDARE
September 28, 1961 - August 30, 1966; NBC

Early Avon/Dells

_____ Young Dr. Kildare; by Max Brand; Avon F-133; c 1938,41 (1st: 1962); $.40

_____ Calling Dr. Kildare; by Max Brand; Dell R123; c 1939,40 (1st: 1961); $.40 [re-issued as #0996]

_____ Dr. Kildare's Trial; by Max Brand; Dell R125; c 1941,42 (1st: 1962); $.40 [re-issued as #1982]

_____ The Secret of Dr. Kildare; by Max Brand; Dell 7712; c 1940 (1st: 1962); $.40

_____ Dr. Kildare's Crisis; by Max Brand; Dell 1980; c 1940+ (1st: 1962); $.40

_____ Dr. Kildare's Search; by Max Brand; Dell 1981; c 1940+ (1st: 1962); $.40

_____ Dr. Kildare Takes Charge; by Max Brand; Dell 1983; c 1940,41 (1st: 1962); $.40

Lancers

_____ Dr. Kildare; by Robert C. Ackworth; Lancer 71-308; c 1962 (1st); $.35 [FC Photo: Richard Chamberlain] [*]

_____ Dr. Kildare [cover-variation]; by Robert C. Ackworth; Lancer 71-308; c 1962 (3rd); $.35 [FC Photo: Chamberlain] [*]

_____ Dr. Kildare [cover-variation]; by Robert C. Ackworth; Lancer 71-308; c 1962 (4th); $.35 [FC Photo: Chamberlain] [*]

[*] Subsequent printings announce "3rd Big Printing" and "4th Big Printing" on their otherwise identical front covers. Their back covers differ, by virtue of different Chamberlain photos. "2nd Big Printings," anyone?

_____ Dr. Kildare's Secret Romance; by Norman Daniels; Lancer 70-007; c 1962 (1st); $.40 [autographed pin-up of Chamberlain inside] [FC Photo: Chamberlain]

_____ Dr. Kildare's Finest Hour; by Norman Daniels; Lancer 70-032; c 1963 (1st); $.40 [FC Photo: Chamberlain; BC Photo: Chamberlain (wallet-size cut-out)]

_____ Dr. Kildare: The Heart Has an Answer; by William Johnston; Lancer 70-043; c 1963 (1st); $.40 [FC Photo: Chamberlain]

_____ Dr. Kildare: The Faces of Love; by William Johnston; Lancer 70-049; c 1963 (1st); $.40 [FC Photo: Chamberlain]

Whitmans

_____ Dr. Kildare: Assigned to Trouble; by Robert C. Ackworth; Whitman 1547; c 1963 (1st) [FC Illus: Chamberlain]

_____ Dr. Kildare: The Magic Key; by William Johnston; Whitman 1519; c 1964 (1st) [FC Illus: Chamberlain]

The show was based on the Max Brand novels and *Dr. Kildare* movies of the 1930's and 40's. Brand, the prolific Western novelist whose real name was Frederick Faust, created the character in the 1938 book *Young Dr. Kildare*, and wrote six sequels by the early 1940's. With the 1961 airing of the TV show the books were re-issued by Avon and Dell, two--*Dr. Kildare Takes Charge* and *Dr. Kildare's Search*--with ad page show-mention (the others are considered inferred TV tie-ins). All are full-length novels, while *Dr. Kildare's Search* also includes the bonus novelette "Dr. Kildare's Hardest Case." The show inspired five Lancer and two Whitman tie-ins, all picturing Richard Chamberlain on the covers. In 1972 the show was remade as *Young Dr. Kildare* (see also it), with the seven Max Brand books being re-issued by Beagle at the time.

DOCTOR WHO
1963 - 1989; Syndicated

Avon

_____ Doctor Who in an Exciting Adventure with the Daleks; by David Whitaker; Avon G1322; c 1964 (1st: 1967); $.50 [novelization of the serial "The Daleks"]

Pinnacles

_____ Doctor Who #1 and the Day of the Daleks; by Terrance Dicks; Pinnacle 40565; c 1974 (1st: 1979); $1.75 [novelization of the serial "Day of the Daleks"]

_____ Doctor Who #2 and the Doomsday Weapon; by Malcolm Hulke; Pinnacle 40566; c 1974 (1st: 1979); $1.75 [novelization of the serial "Colony in Space"]

_____ Doctor Who #3 and the Dinosaur Invasion; by Malcolm Hulke; Pinnacle 40606; c 1976 (1st: 1979); $1.75 [novelization of the serial "Invasion of the Dinosaurs"]

_____ Doctor Who #4 and the Genesis of the Daleks; by Terrance Dicks; Pinnacle 40608; c 1976 (1st: 1979); $1.75 [novelization of the serial "Genesis of the Daleks"]

_____ Doctor Who #5 and the Revenge of the Cybermen; by Terrance Dicks; Pinnacle 40611; c 1976 (1st: 1979); $1.75 [novelization of the serial "Revenge of the Cybermen"]

_____ Doctor Who #6 and the Loch Ness Monster; by Terrance Dicks; Pinnacle 40609; c 1976 (1st: 1979); $1.75 [novelization of the serial "Terror of the Zygons"]

_____ Doctor Who #7 and the Talons of Weng-Chiang; by Terrance Dicks; Pinnacle 40638; c 1977 (1st: 1979); $1.75 [novelization of the serial "The Talons of Weng-Chiang"]

_____ Doctor Who #8 and the Masque of Mandragora; by Philip Hinchcliffe; Pinnacle 40640; c 1977 (1st: 1979); $1.75 [novelization of the serial "The Masque of Mandragora"]

_____ Doctor Who #9 and the Android Invasion; by Terrance Dicks; Pinnacle 40641; c 1978 (1st: 1980); $1.75 [FC Illus: Tom Baker] [novelization of the serial "The Android Invasion"]

_____ Doctor Who #10 and the Seeds of Doom; by Philip Hinchcliffe; Pinnacle 40639; c 1977 (1st: 1980); $1.75 [FC Illus: Tom Baker] [novelization of the serial "The Seeds of Doom"]

Ballantines

_____ Doctor Who #1: Search for the Doctor [Find Your Fate]; by David Martin; Ballantine 33224; c 1986 (1st); $2.50 [FC Illus: Colin Baker]

_____ Doctor Who #2: Crisis in Space [Find Your Fate]; by Michael Holt [David Martin]; Ballantine 33225; c 1986 (1st); $2.50 [FC Illus: Mark Strickson, Nicola Bryant, Colin Baker]

_____ Doctor Who #3: Garden of Evil [Find Your Fate]; by David Martin; Ballantine 33226; c 1986 (1st); $2.50 [FC Illus: Colin Baker]

_____ Doctor Who #4: Mission to Venus [Find Your Fate]; by William Emms; Ballantine 33229; c 1986 (1st); $2.95 [FC Illus: Colin Baker]

_____ Doctor Who #5: Invasion of the Ormazoids [Find Your Fate]; by Philip Martin; Ballantine 33231; c 1986 (1st); $2.95 [FC Illus: Colin Baker]

_____ Doctor Who #6: Race Against Time [Find Your Fate]; by Pip & Jane Baker; Ballantine 33228; c 1986 (1st); $2.50 [FC Illus: Colin Baker, Nicola Bryant]

Produced in England starting in 1963, TV's longest-running science fiction series has been syndicated in over 100 countries, although it wasn't seen widely in the United States until the late 1970's. The show--about a "mysterious, zany ... Time Lord ... who hurtles through space in a stolen Time Machine"--was originally telecast in a serialized format, with each serial made up of several (mostly) 30-minute episodes. In syndication, the show is often seen in a movie format, with the episodes of a given serial being combined into a single viewing. For the first 25 serials, individual titles were used for the episodes; starting in 1966, the episodes were simply telecast as parts 1, 2, 3, etc., of a given serial.

Throughout the show's 26-year run--which saw seven actors play the title role--several publishers issued *Doctor Who* tie-ins, and nearly every serial has been novelized. The above books are those issued in the United States. Target in addition has published an extensive series of British *Doctor Who* tie-ins, with over 150 entries.

Avon's *Doctor Who in an Exciting Adventure with the Daleks* novelizes the show's second story, the seven-episode serial "The Daleks." First telecast in the winter of 1963-64, it turned *Doctor Who* into an overnight sensation, with some 8 million viewers. The Pinnacle *Doctor Who* books include Introductions by Harlan Ellison and novelize stories from the 8th through the 14th seasons. The Ballantines are "Find Your Fate" books, in which the reader takes an active part in the stories.

THE DOCTORS
April 1, 1963 - December 31, 1982; NBC

_____ The Doctors; by Michael Avallone; Popular Library 08115; c 1970 (1st); $.95 [FC Photo: Lydia Bruce, Gerald Gordon, James Pritchett, Elizabeth Hubbard]

DOCTOR'S HOSPITAL
September 10, 1975 - January 14, 1976; NBC

_____ Doctor's Hospital #1: One of Our Own; by Maud Willis [Eileen Lottman]; Pocket 80231; c 1975 (1st); $1.50 [novelization of the TV-movie pilot "One of Our Own" (May-05-1975)] [FC Photo: George Peppard]

DRAGNET
January 3, 1952 - September 6, 1959; NBC
January 12, 1967 - September 10, 1970; NBC

Pockets

_____ Dragnet: Case No. 561; by David Knight [Richard S. Prather]; Pocket 1120; c 1956 (1st); $.25 [FC Photo: Jack Webb]

_____ Dragnet: The Case of the Courteous Killer; by Richard Deming; Pocket 1198; c 1958 (1st); $.25 [FC Photo: Webb]

_____ Dragnet: The Case of the Crime King; by Richard Deming; Pocket 1214; c 1959 (1st); $.25 [FC Photo: Webb]

Crest

_____ Dragnet: The Badge; by Jack Webb; Crest s341; c 1958 (1st: 1959); $.35 [FC Photo: Ben Alexander (middle), Webb (left)]

Popular Library

_____ Dragnet 1968; by David H. Vowell; Popular Library 60-8045; c 1967 (1st: 1968); $.60 [FC Photo: Webb, Harry Morgan] [*]

[*] An additional book entitled "Dragnet 1967" was written by Robert Tralins for Popular Library, but apparently never published.

Whitmans

_____ Dragnet: Case histories from the popular television series; by Richard Deming; Whitman 1527; c 1957 (1st)

_____ Dragnet: Case histories from the popular television series [cover-variation]; by Richard Deming; Whitman 1510; c 1957,70 (unsp: 1970) [FC Illus: Webb, Morgan]

No-nonsense police show started on radio in 1949 and moved to TV three years later, inspiring three early Pocket tie-ins; the books, like the show, are based on actual case histories. Crest's *The Badge* features "the high-powered drama of case histories [producer-director-star Jack Webb] could not present on television."

Whitman's *Case histories from the popular television series* includes 8 stories: "The Jewel Robbery Case," "The Diamond Swindle Case," "The Firebug Case," "The Handcuff Bandit Case," "The Monogrammed Watch Case," "The Strong-Arm Bandit Case," "The Crybaby Case," and "The Hit-and-Run Case." In the stories, Sergeant Joe Friday is paired with Officer Frank Smith, Friday's partner during the show's 1952-59 run. When the show was revived in 1967 (as *Dragnet '67*), Jack Webb returned as Sergeant Friday, but Officer Smith (who'd been played by Ben Alexander) was replaced by the highly similar character in Officer Bill Gannon (played by Harry Morgan). When Whitman re-issued the book in 1970 (minus the stories "The Handcuff Bandit Case" and "The Strong-Arm Bandit Case"), the publisher simply replaced Officer Smith with Officer Gannon throughout, making virtually no other changes.

Dragnet 1968 author David Vowell, who as a writer for the show rode in the black and white patrol units with the officers for his research, enjoyed working for Webb ("outstanding boss ... demanded loyalty and received it ... one of the few people I couldn't say no to") and particularly liked the "gritty, documentary, beautifully directed by Webb" 1950's version of the show.

THE DUKES OF HAZZARD
January 26, 1979 - August 16, 1985; CBS

_____ The Dukes of Hazzard: Gone Racin'; by Eric Alter; Warner 30324; c 1982 (1st: 1983); $2.50 [original story] [FC Illus: Sorrell Booke, Catherine Bach, John Schneider, Tom Wopat; BC Illus: Christopher Mayer, Byron Cherry]

DYNASTY
January 12, 1981 - May 11, 1989; ABC

Bantams

_____ Dynasty; by Eileen Lottman; Bantam 23352; c 1983 (1st); $2.95 [novelization of several episodes] [FC Illus: Jack Coleman, Pamela Sue Martin, Linda Evans, John Forsythe]

_____ Dynasty: Alexis Returns; by Eileen Lottman; Bantam 24431; c 1984 (1st); $2.95 [novelization of several episodes] [FC Illus: (top) Joan Collins, (bottom) Coleman, John James, Martin, Evans, Forsythe]

THE EDGE OF NIGHT
April 2, 1956 - December 28, 1984; CBS/ABC

_____ The Edge of Night #1: The Seventh Mask; by Henry Slesar; Ace 18785; c 1969 (1st); $.60 [FC Photos: (clockwise from top left) Ann Flood, Larry Hugo, Teri Keane, Mandel Kramer, Mary K. Wells, Ray MacDonnell]

Henry Slesar wrote this book during his 15-year stint as headwriter for the show. The award-winning novelist, and one of the busiest TV scriptwriters of the 1960's, Slesar contributed hundreds of scripts for such shows as *Alfred Hitchcock Presents, The Man From U.N.C.L.E.* and *Batman*, seasoning which prepared him for headwritership on the mystery serial *The Edge of Night*. His stint with the show ("I liked writing *Edge*, because it was one of the last daytime series in which an individual voice was allowed to work ... During my 15 years on the show I wrote all storylines, breakdowns, three scripts a week, and edited two...") won him an Emmy in 1974. Long-time admirer Jeff Thompson describes Slesar's *Edge of Night* TV tie-in *The Seventh Mask* as "a thrilling *Edge of Night*-style adventure which, while none of it did happen in the TV series, could have happened in the show just as easily as the book." (Originally written as a promotional piece for the show, Slesar later adapted the story into the teleplay "Please Call It Murder," which aired on ABC's mid-70's late-night anthology show *Wide World of Entertainment*.)

EIGHT IS ENOUGH
March 15, 1977 - August 29, 1981; ABC

_____ Eight is Enough; by Tom Braden; Crest 23002; c 1975 (4th: 1977); $1.75

_____ Eight is Enough [cover-variation]; by Tom Braden; Crest 23002; c 1975 (6th: 1978); $1.95 [FC Photo: (clockwise from top left) Laurie Walters, Willie Aames, Grant Goodeve, Connie Needham, Susan Richardson, Adam Rich, Lani O'Grady, Dianne Key]

The show was based on the 1975 book by Tom Braden, himself a father of eight. Originally published by Fawcett Crest in 1976, the show is first mentioned on the fourth printing (it has the same illustrated cover as the prior printings but to it has been added a banner mentioning the "SENSATIONAL NEW TV SERIES!") and again on the photo cover sixth.

87TH PRECINCT
September 25, 1961 - September 10, 1962; NBC

Permabooks

____ 87th Precinct: Lady, Lady, I did it!; by Ed McBain; Perma M-4253; c 1961 (1st: 1962); $.35

____ 87th Precinct: The Con Man; by Ed McBain; Perma M-4264; c 1957 (2nd: 1962); $.35

____ 87th Precinct: Killer's Payoff; by Ed McBain; Perma M-4265; c 1958 (2nd: 1962); $.35

____ 87th Precinct: The Mugger; by Ed McBain; Perma M-4266; c 1956 (2nd: 1962); $.35

____ 87th Precinct: Killer's Choice; by Ed McBain; Perma M-4267; c 1958 (2nd: 1962); $.35

____ 87th Precinct: Cop Hater; by Ed McBain; Perma M-4268; c 1956 (2nd: 1962); $.35

The show was based on the long-running series of mystery novels by Evan Hunter, as Ed McBain. Hunter had 1954's *The Blackboard Jungle* to his credit when Pocket Books approached him about writing a new detective series. 1956's *Cop Hater, The Mugger,* and *The Pusher* resulted, and provided the springboard for Hunter's long-running *87th Precinct* series, described by George N. Dove in *Twentieth-Century Crime and Mystery Writers* as "the longest, most varied, and by all odds most popular police procedural series in the world." The books inspired three movies in the late 1950's prior to the show, with the airing of which the above books were issued with back cover show-mention.

ELLERY QUEEN
September 11, 1975 - September 19, 1976; NBC

Signets

____ Ellery Queen: The Madman Theory; by Ellery Queen [Jack Vance]; Signet Y6715; c 1966 (1st: 1975); $1.25

____ Ellery Queen: The Finishing Stroke; by Ellery Queen [Dannay/Lee]; Signet Y6819; c 1958 (5th: 1975); $1.25

____ Ellery Queen: Face to Face; by Ellery Queen [Dannay/Lee]; Signet Y6872; c 1967 (3rd: 1975); $1.25

____ Ellery Queen: The House of Brass; by Ellery Queen [Avram Davidson, from Dannay's story outline]; Signet Y6958; c 1968 (3rd: 1975); $1.25

_____ Ellery Queen: Cop Out; by Ellery Queen [Dannay/Lee]; Signet Y6996; c 1969 (4th: 1975); $1.25

_____ Ellery Queen: The Last Woman in His Life; by Ellery Queen [Dannay/Lee]; Signet Y7123; c 1970 (4th: 1975); $1.25

Pyramid

_____ Ellery Queen: The Vanishing Corpse [orig. title "Ellery Queen, Master Detective" - novelization of that 1940 movie]; by Ellery Queen [?]; Pyramid V4094; c 1941 (3rd: 1976); $1.25 [variant 3rd pr. lacks logo and book number on the cover and spine]

The show was based on the long-running series of mystery novels by cousins Frederic Dannay and Manfred B. Lee, whose joint pseudonym of Ellery Queen matched the name of their fictional detective hero. Dannay and Lee created the character in the 1929 book *The Roman Hat Mystery*, and wrote some 35 *Ellery Queen* books through Lee's death in 1971 (Dannay died in 1982). They also edited countless anthologies, founded the highly successful *Ellery Queen's Mystery Magazine* in 1941, co-founded Mystery Writers of America in 1945, and won numerous awards, accomplishments which led profiler Anthony Boucher to remark: "Ellery Queen is the American detective story."

Not all the books the two wrote as Ellery Queen feature Ellery Queen; *Cop Out* and *The Glass Village* are exceptions. Moreover, the Ellery Queen byline was used by other writers in their own stories about Ellery Queen and other characters.

The character inspired nine movies--spanning 1935's *The Spanish Cape Mystery* to 1942's *Enemy Agents Meet Ellery Queen*--a long-running radio series, and three brief 1950's shows before NBC's 1975-76 remake, it leading to the above books being issued with front cover show-mention. Two of the books-- *The Madman Theory* and *Cop Out*--do not feature Ellery Queen but still mention the show.

EMERGENCY!
January 22, 1972 - September 3, 1977; NBC

_____ Emergency!; by Chris Stratton [Richard Hubbard]; Popular Library 08198; c 1972 (1st); $.75 [FC Photos: (top) Randolph Mantooth, Julie London, Bobby Troup, Robert Fuller, (bottom) Mantooth, London, Mantooth, Kevin Tighe]

Original adventures of paramedics Gage and DeSoto of Squad 51 of the Los Angeles County Fire Department (they battle a huge brushfire threatening to engulf L.A.) in this book based on the Jack Webb-produced show.

EXECUTIVE SUITE
September 20, 1976 - February 11, 1977; CBS

_____ Executive Suite; by Cameron Hawley; Popular Library 08578; c 1952 (unsp: 1977); $1.95 [FC Photo: Percy Rodriguez, Mitchell Ryan, Madlyn Rhue, Stephen Elliott]

The show was based on the 1954 movie, which in turn was based on the 1952 book by Cameron Hawley, re-issued by Popular Library as a TV tie-in with the show.

F TROOP
September 14, 1965 - August 31, 1967; ABC

_____ F Troop: The Great Indian Uprising; by William Johnston; Whitman 1544; c 1967 (1st) [FC Photo: Larry Storch, Ken Berry, Forrest Tucker]

FALCON CREST
December 4, 1981 - May 17, 1990; CBS

_____ Falcon Crest; by Patrick Mann [Leslie Waller]; Dell 12437; c 1984 (1st); $3.95 [novelization of several episodes] [FC Illus: Robert Foxworth, Susan Sullivan, Jane Wyman, Lorenzo Lamas, Ana Alicia; BC Photos: (clockwise from top left) Abby Dalton, David Selby, William R. Moses, Mel Ferrer]

FAMILY
March 9, 1976 - June 25, 1980; ABC

Ballantines

_____ Family; by Leila Andrews; Ballantine 25570; c 1976 (1st); $1.50 [novelization of several episodes] [FC Photo: (clockwise from bottom) Kristy McNichol, Gary Frank, James Broderick, Sada Thompson]

_____ Family #2: Transitions; by Leila Andrews; Ballantine 25705; c 1977 (1st); $1.50 [novelization of several episodes] [FC Photo: (clockwise from bottom) McNichol, Frank, Meredith Baxter-Birney, Thompson, Broderick]

_____ Family #3: Commitments; by Leila Andrews; Ballantine 25706; c 1977 (1st); $1.50 [novelization of several episodes] [FC Photos: (clockwise from top left) Broderick, Thompson, McNichol, Frank, Baxter-Birney]

First *Family* book novelizes the first six episodes seen in the spring of 1976; #'s 2 and 3 novelize the first eleven episodes of the 1976-77 season. Leila Andrews may be a house name.

FAMILY AFFAIR
September 12, 1966 - September 9, 1971; CBS

_____ Family Affair: Buffy's Cookbook; by Jody Cameron; Berkley W2092; c 1971 (1st); $1.00 [FC Illus: Anissa Jones, Kathy Garver]

_____ Family Affair: Buffy Finds a Star; by Gladys Baker Bond; Whitman 1567; c 1970 (1st) [FC Illus: (clockwise from top left) Garver, Brian Keith, Sebastian Cabot, Jones, Johnny Whitaker]

Books picture Anissa Jones as eight-year-old Buffy Davis, in the pigtails Cindy Brady later adorned. Jones' death at age 18 of a drug overdose is Hollywood lore.

FAMILY FEUD
July 12, 1976 -; ABC/Syndicated/CBS

_____ Richard Dawson and Family Feud; by Mary Ann Norbom; Signet J9773; c 1981 (1st); $1.95 [FC Photo: Richard Dawson]

FAMILY TIES
September 22, 1982 - September 17, 1989; NBC

_____ Family Ties: Alex Gets the Business; by Joe Claro; Avon 75235; c 1986 (1st); $2.95 [FC Photo: Michael J. Fox; BC Photo: (from left) Fox, Tina Yothers, Justine Bateman, Michael Gross, Meredith Baxter-Birney]

FANTASY ISLAND
January 28, 1978 - August 18, 1984; ABC

Ballantines

_____ Fantasy Island #1; by Jane Seskin; Ballantine 27939; c 1978 (1st); $1.75 [novelization of the teleplays "Lady of the Evening" and "The Racer"] [FC Photo: Herve Villechaize, Ricardo Montalban]

_____ Fantasy Island #2; by Jane Seskin; Ballantine 27940; c 1979 (1st); $1.75 [novelization of the teleplays "The Beachcomber" and "The Last Whodunit"] [FC Photo: Montalban, Villechaize]

Weekly Reader

_____ Fantasy Island; by Roger Elwood; Weekly Reader F435; c 1981 (1st) [FC Photo: Villechaize, Montalban]

    The show consisted of two 30-minute teleplays per episode (three for the 90-minute episodes), and alternated between the stories over the course of the airing. Ballantine's *Fantasy Island* novelizations (Jane Seskin enjoyed writing them, and replacing the character Tattoo's sexist lines with "appropriate" lines) adapt two same-episode teleplays apiece. The Weekly Reader book includes three novelizations of different-episode teleplays ("Mandy's Journey" [from the teleplay "The Devil and Mandy Bream"], "Little Girl Lost" [from the teleplay "Possessed"], and "The Man From Yesterday" [from that teleplay]) and the apparently original story "Flight of Fantasy." See the Episodes Novelized List for details.

FATHER MURPHY
November 3, 1981 - December 28, 1982; NBC

Random Houses

_____ Father Murphy's Promise; by Larry Weinberg; Random House 85318; c 1982 (1st); $1.95 [oversize] [novelization of the episode "By the Bear That Bit Me"] [FC Photo: Merlin Olsen, Scott Mellini]

_____ Father Murphy's First Miracle; by Elizabeth Levy; Random House 85810; c 1983 (1st); $1.95 [oversize] [novelization of the episode "The First Miracle"] [FC Photo: Olsen, Katherine Cannon]

FATHER OF THE BRIDE
September 29, 1961 - September 14, 1962; CBS

_____ Father of the Bride; by Edward Streeter; Popular Library SP162; c 1948,49 (1st: 1962); $.50

The show was based on the 1950 movie, which in turn was based on the 1948 book by Edward Streeter, re-issued by Popular Library as a TV tie-in with the show.

THE FELONY SQUAD
September 12, 1966 - January 31, 1969; ABC

_____ The Felony Squad; by Michael Avallone; Popular Library 60-8036; c 1967 (1st); $.60 [FC Photo: Dennis Cole, Howard Duff]

Michael Avallone's favorite TV tie-in, about a "two-gun kid who challenges beat cops," was "rather glibly duplicated" for an _N.Y.P.D._ episode a year later.

FISH
February 5, 1977 - June 8, 1978; ABC

_____ Fish Strikes Out; by T.J. Hemmings; Ace Tempo Star 24005; c 1977 (1st); $1.25 [FC Photo: (top) Lenny Bari, (middle) Barry Gordon, John Cassisi, Denise Miller, (bottom) Florence Stanley, Abe Vigoda, Sarah Natoli, Todd Bridges]

FLIGHT
1958; Syndicated

_____ Flight; by Edgar Jean Bracco; Berkley G291; c 1959 (1st); $.35

THE FLIP WILSON SHOW
September 17, 1970 - June 27, 1974; NBC

_____ Flip Wilson Close-Up; by James A. Hudson; Avon V2459; c 1971 (1st: 1972); $.75 [FC Photo: Flip Wilson]

_____ Flip Wilson Close-Up; by James A. Hudson; Scholastic Book Services TX1933; c 1971 (1st); $.60 [oversize] [FC Photo: Wilson]

_____ Flip [orig. title "Flip Wilson Close-Up"]; by James A. Hudson; Scholastic Book Services TX2030; c 1971 (1st); $.60 [oversize] [FC Photo: Wilson]

FLIPPER
September 19, 1964 - September 1, 1968; NBC

Whitmans

_____ "flipper": The Mystery of the Black Schooner; by Richard Hardwick; Whitman 2324; c 1966 (1st) [BC Photo: (middle) Tommy Norden, Luke Halpin]

_____ "flipper": Killer Whale Trouble; by George S. Elrick; Whitman Big Little Book 2003; c 1967 (1st)

_____ "flipper": Deep-Sea Photographer; by George S. Elrick; Whitman Big Little Book 2032; c 1969 (1st)

Maritime adventure show about the dolphin that could do it all and the two boys who befriend him inspired the above Whitman tie-ins, one regular-size and two Big Little Books by children's book author George S. Elrick, who once told *Contemporary Authors*: "Big Little Books ... [seem] to have been the most successful literary format of all times, at least in terms of volume sales."

THE FLYING NUN
September 7, 1967 - September 18, 1970; ABC

Avon

_____ The Fifteenth Pelican; by Tere Rios; Avon ZS130; c 1965 (3rd: 1967); $.60

Aces

_____ The Flying Nun: Miracle At San Tanco; by William Johnston; Ace G-702; c 1968 (1st); $.50 [FC Photo: Sally Field; BC Photo: Alejandro Rey]

_____ The Flying Nun: The Littlest Rebels; by William Johnston; Ace G-725; c 1968 (1st); $.50 [FC Photo: Field; BC Photo: Rey, Field]

_____ The Flying Nun #3: Mother of Invention; by William Johnston; Ace 24300; c 1969 (1st); $.50 [FC Photo: (from left) Shelley Morrison, Field, Rey, Marge Redmond]

_____ The Flying Nun #4: The Little Green Men; by William Johnston; Ace 24301; c 1969 (1st); $.60 [FC Photo: (clockwise from top) Morrison, Madeleine Sherwood, Field, Redmond; BC Photo: Rey, with the others]

_____ The Flying Nun #5: The Underground Picnic; by William Johnston; Ace 24302; c 1970 (1st); $.60 [FC Photo: Field; BC Photo: Rey, Field]

The show about airborne Sister Bertrille was based on the 1965 book *The Fifteenth Pelican* by Tere Rios. First published by Avon in 1966 (G1299), it was re-issued as a TV tie-in with the show. The author, who grew up in a Long Island convent, is said to have conceived the idea "when she saw a nun with a stiff cornette headdress caught by a gust of wind which wafted her a short way down the street." Ace's own *Flying Nun* books comprise one of the more desirable sets of TV tie-ins, due to the scarcity of the latter books in the series and the later rise to stardom of Sally Field, pictured on the covers.

FRONTIER
September 25, 1955 - September 9, 1956; NBC

_____ Frontier: 150 Years of the West; by Luke Short, ed. [Frederick D. Glidden]; Bantam A1401; c 1955 (1st); $.35

Inferred TV tie-in, an anthology of Western stories and true articles, is similar to the Western anthology TV show *Frontier*. Though the show isn't mentioned, it aired four months prior to the book's December, 1955 publication.

THE FUGITIVE
September 17, 1963 - August 29, 1967; ABC

_____ The Fugitive: Fear in a Desert Town; by Roger Fuller [Don Tracy]; Pocket 35012; c 1964 (1st); $.35 [novelization of the pilot episode "Fear in a Desert City"] [FC Photo: David Janssen; BC Photos: Barry Morse, Janssen]

David Janssen's classic man-on-the-run saga inspired the above Pocket tie-in. An unauthorized adaptation of the show's pilot episode "Fear in a Desert City," it led to show-creator Roy Huggins' winning a lawsuit over Pocket Books for the infringement. Huggins later executive produced the 1993 hit movie *The Fugitive*, with Harrison Ford starring as the falsely accused hero Dr. Richard Kimble.

FURY
October 15, 1955 - September 3, 1966; NBC

Tempo

_____ Fury: Stallion of Broken Wheel Ranch; by Albert G. Miller; Tempo T14; c 1959 (1st: 1962); $.50

Whitmans

_____ Fury and the Lone Pine Mystery; by William Fenton; Whitman 1537; c 1957 (1st)

_____ Fury and the Mystery at Trappers' Hole; by Troy Nesbit [Franklin Folsom]; Whitman 1557; c 1959 (1st)

GADABOUT GADDIS
1950 - 1965; Syndicated

_____ Gadabout Gaddis: The Flying Fisherman; by R.V. "Gadabout" Gaddis as told to George Sullivan; Pocket 75224; c 1967 (1st); $.75 [biography of Roscoe Vernon, aka Gadabout Gaddis] [FC Photo: Gaddis]

_____ Gadabout Gaddis: Secrets of Successful Fishing; by Henry Shakespeare; Dell First Edition M102; c 1962 (2nd: 1964); $.60 [*]

[*] Certain copies of the second printing were issued with second-page show-mention in an ad for sponsor Liberty Mutual, the book's only reference to the show.

GALACTICA 1980
See BATTLESTAR GALACTICA

THE GANGSTER CHRONICLES
February 21, 1981 - May 8, 1981; NBC

_____ The Gangster Chronicles; by Michael Lasker and Richard Alan Simmons [Richard Elman]; Jove K5808; c 1981 (1st); $2.50

The show about gangsters from the points of view of gangsters featured the exploits of Lucky Luciano and Bugsy Siegel (both real people), and "Michael Lasker" (a composite figure). The above book was written by Richard Elman, as Richard Alan Simmons, from Lasker's memoirs.

GARRISON'S GORILLAS
September 5, 1967 - September 17, 1968; ABC

_____ Garrison's Gorillas; by Jack Pearl; Dell 2798; c 1967 (1st); $.60 [FC Illus: (middle) Ron Harper, (clockwise from top left for balance) Cesare Danova, Rudy Solari, Christopher Cary, Brendon Boone]

_____ Garrison's Gorillas and the Fear Formula; by Jack Pearl; Whitman 1548; c 1968 (1st)

THE GENE AUTRY SHOW
July 23, 1950 - August 7, 1956; CBS

Whitmans

_____ Gene Autry and the Badmen of Broken Bow [dustjacket]; by Snowden Miller; Whitman 2355; c 1951 (1st) [Dustjacket Photo: Gene Autry]

_____ Gene Autry and the Big Valley Grab [dustjacket]; by W.H. Hutchinson; Whitman 2302; c 1952 (1st) [Dustjacket Photo: Autry]

_____ Gene Autry and the Big Valley Grab [laminated cover]; by W.H. Hutchinson; Whitman 2302; c 1952,54 (unsp: 1954) [FC Photo: Autry]

_____ Gene Autry and the Golden Stallion; by Cole Fannin; Whitman 1511; c 1954 (1st) [FC Illus: Autry]

_____ Gene Autry and the Ghost Riders; by Lewis B. Patten; Whitman 1510; c 1955 (1st) [FC Illus: Autry]

_____ Gene Autry and Arapaho War Drums; by Lewis B. Patten; Whitman 1512; c 1957 (1st) [FC Illus: Autry]

Gene Autry was a veteran of some 70 Western films in the 1930's and 40's when he moved to the small-screen in 1950. Whitman, which had been publishing *Gene Autry* books since the 1940's, continued to publish them, with show-mention, once the show aired. *Gene Autry and the Big Valley Grab* was issued in otherwise identical, dustjacket and non-dustjacket versions (Whitman discontinued dustjackets in the early 1950's).

GENERAL HOSPITAL
April 1, 1963 -; ABC

Lancers

_____ General Hospital; by Burt Hirschfeld; Lancer 70-055; c 1963 (1st); $.40 [FC Illus: Emily McLaughlin (left), John Beradino]

_____ General Hospital: Emergency Entrance; by Burt Hirschfeld; Lancer 72-917; c 1965 (1st); $.50 [FC Illus: Beradino (left)]

Awards

_____ General Hospital: A Matter of Life and Death; by Jane Horatio [Edythe Cudlippe]; Award A858S; c 1971 (1st); $.75 [FC Photos: (top) Beradino, Rachel Ames, (bottom) McLaughlin, Beradino]

_____ General Hospital #2: Surgeon's Crisis; by Bruce Cassiday; Award AS1024; c 1972 (1st); $.75 [FC Photos: Beradino, McLaughlin]

_____ General Hospital #3: In the Name of Love; by Bruce Cassiday; Award AN1238; c 1974 (1st); $.95 [FC Photo: Beradino, McLaughlin]

Pioneer Communications Networks

_____ General Hospital #1/#2 [combined]: Forever and a Day, Book One and Two; by Nicole Brooks (#1) and Marcia Lawrence (#2); Pioneer 300; c 1987 (1st); $2.50 [novelization of several episodes]

_____ General Hospital #3: Winds of Change; by Nicole Brooks; Pioneer 301; c 1987 (1st); $2.50 [novelization of several episodes]

The long-running soap inspired tie-ins by Lancer in the 1960's and Award in the 1970's, and picture then-mainstays John Beradino and Emily McLaughlin (Dr. Steve Hardy and Nurse Jessie Brewer) on the covers. The show dropped in the ratings in the mid-1970's before making its legendary late-70's comeback, riding on the shoulders of Luke and Laura. Thom Racina was writing for the show at the time, and created the story that married Luke and Laura eventually. Their wedding took place in November of 1981, as the highest watched program in daytime viewing history. Racina reports it was a "rush" creating popular culture at the time and writing for Elizabeth Taylor, whose character attended the wedding.

GENTLE BEN
September 10, 1967 - August 31, 1969; CBS

_____ Gentle Ben; by Walt Morey; Tempo T-166; c 1965 (1st: 1967); $.60 [FC Photo: Dennis Weaver]

_____ Gentle Ben [cover-variation]; by Walt Morey; Scholastic Book Services TK1084; c 1965 (1st: 1967); $.60

_____ Gentle Ben: Mystery in the Everglades; by Paul S. Newman; Whitman Big Little Book 2035; c 1969 (1st)

The show was based on the 1965 book by Walt Morey, released in two "Starline Editions" in 1967 (one under the Scholastic Book Services imprint and one under the Tempo imprint). Only the Tempo mentions the show; it also mentions the 1967 companion film *Gentle Giant*.

GET SMART
September 18, 1965 - September 11, 1970; NBC/CBS

Tempos

_____ Get Smart!; by William Johnston; Tempo T-103; c 1965 (1st); $.60 [FC Photo: Don Adams]

_____ Get Smart: Sorry, Chief...; by William Johnston; Tempo T-119; c 1966 (1st); $.60 [FC Photo: Adams, Barbara Feldon]

_____ Get Smart Once Again!; by William Johnston; Tempo T-121; c 1966 (1st); $.60 [FC Photo: Adams]

_____ Get Smart #4: Max Smart and the Perilous Pellets; by William Johnston; Tempo T-140; c 1966 (1st); $.60 [FC Photo: Adams, Feldon]

_____ Get Smart #5: Missed It By That Much!; by William Johnston; Tempo T-154; c 1967 (1st); $.60 [FC Photo: Feldon, Adams]

_____ Get Smart #6: And Loving It!; by William Johnston; Tempo T-159; c 1967 (1st); $.60 [FC Photo: Adams]

_____ Get Smart #7: Max Smart - The Spy Who Went Out to the Cold; by William Johnston; Tempo T-174; c 1968 (1st); $.60 [FC Photo: Adams]

_____ Get Smart #8: Max Smart Loses Control; by William Johnston; Tempo T-191; c 1968 (1st); $.60 [FC Photo: Feldon, Adams] [story features Hymie the Robot]

_____ Get Smart #9: Max Smart and the Ghastly Ghost Affair; by William Johnston; Tempo 05326; c 1969 (1st); $.60 [FC Photo: Adams, Feldon]

Bantam

_____ Get Smart: Would You Believe?; by Don Adams & Bill Dana; Bantam 20054; c 1982 (1st); $1.95 [FC Photo: Adams]

Maxwell Smart stumbles through these nine adventures, with sidekick "99" (she and Max are married by the ninth book), the long-suffering Chief (not pictured on the books), the usual *Get Smart* gadgets, and villains in the William Johnston mold.

GETTING TOGETHER
September 18, 1971 - January 8, 1972; ABC

Curtis'

_____ Getting Together; by Judson McCall; Curtis 07173; c 1971 (1st); $.75 [FC Photo: Bobby Sherman]

_____ Getting Together #2: Bobby: Superstar; by Chris Stratton [Richard Hubbard]; Curtis 07180; c 1971 (1st); $.75 [FC Photo: Sherman, Wes Stern]

The short-lived sitcom starred teen-idol recording-artist Bobby Sherman, and was similar to *The Partridge Family* series that spun it, that show featuring teen-idol recording-artist David Cassidy. Curtis Books, then in the midst of their extensive and highly successful *Partridge Family* series, quickly issued two *Getting Together* books before the show's four-month demise.

THE GHOST AND MRS. MUIR
September 21, 1968 - September 18, 1970; NBC/ABC

_____ The Ghost and Mrs. Muir; by Josephine Leslie; Pocket 77761; c 1945,72 (1st: 1974); $.95

_____ The Ghost and Mrs. Muir; by Alice Denham; Popular Library 60-2348; c 1968 (1st); $.60 [FC Photo: Hope Lange, Edward Mulhare]

The show was based on the 1947 movie, which in turn was based on the 1945 book by Josephine Leslie. First published in 1945 by Ziff-Davis under the author's pseudonym of R.A. Dick, the book was re-issued by Pocket in 1974 under the author's real name, and mentions the show on the first page. Popular Library's original *Ghost and Mrs. Muir* book is by former model (and *Playboy* Playmate of the Month) Alice Denham.

GIDGET
September 15, 1965 - September 1, 1966; ABC

Dells

_____ Gidget in Love; by Frederick Kohner; Dell 2872; c 1965 (1st); $.45

_____ Gidget Goes Parisienne; by Frederick Kohner; Dell 2874; c 1966 (1st); $.45

_____ Gidget Goes New York; by Frederick Kohner; Dell 2897; c 1968 (1st); $.50

The show was based on the *Gidget* movies (1959's *Gidget* [it based on the 1957 Frederick Kohner book], 1961's *Gidget Goes Hawaiian*, and 1963's *Gidget Goes to Rome*). The two sequels were novelized by Kohner, and the original book *Gidget* reprinted, by Bantam in the early 1960's. The TV show aired in 1965, with Dell issuing a new series of Kohner-penned *Gidget* books at the time. Only one--*Gidget Goes Parisienne*--mentions the show (on an ad page), the other two are considered inferred TV tie-ins. Sally Field made her acting debut as *Gidget* in the show.

GILLIGAN'S ISLAND
September 26, 1964 - September 4, 1967; CBS

_____ Gilligan's Island; by William Johnston; Whitman 1566; c 1966 (1st) [FC Photo: Bob Denver]

The seven castaways once again fall short of reaching the mainland (thanks to Gilligan) in William Johnston's written version of the show.

THE GIRL FROM U.N.C.L.E.
September 13, 1966 - August 29, 1967; NBC

Signets

_____ The Girl From U.N.C.L.E. #1: The Birds of a Feather Affair; by Michael Avallone; Signet D3012; c 1966 (1st); $.50 [FC Photo: Stefanie Powers]

_____ The Girl From U.N.C.L.E. #2: The Blazing Affair; by Michael Avallone; Signet D3042; c 1966 (1st); $.50 [FC Photo: Powers, Noel Harrison]

This *Man From U.N.C.L.E.* spinoff inspired the above Michael Avallone tie-ins. *The Birds of a Feather Affair* had started as a *Man From U.N.C.L.E.* book "The THRUSH and the Eagles Affair," which Ace had declined to publish. Avallone also wrote "The Devil Down Under Affair" as an intended third *Girl From U.N.C.L.E.* entry, but Signet passed; Avallone later sold the story to *The Saint Mystery Magazine*.

The Birds of a Feather Affair was also published (as #2 in a series) in Britain by Four Square, which issued three additional titles not released here: *#1: The Golden Globules Affair* (by Simon Latter), *#3: The Golden Boats of Taradata Affair* (Latter), and *#4: The Cornish Pixie Affair* (Peter Leslie).

THE GIRL WITH SOMETHING EXTRA
September 14, 1973 - May 24, 1974; NBC

_____ The Girl With Something Extra; by Paul W. Fairman; Lancer 75491; c 1973 (1st); $.95 [FC Photo: John Davidson, Sally Field]

GOMER PYLE, U.S.M.C.
September 25, 1964 - September 19, 1969; CBS

_____ Gomer Pyle, U.S.M.C.; by E. Kitzes Knox [Esther Kitzes and Helen Knox]; Pyramid R-1267; c 1965 (1st); $.50 [FC Illus: Jim Nabors]

Original adventures of America's most naive Marine and the long-suffering Sergeant Carter, with a back-history that's contrary to Gomer's roots as a gas station attendant on *The Andy Griffith Show*. An additional *Gomer Pyle* book was written by Robert Tralins, but apparently never published.

THE GONG SHOW
1976 - 1980; NBC/Syndicated

_____ The Gong Show Book; by Jerry Bowles; Ace Tempo Star 29814; c 1977 (1st); $1.95 [FC Photo: Chuck Barris] [Introduction by Chuck Barris]

GOOD TIMES
February 1, 1974 - August 1, 1979; CBS

_____ Good Times: Jimmie Walker: The Dyn-O-Mite Kid; by Joel H. Cohen; Scholastic Book Services TX3442; c 1976 (1st) [oversize] [FC Photo: Jimmie Walker]

THE GREEN HORNET
September 9, 1966 - July 14, 1967; ABC

_____ The Green Hornet in the Infernal Light; by Ed Friend [Richard Wormser]; Dell 3231; c 1966 (1st); $.50 [FC Photo: Van Williams; BC Illus: Williams, Bruce Lee]

_____ The Greet Hornet: The Case of the Disappearing Doctor; by Brandon Keith; Whitman 1570; c 1966 (1st) [FC Illus: Williams, Lee]

Show based on the 1930's and 40's radio series was enlivened by Bruce Lee's martial arts sequences. Lee, pictured on the above books, parlayed the role into a successful but short-lived movie career. He was found dead in a Hong Kong flat in 1973 of a brain hemorrhage, believed a freak reaction to a combination of painkillers and marijuana.

GRIFF
September 29, 1973 - January 5, 1974; ABC

_____ Griff; by Robert Weverka; Bantam N8339; c 1973 (1st); $.95 [novelization of the TV-movie pilot "Man on the Outside"] [FC Illus: Lorne Greene]

Latter Lorne Greene vehicle began as the pilot telefilm "Man on the Outside," which Robert Weverka novelized in the above book. Dissatisfied with the film, the producers held it from airing until two years following the show's 12-episode run.

GRIZZLY ADAMS
See THE LIFE AND TIMES OF GRIZZLY ADAMS

GROWING PAINS
September 24, 1985 - August 27, 1992; ABC

> *Bantams*

_____ Growing Pains; by N.H. Kleinbaum; Bantam 26881; c 1987 (1st); $2.95 [adapts as chapters 1-5 the episodes "Dirt Bike," "Mike's Madonna Story," "Springsteen," "Standardized Test," and "Reputation"] [FC Photo: (clockwise from top) Alan Thicke, Kirk Cameron, Tracey Gold, Jeremy Miller, Joanna Kerns]

_____ Kirk Cameron: Dream Guy; by Grace Catalano; Bantam 27135; c 1987 (1st); $2.50 [FC Photo: Cameron]

GUESTWARD HO!
September 29, 1960 - September 21, 1961; ABC

_____ Guestward Ho!; by Barbara Hooton and "Patrick Dennis" [Edward Everett Tanner III]; Popular Library SP71; c 1956 (unsp: 1960); $.50 [BC Photo: J. Carrol Naish, Joanne Dru, Mark Miller]

> The show was based on the 1956 book by the above co-authors. First published by Popular Library in 1958 (SP16), it was re-issued as a TV tie-in with the show.

THE GUIDING LIGHT
June 30, 1952 -; CBS

> *Popular Library*

_____ The Guiding Light; by Agnes Nixon; Popular Library 60-8034; c 1967 (1st); $.60 [FC Photo: Bernie Grant] [*]

> *Pioneer Communications Networks*

_____ Guiding Light #1: So Tender, So True; by Angelica Aimes; Pioneer 01; c 1986 (1st); $2.50 [novelization of several episodes]

_____ Guiding Light #2: Two Lives, Two Loves; by Francesca Evans [Angelica Aimes]; Pioneer 02; c 1986 (1st); $2.50 [novelization of several episodes]

_____ Guiding Light #3: Whispered Secrets, Hidden Hearts; by Angelica Aimes; Pioneer 03; c 1986 (1st); $2.50 [novelization of several episodes]

_____ Guiding Light #4: Revenge of the Heart; by Jean Francis Webb; Pioneer 04; c 1986 (1st); $2.50 [novelization of several episodes]

_____ Guiding Light #5: Rush to Love; by Angelica Aimes; Pioneer 05; c 1986 (1st); $2.50 [novelization of several episodes]

_____ Guiding Light #6: Secret Passions; by Kate Lowe Kerrigan [Frances Rickett]; Pioneer 06; c 1986 (1st); $2.50 [novelization of several episodes]

_____ Guiding Light #7: That Special Feeling; by Kate Lowe Kerrigan [Frances Rickett]; Pioneer 07; c 1986 (1st); $2.50 [novelization of several episodes]

_____ Guiding Light #8: Restless Hearts; by Marlene Creed; Pioneer 08; c 1986 (1st); $2.50 [novelization of several episodes]

_____ Guiding Light #9: Playing With Fire; by Marlene Creed; Pioneer 09; c 1987 (1st); $2.50 [novelization of several episodes]

_____ Guiding Light #10: Swept Away; by Marlene Creed; Pioneer 10; c 1987 (1st); $2.50 [novelization of several episodes]

_____ Guiding Light #11: Hidden Fears; by Virginia McDonnell; Pioneer 11; c 1987 (1st); $2.50 [novelization of several episodes]

_____ Guiding Light #12: Tender Loving Care; by Marlene Creed; Pioneer 12; c 1987 (1st); $2.50 [novelization of several episodes]

_____ Guiding Light #13: Love's Fragile Web; by Kacia Bennett; Pioneer 13; c 1987 (1st); $2.50 [novelization of several episodes]

_____ Guiding Light #14: Choices; by Kacia Bennett; Pioneer 14; c 1987 (1st); $2.50 [novelization of several episodes]

    [*] Agnes Nixon, described by Christopher Schemering as "the most respected and influential writer in daytime drama," wrote this book following her six-year stint as headwriter for the show. Nixon--who began her career as an apprentice of Irna Phillips, the "queen of the radio soaps" in the 1930's and creator of _The Guiding Light_ on that medium in 1937--writes in the Introduction of her _Guiding Light_ book that her objective of focusing on one character from the show was best met in the person of Dr. Paul Fletcher, who, "as much as any other character in our story, embodies the true theme of _The Guiding Light_."

GUNSMOKE
September 10, 1955 - September 1, 1975; CBS

Ballantines

_____ Gunsmoke; by Don Ward; Ballantine 236; c 1957 (1st); $.35 [FC Photo: James Arness]

_____ Gunsmoke [cover-variation]; by Don Ward; Ballantine 364K; c 1957 (3rd: 1960); $.35 [FC Photo: Arness]

    [10 short story novelizations of radio and TV scripts: "Reunion '78" (TV script); "Road Ranch" (first radio/then TV script); "Grass" (radio/TV); "Gone Straight" (radio/TV); "Jayhawkers" (radio/TV); "Hot Spell" (TV); "Overland Express" (radio/TV); "There Never Was a Horse" (radio/TV); "The Pesthole" (TV); and "Hickok" (radio). With a 1957 first printing, a 1958 identical Canadian second printing, and a 1960 cover-variation third printing.]

Popular Library

_____ Gunsmoke; by Chris Stratton [Richard Hubbard]; Popular Library 08146; c 1970 (1st); $.60 [FC Photo: Arness]

Awards

_____ Gunsmoke #1: The Renegades; by Jackson Flynn [Donald Bensen]; Award AN1283; c 1974 (1st); $.95 [novelization of the episode "A Game of Death ... An Act of Love"] [FC Photo: Arness]

_____ Gunsmoke #2: Shootout; by Jackson Flynn [Gordon Shirreffs]; Award AN1284; c 1974 (1st); $.95 [original story] [FC Photo: Arness]

_____ Gunsmoke #3: Duel at Dodge City; by Jackson Flynn [Donald Bensen]; Award AN1328; c 1974 (1st); $.95 [novelization of the episode "The Sodbusters"] [FC Photo: Arness]

_____ Gunsmoke #4: Cheyenne Vengeance; by Jackson Flynn [Donald Bensen]; Award AN1403; c 1974 (1st: 1975); $.95 [novelization of the episode "The Drummer"] [FC Photo: Arness]

Whitmans

_____ Gunsmoke; by Robert Turner; Whitman 1587; c 1958 (1st) [FC Illus: Arness, Dennis Weaver] [issued in UK by World Distributors as "Gun Law: The Mystery of Jan Gant's Treasure"]

_____ Gunsmoke: Showdown on Front Street; by Paul S. Newman; Whitman 1520; c 1969 (1st)

_____ Gunsmoke; by Doris Schroeder; Whitman Big Little Book 1647; c 1958 (1st) [FC Illus: Arness]

TV's longest running Western started on radio in 1952 (with William Conrad as Marshal Matt Dillon) and moved to TV three years later, inspiring a smattering of tie-ins over its 20-year run. The first, Ballantine's *Gunsmoke*, novelizes both radio and TV scripts. The Awards were written under the Jackson Flynn house name by the noted authors.

HAPPY DAYS
January 15, 1974 - July 12, 1984; ABC

Tempos

_____ Happy Days 1: Ready To Go Steady; by William Johnston; Tempo 05794; c 1974 (1st); $.95 [FC Photo: Anson Williams, Henry Winkler, Ron Howard]

_____ Happy Days 2: Fonzie Drops In; by William Johnston; Tempo 07452; c 1974 (1st); $.95 [novelization of the episode "Fonzie Drops In"] [FC Photo: Winkler]

_____ Happy Days: Fonzie Drops In [cover-variation]; by William Johnston; Ace Tempo Star 24515; c 1974 (1st Tempo Star: 1977); $1.25 [FC Photo: Winkler]

_____ Happy Days 3: The Invaders; by William Johnston; Tempo 12267; c 1975 (1st); $.95 [FC Photo: Howard, Winkler, Williams]

_____ Happy Days 4: Fonzie, Fonzie, Superstar; by William Johnston; Tempo 12414; c 1976 (1st); $.95 [FC Photo: Winkler]

_____ Happy Days 5: The Fonz & La Zonga; by William Johnston; Tempo 12607; c 1976 (1st); $.95 [FC Photo: Winkler]

_____ Happy Days 6: The Bike Tycoon; by William Johnston; Tempo 12609; c 1976 (1st); $.95 [FC Photo: Winkler] [variant version spine lacks book number, author's name, and the words "The Bike Tycoon"]

_____ Happy Days 7: Dear Fonzie...; by William Johnston; Tempo 12946; c 1977 (1st); $1.25 [FC Photo: Winkler]

_____ Happy Days 8: Fonzie Goes to College; by William Johnston; Tempo 14034; c 1977 (1st); $1.25 [FC Photo: Howard, Winkler]

_____ The Official Fonzie Scrapbook; by Ben Davidson; Tempo 14044; c 1976 (1st); $1.95 [FC Photo: Winkler]

_____ Fonzie's Scrambled Word Find Puzzles; by Linda Doherty; Tempo 12645; c 1976 (1st); $.95 [oversize] [FC Photo: Winkler; BC Photo: Erin Moran, Winkler]

Winkler Biographies

_____ Hollywood's Newest Superstar: Henry Winkler; by Suzanne Munshower; Berkley Z3231; c 1976 (1st); $1.25 [FC Photo: Winkler]

_____ The Fonz: The Henry Winkler Story; by Charles E. Pike; Pocket 80746; c 1976 (1st); $1.50 [FC Photo: Winkler]

_____ The Truth About Fonzie; by Peggy Herz; Scholastic Book Services TK3571; c 1976 (1st) [FC Photo: Winkler]

_____ fonzie!; by Martin A. Grove; Zebra 89083-228; c 1976 (1st); $1.95 [FC Photo: Winkler]

Henry Winkler, as Milwaukee's hip greaser The Fonz, took the show by storm, and is the lone cast member pictured on most of the books in the Tempo series (some were re-issued with higher book numbers). A scarce boxed set includes the first six Tempos.

THE HARDY BOYS/NANCY DREW MYSTERIES
January 30, 1977 - January 21, 1979; ABC

Tempo Puzzle Books

_____ Nancy Drew Mystery Mazes; by Vladimir Koziakin; Tempo 14504; c 1977 (1st); $.95 [oversize] [FC Photo: Pamela Sue Martin]

_____ Hardy Boys Secret Codes; by Evan Morley; Tempo 14505; c 1977 (1st); $.95 [oversize] [FC Photo: Shaun Cassidy, Parker Stevenson]

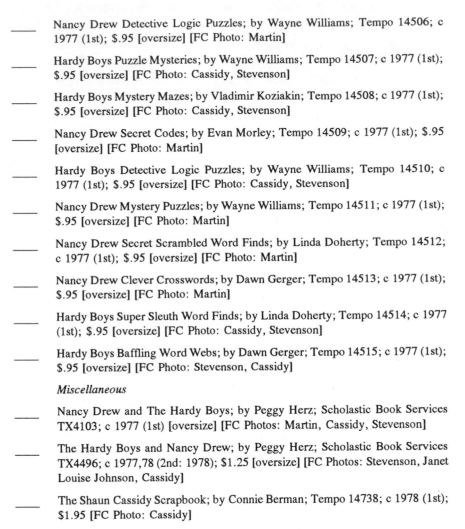

_____ Nancy Drew Detective Logic Puzzles; by Wayne Williams; Tempo 14506; c 1977 (1st); $.95 [oversize] [FC Photo: Martin]

_____ Hardy Boys Puzzle Mysteries; by Wayne Williams; Tempo 14507; c 1977 (1st); $.95 [oversize] [FC Photo: Cassidy, Stevenson]

_____ Hardy Boys Mystery Mazes; by Vladimir Koziakin; Tempo 14508; c 1977 (1st); $.95 [oversize] [FC Photo: Cassidy, Stevenson]

_____ Nancy Drew Secret Codes; by Evan Morley; Tempo 14509; c 1977 (1st); $.95 [oversize] [FC Photo: Martin]

_____ Hardy Boys Detective Logic Puzzles; by Wayne Williams; Tempo 14510; c 1977 (1st); $.95 [oversize] [FC Photo: Cassidy, Stevenson]

_____ Nancy Drew Mystery Puzzles; by Wayne Williams; Tempo 14511; c 1977 (1st); $.95 [oversize] [FC Photo: Martin]

_____ Nancy Drew Secret Scrambled Word Finds; by Linda Doherty; Tempo 14512; c 1977 (1st); $.95 [oversize] [FC Photo: Martin]

_____ Nancy Drew Clever Crosswords; by Dawn Gerger; Tempo 14513; c 1977 (1st); $.95 [oversize] [FC Photo: Martin]

_____ Hardy Boys Super Sleuth Word Finds; by Linda Doherty; Tempo 14514; c 1977 (1st); $.95 [oversize] [FC Photo: Cassidy, Stevenson]

_____ Hardy Boys Baffling Word Webs; by Dawn Gerger; Tempo 14515; c 1977 (1st); $.95 [oversize] [FC Photo: Stevenson, Cassidy]

Miscellaneous

_____ Nancy Drew and The Hardy Boys; by Peggy Herz; Scholastic Book Services TX4103; c 1977 (1st) [oversize] [FC Photos: Martin, Cassidy, Stevenson]

_____ The Hardy Boys and Nancy Drew; by Peggy Herz; Scholastic Book Services TX4496; c 1977,78 (2nd: 1978); $1.25 [oversize] [FC Photos: Stevenson, Janet Louise Johnson, Cassidy]

_____ The Shaun Cassidy Scrapbook; by Connie Berman; Tempo 14738; c 1978 (1st); $1.95 [FC Photo: Cassidy]

The Hardy Boys and Nancy Drew were created in the 1920's by Edward Stratemeyer, and have been featured in two highly successful book series ever since. For the *Hardy Boys* books, the house name Franklin W. Dixon has been used as the byline; for the *Nancy Drew* books, the house name Carolyn Keene has been used. Mr. Stratemeyer, whose publishing empire includes such additional series as *Tom Swift* and *The Bobbsey Twins*, died in 1930. With his death, the reigns were turned over to his daughter Harriet Adams, who helped bring the Hardy Boys and Nancy Drew to TV nearly 50 years later.

They began as two separate series in 1977 (*The Hardy Boys Mysteries* and *The Nancy Drew Mysteries*), alternating bi-weekly in the same time slot, before merging as a single series in 1978. The new series was called *The Hardy*

Boys/Nancy Drew Mysteries, and the three lead characters (brothers Frank and Joe Hardy, and Nancy Drew) appeared jointly in the episodes. Pamela Sue Martin as Nancy Drew left the show with the new arrangement, and was replaced by Janet Louise Johnson. The 1977 book *Nancy Drew and The Hardy Boys*, a behind-the-scenes look at the show, was re-issued as *The Hardy Boys and Nancy Drew* in 1978. The re-issue is identical to the original but for the chapter on Martin being replaced by the chapter on Johnson, and Johnson's picture replacing Martin's on the cover.

The show inspired a series of oversize puzzle books by Tempo, with trivia, stills, and puzzles which "made children think" per Evan Morley, who authored two.

HARRY O
September 12, 1974 - August 12, 1976; ABC

Popular Librarys

_____ Harry O #1; by Lee Hays; Popular Library 00269; c 1975 (1st); $1.25 [FC Photo: David Janssen]

_____ Harry O #2: The High Cost of Living; by Lee Hays; Popular Library 00337; c 1976 (1st); $1.25 [FC Photo: Janssen]

David Janssen's follow-up to *The Fugitive*--in this he played a cynical gumshoe--inspired the above Lee Hays tie-ins.

HAVE GUN, WILL TRAVEL
September 14, 1957 - September 21, 1963; CBS

_____ Have Gun, Will Travel; by Noel Loomis; Dell First Edition B156; c 1960 (1st); $.35 [FC Illus: Richard Boone]

_____ Have Gun, Will Travel: A Man Called Paladin; by Frank C. Robertson; Macfadden 60-191; c 1963 (1st: 1964); $.60 [front cover and spine wrongly print author's middle initial as "G"] [FC Photo: Boone]

_____ Have Gun, Will Travel; by Barlow Meyers; Whitman 1568; c 1959 (1st) [FC Illus: Boone]

HAWAII FIVE-O
September 26, 1968 - April 26, 1980; CBS

Signets

_____ Hawaii Five-O; by Michael Avallone; Signet P3622; c 1968 (1st); $.60 [FC Photo: Jack Lord]

_____ Hawaii Five-O [cover-variation]; by Michael Avallone; Signet T5817; c 1968 (4th: 1970); $.75 [FC Photo: Lord]

_____ Hawaii Five-O #2: Terror in the Sun; by Michael Avallone; Signet P3994; c 1969 (1st); $.60 [FC Photo: Lord]

_____ Hawaii Five-O #2: Terror in the Sun [cover-variation]; by Michael Avallone; Signet T5818; c 1969 (3rd: 1970); $.75 [FC Photo: Lord]

Whitmans

_____ Hawaii Five-O: Top Secret; by Robert Sidney Bowen; Whitman 1511; c 1969 (1st) [FC Illus: Lord]

_____ Hawaii Five-O: The Octopus Caper; by Leo R. Ellis; Whitman 1553; c 1971 (1st) [FC Illus: Lord; BC Illus: James MacArthur]

Tropical crimefighting adventures of Steve McGarrett and his sidekick Dano inspired the above tie-ins--two Michael Avallone Signets ("two of the finest detective novels I ever wrote") and two Whitmans. The Signets were first issued in 1968-69, then re-issued in 1970 (to the otherwise identical covers, banners announcing "THE SMASH CBS-TV SERIES!" were added).

HAWAIIAN EYE
October 7, 1959 - September 10, 1963; ABC

_____ Hawaiian Eye; by Frank Castle; Dell First Edition K112; c 1962 (1st); $.40 [FC Photos: Anthony Eisley, Connie Stevens, Robert Conrad, Grant Williams, Poncie Ponce]

HAWK
September 8, 1966 - December 29, 1966; ABC

_____ Hawk; by Richard Hardwick; Belmont B50-741; c 1966 (1st); $.50 [FC Illus: Burt Reynolds]

The cover pictures Burt Reynolds as Lieutenant Hawk, the full-blooded Iroquois who worked New York City's night beat. Reynolds, himself part Indian, later starred in TV's *Dan August* (no tie-ins), before making the move to the big-screen.

HAZEL
September 28, 1961 - September 5, 1966; NBC/CBS

Bantams

_____ All Hazel; by Ted Key; Bantam A2411; c 1958 (1st: 1962); $.35

_____ All Hazel [cover-variation]; by Ted Key; Bantam J2991; c 1958 (2nd: 1965); $.40

_____ Hazel Time; by Ted Key; Bantam J2990; c 1962 (1st: 1965); $.40

_____ Life With Hazel; by Ted Key; Bantam F3325; c 1965 (1st: 1967); $.50

The show was based on the Ted Key comic strip, which had appeared for nearly 20 years in *The Saturday Evening Post*. The character was also featured in a series of Bantam cartoon books (beginning with 1955's *Hazel*), which the publisher continued to issue, with show-mention, once the TV show aired. The books feature comics reprinted by Bantam.

HEAD OF THE CLASS
September 17, 1986 - January 15, 1991; ABC

_____ Head of the Class; by Susan Beth Pfeffer; Bantam 28190; c 1989 (1st); $2.95 [adapts as chapters 1-6 the episodes "First Day," "A Problem Like Maria," "Crimes of the Heart," "Cello Fever," "Trouble in Perfectville," and "Parents Day"] [FC Photo: Robin Givens (far right), with rest of cast]

HEC RAMSEY
October 8, 1972 - August 25, 1974; NBC

Awards

_____ Hec Ramsey; by Dean Owen [Dudley Dean McGaughy]; Award AN1169; c 1973 (1st); $.95 [novelization of the pilot episode "Hec Ramsey"] [FC Photo: Richard Boone]

_____ Hec Ramsey #2: The Hunted; by Joe Millard; Award AN1232; c 1974 (1st); $.95 [novelization of the episode "Mystery of the Yellow Rose"] [FC Photo: Boone]

HERE COME THE BRIDES
September 25, 1968 - September 18, 1970; ABC

_____ Here Come the Brides; by Chris Stratton [Richard Hubbard]; Curtis 06062; c 1969 (1st); $.60 [FC Photos: (top) David Soul, Robert Brown, Bobby Sherman; (bottom) Sherman, Brown, Bridget Hanley (up top), with extras]

Original adventures of the Bolt brothers and the local townsfolk--Candy, Lottie, Biddie Cloom and the rest--in 1870's Seattle.

HERE'S LUCY
September 23, 1968 - September 2, 1974; CBS

_____ Laugh With Lucy: The Story of Lucille Ball; by Joel H. Cohen; Scholastic Book Services TX2544; c 1974 (1st) [oversize] [FC Photo: Lucille Ball] [See also *The Lucy Show*, which this show succeeded]

THE HIGH CHAPARRAL
September 10, 1967 - September 10, 1971; NBC

Tempos

_____ The High Chaparral: Coyote Gold; by Ed Friend [Richard Wormser]; Tempo 05302; c 1969 (1st); $.60 [FC Photo: Leif Erickson, Linda Cristal; BC Photos: Erickson, Cameron Mitchell, Mark Slade, Cristal, Henry Darrow]

_____ The High Chaparral: Hell and High Water; by Wayne Sotona; Tempo 05319; c 1968 (1st: 1969); $.60 [FC Photo: Erickson, Mitchell, Slade]

Whitman

_____ The High Chaparral: Apache Way; by Steve Frazee; Whitman 1519; c 1969 (1st) [FC Illus: (clockwise from left) Erickson, Slade, Darrow, Cristal, Mitchell]

Western saga of the Cannon family on the sprawling High Chaparral ranch in pre-statehood Arizona inspired the above books. The paperback series was originated in England by World Distributors, which released four titles as "Bandolero Westerns" under the Wayne Sotona byline (*Man of Honour* [BW1], *Gun Runner's Last Ride* [BW2], *Town in Fear* [BW3], and *Hell and High Water* [BW4]). Sotona worked as an export sales agent for Whitman Publishing at the time, and World Distributors was a client. They asked if they could use his name for the bylines (they said it sounded like Zane Grey) and he said "Yes" (while he didn't have anything to do with the stories). *Hell and High Water* was also released in the United States by Tempo, which released an additional title not issued in Britain, *Coyote Gold*.

THE HOLLYWOOD SQUARES
October 17, 1966 - June 20, 1980; NBC

Popular Librarys

_____ Zingers From The Hollywood Squares; by Gail Sicilia, ed.; Popular Library 00221; c 1974 (1st); $1.25 [FC Photos: (top) Peter Marshall, (balance) Jan Murray, Rose Marie, Burt Reynolds, Marty Allen, Paul Lynde, McLean Stevenson, Charley Weaver, Lily Tomlin, Demond Wilson]

_____ More Zingers From The Hollywood Squares; by Gail Sicilia, ed.; Popular Library 04113; c 1978 (1st); $1.50 [FC Photos: Hal Linden, Marie, Stevenson, Allen, Lynde, Mackenzie Phillips, George Gobel, Donna Fargo, LeVar Burton; BC Photos: Karen Valentine, Vincent Price, Roddy McDowall]

HONEY WEST
September 17, 1965 - September 2, 1966; ABC

Pyramids

_____ This Girl for Hire; by G.G. Fickling [Skip and Gloria Fickling]; Pyramid R-1151; c 1957 (4th: 1965); $.50 [issued as G-274 in 1957, with a 1957 second and a 1958 third printing identical but for banners announcing the new printings]

_____ This Girl for Hire [cover-variation]; by G.G. Fickling; Pyramid R-1360; c 1957 (5th: 1965); $.50 [FC Photos: Anne Francis]

_____ A Gun for Honey; by G.G. Fickling; Pyramid R-1167; c 1958 (2nd: 1965); $.50 [issued as G-344 in 1958]

_____ A Gun for Honey [cover-variation]; by G.G. Fickling; Pyramid R-1358; c 1958 (3rd: 1965); $.50 [FC Photos: Francis]

_____ Honey in the Flesh; by G.G. Fickling; Pyramid R-1179; c 1959 (2nd: 1965); $.50 [issued as G-411 in 1959]

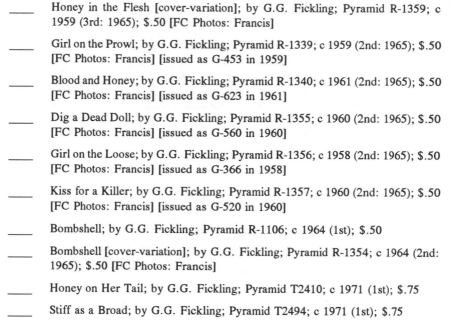

_____ Honey in the Flesh [cover-variation]; by G.G. Fickling; Pyramid R-1359; c 1959 (3rd: 1965); $.50 [FC Photos: Francis]

_____ Girl on the Prowl; by G.G. Fickling; Pyramid R-1339; c 1959 (2nd: 1965); $.50 [FC Photos: Francis] [issued as G-453 in 1959]

_____ Blood and Honey; by G.G. Fickling; Pyramid R-1340; c 1961 (2nd: 1965); $.50 [FC Photos: Francis] [issued as G-623 in 1961]

_____ Dig a Dead Doll; by G.G. Fickling; Pyramid R-1355; c 1960 (2nd: 1965); $.50 [FC Photos: Francis] [issued as G-560 in 1960]

_____ Girl on the Loose; by G.G. Fickling; Pyramid R-1356; c 1958 (2nd: 1965); $.50 [FC Photos: Francis] [issued as G-366 in 1958]

_____ Kiss for a Killer; by G.G. Fickling; Pyramid R-1357; c 1960 (2nd: 1965); $.50 [FC Photos: Francis] [issued as G-520 in 1960]

_____ Bombshell; by G.G. Fickling; Pyramid R-1106; c 1964 (1st); $.50

_____ Bombshell [cover-variation]; by G.G. Fickling; Pyramid R-1354; c 1964 (2nd: 1965); $.50 [FC Photos: Francis]

_____ Honey on Her Tail; by G.G. Fickling; Pyramid T2410; c 1971 (1st); $.75

_____ Stiff as a Broad; by G.G. Fickling; Pyramid T2494; c 1971 (1st); $.75

Honey West, the short-lived but long-recalled show about the "sexiest private eye to ever pull a trigger," was based on the mystery novels by the husband-and-wife writing team of Skip and Gloria Fickling ("G.G. Fickling"). The Ficklings created fiction's first female private detective in the book _This Girl for Hire_ ("on April 24, 1956 a bouncing 120-pound girl was born to my wife and me"), and took it to New York to find a publisher. Pyramid bought it and published it in 1957; the book was a success and led to seven sequels by the early 1960's.

Skip was in the process of writing the ninth _Honey West_ book, _Bombshell_, when he was approached by Dick Powell of Four Star International, who wanted to bring the character to TV. A year of negotiations ensued, and in the Apr-21-1965 _Burke's Law_ episode "Who Killed the Jackpot?" Anne Francis introduced the character of Honey West to TV audiences. The show premiered the following September, with the racy action from the books toned down (she was made into a drawing room detective) and the "pleased and proud" Skip in the role of executive advisor. With the airing of the show Pyramid re-issued the eight original _Honey West_ books, plus _Bombshell_, as TV tie-ins (_This Girl for Hire, A Gun for Honey, Honey in the Flesh,_ and _Bombshell_ were issued twice) and distributed over a million copies at the time. The show attracted a loyal following, Anne Francis was nominated for an Emmy, and there were plans to expand to an hour and go to color episodes, but ABC decided not to renew.

Five years later, two additional *Honey West* books were written, *Honey on Her Tail* and *Stiff as a Broad* (the latter was originally entitled *Angel of Death*). In all, the eleven books were translated into over a dozen languages, with worldwide sales of over 10 million copies (the character, a blonde, was particularly popular in Scandinavia ... and Japan).

The Ficklings cliffside Laguna Beach home ("the house that Honey West built") overlooks Catalina Island, the setting for the first *Honey West* book. Nearly destroyed in the 1993 fires (a portion of the roof caught on fire), it took some "real Honey West moves" on their part to save it. A *Honey West* movie is currently in production.

HOTEL DE PAREE
October 2, 1959 - September 23, 1960; CBS

____ Hotel de Paree: Sundance; by Richard Telfair [Richard Jessup]; Gold Medal 999; c 1960 (1st); $.25 [FC Illus: Earl Holliman]

HOUSE PARTY
See ART LINKLETTER'S HOUSE PARTY

HOW THE WEST WAS WON
February 12, 1978 - April 23, 1979; ABC

____ How the West Was Won; by Lou Cameron; Ballantine 27401; c 1977 (1st: 1978); $1.95 [novelization of several episodes] [FC Illus: James Arness]

The show was based on the 1962 movie, which had also inspired the 1962 Louis L'Amour novelization. Lou Cameron's own *How the West Was Won* book is a novelization of the TV show. "I did it because my then-agent was selling me cheaper than Louis L'Amour or whoever really did Volume I. That's the main reason I left that agency ... It's not as easy to write novelizations as they tell you it is when they cut the deal."

I DREAM OF JEANNIE
September 18, 1965 - September 1, 1970; NBC

____ I Dream of Jeannie; by Dennis Brewster; Pocket 10130; c 1966 (1st); $.60 [oversize] [FC Photo: Barbara Eden]

Features the "hilarious trials and tantalizing tribulations of Astronaut Tony Nelson and his blonde, curvaceous, beguilingly beautiful Genie named Jeannie ... from blast-off to landing."

I LOVE LUCY
October 15, 1951 - June 24, 1957; CBS

____ I Love Lucy: The Real Story of Lucille Ball; by Eleanor Harris; Ballantine 78; c 1954 (1st); $.35 [FC Illus: Lucille Ball]

I SPY
September 15, 1965 - September 2, 1968; NBC

Popular Librarys

_____ I Spy; by John Tiger [Walter Wager]; Popular Library SP400; c 1965 (1st); $.50 [FC Photo: Bill Cosby, Robert Culp]

_____ I Spy #2: Masterstroke; by John Tiger [Walter Wager]; Popular Library 60-2127; c 1966 (1st); $.60 [FC Photos: (bottom) Culp, Cosby]

_____ I Spy #3: Superkill; by John Tiger [Walter Wager]; Popular Library 60-2157; c 1967 (1st); $.60 [FC Photos: Cosby, Culp]

_____ I Spy #4: Wipeout; by John Tiger [Walter Wager]; Popular Library 60-2180; c 1967 (1st); $.60 [FC Illus: Culp, Cosby]

_____ I Spy #5: Countertrap; by John Tiger [Walter Wager]; Popular Library 60-2206; c 1967 (1st); $.60 [FC Photos: Cosby, Culp]

_____ I Spy #6: Doomdate; by John Tiger [Walter Wager]; Popular Library 60-2237; c 1967 (1st); $.60 [FC Photos: Cosby, Culp]

_____ I Spy #7: Death-Twist; by John Tiger [Walter Wager]; Popular Library 60-2311; c 1968 (1st); $.60 [FC Photo: Cosby, Culp]

Whitman

_____ I Spy: Message From Moscow; by Brandon Keith; Whitman 1542; c 1966 (1st) [FC Photo: Cosby, Culp]

Miscellaneous

_____ Robert Culp & Bill Cosby; by Ed Goodgold; Grosset & Dunlap 1097; c 1967 (1st); $1.00 [oversize] [FC Photo: Culp, Cosby]

_____ Cool Cos: The Story of Bill Cosby; by Joel H. Cohen; Scholastic Book Services TX1388; c 1969 (1st); $.60 [FC Photo: Cosby]

    Terrific *I Spy* thrillers by suspense writer Walter Wager, as John Tiger, make good companion reading to the TV show, adding new dimensions to it and expanding on the characters. Wager was already a fan of the show when he was contacted by former college chum James A. Bryans, Editor-in-Chief at Popular Library, who asked him to do an *I Spy* book. It worked, and the six sequels followed. Wager had a "marvelous" time writing them ("at about page 80 the books [virtual first drafts, and once the subject of a graduate level English thesis] took off"), and has considered marketing the film rights for the stories.

    Long-time admirer David Spencer adds: "Such deliberate changes enhanced and made TV tie-ins unique unto their own right in very special cases, as with Walter's *I Spy* books. Creating detailed backstory for the leads; identifying their employer as the CIA (the series never did; in one episode they answered to "The State Department" and in the 1994 reunion TV-movie Kelly had become head of an unidentified government espionage branch that was pointedly <u>not</u> the CIA); giving them a boss: the pudgy, square-but-not-stupid

Carolinian Donald Mars; code-naming the team "Domino," etc. added richness, depth, and a lore that, because it was so evocative, occasionally seems missing from the episodes when they're watched anew."

Among Wager's other works are *58 Minutes* (the story that was the basis for the 1990 hit movie *Die Hard 2*), *Operation Intrigue* (a spy novel he wrote [as Walter Hermann] while an Editor at the United Nations), *My Side* (King Kong's "autobiography"), three "Blue Books" (*Blue Leader, Blue Moon*, and *Blue Murder*, which feature the female private eye Alison Gordon), and two *Mission: Impossible* books. In addition, the 1977 feature films *Telefon* and *Twilight's Last Gleaming* were based on his novels *Telefon* and *Viper Three*. The John Tiger pseudonym, which he used for the *I Spy* and *Mission: Impossible* books because he didn't create the characters, came "out of the blue."

THE IMMORTAL
September 24, 1970 - September 8, 1971; ABC

_____ The Immortal; by James E. Gunn; Bantam S5924; c 1970 (1st); $.75 [novelization of the TV-movie pilot "The Immortal" (Sep-30-1969)] [FC Photo: Christopher George]

The show is rooted in the 1962 book *The Immortals* by James Gunn. The book inspired the Sep-30-1969 TV-movie "The Immortal"; the TV-movie piloted the show, and was then novelized by Gunn in the 1970 book *The Immortal*.

IN SEARCH OF ...
1976 - 1982; Syndicated

Bantams

_____ In Search of Lost Civilizations (#1); by Alan Landsburg; Bantam 10582; c 1976 (1st); $1.95

_____ In Search of Extraterrestrials (#2); by Alan Landsburg; Bantam 10722; c 1976 (1st: 1977); $1.95

_____ In Search of Magic and Witchcraft (#3); by Alan Landsburg; Bantam 10851; c 1977 (1st); $1.95

_____ In Search of Strange Phenomena; by Alan Landsburg; Bantam 10855; c 1977 (1st); $1.95

_____ In Search of Myths and Monsters; by Alan Landsburg; Bantam 11137; c 1977 (1st); $1.95

_____ In Search of Missing Persons; by Alan Landsburg; Bantam 11459; c 1978 (1st); $1.95

Alan Landsburg, "TV's #1 explorer of the unknown," created this documentary series in 1976, basing it in part on his books *In Search of Ancient Mysteries* and *The Outer Space Connection* (issued in 1974 and '75 in conjunction with the films of those names, they were co-written with his wife

Sally Landsburg). The show in turn inspired the above books, each with Forewords by show-host Leonard Nimoy. The first three were issued with series numbers, while books five and six were not, and whether or not the fourth book was is a mystery.

THE INCREDIBLE HULK
March 10, 1978 - May 19, 1982; CBS

Pockets

_____ Stan Lee Presents The Incredible Hulk; by Stan Lee; Pocket 81446; c 1978 (1st); $1.95 [cartoon book]

_____ Stan Lee Presents The Incredible Hulk #2; by Stan Lee; Pocket 82559; c 1978 (1st: 1979); $1.95 [cartoon book]

_____ The Incredible Hulk in Stalker From the Stars; by Len Wein, Marv Wolfman and "Joseph Silva" [Ron Goulart]; Pocket 82084; c 1978 (1st); $1.75 [full-length novel]

_____ The Incredible Hulk in Cry of the Beast; by Richard S. Meyers; Pocket 82085; c 1979 (1st); $1.75 [full-length novel]

_____ The Hulk and Spider-Man in Murdermoon; by Paul Kupperberg; Pocket 82094; c 1979 (1st); $1.95 [full-length novel]

_____ Stan Lee Presents The Incredible Hulk: A Video Novel; by Roy Thomas, ed.; Pocket 82827; c 1979 (1st); $2.75 [photo-novelization of the TV-movie pilot "The Incredible Hulk" (Nov-04-1977)] [FC Photo: Lou Ferrigno]

Tempos

_____ The Incredible Hulk; by Stan Lee and Larry Lieber; Tempo 17179; c 1980 (1st); $1.75 [cartoon book]

_____ The Incredible Hulk Volume 2; by Stan Lee and Larry Lieber; Tempo 17314; c 1981 (1st); $1.95 [cartoon book]

The show was based on the comic strip character created by Stan Lee for *Marvel Comics* in 1962. Lee--who also created *The Fantastic Four*, *Spider-Man*, and *Thor* at the time (additional superheroes whose popularity along with the *Hulk's* put *Marvel Comics* over the top)--was promoted to publisher in 1972, and is widely credited with revolutionizing the comic book industry.

The show was piloted in two TV-movies (Nov-04-1977's "The Incredible Hulk" and Nov-28-1977's "The Return of the Incredible Hulk"), before airing on a weekly basis starting in March of 1978. Pocket Books was publishing a series of books on the *Marvel* characters at the time, including six *Incredible Hulk* books. They include two cartoon books (featuring *Hulk* comic reprints), three original novels (*Stalker From the Stars* is by comic strip novelizer Ron Goulart, as Joseph Silva, from portions started by cartoonists Len Wein and Marv Wolfman; *Murdermoon* also features *Spider-Man*), and a Video Novel which, through novelizing the first TV-movie, tells "the story of the Hulk's incredible origin--in over 150 photos taken from the TV show!"

The *Hulk* was also featured in a syndicated newspaper strip, with Tempo obtaining the reprint rights to them and reprinting them in two cartoon books by Stan Lee and Larry Lieber. (Lee was born Stanley Martin Lieber and had his name legally changed; Lieber is Lee's younger brother.)

THE INVADERS
January 10, 1967 - September 17, 1968; ABC

Pyramids

_____ The Invaders #1; by Keith Laumer; Pyramid R-1664; c 1967 (1st); $.50 [FC Illus: Roy Thinnes] [issued in UK by Corgi as "The Meteor Man," under Laumer's pseudonym of Anthony Le Baron]

_____ The Invaders #2: Enemies From Beyond; by Keith Laumer; Pyramid X-1689; c 1967 (1st); $.60 [FC Photo: Thinnes]

_____ The Invaders #3: Army of the Undead; by Rafe Bernard; Pyramid R-1711; c 1967 (1st); $.50 [FC Photo: Thinnes] [issued in UK by Corgi as "The Halo Highway," as by Bernard]

Whitmans

_____ The Invaders: Dam of Death; by Jack Pearl; Whitman 1545; c 1967 (1st) [FC Illus: Thinnes]

_____ The Invaders: Alien Missile Threat; by Paul S. Newman; Whitman Big Little Book 2012; c 1967 (1st) [FC Illus: Thinnes]

The saga of David Vincent's one-man war against humanoid invaders inspired the above books. In the first Pyramid, author Keith Laumer subtly re-works the show's premise and introductory story, improving their plausibility while maintaining the suspense. (The show's David Vincent is an architect who discovers the invaders outright when he sees a flying saucer; Laumer's David Vincent is an industrial engineer who is more plausibly drawn into the invaders' conspiracy through a series of events.) Laumer agreed to take the assignment only on the condition he could so modify the concept.

The first and third *Invaders* books were also published in Britain by Corgi (as noted above), which published two additional titles not released here: *Night of the Trilobites* and *The Autumn Accelerator*, both by Peter Leslie.

THE INVISIBLE MAN
September 8, 1975 - January 19, 1976; NBC

_____ The Invisible Man; by Michael Jahn; Fawcett Gold Medal P3460; c 1975 (1st); $1.25 [novelization of the TV-movie pilot "The Invisible Man" (May-06-1975)] [FC Photo: David McCallum]

THE IRON HORSE
September 12, 1966 - January 6, 1968; ABC

_____ The Iron Horse; by William Johnston; Popular Library 60-2156; c 1967 (1st); $.60 [FC Photo: Dale Robertson]

IRONSIDE
September 14, 1967 - January 16, 1975; NBC

_____ Ironside; by Jim Thompson; Popular Library 60-2244; c 1967 (1st); $.60 [FC Photo: (standing) Barbara Anderson, Don Galloway, Don Mitchell, (seated) Raymond Burr] [*]

_____ Ironside: The Picture Frame Frame-Up; by William Johnston; Whitman 1521; c 1969 (1st) [FC Illus: Burr]

[*] This, Jim Thompson's only TV tie-in, makes a nice addition to his other works. Thompson's fine crime novels are among the most highly sought vintage paperbacks published.

IT TAKES A THIEF
January 9, 1968 - September 14, 1970; ABC

Aces

_____ It Takes a Thief #1: The Devil in Davos; by Gil Brewer; Ace 37598; c 1969 (1st); $.60 [FC Photo: Robert Wagner]

_____ It Takes a Thief #2: Mediterranean Caper; by Gil Brewer; Ace 37599; c 1969 (1st); $.60 [FC Photo: Wagner]

_____ It Takes a Thief #3: Appointment in Cairo; by Gil Brewer; Ace 37600; c 1970 (1st); $.60 [FC Photo: Wagner; BC Photo: Wagner, Malachi Throne]

European adventure series starring Robert Wagner as Alexander Mundy inspired the above Gil Brewer tie-ins, set in Switzerland, France, and Cairo, respectively.

IT'S YOUR MOVE
September 26, 1984 - August 10, 1985; NBC

_____ It's Your Move; by William Rotsler; Archway 54716; c 1984 (1st); $2.25 [FC Photo: Caren Kaye, Jason Bateman, David Garrison]

THE JACK PAAR TONIGHT SHOW
July 29, 1957 - March 30, 1962; NBC

_____ Charley Weaver's Letters from Mamma; by Cliff Arquette; Dell D347; c 1959 (1st: 1960); $.35 [FC Photo: Jack Paar, Cliff Arquette/Charley Weaver]

_____ Yours Truly, Hugh Downs; by Hugh Downs; Avon F-106; c 1960 (1st); $.40 [FC Photo: Downs]

___ I Kid You Not; by Jack Paar; Cardinal GC-103; c 1959,60 (1st: 1961); $.50 [FC Photo: Paar]

___ My Saber is Bent; by Jack Paar; Cardinal GC-148; c 1961 (1st: 1962); $.50 [FC Photo: Paar]

___ The Real Jack Paar; by George Johnson; Gold Medal s1263; c 1962 (1st); $.35 [FC Photo: Paar]

___ What is Jack Paar Really Like?; by William H.A. Carr; Lancer 70-005; c 1962 (1st); $.40 [FC Photo: Paar]

Above books were issued in conjunction with Jack Paar's five-year stint as host of *The Tonight Show*, then called *The Jack Paar Tonight Show*. Cliff Arquette made frequent guest appearances on the show under his stage name Charley Weaver; Hugh Downs was Paar's announcer and sidekick.

JAMES AT 15
October 27, 1977 - July 27, 1978; NBC

Dells

___ James at 15; by April Smith; Dell 14389; c 1977 (1st); $1.50 [novelization of the TV-movie pilot "James at 15" (Sep-05-1977)] [FC Photo: Lance Kerwin; BC Photo: (seated) Linden Chiles, (standing) Deirdre Berthrong, Kerwin, Kim Richards, Lynn Carlin]

___ James at 15 [cover-variation]; by April Smith; Dell 94389; c 1977 (1st Laurelleaf: 1980); $1.50

___ James at 15: Friends; by April Smith; Dell 12666; c 1978 (1st); $1.50 [novelization of the episode "Friends"] [FC Photo: David Hubbard, Lisa Pelikan, Kerwin, Susan Myers]

___ James at 15: Friends [cover-variation]; by April Smith; Dell 92666; c 1978 (1st Laurelleaf: 1980); $1.50

JERICHO
September 15, 1966 - January 19, 1967; CBS

___ Code Name: Jericho - Operation Goldkill; by Bruce Cassiday; Award A211F K; c 1967 (1st); $.50 [FC Photo: John Leyton, Don Francks, Marino Mase]

The book was based on the author's experiences as a U.S. Air Force staff sergeant during World War II. The show was about three Allied resistance fighters who worked--under the code name Jericho--behind enemy lines. Cassiday based the story on an actual event in which the Allied forces attempted to deliver a shipment of gold bullion to the partisan forces fighting in Northern Italy.

JIM BOWIE
September 7, 1956 - August 29, 1958; ABC

_____ The Adventures of Jim Bowie; by Lewis B. Patten; Whitman Big Little Book 1648; c 1958 (1st) [FC Illus: Scott Forbes]

JOANIE LOVES CHACHI
March 23, 1982 - September 13, 1983; ABC

Wanderers

_____ Joanie Loves Chachi #1: Secrets; by William Rotsler; Wanderer 46010; c 1982 (1st); $2.95 [oversize] [FC Photo: Erin Moran, Scott Baio]

_____ Joanie Loves Chachi #2: A Test of Hearts; by William Rotsler; Wanderer 46011; c 1982 (1st); $2.95 [oversize] [FC Photo: Moran, Baio]

Weekly Reader

_____ Joanie Loves Chachi; by Roger Elwood; Weekly Reader F536; c 1982 (1st) [FC Photo: Moran, Baio]

JOHNNY STACCATO
September 10, 1959 - September 25, 1960; NBC/ABC

_____ Johnny Staccato; by Frank Boyd [Frank Kane]; Gold Medal 980; c 1960 (1st); $.25 [FC Illus: John Cassavetes]

JUDD FOR THE DEFENSE
September 8, 1967 - September 19, 1969; ABC

Paperback Librarys

_____ Judd for the Defense; by Lawrence Louis Goldman; Paperback Library 53-625; c 1968 (1st); $.60 [FC Photo: Carl Betz, Stephen Young]

_____ Judd for the Defense #2: The Secret Listeners; by Lawrence Louis Goldman; Paperback Library 53-721; c 1968 (1st); $.60 [FC Photo: Betz, Young]

KNIGHT RIDER
September 26, 1982 - August 8, 1986; NBC

Pinnacles

_____ Knight Rider; by Glen A. Larson and Roger Hill; Pinnacle 42170; c 1983 (1st); $2.50 [novelization of the pilot episode "Knight Rider"] [FC Photo: David Hasselhoff]

_____ Knight Rider #2: Trust Doesn't Rust; by Glen A. Larson and Roger Hill; Pinnacle 42181; c 1984 (1st); $2.50 [novelization of the episode "Trust Doesn't Rust"] [FC Photo: Hasselhoff]

____ Knight Rider #3: Hearts of Stone; by Glen A. Larson and Roger Hill; Pinnacle 42182; c 1984 (1st); $2.50 [novelization of the episode "Hearts of Stone"] [FC Photo: Hasselhoff]

Show-creator/executive producer Glen A. Larson is given co-author credit for the above books, but wasn't involved in the writing. The books were also published in Britain, by Star (#'s 1 and 2) and Target (#3), sister imprints under the W.H. Allen umbrella. Target issued two additional *Knight Rider* books (under the same co-authorship) that weren't issued here: *#4: The 24-Carat Assassin* and *#5: Mirror Image*.

KNOTS LANDING
December 27, 1979 - May 13, 1993; CBS

Pioneer Communications Networks

____ Knots Landing #1: Secrets of Knots Landing; by Mary Ann Cooper; Pioneer 61; c 1986 (1st); $2.50 [novelization of several episodes]

____ Knots Landing #2: Uncharted Love; by Samantha Phillips [Sandi Gelles-Cole]; Pioneer 62; c 1986 (1st); $2.50 [novelization of several episodes]

____ Knots Landing #3: Love Unbound; by Anne Cavaliere; Pioneer 63; c 1986 (1st); $2.50 [novelization of several episodes]

____ Knots Landing #4: Misguided Hearts; by Scott Cunningham; Pioneer 64; c 1986 (1st); $2.50 [novelization of several episodes]

____ Knots Landing #5: Mothers and Daughters; by Samantha Phillips [Sandi Gelles-Cole]; Pioneer 65; c 1986 (1st); $2.50 [novelization of several episodes]

____ Knots Landing #6: Starting Over; by Brian Wolff; Pioneer 66; c 1986 (1st); $2.50 [novelization of several episodes]

____ Knots Landing #7: Tell Me No Lies; by Scott Cunningham; Pioneer 67; c 1986 (1st); $2.50 [novelization of several episodes]

____ Knots Landing #8: Once in a Lifetime; by Victoria Dann; Pioneer 68; c 1986 (1st); $2.50 [novelization of several episodes]

____ Knots Landing #9: A House Divided; by Anne Cavaliere; Pioneer 69; c 1987 (1st); $2.50 [novelization of several episodes]

____ Knots Landing #10: Family Affairs; by Marcia Lawrence; Pioneer 70; c 1987 (1st); $2.50 [novelization of several episodes]

____ Knots Landing #11: A Second Chance; by Amanda Preble; Pioneer 200; c 1987 (1st); $2.50 [novelization of several episodes]

____ Knots Landing #12: _____ ; by _____ ; Pioneer 201; c 1987 (1st); $2.50

____ Knots Landing #13: Dangerous Games; by D.L. Adler; Pioneer 202; c 1987 (1st); $2.50 [novelization of several episodes]

Covers of the above *Knots Landing* books picture unspecified actors. A fourteenth title may also exist.

KOJAK
October 24, 1973 - April 15, 1978; CBS

Pockets

_____ Kojak #1: Siege; by Victor B. Miller; Pocket 78487; c 1974 (1st); $1.25 [novelization of the pilot episode "Siege of Terror"] [FC Photo: Telly Savalas]

_____ Kojak #2: Requiem for a Cop; by Victor B. Miller; Pocket 78488; c 1974 (1st); $1.25 [novelization of the episode "Requiem for a Cop"] [FC Photo: Savalas]

_____ Kojak #3: Girl in the River; by Victor B. Miller; Pocket 78817; c 1975 (1st); $1.25 [novelization of the episode "Girl in the River"] [FC Photo: Savalas]

_____ Kojak #4: Therapy in Dynamite; by Victor B. Miller; Pocket 78865; c 1975 (1st); $1.25 [novelization of the episode "Therapy in Dynamite"] [FC Photo: Savalas]

_____ Kojak #5: Death Is Not a Passing Grade; by Victor B. Miller; Pocket 78912; c 1975 (1st); $1.25 [novelization of the episode "Death Is Not a Passing Grade"] [FC Photo: Savalas]

_____ Kojak #6: A Very Deadly Game; by Victor B. Miller; Pocket 78960; c 1975 (1st); $1.25 [novelization of the episode "A Very Deadly Game"] [FC Photo: Savalas]

_____ Kojak #7: Take-over; by Victor B. Miller; Pocket 78996; c 1975 (1st); $1.25 [novelization of the episode "The Chinatown Murders"] [FC Photo: Savalas]

_____ Kojak #8: Gun Business; by Victor B. Miller; Pocket 78998; c 1975 (1st); $1.25 [novelization of the episode "Nursemaids"] [FC Photo: Savalas]

_____ Kojak #9: The Trade-off; by Victor B. Miller; Pocket 80045; c 1975 (1st); $1.25 [novelization of the episode "The Trade-off"] [FC Photo: Savalas]

Berkleys

_____ Kojak in San Francisco; by Thom Racina; Berkley Z3237; c 1976 (1st); $1.25 [original story - front cover says "the story that couldn't be shown on TV!"] [FC Photo: Savalas]

_____ Telly Savalas: TV's Golden Greek; by Marsha Daly; Berkley Z3021; c 1975 (1st); $1.25 [FC Photo: Savalas]

Kojak was an instant hit as well as a highly regarded police show, and Pocket Books rushed to get a series of *Kojak* novelizations on the market. Victor Miller was signed to write the first three books, and on the basis of those manuscripts he was signed to write the second three, then the third, without any of the books having been marketed. With the popularity of the show in hand with the well-written manuscripts, Pocket was sure the books would do well, but sales were disappointing. (It was later thought the books' covers may have been too similar.)

Miller wrote the books first person, re-working the third person TV-scripts. (In the show the viewer sees the crime committed and watches Kojak solve it; in the books the reader discovers the crime along with Kojak and works with him to solve it, not finding out who-did-it until the end.) Kojak's sidekick Crocker is a less important figure in the books than the show, for Kojak shares his thoughts with the readers instead. Miller spiced the books (which at $1,500 apiece provided his springboard into free-lance writing) with the appropriate truisms (the Kojak lollipops and catchphrases) and enjoyed taking on the Telly Savalas persona.

KRAFT TELEVISION THEATER
May 7, 1947 - October 1, 1958; NBC/ABC

_____ Patterns; by Rod Serling; Bantam F1832; c 1955+ (1st: 1958); $.50 [FC Photo: Rod Serling]

Book includes "four famous plays by a brilliant young writer [the pre-*Twilight Zone* Rod Serling] for the world's newest form of entertainment--TV." Two of the plays appeared on *Kraft Television Theater*: "Patterns" (Jan-12-1955) and "Old MacDonald Had a Curve" (Aug-5-1953). The others appeared on *Playhouse 90* ("Requiem for a Heavyweight," Oct-11-1956) and *The U.S. Steel Hour* ("The Rack," Apr-12-1955). "Patterns" and "Requiem for a Heavyweight" won Emmys for Serling.

KUNG FU
October 14, 1972 - June 28, 1975; ABC

Warners

_____ Kung Fu #1: The Way of the Tiger, the Sign of the Dragon; by Howard Lee [Barry N. Malzberg]; Warner 76-464; c 1973 (1st); $1.25 [novelization of the TV-movie pilot "Kung Fu" (Feb-22-1972)] [FC Photo: David Carradine]

_____ Kung Fu #2: Chains; by Howard Lee [Ron Goulart]; Warner 76-465; c 1973 (1st); $1.25 [novelization of the episode "Chains"] [FC Photo: Carradine]

_____ Kung Fu #3: Superstition; by Howard Lee [Ron Goulart]; Warner 76-466; c 1973 (1st); $1.25 [novelization of the episode "Superstition"] [FC Photo: Carradine]

_____ Kung Fu #4: A Praying Mantis Kills; by Howard Lee [Lou Cameron]; Warner 76-467; c 1974 (1st); $1.25 [novelization of the episode "A Praying Mantis Kills"] [FC Photo: Carradine]

Pyramid

_____ Kung Fu: The Peaceful Way; by Richard Robinson; Pyramid 03315; c 1974 (1st); $.95 [*]

Popular series about mystic nomad/martial arts expert Kwai Chang Caine inspired four Warner novelizations, written under the Howard Lee house name by the noted authors. The "Howard" came from Howard Kaminsky, President of Warner Books; the "Lee" was chosen for its Oriental touch.

[*] This book, with 8 pages of photos various *Kung Fu* stars (Bruce Lee from the *Kung Fu* movies, David Carradine, Philip Ahn, and Radames Pera from the show), takes the reader on "a fascinating journey ... into the secret world where the ancient skills and wisdom of Kung Fu are taught."

LANCER
September 24, 1968 - June 23, 1970; CBS

_____ Lancer; by Paul W. Fairman; Popular Library 60-2349; c 1968 (1st); $.60 [FC Photos: Elizabeth Baur, Andrew Duggan, James Stacy, Wayne Maunder]

LAND OF THE GIANTS
September 22, 1968 - September 6, 1970; ABC

Pyramids

_____ Land of the Giants; by Murray Leinster [Will F. Jenkins]; Pyramid X-1846; c 1968 (1st); $.60 [FC Photos: Gary Conway, Don Matheson]

_____ Land of the Giants #2: The Hot Spot; by Murray Leinster [Will F. Jenkins]; Pyramid X-1921; c 1969 (1st); $.60 [FC Photo: Matheson, Conway, Heather Young]

_____ Land of the Giants #3: Unknown Danger; by Murray Leinster [Will F. Jenkins]; Pyramid X-2105; c 1969 (1st); $.60 [FC Photo (from top): Don Marshall, Deanna Lund, Kurt Kasznar, Conway, Stefan Arngrim]

Whitman

_____ Land of the Giants: Flight of Fear; by Carl Henry Rathjen; Whitman 1516; c 1969 (1st)

Highly farfetched show asked a lot in the suspension of belief department (an alien planet with Chevrolets, tiny earthlings being able to survive there) but was entertaining and had great props. In the above books, the seven earthlings battle an assortment of giant insects, housepets, menacing humans, and so on, always managing to find safety in the end, if not a return to earth.

LASSIE
September 12, 1954 - September 12, 1971; CBS
1971 - 1974; Syndicated

Whitman Regular Size

_____ Lassie and the Mystery at Blackberry Bog; by Dorothea J. Snow; Whitman 1536; c 1956 (1st)

_____ Lassie and the Mystery at Blackberry Bog [cover-variation]; by Dorothea J. Snow; Whitman 1509; c 1956 (unsp: 1966)

_____ Lassie and the Secret of Summer; by Dorothea J. Snow; Whitman 1589; c 1958 (1st)

_____ Lassie and the Secret of Summer [cover-variation]; by Dorothea J. Snow; Whitman 1500; c 1958 (unsp: 1964)

_____ Lassie: Forbidden Valley; by Doris Schroeder; Whitman 1508; c 1959 (1st) [FC Photo: Jon Provost]

_____ Lassie: Treasure Hunter; by Charles S. Strong; Whitman 1552; c 1960 (1st)

_____ Lassie: The Wild Mountain Trail; by I.G. Edmonds; Whitman 1513; c 1966 (1st) [BC Photo: Robert Bray]

_____ Lassie: The Mystery of Bristlecone Pine; by Steve Frazee; Whitman 1505; c 1967 (1st)

_____ Lassie: The Secret of the Smelters' Cave; by Steve Frazee; Whitman 1514; c 1968 (1st)

_____ Lassie: Lost in the Snow; by Steve Frazee; Whitman 1504; c 1969 (1st)

_____ Lassie: Trouble at Panter's Lake; by Steve Frazee; Whitman 1515; c 1972 (1st)

Whitman Big Little Books

_____ Lassie: Adventure in Alaska; by George S. Elrick; Whitman Big Little Book 2004; c 1967 (1st)

_____ Lassie and the Shabby Sheik; by George S. Elrick; Whitman Big Little Book 2027; c 1968 (1st)

The adventures of America's most beloved collie inspired a smattering of Whitman tie-ins over its 20-year run, including several regular size titles (all but *Trouble at Panter's Lake* include the Whitman "TV" logo on the covers or spines) and two Big Little Books. Several of the copyrights are held by "Lassie Television."

LAUGH-IN
January 22, 1968 - May 14, 1973; NBC

Signets

_____ Rowan & Martin's Laugh-In #1; by Morgul the Friendly Drelb; Signet T3844; c 1969 (1st); $.75 [FC Photo: Dan Rowan, Dick Martin; BC Photo: (bottom) Rowan, Martin, (second row) Judy Carne, Henry Gibson, Ruth Buzzi, JoAnne Worley, (third row) Dave Madden, Chelsea Brown, Goldie Hawn, Arte Johnson, Alan Sues, (top) Dick Whittington] [humor book with stills, blackouts, Sock-it-to-Me sketches, etc.]

_____ Rowan & Martin's Laugh-In #2: Mod, Mod World; by Roy Doty; Signet T3845; c 1968,69 (1st: 1969); $.75 [cartoon book based on the Roy Doty strip]

_____ Rowan & Martin's Laugh-In #3: Inside Laugh-In; by James E. Brodhead; Signet T4059; c 1969 (1st); $.75 [FC Photo: (top) Buzzi, Carne, Sues, Johnson, Gary Owens, (middle) Madden, Brown, Gibson, Hawn, Worley, (bottom) Rowan, Martin] [behind-the-scenes look at the show]

_____ Rowan & Martin's Laugh-In #4: JoAnne Worley's Chicken Joke Book; by JoAnne Worley with Dick Matthews; Signet T4060; c 1969 (1st); $.75 [FC Photo: Worley] [book of chicken jokes]

Popular Library

_____ Here Come the Judge!; by Dewey "Pigmeat" Markham with Bill Levinson; Popular Library 60-8080; c 1969 (1st); $.60 [FC Photos: Markham] [Markham, a regular during the show's first season, was famous for the catchphrase of the book's title]

LAVERNE AND SHIRLEY
January 27, 1976 - May 10, 1983; ABC

Warners [*]

_____ Laverne and Shirley #1: Teamwork; by Con Steffanson [Ron Goulart]; Warner 88-294; c 1976 (1st); $1.50 [FC Photo: Penny Marshall, Cindy Williams]

_____ Laverne and Shirley #2: Easy Money; by Con Steffanson [Ron Goulart]; Warner 88-295; c 1976 (1st); $1.50 [FC Photo: Williams, Marshall]

_____ Laverne and Shirley #3: Gold Rush; by Con Steffanson [Ron Goulart]; Warner 88-296; c 1976 (1st); $1.50 [FC Photo: Marshall, Williams]

Tempo

_____ Penny Marshall & Cindy Williams; by Connie Berman; Tempo 12937; c 1977 (1st); $1.25 [FC Photo: Marshall, Williams]

[*] Original novels based on the popular sitcom by distinguished science fiction and mystery novelist Ron Goulart, as Con Steffanson. A spinoff of *Happy Days*, that show's Fonzie appeared in a few *Laverne and Shirley* episodes, and as such Goulart wrote the character into the first *Laverne and Shirley* book. Paramount wouldn't allow it, however (they'd only sold the rights to the one show), so Goulart kept the character but changed his name to Arthur Caruso.

The book *Easy Money* was a takeoff of the quiz show scandals of the 1950's. In the book, Laverne wins contestantship on the Hollywood quiz show "Easy Money," flies to Los Angeles to be on it (Shirley goes with her), is provided the answers to the questions by a wealthy admirer, threatens to expose him, is kidnapped, escapes, and through it all exposes the scandal and causes the show's cancellation.

The Con Steffanson pseudonym, which Goulart also used for his *Flash Gordon* series (one of several comic strips he novelized), was derived from the Connecticut-based "Con-Edison" utility company, and his son Steffan.

THE LAWRENCE WELK SHOW
1955 - 1982; ABC/Syndicated

Whitmans

_____ The Lennon Sisters: The Secret of Holiday Island; by Doris Schroeder; Whitman 1544; c 1960 (1st) [FC Photos: (clockwise from top left) Dianne, Peggy, Janet, and Kathy Lennon]

_____ Janet Lennon: Adventure at Two Rivers; by Barlow Meyers; Whitman 1536; c 1961 (1st) [FC Illus: Janet Lennon]

_____ Janet Lennon at Camp Calamity; by Barlow Meyers; Whitman 1539; c 1962 (1st) [FC Illus: Janet Lennon]

_____ Janet Lennon and the Angels; by Barlow Meyers; Whitman 1583; c 1963 (1st) [FC Illus: Janet Lennon]

Adventure stories featuring the Lennon sisters (Dianne, Peggy, Kathy, and Janet), regular singers on *The Lawrence Welk Show* from 1955-68.

LEAVE IT TO BEAVER
October 4, 1957 - September 12, 1963; CBS/ABC

Berkleys

_____ Leave it to Beaver; by Beverly Cleary; Berkley Medallion G406; c 1960 (1st); $.35 [FC Photo: Tony Dow, Jerry Mathers]

_____ Leave it to Beaver [cover-variation]; by Beverly Cleary; Berkley Highland F1331; c 1960 (3rd: 1966); $.50 [FC Photo: Dow, Mathers]

_____ Here's Beaver; by Beverly Cleary; Berkley Medallion G497; c 1961 (1st); $.35 [FC Photo: Mathers, Dow]

_____ Here's Beaver [cover-variation]; by Beverly Cleary; Berkley Highland F1332; c 1961 (2nd: 1966); $.50 [FC Photo: Mathers, Dow]

_____ Beaver and Wally; by Beverly Cleary; Berkley Medallion G557; c 1961 (1st); $.35 [FC Photos: Dow, Mathers]

_____ Beaver and Wally [cover-variation]; by Beverly Cleary; Berkley Highland F1333; c 1961 (3rd: 1966); $.50 [FC Photos: Dow, Mathers]

Whitman

_____ Leave it to Beaver; by Cole Fannin; Whitman 1526; c 1962 (1st) [FC Illus: Mathers]

Popular sitcom inspired the above books, including three collections of short story novelizations by renowned children's book author Beverly Cleary. The books, fun reading and true to the show, were first issued as Berkley Medallions in 1960-61, then re-issued (with the same photos but different cover and spine designs) as Berkley Highlands in 1966.

Stories in *Leave it to Beaver* are: "Beaver and the Pigeons" (from the episode "Beaver's Pigeon's"), "Beaver's Hero," "Beaver Gets Adopted," "Beaver Goes Shopping" (from the episode "Beaver's Short Pants"), "Beaver's Big Game" (from the episode "Beaver and Henry"), and "Beaver and Wally" (from the episodes "Wally's Job" and "Lonesome Beaver").

Stories in *Here's Beaver* are: "Beaver the Magician," "Beaver Plays Ball" (from the episode "Beaver the Athlete"), "Beaver and the School Sweater" (from the episode "School Sweater"), "Wally's Haircomb," "Wally Goes Into Business" (from the episode "Wally, the Businessman"), "Beaver Makes a Loan," and "Beaver's Baby Picture" (from the episode "Baby Picture").

Stories in *Beaver and Wally* are: "Beaver Goes to the Carnival" and "The Horse Named Nick" (two stories adapted from the episode "The Horse Named Nick"), "Chuckie's New Shoes," "Wally's Play," "Wally, the Lifeguard," "Beaver's Accordion," "Wally's Glamour Girl," and "Beaver and Violet."

Due to potential confusion surrounding the books' multiple printing statuses, each book is described following:

Leave it to Beaver includes three printings: 1) Berkley Medallion G406 [copyright page says "BERKLEY EDITION, FEBRUARY, 1960"]; 2) Berkley Medallion G406 ["BERKLEY MEDALLION EDITION, FEBRUARY, 1960/2nd Printing, September, 1960"]; 3) Berkley Highland F1331 ["BERKLEY MEDALLION EDITION, FEBRUARY, 1960/2nd Printing, September, 1960/BERKLEY HIGHLAND EDITION, AUGUST, 1966 (3rd printing)"].

Here's Beaver includes two printings: 1) Berkley Medallion G497 ["BERKLEY EDITION, JANUARY, 1961"]; 2) Berkley Highland F1332 ["BERKLEY MEDALLION EDITION, JANUARY, 1961/BERKLEY HIGHLAND EDITION, AUGUST, 1966 (2nd printing)"].

Beaver and Wally includes three printings: 1) Berkley Medallion G557 ["BERKLEY EDITION, SEPTEMBER, 1961"]; 2) Berkley Medallion G557 ["BERKLEY EDITION, SEPTEMBER, 1961/2nd Printing, April, 1963"]; 3) Berkley Highland F1333 ["BERKLEY MEDALLION EDITION, OCTOBER, 1961/2nd Printing, May, 1963/BERKLEY HIGHLAND EDITION, AUGUST, 1966"].

THE LENNON SISTERS
See THE LAWRENCE WELK SHOW

LET'S MAKE A DEAL
December 20, 1963 - July 9, 1976; NBC/ABC

____   Let's Make a Deal: Emcee Monty Hall; by Monty Hall and Bill Libby; Ballantine 24370; c 1973 (1st: 1975); $1.50 [FC Photo: Monty Hall]

THE LIFE AND TIMES OF GRIZZLY ADAMS
February 9, 1977 - July 26, 1978; NBC

_____ The Life and Times of Grizzly Adams; by Charles E. Sellier, Jr.; Schick Sunn 917214; c 1977 (1st); $1.75 [FC Illus: Dan Haggerty] [novelization of the 1976 feature film and subsequent series - Sellier produced both]

THE LINEUP
October 1, 1954 - January 20, 1960; CBS

_____ The Lineup; by Frank Kane; Dell First Edition B125; c 1959 (1st); $.35 [FC Illus: Warner Anderson, Tom Tully; BC Illus: Tully, Anderson]

THE LINKLETTER SHOW
See ART LINKLETTER'S HOUSE PARTY

LITTLE HOUSE ON THE PRAIRIE
September 11, 1974 - September 5, 1983; NBC

_____ Little House on the Prairie; by Laura Ingalls Wilder; Perennial Library P357; c 1935 (1st: 1975); $1.25 [FC Photo: (top) Sidney Greenbush, Michael Landon, Karen Grassle, Melissa Gilbert, (bottom) Melissa Sue Anderson]

       Popular Michael Landon series was based on the "Little House" books by Laura Ingalls Wilder, which tell of the author's girlhood frontier experiences. Described in *Contemporary Authors* as "an honest, unsentimental, and vivid combination of storytelling, history, and autobiography," Wilder's third such book was entitled *Little House on the Prairie*, and re-issued as a TV tie-in with the show.

THE LITTLE PEOPLE
September 15, 1972 - August 30, 1974; NBC

_____ Debbie Preston Teenage Reporter in the Michael Gray Hawaiian Mystery; by James Carter; Tiger Beat XQ2024; c 1973 (1st: 1971); $.95 [FC Photo: Michael Gray]

       Unusual TV tie-in is the story of fictitious Debbie Preston trying to rescue real-life Michael Gray, star of TV's *The Little People*, from bank robbers. The show was renamed *The Brian Keith Show* for its second season.

LONGSTREET
September 16, 1971 - August 10, 1972; ABC

Lancers

_____ Longstreet: The Last Express; by Baynard Kendrick; Lancer 74779; c 1937 (1st: 1971); $.75

_____ Longstreet: Reservations For Death; by Baynard Kendrick; Lancer 74784; c 1956,57 (1st: 1971); $.75

_____ Longstreet: Blind Man's Bluff; by Baynard Kendrick; Lancer 74788; c 1943 (1st: 1971); $.75

_____ Longstreet: Out of Control; by Baynard Kendrick; Lancer 75287; c 1945 (1st: 1972); $.95

_____ Longstreet: You Die Today!; by Baynard Kendrick; Lancer 75305; c 1952 (1st: 1972); $.95

Show about the sight-impaired insurance investigator was based on the Baynard Kendrick mysteries, which feature the blind Captain Duncan Maclain. Kendrick created the character in the 1937 book *The Last Express*, and wrote 11 additional titles through 1961's *Frankincense and Murder*. The books spawned a brief series of movies in the 1930's and 40's, and with the 1971 airing of the TV show the above titles were re-issued by Lancer. The books' covers note: "The famous series about the blind detective on whom TV's *Longstreet* is based." Each book notes its *Duncan Maclain* series number on the cover; in the order above, the books are numbers 1 through 5 in the series.

LOST IN SPACE
September 15, 1956 - September 11, 1968; CBS

_____ Lost in Space; by Dave Van Arnam and "Ron Archer" [Ted White]; Pyramid X-1679; c 1967 (1st); $.60

Original adventures of the Robinson family, lost in space aboard the Jupiter II with pilot Don West, the Robot, and the incorrigible Dr. Smith.

LOVE, AMERICAN STYLE
September 29, 1969 - January 11, 1974; ABC

_____ Love, American Style; by Paul Fairman; Pinnacle P047-N; c 1971 (1st); $.95 [4 original stories: "Love and the Ulterior Motive," "Love and the Good Earth," "Love and the Beautiful Loan Shark," and "Love and the Store-Bought Wife"]

_____ Love, American Style, 2; by Paul Fairman; Pinnacle P081-N; c 1972 (1st); $.95 [4 original stories: "Love and the Valentine Caper," "Love and the Jupiter Trine," "Love and the Late Shift," and "Love and the Luscious Amazon"]

THE LOVE BOAT
September 24, 1977 - September 5, 1986; ABC

_____ The Love Boats; by Jeraldine Saunders; Pinnacle 240698; c 1974 (2nd: 1976); $1.75

_____ The Love Boat #1: Voyage of Love [Plot-it-Yourself]; by William Rotsler; Wanderer 49802; c 1983 (1st); $3.95 [oversize] [FC Photos: (top) Jill Whelan, Gavin MacLeod, Lauren Tewes, (bottom) Bernie Kopell, Ted Lange, Fred Grandy]

Long-running series was based on the 1974 book *The Love Boats*, about author Jeraldine Saunders' "incredible but true adventures and misadventures [as] the world's only female cruise director." The book, first issued in 1975, was re-issued with a new cover in 1976 in conjunction with the three TV-specials that piloted the show: "The Love Boat" (Sep-17-1976), "The Love Boat II," (Jan-21-1977), and "The Love Boat III" aka "The New Love Boat" (May-5-1977).

LOVE OF LIFE
September 24, 1951 - February 1, 1980; CBS

_____ Love of Life; by Margaret Manners; Dell First Edition B183; c 1961 (1st); $.35 [FC Illus: Audrey Peters]

_____ Love of Life: The Perilous Summer; by Joan Hughes; Pocket 75445; c 1970 (1st); $.75 [FC Photo: actors unkn.]

LUCAN
September 12, 1977 - December 4, 1978; ABC

_____ Lucan; by C.K. Chandler; Ballantine 27402; c 1977 (1st: 1978); $1.95 [novelization of the TV-movie pilot "Lucan" (May-22-1977) - about a boy raised by wolves] [FC Photo: Kevin Brophy]

LUCAS TANNER
September 11, 1974 - August 20, 1975; NBC

Pyramids

_____ Lucas Tanner: A Question of Guilt; by Richard Posner; Pyramid V3777; c 1975 (1st); $1.25 [novelization of the TV-movie pilot "Lucas Tanner" (May-08-1974)] [FC Illus: David Hartman]

_____ Lucas Tanner #2: A Matter of Love; by Richard Posner; Pyramid V3928; c 1975 (1st); $1.25 [novelization of the episodes "A Matter of Love" and "Three Letter Word"] [FC Illus: Hartman]

_____ Lucas Tanner #3: For Her to Decide; by Richard Posner; Pyramid V4042; c 1976 (1st); $1.25 [original story] [FC Illus: Hartman]

THE LUCY SHOW
October 1, 1962 - September 16, 1968; CBS

_____ Lucy and the Madcap Mystery; by Cole Fannin; Whitman 1505; c 1963 (1st) [FC Illus: Candy Moore, Jimmy Garrett, Lucille Ball] [See also *Here's Lucy*, this show's successor.]

This book based on the first lady of television's second sitcom features the madcap adventures of Lucy Carmichael as she "turns the entire United States Air Force upside down."

MCCLOUD
September 16, 1970 - August 28, 1977; NBC

Awards

_____ McCloud #1; by Collin Wilcox; Award AN1203; c 1973 (1st); $.95 [novelization of the episode "The Disposal Man"] [FC Photo: Dennis Weaver]

_____ McCloud #2: The New Mexico Connection; by Collin Wilcox; Award AN1259; c 1974 (1st); $.95 [novelization of the episode "The New Mexico Connection"] [FC Photos: Weaver]

_____ McCloud #3: The Killing; by David Wilson; Award AN1281; c 1974 (1st); $.95 [novelization of the episode "Butch Cassidy Rides Again"] [FC Photos: Weaver]

_____ McCloud #4: The Corpse-Maker; by David Wilson; Award AN1365; c 1974 (1st); $.95 [novelization of the episode "The Solid Gold Swingers"] [FC Photo: Weaver]

_____ McCloud #5: A Dangerous Place to Die; by David Wilson; Award AN1368; c 1975 (1st); $.95 [novelization of the episode "The Barefoot Stewardess Caper"] [FC Photo: Weaver]

_____ McCloud #6: Park Avenue Executioner; by David Wilson; Award AQ1463; c 1975 (1st); $1.25 [novelization of the episode "Lady on the Run"] [FC Photo: Weaver]

NBC Mystery Movie segment about the displaced U.S. Marshal inspired the above books, the first two by suspense writer Collin Wilcox. David Wilson, the byline of the sequels, may be a house name.

MCCOY
October 5, 1975 - March 28, 1976; NBC

_____ McCoy; by Sam Stewart [Linda Stewart]; Dell 05293; c 1976 (1st); $1.25 [novelization of the TV-movie pilot "The Big Ripoff" (Mar-11-1975)] [FC Photo: Tony Curtis]

MACKENZIE'S RAIDERS
1958 - 1959; Syndicated

_____ Mackenzie's Raiders: The Mackenzie Raid; by Colonel Red Reeder; Ballantine 460K; c 1955 (unsp: 1960); $.35

The show was based on the adventures of Col. Ranald Mackenzie, the U.S. Army officer who battled the Mexican bandits in the Texas border wars of the 1870's. *The Mackenzie Raid*, the 1955 book chronicling these wars, was first published by Ballantine in 1955 (#110), and re-issued in 1960. The re-issue has the same cover but to it has been added a blurb mentioning "The original book of the popular TV series 'Mackenzie's Raiders'".

M SQUAD
September 20, 1957 - September 13, 1960; NBC

_____ M Squad: The Case of the Chicago Cop-Killer; by David Saunders [Dan Sontup]; Belmont 91-254; c 1962 (1st); $.35 [FC Photo: Lee Marvin]

M*A*S*H
September 17, 1972 - September 19, 1983; CBS

Pockets

_____ M*A*S*H; by Richard Hooker; Pocket 77232; c 1968 (16th: 1973); $.95

_____ M*A*S*H Goes to Maine; by Richard Hooker; Pocket 78815; c 1971 (10th: 1975); $1.50

_____ M*A*S*H Goes to New Orleans; by Richard Hooker and William E. Butterworth; Pocket 78490; c 1975 (1st); $1.50

_____ M*A*S*H Goes to Paris; by Richard Hooker and William E. Butterworth; Pocket 78491; c 1974 (1st: 1975); $1.50

_____ M*A*S*H Goes to London; by Richard Hooker and William E. Butterworth; Pocket 78941; c 1975 (1st); $1.50

_____ M*A*S*H Goes to Morocco; by Richard Hooker and William E. Butterworth; Pocket 80264; c 1976 (1st); $1.50

_____ M*A*S*H Goes to Las Vegas; by Richard Hooker and William E. Butterworth; Pocket 80265; c 1976 (1st); $1.50

_____ M*A*S*H Goes to Hollywood; by Richard Hooker and William E. Butterworth; Pocket 80408; c 1976 (1st); $1.50

_____ M*A*S*H Goes to Vienna; by Richard Hooker and William E. Butterworth; Pocket 80458; c 1976 (1st); $1.50

_____ M*A*S*H Goes to Miami; by Richard Hooker and William E. Butterworth; Pocket 80705; c 1976 (1st); $1.50

_____ M*A*S*H Goes to San Francisco; by Richard Hooker and William E. Butterworth; Pocket 80786; c 1976 (1st); $1.50

_____ M*A*S*H Goes to Texas; by Richard Hooker and William E. Butterworth; Pocket 80892; c 1977 (1st); $1.50

_____ M*A*S*H Goes to Montreal; by Richard Hooker and William E. Butterworth; Pocket 80910; c 1977 (1st); $1.50

_____ M*A*S*H Goes to Moscow; by Richard Hooker and William E. Butterworth; Pocket 80911; c 1977 (1st); $1.50

_____ M*A*S*H Mania; by Richard Hooker; Pocket 82178; c 1977 (1st: 1979); $1.95

Miscellaneous

_____ All About "M*A*S*H"; by Peggy Herz; Scholastic Book Services TK3237; c 1975 (1st) [FC Photo: Loretta Swit, Alan Alda]

_____ M*A*S*H: The Official 4077 Quiz Manual; by Paul Bertling; Signet AE4135; c 1984 (1st: 1986); $2.50 [FC Photo: (top) Jamie Farr, William Christopher, (middle) Swit, Alda, Mike Farrell, (bottom) Larry Linville, Harry Morgan, Gary Burghoff]

_____ M*A*S*H Trivia: The Unofficial Quiz Book; by George St. John; Warner 32000; c 1983 (1st); $2.50

Alan Alda's anti-war hit was based on the 1970 movie, which in turn was based on the 1968 best-selling book by Richard Hornberger. Hornberger had himself served as a M*A*S*H unit surgeon during the Korean War, and the book was issued under a pen name in order to keep his stateside identity a secret. First issued by Pocket in 1969 with an olive green cover (#75453), the book saw numerous nearly identical white-cover subsequent printings. All include a picture of a pair of shapely legs turning into a hand making a peace sign, but differ in blurbs and title-lettering. The show is first mentioned on the cover of the 16th printing.

The book spawned numerous sequels, the first being *M*A*S*H Goes to Maine* (with show-mention upon the 10th printing). The sequels are premised on a post-Korean War Hawkeye Pierce who, as Chief Surgeon for Spruce Harbor, Maine, Medical Center, continuously becomes involved with his former M*A*S*H co-workers in adventures in various locations. While most of the sequels give Richard Hooker and William Butterworth co-author credit, they were reportedly written by Butterworth alone. The back covers include cast lists, which changed as the show progressed.

MAGNUM, P.I.
December 11, 1980 - September 12, 1988; CBS

_____ Tom Selleck: An Unauthorized Biography; by Jason Bonderoff; Signet AE2063; c 1983 (1st); $2.95 [FC Photo: Tom Selleck]

_____ Magnum, P.I. #1: Maui Mystery [Plot-It-Yourself]; by William Rotsler; Wanderer 49607; c 1983 (1st); $3.95 [oversize] [FC Photos: Selleck]

MAMA
July 1, 1949 - March 17, 1957; CBS

_____ Mama's Bank Account; by Kathryn Forbes; Bantam 1513; c 1943 (2nd: 1956); $.25 [FC Illus: Irene Dunne]

The show was based on the 1943 book *Mama's Bank Account*, which had previously inspired the 1944 play and 1948 movie, those both entitled *I Remember Mama*. First published by Bantam as a movie tie-in in 1947 (#135), the book was re-issued as a TV tie-in with the show.

MAN FROM ATLANTIS
September 22, 1977 - July 25, 1978; NBC

Dells

_____ Man From Atlantis #1; by Richard Woodley; Dell 15368; c 1977 (1st); $1.50 [novelization of the TV-movie pilot "Man From Atlantis" (Mar-04-1977)] [FC Photo: Patrick Duffy]

_____ Man From Atlantis #2: Death Scouts; by Richard Woodley; Dell 15369; c 1977 (1st); $1.50 [novelization of the TV-sequel "Death Scouts"] [FC Photo: Duffy]

_____ Man From Atlantis #3: Killer Spores; by Richard Woodley; Dell 15926; c 1978 (1st); $1.50 [novelization of the TV-sequel "Killer Spores"] [FC Illus: Duffy]

_____ Man From Atlantis #4: Ark of Doom; by Richard Woodley; Dell 15927; c 1978 (1st); $1.50 [novelization of the TV-sequel "The Disappearances"] [FC Illus: Duffy]

     Underwater adventure show began as a series of TV-movies in the spring of 1977, before airing that September on a weekly basis. All four telefilms were novelized by Richard Woodley. Star Patrick Duffy parlayed the short-lived role into that of Bobby Ewing in the immensely popular *Dallas* (see also that show), which premiered soon after.

THE MAN FROM U.N.C.L.E.
September 22, 1964 - January 15, 1968; NBC

Aces

_____ The Man From U.N.C.L.E.; by Michael Avallone; Ace G-553; c 1965 (1st); $.50 [title aka "The Thousand Coffins Affair"] [FC Photo: Robert Vaughn] [#1 in UK]

_____ The Man From U.N.C.L.E. #2: The Doomsday Affair; by Harry Whittington; Ace G-560; c 1965 (1st); $.50 [FC Photos: Robert Vaughn, David McCallum] [#2 in UK]

_____ The Man From U.N.C.L.E. #3: The Copenhagen Affair; by John Oram [John Oram Thomas]; Ace G-564; c 1965 (1st); $.50 [FC Photo: Vaughn, McCallum] [UK original/#3 in UK]

_____ The Man From U.N.C.L.E. #4: The Dagger Affair; by David McDaniel; Ace G-571; c 1965 (1st: 1966); $.50 [FC Photo: McCallum, Vaughn; BC Photo: Vaughn, Leo G. Carroll, McCallum] [#6 in UK]

_____ The Man From U.N.C.L.E. #5: The Mad Scientist Affair; by John T. Phillifent; Ace G-581; c 1966 (1st); $.50 [FC Photos: Vaughn, McCallum] [UK original/#8 in UK]

_____ The Man From U.N.C.L.E. #6: The Vampire Affair; by David McDaniel; Ace G-590; c 1966 (1st); $.50 [FC Photo: McCallum, Vaughn] [#9 in UK]

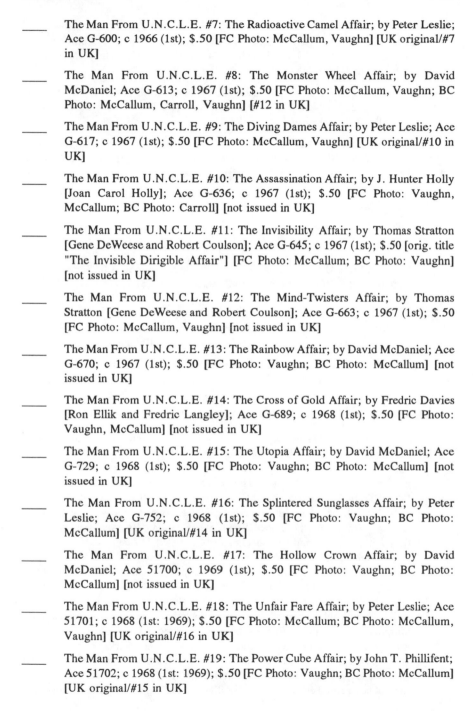

_____ The Man From U.N.C.L.E. #7: The Radioactive Camel Affair; by Peter Leslie; Ace G-600; c 1966 (1st); $.50 [FC Photo: McCallum, Vaughn] [UK original/#7 in UK]

_____ The Man From U.N.C.L.E. #8: The Monster Wheel Affair; by David McDaniel; Ace G-613; c 1967 (1st); $.50 [FC Photo: McCallum, Vaughn; BC Photo: McCallum, Carroll, Vaughn] [#12 in UK]

_____ The Man From U.N.C.L.E. #9: The Diving Dames Affair; by Peter Leslie; Ace G-617; c 1967 (1st); $.50 [FC Photo: McCallum, Vaughn] [UK original/#10 in UK]

_____ The Man From U.N.C.L.E. #10: The Assassination Affair; by J. Hunter Holly [Joan Carol Holly]; Ace G-636; c 1967 (1st); $.50 [FC Photo: Vaughn, McCallum; BC Photo: Carroll] [not issued in UK]

_____ The Man From U.N.C.L.E. #11: The Invisibility Affair; by Thomas Stratton [Gene DeWeese and Robert Coulson]; Ace G-645; c 1967 (1st); $.50 [orig. title "The Invisible Dirigible Affair"] [FC Photo: McCallum; BC Photo: Vaughn] [not issued in UK]

_____ The Man From U.N.C.L.E. #12: The Mind-Twisters Affair; by Thomas Stratton [Gene DeWeese and Robert Coulson]; Ace G-663; c 1967 (1st); $.50 [FC Photo: McCallum, Vaughn] [not issued in UK]

_____ The Man From U.N.C.L.E. #13: The Rainbow Affair; by David McDaniel; Ace G-670; c 1967 (1st); $.50 [FC Photo: Vaughn; BC Photo: McCallum] [not issued in UK]

_____ The Man From U.N.C.L.E. #14: The Cross of Gold Affair; by Fredric Davies [Ron Ellik and Fredric Langley]; Ace G-689; c 1968 (1st); $.50 [FC Photo: Vaughn, McCallum] [not issued in UK]

_____ The Man From U.N.C.L.E. #15: The Utopia Affair; by David McDaniel; Ace G-729; c 1968 (1st); $.50 [FC Photo: Vaughn; BC Photo: McCallum] [not issued in UK]

_____ The Man From U.N.C.L.E. #16: The Splintered Sunglasses Affair; by Peter Leslie; Ace G-752; c 1968 (1st); $.50 [FC Photo: Vaughn; BC Photo: McCallum] [UK original/#14 in UK]

_____ The Man From U.N.C.L.E. #17: The Hollow Crown Affair; by David McDaniel; Ace 51700; c 1969 (1st); $.50 [FC Photo: Vaughn; BC Photo: McCallum] [not issued in UK]

_____ The Man From U.N.C.L.E. #18: The Unfair Fare Affair; by Peter Leslie; Ace 51701; c 1968 (1st: 1969); $.50 [FC Photo: McCallum; BC Photo: McCallum, Vaughn] [UK original/#16 in UK]

_____ The Man From U.N.C.L.E. #19: The Power Cube Affair; by John T. Phillifent; Ace 51702; c 1968 (1st: 1969); $.50 [FC Photo: Vaughn; BC Photo: McCallum] [UK original/#15 in UK]

____ The Man From U.N.C.L.E. #20: The Corfu Affair; by John T. Phillifent; Ace 51703; c 1967 (1st: 1970); $.50 [FC Photo: Vaughn; BC Photo: McCallum] [UK original/#13 in UK]

____ The Man From U.N.C.L.E. #21: The Thinking Machine Affair; by Joel Bernard; Ace 51704; c 1967 (1st: 1970); $.50 [FC Photo: Vaughn; BC Photo: McCallum] [UK original/#11 in UK]

____ The Man From U.N.C.L.E. #22: The Stone-Cold Dead in the Market Affair; by John Oram [John Oram Thomas]; Ace 51705; c 1966 (1st: 1971); $.50 [FC Photo: Vaughn, McCallum] [UK original/#4 in UK]

____ The Man From U.N.C.L.E. #23: The Finger in the Sky Affair; by Peter Leslie; Ace 51706; c 1966 (1st: 1971); $.50 [FC Photo: Carroll, Vaughn; BC Photo: McCallum] [UK original/#5 in UK]

Signet

____ The Man From U.N.C.L.E.'s ABC of Espionage; by John Hill; Signet D3045; c 1966 (1st); $.50 [FC Photo: Carroll, Vaughn, McCallum]

Whitmans

____ The Man From U.N.C.L.E. and the Affair of the Gentle Saboteur; by Brandon Keith; Whitman 1541; c 1966 (1st) [FC Photos: McCallum, Vaughn]

____ The Man From U.N.C.L.E. and the Affair of the Gunrunners' Gold; by Brandon Keith; Whitman 1543; c 1967 (1st) [FC Illus: McCallum, Vaughn]

____ The Man From U.N.C.L.E.: The Calcutta Affair; by George S. Elrick; Whitman Big Little Book 2011; c 1967 (1st) [FC Illus: McCallum, Vaughn]

Ace's *Man From U.N.C.L.E.* books, based on the tongue-in-cheek adventures of U.N.C.L.E. agents Napoleon Solo and Illya Kuryakin and their ongoing battle with the enemy organization THRUSH, comprise one of the most prominent sets of TV tie-ins. The series was born in late 1964, when Ace Editor Terry Carr approached Michael Avallone with the idea of writing an *U.N.C.L.E.* book. Both felt that although the show was unproven, the time was ripe to cash in on the James Bond phenomenon, "so Ace said Yes and [Avallone] said Yes and the wheel of fortune rolled." Ace paid MGM $6,000 for the rights to do the book (it was intended as a one-shot) and paid Avallone $1,000 to write it, which he did in a single day in December of 1964. Subtitled "The Thousand Coffins Affair," its release coincided with the show's rise in popularity, and both met great success. The show became an international hit and the book sold several million copies, including numerous foreign editions. Moreover, as Avallone's first TV tie-in (he'd done movie tie-ins), it gave him widespread exposure and established him firmly in that market niche.

Wishing to capitalize on the book's success, Ace signed several other writers and began churning out original *U.N.C.L.E.* novels. (Avallone's own attempt at a second entry--"The THRUSH and the Eagles Affair"--was declined by Ace; Avallone later turned the story into "The Birds of a Feather Affair" and sold it to Signet as their first *Girl From U.N.C.L.E.* book).

Ace issued 23 titles in all (the higher numbers are scarcer), sixteen of which were also published in Britain by Souvenir Press, but with different series numbers from the American editions. A shared arrangement between the two publishers allowed each publisher to sign writers from its own country for the first printings, and to buy the reprint rights for the existing books from the other publisher. Thus, Souvenir Press signed Britons Peter Leslie, John T. Phillifent, John Oram, and Joel Bernard, and bought from Ace the reprint rights for the American books by veteran Harry Whittington, newcomer David McDaniel, and Avallone. Of the 16 Souvenir Press books, eleven were originals, and five were reprints of American editions. Of the 23 Ace books, twelve were originals, and eleven were reprints of the British editions.

David McDaniel was the most prolific--and popular--*U.N.C.L.E.* books author, writing seven titles in all, including one which was not published. In *The Dagger Affair* (#4 in the Ace series and his own first entry), he coined the THRUSH acronym "The Technological Hierarchy for the Removal of Undesirables and the Subjugation of Humanity." In the TV show, only the U.N.C.L.E. acronym "The United Network Command for Law and Enforcement" had been coined.

McDaniel dedicated *The Utopia Affair* (#15) to Ron Ellik. Ellik had just finished writing *The Cross of Gold Affair* (#14) with Fredric Langley (the two co-wrote it as "Fredric Davies"), when Ellik was killed in a car accident.

McDaniel was a fan of *Dark Shadows*, for in *The Hollow Crown Affair* (#17), Napoleon and Illya go to Collinsport, Maine, where they meet Sheriff Patterson (a semi-regular on *Dark Shadows*) and see the inscription "Barnabas Loves Josette" carved into a tree. The book was published in 1969, the year following the show's cancellation, and was to be the last Ace original. However, McDaniel followed with his seventh *U.N.C.L.E.* book, "The Final Affair," in which both THRUSH and U.N.C.L.E. were destroyed. Ace passed, however, as they wanted to continue issuing the last batch of British reprints (which they did through 1971) and to follow "The Final Affair" with them wouldn't have worked. McDaniel died in 1977 in a household accident (see *The Prisoner* for more on this author).

The Man From U.N.C.L.E's ABC of Espionage is a non-fiction book about "how the world's great spies are trained in the deadly job of espionage--from the USA to the USSR." The show also inspired a Grosset & Dunlap novelette by Walter B. Gibson (creator of *The Shadow*), a series of *Man From U.N.C.L.E.* Magazines, a *Gold Key* comic book series, and a Whitman coloring book.

MANNIX
September 16, 1967 - August 27, 1975; CBS

Popular Library

_____ Mannix; by Michael Avallone; Popular Library 60-2256; c 1968 (1st); $.60 [FC Photos: Mike Connors]

Belmont Towers

____   Mannix #1: The Faces of Murder; by J.T. MacCargo; Belmont Tower 50793;
c 1975 (1st); $1.25 [novelization of the episode "The Faces of Murder"] [FC
Photos: Connors]

____   Mannix #2: A Fine Day for Dying; by J.T. MacCargo [Peter Rabe]; Belmont
Tower 50823; c 1975 (1st); $1.25 [novelization of the episode "A Fine Day For
Dying"] [FC Photo: Connors]

____   Mannix #3: A Walk on the Blind Side; by J.T. MacCargo; Belmont Tower
50825; c 1975 (1st); $1.25 [novelization of the episode "A Walk on the Blind
Side"] [FC Photo: Connors]

____   Mannix #4: Round Trip to Nowhere; by J.T. MacCargo [Peter Rabe]; Belmont
Tower 50834; c 1975 (1st); $1.25 [novelization of the episode "Round Trip to
Nowhere"] [FC Photo: Connors]

Action-filled series about the exploits of Los Angeles-based private eye Joe
Mannix and his gal-Friday Peggy inspired the above books--an original Popular
Library during its first season and four Belmont Tower novelizations (written
under the J.T. MacCargo house name) during its last. Peter Rabe wrote the
second and fourth novelizations; the first and third titles may have been by
"J.W. O'Dell."

In *Round Trip to Nowhere*, Peggy's last name is given as Fast while in the
show she was Peggy Fair. Moreover, in expanding the source script the author
apparently misinterpreted key lines of dialog, for "Toby" is given as Peggy's
husband. In the show, Peggy is a widow whose husband was a cop and friend
of Mannix's who was killed in the line of duty. Mannix has since hired Peggy,
not just because she was good but to insure the well-being of his late friend's
wife and her young son, Toby.

THE MANY LOVES OF DOBIE GILLIS
September 29, 1959 - September 18, 1963; CBS

____   The Many Loves of Dobie Gillis; by Max Shulman; Bantam F2041; c 1945+
(1st: 1960); $.50

The show was based on the short stories by Max Shulman, which had
appeared in *Good Housekeeping* and *The Saturday Evening Post* magazines in
the 1940's. The stories were published as a collection in the 1951 book *The
Many Loves of Dobie Gillis*, which in turn inspired the 1953 movie *The Affairs
of Dobie Gillis*. With the airing of the TV show in 1959 the book was re-issued
by Bantam as a TV tie-in. (Its stories are "The Unlucky Winner," "She Shall
Have Music," "Love is a Fallacy," "The Sugar Bowl," "Everybody Loves My
Baby," "Love of Two Chemists," "The Face is Familiar But--" "The Mock
Governor," "Boy Bites Man," "The King's English," and "You Think You Got
Trouble?")

MARCUS WELBY, M.D.
September 23, 1969 - May 11, 1976; ABC

Aces

_____ Marcus Welby, M.D.: Rock a Cradle Empty; by Bruce Cassiday; Ace 51938; c 1970 (1st); $.75 [FC Photo: Robert Young; BC Photo: Young, James Brolin]

_____ Marcus Welby, M.D. #2: The Acid Test; by Bruce Cassiday; Ace 51939; c 1970 (1st); $.75 [FC Photo: Young; BC Photo: Young, Brolin]

_____ Marcus Welby, M.D. #3: The Fire's Center; by Bruce Cassiday; Ace 51941; c 1971 (1st); $.75 [FC Photo: Brolin, Young]

Original novels with a mild mystery angle based on the popular medical series starring Robert Young.

MARKHAM
May 2, 1959 - September 22, 1960; CBS

_____ Markham: The Case of the Pornographic Photos; by Lawrence Block; Belmont 236; c 1961 (1st); $.35 [FC Illus: Ray Milland]

MARY HARTMAN, MARY HARTMAN
1976 - 1978; Syndicated

_____ Louise Lasser, Louise Lasser; by Kate Brosnan; Belmont Tower 50992; c 1976 (1st); $.95 [FC Photo: Louise Lasser]

_____ The Mary Hartman Story; by Daniel Lockwood; Bolder 9098; c 1976 (1st); $1.75 [FC Illus: (center) Lasser, (clockwise from left for balance) Philip Bruns, Dody Goodman, Greg Mullavey, Mary Kay Place, Graham Jarvis]

THE MARY TYLER MOORE SHOW
September 19, 1970 - September 3, 1977; CBS

_____ The Real Mary Tyler Moore; by Chris Bryars; Pinnacle 230988; c 1976 (1st: 1977); $1.50 [FC Photo: Mary Tyler Moore]

MATT LINCOLN
September 24, 1970 - January 14, 1971; ABC

Lancers

_____ Matt Lincoln #1: The Revolutionist; by Ed Garth [William Johnston]; Lancer 73201; c 1970 (1st); $.60 [FC Photo: Vince Edwards]

_____ Matt Lincoln #2: The Hostage; by Ed Garth [William Johnston]; Lancer 73211; c 1971 (1st); $.60 [FC Photo: Edwards]

Original novels based on the short-lived show starring Vince Edwards of *Ben Casey* fame--in this he played a hip psychiatrist running a Hotline for troubled teens.

MAVERICK
September 22, 1957 - July 8, 1962; ABC

Dells

____ Poker According to Maverick [BC: Royal Flush]; by J. Hoyt Cummings; Dell First Edition B142; c 1959 (1st); $.35 [FC Photo: James Garner, Jack Kelly]

____ Poker According to Maverick [BC: Ad for Kaiser Aluminum Foil Products]; by J. Hoyt Cummings; Dell First Edition B142; c 1959 (1st); $.35 [FC Photo: Garner, Kelly]

____ Poker According to Maverick [BC: Ad for Jeep Vehicles]; by J. Hoyt Cummings; Dell First Edition B142; c 1959 (1st); $.35 [FC Photo: Garner, Kelly]

____ Poker According to Maverick [BC: Ad for Drackett Cleaning Products]; by J. Hoyt Cummings; Dell First Edition B142; c 1959 (1st); $.35 [FC Photo: Garner, Kelly]

____ Poker According to Maverick [BC: Ad for Kaiser Aluminum, with Logo]; by J. Hoyt Cummings; Dell First Edition B142; c 1959 (1st); $.35 [FC Photo: Garner, Kelly]

____ Poker According to Maverick [BC: Ad for Kaiser Aluminum, without Logo]; by J. Hoyt Cummings; Dell First Edition B142; c 1959 (2nd: 1960); $.35 [FC Photo: Garner, Kelly]

Whitman

____ Maverick ["Authorized TV Edition" logo on front cover]; by Charles I. Coombs; Whitman 1566; c 1959 (1st) [FC Illus: Garner]

____ Maverick ["Authorized TV Adventure" logo on spine]; by Charles I. Coombs; Whitman 1566; c 1959 (1st) [FC Illus: Garner]

Classic Western with James Garner as the maverick cardsharp inspired Dell's how-to-book *Poker According to Maverick*, which by virtue of its different back covers includes the six noted "cover-variations." The front covers are identical, but for the cover of the first variation lacking a white circle around the cover price.   The first variation was issued for normal newsstand distribution; the balance were distributed by the various sponsors of the show, and include ads for the sponsors on the back covers. The book's first draft was by an uncredited J. Hoyt Cummings, while Peter Margolies edited it into the voice of Maverick.   The six cover variations are described in further detail following:

1) Back cover includes a royal flush poker hand. Identical first, second, third, and fourth printings.

2) Back cover includes an ad for Kaiser Aluminum Foil products and a photo of James Garner and Jack Kelly. Inside back cover includes an ad for the Kaiser product ShadeScreen. First printing.

3)   Back cover includes an ad for Jeep vehicles. Inside back cover includes an additional Jeep ad. First printing.
4)   Back cover includes an ad for Drackett Company cleaning products. Inside back cover includes an additional Drackett ad. First printing.
5)   Back cover is mostly white and includes an ad for Kaiser Aluminum, with the Kaiser logo. First printing.
6)   Back cover is mostly white and includes an ad for Kaiser Aluminum, without the Kaiser logo. Second printing.

In 1994 the movie *Maverick* was released, with Mel Gibson as Maverick and James Garner in a supporting role. With the release of the movie the book *Poker According to Maverick* was re-issued (as *Maverick's Guide to Poker*) by Charles E. Tuttle.

MAYA
September 16, 1967 - February 10, 1968; NBC

_____   Maya #1: The Forbidden City; by Norman Daniels; Berkley F1538; c 1967 (1st); $.50 [FC Photo: Sajid Khan, Jay North]

MEDICAL CENTER
September 24, 1969 - September 6, 1976; CBS

_____   Medical Center; by Chris Stratton [Richard Hubbard]; Popular Library 01336; c 1970 (1st); $.75 [FC Photo: Chad Everett]

MEDICAL STORY
September 4, 1975 - January 8, 1976; NBC

Signets

_____   Medical Story; by Abby Mann; Signet W6785; c 1975 (1st); $1.50 [novelization of the pilot episode "Medical Story"] [FC Photos: Beau Bridges, Jose Ferrer]

_____   Medical Story #2: Kill Me, Please...; by William Johnston; Signet W6802; c 1976 (1st); $1.50 [novelization of the episode "The Right to Die"]

Medical anthology series about the shortcomings of doctors inspired two Signet tie-ins. A third title was reportedly commissioned by Signet but never released, due to the abrupt cancellation of the show.

THE MEN FROM SHILOH
September 16, 1970 - September 8, 1971; NBC

_____   The Men From Shiloh #1: Lone Trail for the Virginian; by Dean Owen [Dudley Dean McGaughy]; Lancer 74775; c 1971 (1st); $.75 [FC Photo: Doug McClure, James Drury]

Long-running show *The Virginian* (see also it) was renamed *The Men From Shiloh* in 1970, and inspired the above Lancer tie-in.

MEN INTO SPACE
September 30, 1959 - September 7, 1960; CBS

_____ Men Into Space; by Murray Leinster [Will F. Jenkins]; Berkley G461; c 1960 (1st); $.35 [BC Photo: William Lundigan]

MIAMI UNDERCOVER
1961; Syndicated

_____ Miami Undercover; by Evan Lee Heyman; Popular Library G554; c 1961 (1st); $.35 [FC Photo: Rocky Graziano, Lee Bowman]

MIAMI VICE
September 16, 1984 - July 26, 1989; NBC

Avons

_____ Miami Vice #1: The Florida Burn; by Stephen Grave [David J. Schow]; Avon 89930; c 1985 (1st); $2.95 [novelization of the pilot episode "Brother's Keeper" aka "Miami Vice"] [FC Photo: (center) Philip Michael Thomas, Don Johnson]

_____ Miami Vice #2: The Vengeance Game; by Stephen Grave [David J. Schow]; Avon 89931; c 1985 (1st); $2.95 [novelization of the episodes "Hit List" and "Calderone's Dream"] [FC Photo: (center) Thomas, Johnson]

Miscellaneous

_____ Miami Magic; by Caroline Latham; Zebra 8217-1800; c 1985 (1st); $2.95 [FC Photo: Johnson, Thomas]

_____ Don Johnson; by David Hershkovits; St. Martin's Press 90165; c 1986 (1st); $3.50 [FC Photo: Johnson]

_____ Don Johnson: An Unauthorized Biography; by Suzanne Munshower; Signet AE4345; c 1986 (1st); $2.95 [FC Photo: Johnson]

_____ The Making of Miami Vice; by Trish Janeshutz and Rob MacGregor; Ballantine 33669; c 1986 (1st); $3.95 [FC Photo: Johnson, Thomas] [husband-and-wife co-authors enjoyed writing/researching, from the shores of Miami to the editing rooms of Hollywood]

Avon novelizations based on the splashy crime show by David J. Schow as Stephen Grave were also published in Britain by Star, which issued four additional Schow as Grave titles not released here: *The Razor's Edge, China White, Hellhole*, and *Probing by Fire*. The books ("Schow did a great job getting the rhythm and cadence from the show into the stories" per Senior Editor Joe Blades) were published in at least seven other languages, including hardcover editions in Hebrew. Show-creator Anthony Yerkovich wrote the award-winning pilot episode "Brother's Keeper," upon which *The Florida Burn* was based, and later created the film noir TV series *Private Eye* (see also it). Schow later co-wrote the 1994 Brandon Lee swan song *The Crow*.

MICHAEL SHAYNE
September 30, 1960 - September 22, 1961; NBC

Dells

_____ Michael Shayne: Murder Takes No Holiday; by Brett Halliday [Robert Terrall]; Dell D379; c 1960 (1st: 1961); $.35 [BC Photo: Richard Denning]

_____ Michael Shayne: The Corpse Came Calling; by Brett Halliday [Davis Dresser]; Dell D401; c 1942 (1st new Dell: 1961); $.35 [title aka "The Case of the Walking Corpse"]

_____ Michael Shayne's Long Chance; by Brett Halliday [Davis Dresser]; Dell D416; c 1944 (1st new Dell: 1961); $.35 [BC Photo: Denning]

_____ Michael Shayne: Death Has Three Lives; by Brett Halliday [Davis Dresser]; Dell D423; c 1955 (1st new Dell: 1961); $.35 [BC Photo: Denning]

_____ Michael Shayne: Dolls Are Deadly; by Brett Halliday [Ryerson Johnson] Dell D424; c 1960 (1st: 1961); $.35 [BC Photo: Denning]

_____ Michael Shayne: Stranger in Town; by Brett Halliday [Davis Dresser]; Dell D425; c 1955 (1st new Dell: 1961); $.35 [BC Photo: Denning]

_____ Michael Shayne: The Homicidal Virgin; by Brett Halliday [Davis Dresser]; Dell D437; c 1960 (1st: 1961); $.35 [BC Photo: Denning]

_____ Michael Shayne: Killers From the Keys; by Brett Halliday [Ryerson Johnson]; Dell 4476; c 1961 (1st: 1962); $.40

The show was based on the character created by Davis Dresser in the 1939 book *Dividend on Death*. Dresser used the Brett Halliday pseudonym for this and all his subsequent *Michael Shayne* books, writing over 30 titles through 1960. The series continued into the 1970's, with other writers using the Brett Halliday byline. Some 60 books total were written, through 1976's *Win Some, Lose Some*. The books inspired a series of movies in the 1940's, a radio series, and the *Mike Shayne Mystery Magazine* all prior to the TV show, with the airing of which the above books were issued as show-mentioning TV tie-ins.

THE MICHAELS IN AFRICA
1958; Syndicated

_____ The Michaels in Africa: I Married a Hunter; by Marjorie Michael; Pyramid PR 14; c 1957 (1st: 1958); $.35 [FC Photo: George and Marjorie Michael]

THE MICKEY MOUSE CLUB
October 3, 1955 - September 24, 1959; ABC

Spin and Marty Books

_____ Walt Disney's Spin and Marty [orig. title "Marty Markham"]; by Lawrence Edward Watkin; Whitman 1535; c 1942 (1st: 1956) [FC Illus: Tim Considine, David Stollery]

_____ Walt Disney's Spin and Marty: Trouble at Triple-R; by Doris Schroeder; Whitman 1577; c 1958 (1st)

Annette Books

_____ Walt Disney's Annette: Sierra Summer; by Doris Schroeder; Whitman 1585; c 1960 (1st) [FC Illus: Annette Funicello]

_____ Walt Disney's Annette: The Desert Inn Mystery; by Doris Schroeder; Whitman 1546; c 1961 (1st) [FC Illus: Funicello]

_____ Walt Disney's Annette and the Mystery at Moonstone Bay; by Doris Schroeder; Whitman 1537; c 1962 (1st) [FC Illus: Funicello]

_____ Walt Disney's Annette and the Mystery at Smugglers' Cove; by Doris Schroeder; Whitman 1574; c 1963 (1st) [FC Illus: Funicello]

_____ Walt Disney's Annette: Mystery at Medicine Wheel; by Barlow Meyers; Whitman 1512; c 1964 (1st) [FC Illus: Funicello]

Miscellaneous

_____ The Secret World of Roy Williams; by Roy Williams; Bantam 1697; c 1957 (1st); $.25 [*]

[*] Long-time Disney cartooner Roy Williams was featured as "The Big Mouseketeer" on this weekday children's show, for which he drew the mouse cartoons. In contrast, his book *The Secret World of Roy Williams* includes the "weird, wacky, wonderful" cartoons he drew when the kids were asleep.

The show included several serials, two with Whitman tie-ins: *Annette* (starring Annette Funicello as country girl Annette in a career-launching role) and *Spin and Marty* (the story of two boys--Spin Evans and Marty Markham--at the summer boys' camp the Triple-R Ranch). The latter serial was based on the 1942 book *Marty Markham*, renamed *Spin and Marty* for its 1956 Whitman re-issue.

MISSION: IMPOSSIBLE
September 17, 1966 - September 8, 1973; CBS

Popular Librarys

_____ Mission: Impossible; by John Tiger [Walter Wager]; Popular Library 60-8042; c 1967 (1st); $.60 [FC Photo: Steven Hill, Martin Landau]

_____ Mission: Impossible #2: Code Name: Judas; Max Walker; Popular Library 60-2261; c 1968 (1st); $.60 [FC Photo: Peter Graves; BC Photo: Graves, Barbara Bain]

_____ Mission: Impossible #3: Code Name: Rapier; Max Walker; Popular Library 60-2325; c 1968 (1st); $.60 [FC Photo: Graves, Bain]

_____ Mission: Impossible #4: Code Name: Little Ivan; by John Tiger [Walter Wager]; Popular Library 60-2464; c 1969 (1st); $.60 [FC Photo: Graves]

Whitmans

____ Mission: Impossible: The Priceless Particle; by Talmage Powell; Whitman 1515; c 1969 (1st) [FC Illus: (clockwise from top left) Bain, Landau, Greg Morris, Graves, Peter Lupus]

____ Mission: Impossible: The Money Explosion; by Talmage Powell; Whitman 1512; c 1970 (1st) [FC Illus: Lupus, Leonard Nimoy, Graves, Morris]

The show with the most memorable theme music inspired TV tie-ins by Popular Library and Whitman. Good companion reading and true to the show, the books feature the different characters that evolved through cast changes as the show progressed. (Peter Graves as Jim Phelps replaced Steven Hill as Dan Briggs after the first season; Leonard Nimoy as Paris replaced Martin Landau as Rollin Hand, and various women replaced Barbara Bain as Cinnamon Carter, after the third season.) Dan Briggs is gone after the first book, replaced by Jim Phelps for the balance. Rollin and Cinnamon are gone after the third Popular Library book and the first Whitman. The fourth Popular Library (the Leipzig-based *Code Name: Little Ivan*) and the second Whitman (*The Money Explosion*) were written with Rollin and Cinnamon originally, but were re-written for the new characters. Rollin was replaced by Paris in both books, while Cinnamon was replaced by "Annabelle Drue" (a character not in the show) in *Code Name: Little Ivan* (the book, hastily re-written by the editorial staff, still mentions Cinnamon's name on the back cover) and by Tracey (played by Lee Meriwether) in *The Money Explosion* (author Talmage Powell was paid a bonus to re-write the book). Barney Collier and Willy Armitage, who were with the Impossible Missions Force--the IMF--for the run of the show, are featured throughout the books.

MR. ED
October 1, 1961 - September 8, 1965; Syndicated/CBS

____ The Original Mr. Ed; by Walter Brooks; Bantam J2530; c 1963 (1st); $.40

The show is rooted in the short stories by Walter Brooks, which had appeared in the *Saturday Evening Post* and *Liberty* magazines in the 1930's and 40's. With the airing of the TV show, 9 of the stories were published by Bantam as a collection in the above book: "Ed Shoots It Out," "The Midnight Ride of Mr. Ed," "The Royal Harness," "Ed Quenches an Old Flame," "Medium Rare," "Ed Gets a Mother Complex," "Ed Takes the Cockeyed Initiative," "Just a Song at Twilight" and "Ed Takes the Brush in His Teeth."

Note: The stories first inspired the 1946 David Stern novel *Francis* (about the talking mule); the novel in turn inspired seven *Francis the Talking Mule* motion pictures (1949-56). The first six pictures were directed by Arthur Lubin, who later learned of the Mr. Ed character, purchased the rights to the character, and in 1961 succeeded in bringing him to TV. The show began in syndication before being picked up by CBS.

MR. LUCKY
October 24, 1959 - September 3, 1960; CBS

_____   Mr. Lucky; by Albert Conroy [Marvin H. Albert]; Dell First Edition B165; c
         1960 (1st); $.35 [FC Illus: John Vivyan]

MR. MERLIN
October 7, 1981 - September 15, 1982; CBS

Wanderers

_____   Mr. Merlin Episode 1; by William Rotsler; Wanderer 44479; c 1981 (1st);
         $2.95 [oversize] [novelization of the pilot episode "Mr. Merlin"] [FC Photo:
         Clark Brandon, Jonathan Prince, Barnard Hughes]

_____   Mr. Merlin Episode 2; by William Rotsler; Wanderer 44480; c 1981 (1st);
         $2.95 [oversize] [original story] [FC Photo: Hughes, Elaine Joyce, Brandon]

         Short-lived sitcom about Merlin the Magician (the fictional character from
King Arthur's Court) transported to present-day San Francisco had just gone into
production when Wanderer Books bought the rights to do two books on the
show. William Rotsler had completed the first book, a novelization of the pilot
script, when the Writer's Guild began its 13-week strike in 1981, thus
preventing any additional scripts from being written and available for the second
novelization. As the money had already been paid and a publication date set,
mild panic set in, but was defused when Rotsler suggested he write an original
novel instead.

THE MOD SQUAD
September 24, 1968 - August 23, 1973; ABC

Pyramids

_____   The Mod Squad #1: The Greek God Affair; by Richard Deming; Pyramid
         X-1888; c 1968 (1st); $.60 [FC Photo: Michael Cole, Peggy Lipton, Clarence
         Williams, III]

_____   The Mod Squad: The Greek God Affair [cover-variation]; by Richard Deming;
         Pyramid X2319; c 1968 (2nd: 1970); $.60 [FC Photo: Cole, Lipton, Williams]

_____   The Mod Squad #2: A Groovy Way to Die; by Richard Deming; Pyramid
         X-1908; c 1968 (1st); $.60 [FC Photo: Lipton, Cole, Williams]

_____   The Mod Squad #3: The Sock-it-to-Em Murders; by Richard Deming; Pyramid
         X-1922; c 1968 (1st); $.60 [FC Photo: Williams, Lipton, Tige Andrews, Cole]
         [$.75 variant version lacks logo, book number]

_____   The Mod Squad #4: Spy-In; by Richard Deming; Pyramid X-1986; c 1969 (1st);
         $.60 [FC Photo: Williams, Lipton, Cole]

_____   The Mod Squad #5: The Hit; by Richard Deming; Pyramid X-2214; c 1970
         (1st); $.60 [FC Photo: Lipton]

Pinnacle

_____ Mod Squad: Home is Where the Quick Is; by William Johnston; Pinnacle P027-N; c 1971 (1st); $.95 [FC Photo: Cole, Lipton, Williams]

Whitmans

_____ The Mod Squad: Assignment: The Arranger; by Richard Deming; Whitman 1538; c 1969 (1st) [FC Illus: Cole, Williams, Andrews, Lipton]

_____ The Mod Squad: Assignment: The Hideout; by Richard Deming; Whitman 1517; c 1970 (1st) [FC Illus: Lipton, Cole, Williams, Andrews]

TV's hip cops Pete, Linc, and Julie--*The Mod Squad*--inspired seven Richard Deming tie-ins and a William Johnston Pinnacle. While not as popular in syndication as other 70's camp (at least not yet), but replete with the appropriate speech, fashion, and hairstyles, two of the show's cast members were reunited (Peggy Lipton as a regular, Clarence Williams, III as a guest star) in the early-90's David Lynch series *Twin Peaks*.

THE MONKEES
September 12, 1966 - August 19, 1968; NBC

Popular Librarys

_____ The Monkees; by Gene Fawcette and Howard Liss; Popular Library 50-8026; c 1966 (1st); $.50 [BC Photos: Davy Jones, Mickey Dolenz, Peter Tork, Mike Nesmith] [Cartoon book featuring "The Monkees in 'Way-Out' West," "The Monkees in Beauty and the Beach," "The Monkees in Chicken A Go-Go," and "The Monkees in Fair and Cool It"]

_____ The Monkees Go Mod; by Patrick O'Connor; Popular Library 60-8046; c 1967 (1st); $.60 [humor book with stills, trivia, bios] [FC Photo: Jones, Nesmith, Tork, Dolenz]

_____ Love Letters to the Monkees; by Bill Adler, ed.; Popular Library 60-8049; c 1967 (1st); $.60 [compilation of fan mail, with illustrations by Jack Davis] [FC Illus: (clockwise from top) Nesmith, Dolenz, Jones, Tork]

_____ The Monkees Go Ape; by Bill Adler, ed.; Popular Library 60-8069; c 1968 (1st); $.60 [scarce humor book with stills from the 1968 Monkees movie *Head*] [FC Photos: Tork, Jones, Nesmith (top), Dolenz]

Whitman

_____ The Monkees in Who's Got the Button?; by William Johnston; Whitman 1539; c 1968 (1st) [original story] [FC Photos: Jones, Dolenz, Tork, Nesmith]

Far-out sitcom, based on the 1964 Beatles film *A Hard Day's Night*, inspired the above books. *The Monkees Go Mod* was written by Senior Editor Patrick O'Connor in three days ("I found something on my desk called *The Monkees* and they wanted a book fast ... I couldn't find anyone to write it because no one knew anything about it ... all I had were the pictures...") and sold over a million copies.

MORK & MINDY
September 14, 1978 - August 12, 1982; ABC

Pockets

_____ Mork & Mindy; by Ralph Church; Pocket 82729; c 1979 (1st); $1.95 [novelization of the pilot episode "Mork Moves In" (aka "Mork Hour Special") and the episode "Mork Runs Away"] [FC Photo: Robin Williams, Pam Dawber]

_____ Mork & Mindy 2: The Incredible Shrinking Mork; by Robin S. Wagner; Pocket 83677; c 1980 (1st); $1.95 [original story] [FC Photos: Dawber, Williams]

_____ Mork & Mindy: A Video Novel; by Richard J. Anobile; Pocket 82754; c 1978 (1st: 1979); $2.75 [photo-novelization of the pilot episode "Mork Moves In"] [FC Photo: Williams, Dawber]

Miscellaneous

_____ The Robin Williams Scrapbook; by Mary Ellen Moore; Ace Tempo Star 73200; c 1979 (1st); $1.95 [FC Photo: Williams]

_____ Robin Williams ["The Robin Williams Scrapbook" abridged]; by Mary Ellen Moore; Grosset & Dunlap; c 1979 (1st); $1.95 [FC Photo: Williams]

_____ Mork & Mindy: Code Puzzles From Ork; by D.J. Arneson; Cinnamon House 15879; c 1979 (1st); $1.25 [FC Photo: Williams, Dawber]

_____ Mork & Mindy Puzzlers; by Mary Beth Lewis; Cinnamon House 15880; c 1979 (1st); $1.25 [FC Photo: Williams, Dawber]

_____ The Mork & Mindy Story; by Peggy Herz; Scholastic Book Services TX4757; c 1979 (1st) [oversize] [re-issued as #05756] [FC Photo: Williams, Dawber]

Robin Williams' launchpad, this *Happy Days* spinoff featured Henry Winkler (as Fonzie from *Happy Days*) and Penny Marshall (as Laverne from *Laverne and Shirley*) in its pilot episode "Mork Moves In." The episode was adapted into the novel *Mork & Mindy* and the video-novel *Mork & Mindy: A Video Novel*, the latter omitting the segments with Winkler and Marshall. (The *Video Novel* is by Richard Anobile, who originated the idea of translating film into book form ["... selecting frames to act as the narrative portion of the novel, coupled with dialog that included descriptive attitude..."], and had trademarked the "Movie Novel" earlier.)

THE MOST DEADLY GAME
October 10, 1970 - January 16, 1971; ABC

Lancers

_____ The Most Deadly Game #1: The Corpse in the Castle; by Ed Friend [Richard Wormser]; Lancer 73200; c 1970 (1st); $.60 [FC Photo: George Maharis, Yvette Mimieux, Ralph Bellamy]

_____ The Most Deadly Game #2: The One-Armed Murder; by Richard Gallagher; Lancer 73216; c 1971 (1st); $.60 [FC Photo: Maharis, Bellamy, Mimieux]

Author Richard Gallagher points out a flaw in the second *Most Deadly Game* book, in which the one-armed character in the story "lifts both hands palms up..."

THE MUNSTERS
September 24, 1964 - September 1, 1966; CBS

Avon

_____ The Munsters; by Morton Cooper; Avon G1237; c 1964 (1st); $.50 [FC Photo: (clockwise from top) Fred Gwynne, Pat Priest, Al Lewis, Butch Patrick, Yvonne DeCarlo] [*]

Whitmans

_____ The Munsters and the Great Camera Caper; by William Johnston; Whitman 1510; c 1965 (1st) [FC Illus: (left) Lewis, (clockwise from top for balance) Gwynne, Priest, Patrick, DeCarlo]

_____ The Munsters: The Last Resort; by William Johnston; Whitman 1567; c 1966 (1st) [FC Illus: Gwynne, DeCarlo, Gwynne, Priest, Patrick, Lewis]

[*] In this scarce and "Monster-ously Funny" book, the Munsters travel to New York City, where they "innocently invade the appalled world of TV and advertising," and to Washington, D.C., where Grandpa "accidentally catches a pair of spies and becomes a national hero."

MURDER, SHE WROTE
September 30, 1984 -; CBS

Avons

_____ Murder, She Wrote: The Murder of Sherlock Holmes; by James Anderson; Avon 89702; c 1985 (1st); $2.95 [novelization of the pilot episode "The Murder of Sherlock Holmes"] [FC Photos: Angela Lansbury]

_____ Murder, She Wrote #2: Horray for Homicide; by James Anderson; Avon 89937; c 1985 (1st); $2.95 [novelization of the episodes "Horray for Homicide" and "Deadly Lady"] [FC Photos: Lansbury]

_____ Murder, She Wrote #3: Lovers and Other Killers; by James Anderson; Avon 89938; c 1986 (1st); $2.95 [novelization of the episodes "Lovers and Other Killers" and "It's a Dog's Life"] [FC Photos: Lansbury]

Three books based on the long-running whodunit were also published in Britain by Star, which released a fourth title not issued here: *Murder in Two Acts*, by David Deutsch. The show, especially popular among senior citizens, is about a widowed mystery writer and most famous resident of Cabot Cove, Maine, who continually becomes involved in real-life murder mysteries.

MY FRIEND TONY
January 5, 1969 - August 31, 1969; NBC

____   My Friend Tony; by William Johnston; Lancer 73-838; c 1969 (1st); $.60 [FC
        Photo: James Whitmore, Enzo Cerusico]

THE NAKED CITY
September 30, 1958 - September 29, 1959; ABC
October 12, 1960 - September 11, 1963; ABC

____   The Naked City; by Charles Einstein; Dell First Edition A180; c 1959 (1st);
        $.25 [BC Photo: James Franciscus, John McIntire]

        Includes 8 short story novelizations by Charles Einstein, adapted from the
        teleplays written by show-creator Stirling Silliphant (to whom the book's
        authorship is credited on the cover and spine). Stories are "Meridian" (from the
        pilot episode), "Line of Duty," "Nickel Ride," "The Violent Circle,"
        "Susquehanna 7-8367," "The Other Face of Goodness," "Lady Bug, Lady
        Bug...," and "And a Merry Christmas to the Force on Patrol." The episodes
        are from the show's first season, when it was introduced in a 30-minute format.
        The show was dropped for a year and returned in 1960 in a 60-minute format,
        lasting an additional four seasons.

NAKIA
September 21, 1974 - December 28, 1974; ABC

____   Nakia; by Lee Hays; Popular Library 08325; c 1975 (1st); $1.25 [FC Illus:
        Robert Forster]

THE NAME OF THE GAME
September 20, 1968 - September 10, 1971; NBC

____   Name of the Game: Los Angeles: A.D. 2017; by Philip Wylie; Popular Library
        00272; c 1971 (1st); $.95 [novelization of the episode "Los Angeles: 2017"] [FC
        Photo: Gene Barry]

NANCY
September 17, 1970 - January 7, 1971; NBC

____   Nancy; by Jack Pearl; Pyramid T2339; c 1970 (1st); $.75 [FC Photo: John
        Fink, Renne Jarrett]

NANCY DREW
See THE HARDY BOYS/NANCY DREW MYSTERIES

NANNY AND THE PROFESSOR
January 21, 1970 - December 27, 1971; ABC

Lancers

_____ Nanny and the Professor; by William Johnston; Lancer 73876; c 1970 (1st); $.60 [FC Photos: (top) Juliet Mills, (bottom) Kim Richards, Trent Lehman, David Doremus, Richard Long]

_____ Nanny and the Professor #2: What Hath Nanny Wrought?; by William Johnston; Lancer 73889; c 1970 (1st); $.60 [FC Photos: (top) Mills, (bottom) Doremus, Richards, Long, Lehman]

_____ Nanny and the Professor #3: The Bloop Box; by William Johnston; Lancer 73205; c 1970 (1st); $.60 [orig. title "Nanny's Miracle"] [FC Photo: (clockwise from top left) Mills, Long, Doremus, Lehman, Richards]

In these books based on the *Mary Poppins* takeoff, find out, maybe, if Nanny--who "breezed in from Britain unannounced to captivate the household of the Professor and his three motherless children"--really has magical powers. Butch and Prudence believe so.

Note: Richard Long, who played Professor Harold Everett, died of a heart attack three years following the show's cancellation. Trent Lehman, who played nine-year-old Butch, sadly hanged himself in a San Fernando Valley schoolyard nearly ten years to the day following the show's cancellation. A casualty of the former child actor syndrome, Lehman had been despondent and was having trouble making the transition to normal adulthood. Roles had been difficult to come by as he grew into adolescence and additional problems had mounted; his final moments were spent at his former elementary school and sign of happier times.

THE NEW AVENGERS
September 5, 1978 - March 23, 1979; CBS

Berkleys

_____ The New Avengers #1: House of Cards; by Peter Cave; Berkley 03993; c 1976 (1st: 1978); $1.50 [novelization of the episode "House of Cards"] [FC Photos: Joanna Lumley, Patrick Macnee]

_____ The New Avengers #2: The Eagle's Nest; by John Carter; Berkley 03994; c 1976 (1st: 1978); $1.50 [novelization of the pilot episode "The Eagle's Nest"] [FC Photos: Lumley, Macnee, Gareth Hunt]

_____ The New Avengers #3: To Catch a Rat; by Walter Harris; Berkley 03995; c 1976 (1st: 1978); $1.50 [novelization of the episode "To Catch a Rat"] [FC Photo: Hunt, Lumley, Macnee]

Novelizations based on the unsuccessful *Avengers* remake (Patrick Macnee returned, but as a father figure Steed overseeing two younger agents) were also published in Britain by Futura, which published three additional titles not issued here: *#4: Fighting Men* (by Justin Cartright), *#5: Last of The Cybernauts* (Peter Cave), and *#6: Hostage* (Peter Cave).

THE NEW BREED
October 3, 1961 - September 25, 1962; ABC

_____ The New Breed; by Lee Costigan [Hank Searls]; Gold Medal s1186; c 1962 (1st); $.35 [novelization of the pilot episode "No Fat Cops"] [BC Photo: Leslie Nielsen, John Beradino, John Clarke, Greg Roman]

Absorbing Hank Searls creation--noted for its realistic portrayal of police work, guest stars that later became famous, and liberal use of on-location scenery in the streetscapes of L.A.--gave Leslie Nielsen his first starring role. Nielsen continued his prolific TV career throughout the 1960's and 70's before hitting it big with 1980's *Airplane!*

THE NEW PEOPLE
September 22, 1969 - January 12, 1970; ABC

_____ The New People: They Came From the Sea; by Alex Steele [William Johnston]; Tempo 05308; c 1969 (1st); $.75 [FC Photo: David Moses, Jill Jaress, Dennis Olivieri, Peter Ratray, Tiffany Bolling, Zooey Hall]

A planeload of hip youths crash-lands on a deserted island and the survivors start a hip society in this short-lived show. The question posed by the above TV tie-in: "Can the new people create a better society than the one they left behind?"

THE NEWLYWED GAME
July 11, 1966 - December 20, 1974; ABC

_____ "The Newlywed Game" Cookbook; by Jody Cameron Malis; Pocket 75652; c 1971 (1st); $.75 [FC Photo: Bob Eubanks]

NIGHT GALLERY
December 16, 1970 - May 27, 1973; NBC

_____ Night Gallery; by Rod Serling; Bantam S7160; c 1971 (1st); $.75 [FC Illus: Rod Serling] [stories "The Soul Survivor," "Make Me Laugh," "Pamela's Voice," "Does the Name Grimsby Do Anything to You?" (*), "Clean Kills and Other Trophies," and "They're Tearing Down Tim Riley's Bar"]

_____ Night Gallery 2; by Rod Serling; Bantam SP7203; c 1972 (1st); $.75 [FC Illus: Serling] [stories "Collector's Items" (*), "The Messiah on Mott Street," "The Different Ones," "Lindemann's Catch," and "Suggestion" (*)]

Following *The Twilight Zone* Rod Serling created, hosted, and wrote for this supernatural anthology show. The above books are collections of Serling's own story novelizations of a selection of his teleplays, and apparently original stories (those coded "*").

THE NIGHT STALKER
September 13, 1974 - August 30, 1975; ABC

Pockets

_____ The Night Stalker; by Jeff Rice; Pocket 78343; c 1973 (1st); $1.25 [original story] [FC Photo: Darren McGavin]

_____ The Night Strangler; by Jeff Rice; Pocket 78352; c 1974 (1st); $1.25 [novelization of the TV-movie]

Brief Darren McGavin cult favorite was based on the hit TV-movies "The Night Stalker" (Jan-11-1972) and "The Night Strangler" (Jan-16-1973). Jeff Rice's book *The Night Stalker* inspired the first movie; his book *The Night Strangler* was adapted from the teleplay of the second. Richard Matheson wrote both teleplays.

THE NURSES
September 27, 1962 - September 7, 1965; CBS

_____ The Nurses; by William Johnston; Bantam F2497; c 1963 (1st); $.50 [FC Illus: Zina Bethune] [variant second printing has "2ND BIG PRINTING" stamp on the cover]

ONE LIFE TO LIVE
July 15, 1968 - ; ABC

_____ One Life to Live #1/#2 [combined]: Moonlight Obsession, Books One and Two; by Gwendolynn Arden; Pioneer 400; c 1987 (1st); $2.50 [novelization of several episodes]

ONE STEP BEYOND
January 20, 1959 - October 3, 1961; ABC

_____ One Step Beyond: The World Grabbers; by Paul W. Fairman; Monarch 471; c 1964 (1st); $.40

Original novel based on the ESP-anthology show by Paul Fairman, whose body of work Marvin W. Hunt in *Twentieth-Century Science-Fiction Writers* describes as "graceful, precise, and imaginative, yet tastefully restrained."

THE OUTCASTS
September 23, 1968 - September 15, 1969; ABC

_____ The Outcasts; by Steve Frazee; Popular Library 60-2345; c 1968 (1st); $.60 [FC Photos: Don Murray, Otis Young]

THE OUTSIDER
September 18, 1968 - September 3, 1969; NBC

_____ The Outsider; by Lou Cameron; Popular Library 60-2373; c 1969 (1st); $.60 [FC Photos: Darren McGavin]

THE PAPER CHASE
September 12, 1978 - July 17, 1979; CBS
April 15, 1983 - August 9, 1986; Showtime

_____ The Paper Chase; by John Jay Osborn, Jr.; Popular Library 04357; c 1971 (1st: 1978); $1.95 [FC Photos: (top) James Stephens, (bottom) John Houseman]

_____ The Paper Chase [cover-variation]; by John Jay Osborn, Jr.; Warner 31141; c 1971 (1st: 1983); $2.95 [FC Photos: (top) Stephens, (bottom) Houseman]

 Law school drama was based on the 1973 movie, which in turn was based on the 1971 book by John Jay Osborn, himself a former Harvard Law School student. The above book was issued by Popular Library when the show aired in 1978, and re-issued with a slightly different cover by Warner when the show was revived (as *The Paper Chase: The Second Year*) by the cable network Showtime in 1983.

PAPER DOLLS
September 23, 1984 - December 25, 1984; ABC

_____ Paper Dolls; by Susan Beth Pfeffer; Dell 96777; c 1984 (1st); $2.25 [novelization of the TV-movie pilot "Paper Dolls" (May-24-1982)] [FC Photos: Daryl Hannah (both left), Alexandra Paul (both right)]

_____ Paper Dolls [cover-variation]; by Susan Beth Pfeffer; Dell 96777; c 1984 (2nd); $2.50 [FC Photos: Hannah (left), Paul (right)]

 This novelization of the May-24-1982 TV-movie "Paper Dolls" was copyrighted in 1984 and issued by Dell several times that year, in conjunction with the spinoff show. All issues include the same photo cover of Daryl Hannah and Alexandra Paul--from the TV-movie--but different banners. The banner on the May, 1984 first printing and undated fourth printing says: "The World of High Fashion Modeling--Is It Really a Dream Come True?" The banner on the September, 1984 second printing and November, 1984 third printing says: "Now a Major Television Series From ABC," the book's only reference to the show.

PAPER MOON
September 12, 1974 - January 2, 1975; ABC

_____ Paper Moon [orig. title "Addie Pray"]; by Joe David Brown; Signet W6409; c 1971 (15th: 1974); $1.50 [FC Photo: Christopher Connelley, Jodie Foster]

 The show was based on the 1973 movie of the same name, which in turn was based on the 1971 book *Addie Pray*, first published by Signet as *Paper Moon* in 1973. Several identical printings (Y5418) and cover-variation printings (Y5822) followed, before the book was re-issued as a 15th printing TV tie-in (W6409).

THE PARTRIDGE FAMILY
September 25, 1970 - August 31, 1974; ABC

Curtis Numbered Series

_____ The Partridge Family; by Michael Avallone; Curtis 05003; c 1970 (1st); $.60 [FC Photo: (rear) Jeremy Gelbwaks, Shirley Jones, Danny Bonaduce, David Cassidy, (front) Susan Dey, Suzanne Crough]

_____ The Partridge Family #2: The Haunted Hall; by Michael Avallone; Curtis 05004; c 1970 (1st); $.60 [FC Photo: Dey]

_____ The Partridge Family #3: Keith, the Hero; by Michael Avallone; Curtis 05005; c 1970 (1st); $.60 [FC Photo: Cassidy]

_____ The Partridge Family #4: The Ghost of Graveyard Hill; by Paul W. Fairman; Curtis 06147; c 1971 (1st); $.60 [FC Photos: Cassidy, Dey]

_____ The Partridge Family #5: Terror by Night; by Vic Crume; Curtis 06148; c 1971 (1st); $.60 [FC Photo: Cassidy, Crough, Bonaduce, Gelbwaks, Dey, Jones]

_____ The Partridge Family #6: Keith Partridge, Master Spy; by Vance Stanton [Michael Avallone]; Curtis 06150; c 1971 (1st); $.60 [FC Photo: Cassidy]

_____ The Partridge Family #7: The Walking Fingers; by Vance Stanton [Michael Avallone]; Curtis 06162; c 1972 (1st); $.60 [FC Photo: Cassidy]

_____ The Partridge Family #8: The Treasure of Ghost Mountain; by Paul W. Fairman; Curtis 06164; c 1972 (1st); $.60 [FC Photo: Jones, Bonaduce, Brian Forster, Crough, Dey, Cassidy]

_____ The Partridge Family #9: The Fat and Skinny Murder Mystery; by Vance Stanton [Michael Avallone]; Curtis 06180; c 1972 (1st); $.60 [FC Photo: Cassidy]

_____ The Partridge Family #10: Marked for Terror; by Vic Crume; Curtis 06182; c 1972 (1st); $.60 [FC Photo: Cassidy]

_____ The Partridge Family #11: Who's That Laughing in the Grave?; by Vance Stanton [Michael Avallone]; Curtis 06184; c 1972 (1st); $.60 [FC Photo: Cassidy]

_____ The Partridge Family #12: The Phantom of the Rock Concert; by Lee Hays; Curtis 06189; c 1973 (1st); $.60 [FC Photo: Cassidy]

_____ The Partridge Family #13: The Mystery of the Mad Millionairess; by Edward Fenton; Curtis 06186; c 1973 (1st); $.60 [FC Photo: Cassidy]

_____ The Partridge Family #14: Thirteen at Killer Gorge; by Vic Crume; Curtis 06190; c 1973 (1st); $.60 [FC Photo: Cassidy]

_____ The Partridge Family #15: The Disappearing Professor; by Lee Hays; Curtis 06191; c 1973 (1st); $.60 [FC Photo: Cassidy]

_____ The Partridge Family #16: The Stolen Necklace; by Lee Hays; Curtis 07321; c 1973 (1st); $.75 [FC Photo: Cassidy]

_____ The Partridge Family #17: Love Comes to Keith Partridge; by Michael Avallone; Curtis 07335; c 1973 (1st); $.75 [FC Photo: Cassidy]

Curtis Additional Titles

_____ The David Cassidy Story; by Carol Deck; Curtis 06154; c 1972 (1st); $.60 [FC Photo: Cassidy]

_____ David, David, David; by James Gregory; Curtis 06167; c 1972 (1st); $.60 [FC Photo: Cassidy]

_____ The Partridge Family Cookbook; by Sylvia Resnick; Curtis 09219; c 1973 (1st); $.95 [FC Illus: (rear) Cassidy, Jones, Dey, (front) Forster, Crough, Bonaduce; BC Photo: Cassidy]

Miscellaneous Titles

_____ Young Mr. Cassidy; by James A. Hudson; Scholastic Book Services TK2070; c 1972 (1st); $.60 [FC Photo: Cassidy]

_____ Meet David Cassidy [abridged Special Arrow Edition of "Young Mr. Cassidy"]; by James A. Hudson; Scholastic Book Services TX2123; c 1972 (1st); $.60 [oversize] [FC Photo: Cassidy]

_____ For Girls Only; by Susan Dey as told to Rochelle Reed; Tiger Beat XQ2001; c 1972 (1st); $.95 [FC Photo: Dey]

_____ Susan Dey's Secrets On Boys, Beauty & Popularity [formerly "For Girls Only"]; by Susan Dey as told to Rochelle Reed; Tiger Beat LAU 1; c 1972 (2nd); $.95 [FC Photo: Dey] [Scholastic Book Club Edition]

TV's crooning clan inspired the extensive series of tie-ins by Curtis, which "kept Curtis Books alive" per Editor-in-Chief Patrick O'Connor. With 17 original mysteries, two David Cassidy bios, and the scarce *Partridge Family Cookbook*. Spearheaded by James A. Bryans, Editor-in-Chief at parent company Popular Library, Michael Avallone was signed to write the first three books. He wrote eight in all ("after the third book a difficult editor forced me to hide behind the Vance Stanton byline") and made out well ("... fortunately I had a royalty slice on *Partridge* and made a great deal of money when #2 sold 2-1/2 million copies in six months of 1971"). *The Haunted Hall* may indeed be the most common TV tie-in ever published. Picturing Susan Dey on the cover, it involves a family trip to a haunted mansion that Laurie Partridge remarks "looks like Collins House on *Dark Shadows*." Numbers 5 and 10 in the series are also quite common; with her royalties from those books author Vic Crume retired.

The show--and simultaneous debut of the group's real-life hit single "I Think I Love You"--skyrocketed David Cassidy to teen-idol fame, and he alone is pictured on 14 of the books in the Curtis series (and all of them from the ninth one on).

Jeremy Gelbwaks as Christopher Partridge left the show after the first season (his father got transferred and moved the family out of L.A.) and was replaced by Brian Forster. Gelbwaks is pictured on the first and fifth *Partridge Family* books, Forster on the eighth book and the *Cookbook*. (Note: Forster didn't bear any resemblance at all to Gelbwaks ... but then again, neither did Dick Sargent to Dick York--as the two Darrins--in *Bewitched*.)

THE PATTY DUKE SHOW
September 18, 1963 - August 31, 1966; ABC

Whitmans

_____ Patty Duke and Mystery Mansion; by Doris Schroeder; Whitman 1514; c 1964 (1st) [FC Photo: Duke]

_____ Patty Duke and the Adventure of the Chinese Junk; by Doris Schroeder; Whitman 2334; c 1966 (1st) [FC Illus: Duke]

Ace

_____ The Patty Duke Show: Patty goes to Washington; by Frances Spatz Leighton; Ace F-278; c 1964 (1st); $.40 [FC Photos: Duke] [*]

[*] Brooklyn Heights, New York, residents Patty and Cathy Lane (cousins played jointly by Patty Duke) travel to Washington, D.C. in this book filled with "fascinating facts about famous people and places" by Washington correspondent and social historian Frances Spatz Leighton.

PEOPLE ARE FUNNY
September 19, 1954 - April 2, 1961; NBC

_____ People Are Funny; by Art Linkletter; Cardinal C-384; c 1947,60 (1st: 1960); $.35 [FC Photo: Art Linkletter]

PERRY MASON
September 21, 1957 - September 4, 1966; CBS

Cardinals

_____ Perry Mason: The Case of the Gilded Lady; by Erle Stanley Gardner; Cardinal C-337; c 1956 (1st: 1959); $.35 [BC Photo: Raymond Burr]

_____ Perry Mason: The Case of the Dubious Bridegroom; by Erle Stanley Gardner; Cardinal C-376; c 1949 (1st: 1959); $.35 [BC Photo: Burr]

_____ Perry Mason: The Case of the Screaming Woman; by Erle Stanley Gardner; Cardinal C-377; c 1957 (1st: 1959); $.35 [BC Photo: Burr]

_____ Perry Mason: The Case of the Perjured Parrot; by Erle Stanley Gardner; Cardinal C-379; c 1939 (1st: 1959); $.35 [BC Photo: Burr]

_____ Perry Mason: The Case of the Hesitant Hostess; by Erle Stanley Gardner; Cardinal C-381; c 1953 (1st: 1959); $.35 [BC Photo: Burr] [$.25 variant version issued as Pocket 1127]

Pockets

_____ Perry Mason: The Case of the Fan-Dancer's Horse; by Erle Stanley Gardner; Pocket 886; c 1947 (4th: 1957)

_____ Perry Mason: The Case of the Daring Decoy; by Erle Stanley Gardner; Pocket 6001; c 1957 (1st: 1960); $.35 [BC Photo: Burr]

_____ Perry Mason: The Case of the Lonely Heiress; by Erle Stanley Gardner; Pocket 6027; c 1948 (4th: 1960); $.35 [BC Photo: Burr]

_____ Perry Mason: The Case of the Calendar Girl; by Erle Stanley Gardner; Pocket 6040; c 1958 (1st: 1960); $.35 [BC Illus: Burr] [$.25 variant version issued as Pocket 1275]

_____ Perry Mason: The Case of the Fiery Fingers; by Erle Stanley Gardner; Pocket 6044; c 1951 (6th: 1960); $.35 [BC Illus: Burr]

TV's most famous courtroom drama was based on the long-running series of mysteries by Erle Stanley Gardner. Gardner, himself a lawyer, created the character in the 1933 book *The Case of the Velvet Claws*, and wrote 82 *Perry Mason* books in all through 1973's posthumously published *The Case of the Postponed Murder* (Gardner died in 1970). The character inspired a brief series of movies in the 1930's and a long-running radio series all prior to the TV show, with the airing of which the above books were issued with back cover show-mention. All but *The Case of the Fan-Dancer's Horse* mention the show alongside a small inset of Raymond Burr; *The Fan-Dancer's Horse* mentions it on the back and inside front covers, in ads for sponsor Libbey-Owens-Ford.

THE PERSUADERS
September 18, 1971 - June 14, 1972; ABC

Ballantines

_____ The Persuaders! Book One: The Heart-Shaped Birthmark; by Frederick E. Smith; Ballantine 02630; c 1971 (1st: 1972); $.95 [FC Photo: Roger Moore] [includes the novelizations "Overture" and "Angie, Angie"]

_____ The Persuaders! Book Two: Five Miles to Midnight; by Frederick E. Smith; Ballantine 02633; c 1971 (1st: 1972); $.95 [FC Photo: Moore] [includes the novelizations "Five Miles to Midnight" and "Someone Like Me"]

European adventure series paired Tony Curtis and Roger Moore from the big-screen and inspired the above books. *Book Two's* title comes from its first novelization. *Book One* was apparently mistitled; its story "Overture" includes a character with a heart-shaped birthmark.

Note: The books were also published in Britain by Pan, which released a third title not issued here: Frederick Smith's *The Persuaders! Book Three*, with the novelizations "The Gold Napoleon," "Greensleeves," and "The Old, The New, and The Deadly." *Books Two* and *Three* were re-issued in 1977 by State Mutual, as *The Persuaders Again!* and *The Persuaders at Large*.

PETER GUNN
September 22, 1958 - September 25, 1961; NBC/ABC

_____ Peter Gunn; by Henry Kane; Dell First Edition B155; c 1960 (1st); $.35 [FC Photo: Craig Stevens; BC Photo: Lola Albright, Stevens]

PEYTON PLACE
September 15, 1964 - June 2, 1969; ABC

Pockets

_____ Peyton Place; by Grace Metalious; Pocket 75087; c 1956 (1st: 1965); $.75

_____ Peyton Place [cover-variation]; by Grace Metalious; Pocket 75087; c 1956 (13th: 1968); $.75

_____ Again Peyton Place; by Roger Fuller; Pocket 75196; c 1967 (1st); $.75

_____ Carnival in Peyton Place; by Roger Fuller; Pocket 75250; c 1967 (1st); $.75

_____ Pleasures of Peyton Place; by Roger Fuller; Pocket 75267; c 1968 (1st); $.75

_____ Secrets of Peyton Place; by Roger Fuller; Pocket 75285; c 1968 (1st); $.75

_____ The Evils of Peyton Place; by Roger Fuller; Pocket 75334; c 1969 (1st); $.75

_____ Hero in Peyton Place; by Roger Fuller; Pocket 75367; c 1969 (1st); $.75

_____ The Temptations of Peyton Place; by Roger Fuller; Pocket 75423; c 1970 (1st); $.75

_____ Thrills of Peyton Place; by Roger Fuller; Pocket 75457; c 1969 (1st); $.75

_____ Nice Girl from Peyton Place; by Roger Fuller; Pocket 75470; c 1970 (1st); $.75

Dell

_____ The Girl From "Peyton Place"; by George Metalious and June O'Shea; Dell 2888; c 1965 (1st); $.60

The show was based on the 1957 movie, which in turn was based on the 1956 Grace Metalious novel, the huge best-seller that put Dell Books on the map and whose title became a household word. In 1960 Dell also published the Metalious novels *Return to Peyton Place* (it inspired that 1961 movie) and *The Tight White Collar*, and issued numerous printings of all three titles through the mid-1960's.

The show aired in 1964 (Metalious died that year), with Pocket Books obtaining the reprint rights to the book *Peyton Place* and thus launching their own *Peyton Place* series. It includes nine Roger Fuller sequels (those titles noted above), and two additional Metalious titles (*The Tight White Collar* and *No Adam in Eden* - stories set in locations other than "Peyton Place" and not included here). The only book in the series to mention the show is *Peyton Place* (among its subsequent printings is a cover-variation 13th printing released during the run of the show); the Fuller sequels are considered inferred TV tie-ins.

In 1965 Dell published the Metalious biography *The Girl From "Peyton Place,"* co-authored by her husband George. Pocket Books, then in control of the paperback rights to the *Peyton Place* novels, attempted to block its sale, claiming its cover misrepresented it as a *Peyton Place* sequel, but lost the battle in court.

THE PHIL SILVERS SHOW
September 20, 1955 - September 11, 1959; CBS

Ballantines

____ Sergeant Bilko [mouth open version]; by Nat Hiken; Ballantine 229; c 1957 (1st); $.35 [FC Photo: Phil Silvers; BC Photos: Maurice Gosfield (top left, bottom), Paul Ford, Silvers]

____ Sergeant Bilko [mouth closed version]; by Nat Hiken; Ballantine 229; c 1957 (1st); $.35 [FC Photo: Silvers; BC Photos: Gosfield (top left, bottom), Ford, Silvers]

____ Sgt. Bilko Joke Book; Ballantine 289K; c 1959 (1st); $.35 [FC Photo: Silvers]

Award-winning Nat Hiken creation inspired the above books. The book *Sergeant Bilko* was issued with two slightly different covers, both with photos of star Phil Silvers. The simplest way to describe the difference in the photos-- and distinguish the books--is to say that in one photo his mouth is open and in the other it's closed ... and thus, the "mouth open" and "mouth closed" versions. The former version has two printings, including a stated second printing; the latter has one printing only.

The *Sgt. Bilko Joke Book's* 289K serial number is shared by another Ballantine, Chad Merriman's Western *The Avengers*. Reportedly, *The Avengers* was intended to be issued as Ballantine 298K but was mistakenly issued as 289K; consequently, there is no book number 298K in the Ballantine series.

Sergeant Bilko is a collection of 10 shooting scripts: "Personal Transportation Provided," "Bilko's Battle With Hollywood," "The Bivouac," "Bilko in Wall Street," "Dinner at Sowici's," "The Millionaire," "The Motor Pool Mardi Gras," "The Visiting Congressman," "The Big Uranium Strike," and "The Case of Harry Speakup." *Sgt. Bilko Joke Book* includes 4 shooting scripts ("The Con Men," "Rest Cure," "The Singing Contest," and "Transfer") plus 10 chapters of jokes. The shooting scripts contain dialog that was cut during the editing process and didn't make it to the screen.

Note: The show, which swept the Emmys for Best Comedy Series and Best Comedy Writing in each of its first three seasons, was originally entitled *You'll Never Get Rich*, but was renamed *The Phil Silvers* Show during its first season; the reruns are syndicated as *Sergeant Bilko*.

PHYLLIS DILLER

Crests

_____ Phyllis Diller's Housekeeping Hints; by Phyllis Diller; Crest R1082; c 1966 (1st: 1968); $.60 [FC Photo: Phyllis Diller]

_____ Phyllis Diller's Housekeeping Hints [cover-variation]; by Phyllis Diller; Crest T2027; c 1966 (unsp: 1969); $.75 [FC Photo: Diller]

_____ Phyllis Diller's Marriage Manual; by Phyllis Diller; Crest R1245; c 1967 (1st: 1969); $.60 [FC Photo: Diller]

      Comedienne Phyllis Diller starred in two 1960's shows: ABC's sitcom *The Pruitts of Southampton*, renamed *The Phyllis Diller Show* (September 6, 1966 - September 1, 1967), and NBC's variety show *The Beautiful Phyllis Diller Show* (September 15, 1968 - December 22, 1968). The above books were issued at the time of the shows, but fail to mention them.

PLANET OF THE APES
September 13, 1974 - December 27, 1974; CBS

Awards

_____ Planet of the Apes #1: Man the Fugitive; by George Alec Effinger; Award AN1373; c 1974 (1st); $.95 [novelization of the episodes "The Cure" and "The Good Seeds"] [FC Photo: Ron Harper, Roddy McDowall, James Naughton]

_____ Planet of the Apes #2: Escape to Tomorrow; by George Alec Effinger; Award AN1407; c 1974,75 (1st: 1975); $.95 [novelization of the episodes "The Surgeon" and "The Deception"] [FC Photo: Harper, Naughton, McDowall]

_____ Planet of the Apes #3: Journey Into Terror; by George Alec Effinger; Award AN1436; c 1974,75 (1st: 1975); $.95 [novelization of the episodes "The Legacy" and "The Horse Race"] [FC Photo: McDowall]

_____ Planet of the Apes #4: Lord of the Apes; by George Alec Effinger; Award AN1488; c 1974,76 (1st: 1976); $.95 [novelization of the episodes "The Tyrant" and "The Gladiators"] [FC Photo: Naughton, McDowall, Harper]

      The show was based on the 1968 movie *Planet of the Apes* and its sequels. The show inspired four TV tie-ins by Award, which had published movie tie-ins on the sequels. (Pierre Boulle's 1963 novel *Planet of the Apes*, upon which the original movie was based, was published by Signet.) Ballantine in addition published three books based on NBC's 1975-76 animated remake series *Return to the Planet of the Apes* (see also it).

PLAYHOUSE 90
October 4, 1956 - May 18, 1960; CBS

_____   The Comedian and Other Stories; by Ernest Lehman; Signet 1446; c 1946+
          (1st: 1957); $.25 [FC Photo: Mickey Rooney] [*]

_____   No Time At All; by Charles Einstein; Dell D224; c 1957 (1st: 1958); $.35 [**]

     [*] Includes 8 Ernest Lehman stories: "The Comedian" (upon which the
show's Feb-14-1957 episode was based), "The Happy Hangover," "Hunsecker
Fights the World," "End of Summer," "Clear Connection," "The Unguarded
Moment," "Clear Havana Filler," and "It's the Little Things That Count." Rod
Serling wrote the Emmy-winning teleplay "The Comedian," based on the
Lehman story.
     [**] The show's Feb-13-1958 episode "No Time at All" was based on this
1957 Charles Einstein novel, issued in February of 1958 in conjunction with the
episode.

PLEASE DON'T EAT THE DAISIES
September 14, 1965 - September 2, 1967; NBC

_____   Please Don't Eat the Daisies; by Jean Kerr; Crest d834; c 1953+ (unsp: 1965);
          $.50

_____   Please Don't Eat the Daisies [cover-variation]; by Jean Kerr; Crest d834; c
          1953+ (13th: 1966); $.50

     The show was based on the 1960 movie, which in turn was based on the
Jean Kerr book, a collection of humorous essays based on the author's
experiences as a playwright and mother of four (her children once ate the daisies
from a vase on the dining room table). First published by Crest in 1959 with
a yellow cover, the book saw numerous nearly-identical subsequent printings
prior to, during, and beyond the run of the show. It was first issued as s263
(printings one through five, including a cover-variation movie tie-in fourth
printing), then as s588 (printings six through nine), then as d834, it with two
printings with front cover show-mention: One includes a large logo in the upper
left hand corner of the cover and the cover price in the upper right; its copyright
page lacks an issue date and printing status notation. The other includes a small
logo in the upper left hand corner, with the cover price included in the logo; its
copyright page notes "Thirteenth Fawcett Crest printing, November 1966."

POLICE WOMAN
September 13, 1974 - August 30, 1978; NBC

     Awards

_____   Police Woman #1: The Rape; by Leslie Trevor; Award AQ1438; c 1975 (1st);
          $1.25 [novelization of the episode "Warning: All Wives..."] [FC Photo: Angie
          Dickinson]

_____ Police Woman #2: Code 1013: Assassin; by Leslie Trevor; Award AQ1452; c 1975 (1st); $1.25 [original story] [FC Photo: Dickinson]

_____ Police Woman #3: Death of a Call Girl; by Leslie Trevor; Award AQ1487; c 1975 (1st); $1.25 [novelization of the episode "The Beautiful Die Young"] [FC Photo: Dickinson]

Popular police show starring Angie Dickinson as the sexy undercover agent Pepper Anderson inspired the above books. Leslie Trevor may be a pseudonym.

PRIMUS
1971; Syndicated

_____ Primus; by Bradford Street [Al Hine]; Bantam S7262; c 1971 (1st); $.75 [FC Photo: Robert Brown] [variant Special Edition issued as #9153]

THE PRISONER
June 1, 1968 - September 21, 1968; CBS

Aces

_____ The Prisoner; by Thomas M. Disch; Ace 67900; c 1969 (1st); $.60 [FC Photo: Patrick McGoohan]

_____ The Prisoner #2: Number Two; by David McDaniel; Ace 67901; c 1969 (1st); $.60 [FC Photo: McGoohan]

_____ The Prisoner #3: A Day in the Life; by Hank Stine; Ace 67902; c 1970 (1st); $.60 [FC Photo: McGoohan]

The show's bizarre and esoteric surrealism made Thomas Disch an ideal candidate to write the first _Prisoner_ book. Disch, only 28 at the time, perfectly captures the sophisticated and macabre feel of the show, in what is one of the finest TV tie-ins ever written. Said one: "The kind of sophistication implied in the show really comes out in the book."

In the show Patrick McGoohan starred as "Number 6," in a continuation of the role he played in _Danger Man_ and _Secret Agent_ (see also those shows). In the three _Prisoner_ books, he escapes at the end of #1, seems to have escaped at the end of #2, and remains a prisoner at the end of #3.

David McDaniel wrote the second _Prisoner_ book, dedicating it to Dan Curtis and Art Wallace of _Dark Shadows_ (Curtis was that show's creator and executive producer, Wallace wrote the first 13 weeks' episodes). McDaniel's own life, like Number 6's, was somewhat bizarre, as fellow Los Angeles Science Fiction Society member William Rotsler recounts: "It was the early 1960's and I had an office at a motion picture company. One weekend we shot a black magic photo-set of still pictures. I got a number of science fiction fans to attend and hired several models, and McDaniel was one of them. A magazine then published the pictures, which were shot sort of like a movie. Later, McDaniel was going to write a book about the Salem witch trials, so he rides his motorcycle back to Massachusetts. He comes to the hill they used, which was very barren, and wanders around and comes upon the remains of a recent campfire. The fire is still smoldering, and he sees the remnants of a magazine, which he kicks open to reveal a picture of himself! They were the black magic photos we had shot at the studio."

PRISONER: CELL BLOCK H
1979 - 1981; Syndicated

Pinnacles

_____   Prisoner: Cell Block H; by Murray Sinclair; Pinnacle 41113; c 1980 (1st); $2.25 [BC Photos (clockwise from top left): Carol Burns, Pieta Tommano, Val Lehman, Kerry Armstrong]

_____   Prisoner: Cell Block H #2: The Franky Doyle Story; by Henry Clement [Edward Fenton]; Pinnacle 41175; c 1981 (1st); $2.25 [FC Photo: Burns; BC Photos: (top) Burns, Colette Mann, (bottom) Lehman]

_____   Prisoner: Cell Block H #3: The Karen Travers Story; by Maggie O'Shell; Pinnacle 41176; c 1981 (1st); $2.25 [FC Photo: Tommano]

_____   Prisoner: Cell Block H #4: The Frustrations of Vera; by Michael Kerr [Robert Hoskins]; Pinnacle 41215; c 1981 (1st); $2.25 [FC Photo: Fiona Spence]

_____   Prisoner: Cell Block H #5: The Reign of Queen Bea; by Angela Michaels; Pinnacle 41403; c 1981 (1st); $2.25 [FC Photo: Lehman]

_____   Prisoner: Cell Block H #6: Trials of Erica; by Mary Carter; Pinnacle 41404; c 1981 (1st); $2.25 [FC Photo: Patsy King]

Trashy women's prison series imported from Australia inspired the above books, each with the statement "RECOMMENDED FOR MATURE READERS" on the cover. The stories are drawn mostly from the episodes, with plenty of new material added, including material--such as explicit lesbian sex-- not allowed in the already frank and violent show. Editor-in-Chief Patrick O'Connor "loved the show! We thought the books would be a smash, but they weren't."

PRIVATE EYE
September 13, 1987 - January 8, 1988; NBC

Ivys

_____   Private Eye #1; by T.N. Robb [Rob MacGregor]; Ivy 0269; c 1988 (1st); $3.50 [novelization of the pilot episode "Private Eye"] [FC Photo: Josh Brolin, Michael Woods]

_____   Private Eye #2: Blue Movie; by David Elliott [David Elliott Pedneau]; Ivy 0270; c 1988 (1st); $3.50 [novelization of the episodes "Blue Movie" and "Nicky The Rose"] [FC Photo: Woods, Brolin]

____ Private Eye #3: Flip Side; by T.N. Robb [Rob MacGregor]; Ivy 0271; c 1988 (1st); $3.50 [novelization of the episode "Flip Side"] [FC Photo: Brolin, Woods]

____ Private Eye #4: Nobody Dies in Chinatown; by Max Lockhart [Doris R. Meredith]; Ivy 0272; c 1988 (1st); $3.50 [novelization of the episodes "Nobody Dies in Chinatown" and "War Buddy"] [FC Photo: Woods, Brolin]

Stylish private eye series by the creators of *Miami Vice* set in 1950's L.A. didn't catch on fast enough and was dropped mid-season, before the above books hit the stands. Ballantine suffered heavy losses as a result, and the experience cast a dark view on the publisher's feelings about TV tie-ins in general. Sales were negligible, most books were stripped and returned, few copies made it to the public, and as a result these books have become collectible early.

The writers were required to choose pen names which the publisher controlled. Husband and wife Rob MacGregor and Trish Janeshutz were to have collaborated on his titles originally (hence the pseudonym T.N. Robb), but she passed. Doris Meredith's pseudonym of Max Lockhart, which she used for *Nobody Dies in Chinatown*, was suggested by her son from a character in a role-playing board game. Meredith enjoyed writing the book ("we were required to use every word from the scripts ... finding a common thread between the two unrelated stories and my own portion of the material was the most challenging part") and it paid well. The car chase scene in her *Chinatown* novelization was dropped from the filming in an attempt to cut losses.

QUINCY, M.E.
October 3, 1976 - September 5, 1983; NBC

Aces

____ Quincy, M.E.; by Thom Racina; Ace 69945; c 1977 (1st); $1.50 [novelization of the pilot episode "Go Fight City Hall--To the Death"] [FC Photo: Jack Klugman]

____ Quincy, M.E. #2; by Thom Racina; Ace 69946; c 1977 (1st); $1.50 [novelization of the episode "The Thigh Bone's Connected to the Hip Bone"] [FC Photo: Klugman]

Thom Racina mysteries based on the popular NBC-show, starring Jack Klugman as the intense medical examiner Dr. Quincy.

THE RAT PATROL
September 12, 1966 - September 16, 1968; ABC

Paperback Librarys

____ The Rat Patrol; by Norman Daniels; Paperback Library 53-387; c 1966 (1st); $.60 [BC Photos: Christopher George, Gary Raymond, Lawrence Casey, Justin Tarr]

____ The Rat Patrol #2 in Desert Danger; by David King; Paperback Library 53-411; c 1967 (1st); $.60 [FC Photo: Casey, George, Tarr; BC Photos: George, Raymond, Casey, Tarr]

___ The Rat Patrol #3 in The Trojan Tank Affair; by David King; Paperback Library 53-477; c 1967 (1st); $.60

___ The Rat Patrol #4 in Two-Faced Enemy; by David King; Paperback Library 53-566; c 1967 (1st); $.60 [FC Photo: (top) Raymond, George, (bottom) Tarr, Casey]

___ The Rat Patrol #5 in Target for Tonight; by David King; Paperback Library 53-628; c 1968 (1st); $.60 [FC Photo: (top) Raymond, Tarr, (bottom) Casey, George]

___ The Rat Patrol #6 in Desert Masquerade; by David King; Paperback Library 53-696; c 1968 (1st); $.60 [FC Photo: Raymond, George, Casey, Tarr]

Whitman

___ The Rat Patrol: The Iron Monster Raid; by I.G. Edmonds; Whitman 1547; c 1968 (1st)

World War II drama set in the North African campaign inspired the above tie-ins. Norman Daniels wrote the first Paperback Library but passed on the sequels ("they were long books and wouldn't pay enough" - even for the prolific Daniels, apparently, who "typed two fingers 10,000 words a day," typically, throughout his career). The David King byline of the sequels is a pseudonym of Howard Pehrson; they may have been written by Pehrson or ghosted by others.

RAWHIDE
January 9, 1959 - January 4, 1966; CBS

___ Rawhide; by Frank C. Robertson; Signet S1910; c 1961 (1st); $.35 [FC Illus: Sheb Wooley, Eric Fleming, Clint Eastwood]

Cover pictures Clint Eastwood as Rowdy Yates in the classic TV Western. Eastwood parlayed the role into that of the "Man With No Name" in the 1964 spaghetti-Western *A Fistful of Dollars* (released in the United States in 1967) and stardom.

THE REAL MCCOYS
October 3, 1957 - September 22, 1963; ABC/CBS

___ The Real McCoys and Danger at the Ranch; by Cole Fannin; Whitman 1577; c 1961 (1st) [FC Illus: (back seat) Michael Winkleman, Lydia Reed, Richard Crenna, (front seat) Kathy Nolan, Walter Brennan]

THE REBEL
October 4, 1959 - September 17, 1961; ABC

___ Rebel of Broken Wheel; by Dean Owen [Dudley Dean McGaughy]; Monarch 218; c 1961 (1st); $.35 [FC Photo: Nick Adams]

_____ The Rebel; by H.A. De Rosso; Whitman 1548; c 1961 (1st) [FC Illus: Adams]

Books picture Nick Adams as Rebel Johnny Yuma. Adams, who later saw his once promising screen career falter, was found dead of a drug overdose in 1968.

THE RESTLESS GUN
September 23, 1957 - September 14, 1959; NBC

Signets

_____ The Restless Gun; by Will Hickok [C. William Harrison]; Signet 1541; c 1958 (1st); $.25 [FC Illus: John Payne]

_____ Trail of the Restless Gun; by Will Hickok [C. William Harrison]; Signet 1675; c 1959 (1st); $.25 [FC Illus: Payne]

Whitman

_____ The Restless Gun; by Barlow Meyers; Whitman 1559; c 1959 (1st) [FC Illus: Payne]

RETURN TO THE PLANET OF THE APES
September 6, 1975 - September 4, 1976; NBC

Ballantines

_____ Return to the Planet of the Apes #1: Visions from Nowhere; by William Arrow [William Rotsler]; Ballantine 25122; c 1976 (1st); $1.50 [novelization of the episodes "Flames of Doom," "Escape from Ape City," and "A Date with Judy"]

_____ Return to the Planet of the Apes #2: Escape from Terror Lagoon; by William Arrow [Don Pfeil]; Ballantine 25167; c 1976 (1st); $1.50 [novelization of the episodes "Tunnel of Fear," "Lagoon of Peril," and "Terror on Ice Mountain"]

_____ Return to the Planet of the Apes #3: Man, the Hunted Animal; by William Arrow [William Rotsler]; Ballantine 25211; c 1976 (1st); $1.50 [novelization of the episodes "River of Flames," "Screaming Wings," and "Trail to the Unknown"]

This *Planet of the Apes* cartoon spinoff inspired the above books, each a novelization of three consecutive episodes, beginning with the pilot episode "Flames of Doom." The William Arrow house name was derived from the authors; the "William" was from science fiction author William Rotsler, the "Arrow" was from former Hell's Angel Don Pfeil (pronounced "file," it means "arrow" in German).

RHODA
September 9, 1974 - December 9, 1978; CBS

_____ All About "Rhoda"; by Peggy Herz; Scholastic Book Services TK3121; c 1975 (1st) [FC Photos: (top) David Groh, Valerie Harper, (bottom) Julie Kavner, Harper]

THE RIFLEMAN
September 30, 1958 - July 1, 1963; ABC

_____   The Rifleman ["Authorized TV Edition" logo on front cover]; by Cole Fannin;
         Whitman 1569; c 1959 (1st) [FC Photo: Johnny Crawford, Chuck Connors]

_____   The Rifleman ["Authorized TV Adventure" logo on spine]; by Cole Fannin;
         Whitman 1569; c 1959 (1st) [FC Photo: Crawford, Connors]

         Popular Western saga of father and son Lucas and Mark McCain inspired
the above book; its two versions are identical except for the logos.

RIN TIN TIN
October 15, 1954 - August 28, 1959; ABC

         Whitmans

_____   Rin Tin Tin's Rinty; by Julie Campbell; Whitman 1542; c 1954 (1st)

_____   Rin Tin Tin and The Ghost Wagon Train; by Cole Fannin; Whitman 1579; c
         1958 (1st) [FC Illus: Lee Aaker]

_____   Rin Tin Tin and Call to Danger; by Doris Schroeder; Whitman 1539; c 1957
         (1st)

         TV's other dog show--this one featuring a German Shepherd--inspired the
above books. The book *Rin Tin Tin's Rinty* lacks, and the other two books
include, the "TV" logos found on most Whitman TV tie-ins.

RIPCORD
1961 - 1963; Syndicated

_____   Ripcord; by D.S. Halacy, Jr.; Whitman 1522; c 1962 (1st) [FC Illus: Ken
         Curtis]

RIPLEY'S BELIEVE IT OR NOT!
September 26, 1982 - September 4, 1986; ABC

         Signets

_____   Ripley's Believe It or Not! #31; Signet AE2212; c 1982 (1st); $2.25

_____   Ripley's Believe It or Not! #32; Signet AE2213; c 1982 (1st); $2.25

_____   Ripley's Believe It or Not! #33; Signet AE2214; c 1982 (1st); $2.25

_____   Ripley's Believe It or Not! #34; Signet AE2215; c 1982 (1st); $2.25

         The show was based on the comic strip created by cartoonist Robert L.
Ripley, host of the 1940's radio series and 1949-50 TV series *Believe It or Not*
until his death in 1949. Extensive *Believe It or Not* paperback series by Pocket
runs through 1979's 30th entry; Signet resumed the series in 1982 with #'s 31
through 34, which mention the ABC show on the covers.

ROALD DAHL'S TALES OF THE UNEXPECTED
1979 - 1985; Syndicated

_____ Roald Dahl's Tales of the Unexpected; by Roald Dahl; Vintage 74081; c 1948+
(1st: 1979); $2.95 [FC Photo: Roald Dahl]

Dramatic anthology series created by Roald Dahl led to the above book.
Of Dahl's 24 short stories appearing in the book, all but "The Butler" were
adapted into episodes. Stories are: "Taste," "Lamb to the Slaughter," "Man
from the South," "My Lady Love, My Dove," "Dip in the Pool," "Galloping
Foxley," "Skin," "Neck," "Nunc Dimittis" (adapted as "Depart in Peace"), "The
Landlady," "William and Mary," "The Way Up to Heaven," "Parson's
Pleasure," "Mrs. Bixby and the Colonel's Coat," "Royal Jelly," "Edward the
Conqueror," "The Sound Machine," "Georgy Porgy," "The Hitchhiker,"
"Poison," "The Boy Who Talked with Animals," "The Umbrella Man,"
"Genesis and Catastrophe," and "The Butler." Note: The show was renamed
Tales of the Unexpected in 1981, and shouldn't be confused with the 1977 NBC
show of the same name.

THE ROARING 20'S
October 15, 1960 - September 21, 1962; ABC

_____ The Roaring 20's: Sing Out Sweet Homicide; by John Roeburt; Dell First
Edition K105; c 1961 (1st); $.40 [FC Illus: Dorothy Provine]

THE ROCKFORD FILES
September 13, 1974 - July 25, 1980; NBC

Popular Librarys

_____ The Rockford Files #1: The Unfortunate Replacement; by Mike Jahn; Popular
Library 00318; c 1975 (1st); $1.25 [novelization of the TV-movie pilot "The
Rockford Files" (Mar-27-1974)] [FC Photo: James Garner]

_____ The Rockford Files #2: The Deadliest Game; by Mike Jahn; Popular Library
00354; c 1976 (1st); $1.25 [novelization of the episodes "The Kirkoff Case" and
"This Case is Closed"] [FC Photo: Garner]

The James Garner classic inspired two Mike Jahn tie-ins, among Jahn's
favorites to write. (Jahn's later character Bill Donovan, created in the 1982
book _Night Rituals_, was influenced by the chronically-in-trouble, world-weary
Rockford.) Garner, who won an Emmy in 1977 for the role, resurrected it in
a series of TV-movies in the 1990's. The first, Nov-27-1994's "I Still Love
L.A.," has Rockford dealing with the L.A. riots, brushfires, and earthquakes,
and his ex-wife, as he solves his case. The movie was dedicated to the late
Noah Beery, Rockford's father "Rocky" in the TV show, who died a few weeks
before it was released.

THE ROOKIES
September 11, 1972 - June 29, 1976; ABC

_____   The Rookies; by Claire Parker; Bantam N7703; c 1973 (1st); $.95 [novelization of the TV-movie pilot "The Rookies" (Mar-07-1972)] [FC Photo: Michael Ontkean, Kate Jackson, Sam Melville, Georg Stanford Brown] [variant Special Book Club Edition issued as #9199]

ROOM 222
September 17, 1969 - January 11, 1974; ABC

Tempos

_____   Room 222: What Ever Happened to Mavis Rooster?; by William Johnston; Tempo 05339; c 1970 (1st); $.75 [FC Photo: Lloyd Haynes; BC Photo: Denise Nicholas, Haynes, Karen Valentine, Michael Constantine]

_____   Room 222 #2: Monday Morning Father; by William Johnston; Tempo 05342; c 1970 (1st); $.75 [FC Photo: Haynes; BC Photo: Nicholas, Haynes, Valentine, Constantine]

_____   Room 222 #3: Love is a Three Letter Word; by William Johnston; Tempo 05358; c 1970 (1st); $.75 [FC Photo: Haynes; BC Photo: Nicholas, Haynes, Valentine, Constantine]

_____   Room 222 #4: Bomb in the Classroom; by William Johnston; Tempo 05372; c 1971 (1st); $.75 [FC Photo: Haynes, Constantine; BC Photo: Nicholas, Haynes, Valentine, Constantine] [$.95 variant version issued as #05591]

_____   Room 222 #5: A Little Grass On The Side; by William Johnston; Tempo 05414; c 1971 (1st); $.75 [FC Photo: Haynes, Howard Rice (black student); BC Photo: Nicholas, Haynes, Valentine, Constantine]

_____   Room 222 #6: Have you heard about Kelly?; by William Johnston; Tempo 05594; c 1973 (1st); $.95 [FC Photo: Judy Strangis, Haynes; BC Photo: Nicholas, Haynes, Valentine, Constantine]

Early-70's comedy-drama set at racially-integrated Walt Whitman High inspired the above books. Hailed by educational and civil rights groups at the time, but rarely seen in syndication, many of the issues the show and books dealt with are timeless (prejudice, peer pressure, staying in school, etc.), while others have been overshadowed by the more serious issues of today: sex education by AIDS awareness, teen pregnancy by date rape, smog by global warming, school yard bullies by gang members, marijuana by crack cocaine ...

ROWAN & MARTIN'S LAUGH-IN
See LAUGH-IN

THE ROY ROGERS SHOW
December 30, 1951 - June 23, 1957; NBC

Whitmans

_____ Roy Rogers and the Rimrod Renegades [dustjacket]; by Snowden Miller; Whitman 2305; c 1952 (1st) [Dustjacket Photo: Roy Rogers]

_____ Roy Rogers and the Rimrod Renegades [laminated cover]; by Snowden Miller; Whitman 2305; c 1952,54 (unsp: 1954) [FC Photo: Rogers]

_____ Roy Rogers and the Enchanted Canyon; by Jim Rivers; Whitman 1502; c 1954 (1st) [FC Illus: Rogers] [also issued as Whitman 2373]

_____ Roy Rogers on the Trail of the Zeroes; by Packer Elton; Whitman 2361; c 1954 (1st) [FC Photo: Rogers]

_____ Roy Rogers and The Brasada Bandits; by Cole Fannin; Whitman 1500; c 1955 (1st) [FC Photo: Rogers]

_____ Roy Rogers: King of the Cowboys; by Cole Fannin; Whitman 1503; c 1956 (1st) [FC Illus: Rogers]

_____ Roy Rogers and Dale Evans in River of Peril; by Cole Fannin; Whitman 1504; c 1957 (1st) [FC Photo: Rogers]

_____ Dale Evans and Danger in Crooked Canyon; by Helen Hale [Lucille Burnett Mulcahy]; Whitman 1506; c 1958 (1st) [FC Illus: Dale Evans]

      Roy Rogers was a veteran of some 70 Western films in the 1930's and 40's when he and his wife Dale Evans moved to the small-screen in 1951. Whitman, which had been publishing *Roy Rogers* books since the 1940's, continued to publish them, with show-mention, once the show aired. *Roy Rogers and the Rimrod Renegades* was issued in otherwise identical, dustjacket and non-dustjacket versions (Whitman discontinued dustjackets in the early 1950's).

S.W.A.T.
February 24, 1975 - June 29, 1976; ABC

_____ S.W.A.T. #1: Crossfire!; by Dennis Lynds; Pocket 80241; c 1975 (1st); $1.25 [novelization of the episode "Death Score" aka "Red September"] [FC Photos: (top) Steve Forrest, (middle) Forrest, Robert Urich, Mark Shera, (bottom) Rod Perry]

THE SAINT
1963 - 1966; May 21, 1967 - September 12, 1969; Syndicated/NBC

Fictions

_____ The Saint Steps In; by Leslie Charteris; Fiction K101; c 1942,43 (1st: 1963); $.50 [full-length novel] [FC Photo: Roger Moore]

_____ The Saint Sees it Through; by Leslie Charteris; Fiction K102; c 1946 (1st: 1963); $.50 [full-length novel] [FC Photo: Moore]

_____ The Saint Closes the Case; by Leslie Charteris; Fiction K103; c 1930 (1st: 1964); $.50 [full-length novel] [FC Photo: Moore]

_____ The Avenging Saint; by Leslie Charteris; Fiction K104; c 1930,31 (1st: 1964); $.50 [full-length novel] [FC Photo: Moore]

_____ The Saint's Getaway; by Leslie Charteris; Fiction K105; c 1932,33 (1st: 1964); $.50 [full-length novel] [FC Photo: Moore]

_____ The Saint in New York; by Leslie Charteris; Fiction K106; c 1934,35 (1st: 1964); $.50 [full-length novel] [FC Photo: Moore]

_____ Enter the Saint; by Leslie Charteris; Fiction K107; c 1930,31 (1st: 1964); $.50 [stories "The Policeman With Wings" and "The Lawless Lady"] [FC Photo: Moore]

_____ The Saint Meets His Match; by Leslie Charteris; Fiction K108; c 1941 (1st: 1964); $.50 [full-length novel] [FC Photo: Moore]

_____ Featuring the Saint; by Leslie Charteris; Fiction K109; c 1931 (1st: 1964); $.50 [stories "The Logical Adventure," "The Wonderful War," and "The Man Who Could Not Die"] [FC Photo: Moore]

_____ Alias the Saint; by Leslie Charteris; Fiction K110; c 1931 (1st: 1964); $.50 [stories "The Story of a Dead Man," "The Impossible Crime," and "The National Debt"] [FC Photo: Moore]

_____ The Saint Overboard; by Leslie Charteris; Fiction K111; c 1935,36 (1st: 1964); $.50 [full-length novel] [FC Photo: Moore]

_____ The Saint - The Brighter Buccaneer; by Leslie Charteris; Fiction K112; c 1933 (1st: 1964); $.50 [15 stories] [FC Photo: Moore]

_____ The Saint vs The Scotland Yard; by Leslie Charteris; Fiction K113; c 1932 (1st: 1964); $.50 [stories "The Inland Revenue," "The Million Pound Day," and "The Melancholy Journey of Mr. Teal"] [FC Photo: Moore]

_____ The Saint and Mr. Teal; by Leslie Charteris; Fiction K114; c 1933 (1st: 1964); $.50 [stories "The Gold Standard," "The Man From St. Louis," and "The Death Penalty"] [FC Photo: Moore]

Macfaddens

_____ The Saint in the Sun; by Leslie Charteris; Macfadden 60-238; c 1963 (1st: 1966); $.60 [stories "The Better Mousetrap," "The Ugly Impresario," "The Prodigal Miser," "The Fast Women," "The Jolly Undertaker," "The Russian Prisoner," and "The Hopeless Heiress"] [FC Photo: Roger Moore]

_____ The Saint Goes West; by Leslie Charteris; Macfadden 60-246; c 1942 (1st: 1966); $.60 [stories "Palm Springs" and "Hollywood"]

_____ Saint Errant; by Leslie Charteris; Macfadden 60-247; c 1933+ (1st: 1966); $.60 [stories "Judith," "Iris," "Lida," "Jeannine," "Lucia," "Teresa," "Luella," "Emily," and "Dawn"]

_____ The Saint on the Spanish Main; by Leslie Charteris; Macfadden 60-252; c 1949+ (1st: 1966); $.60 [stories "Bimini: The Effete Angler," "Nassau: The Arrow of God," "Jamaica: The Black Commissar," "Puerto Rico: The Unkind Philanthropist," "The Virgin Islands: The Old Treasure Story," and "Haiti: The Questing Tycoon"]

_____ Trust the Saint; by Leslie Charteris; Macfadden 60-253; c 1962 (1st: 1966); $.60 [stories "The Helpful Pirate," "The Bigger Game," "The Cleaner Cure," "The Intemperate Reformer," "The Uncured Ham," and "The Convenient Monster"]

_____ The Saint Around the World; by Leslie Charteris; Macfadden 60-260; c 1954+ (1st: 1966); $.60 [stories "Bermuda: The Patient Playboy," "England: The Talented Husband," "France: The Reluctant Nudist," "Middle East: The Lovelorn Sheik," "Malaya: The Pluperfect Lady," "Vancouver: The Sporting Chance"]

_____ The Saint Intervenes; by Leslie Charteris; Macfadden 60-262; c 1934 (1st: 1966); $.60 [14 stories]

_____ The Saint Goes On; by Leslie Charteris; Macfadden 60-265; c 1934,35 (1st: 1966); $.60 [stories "The High Fence," "The Elusive Ellshaw," and "The Case of the Frightened Innkeeper"]

_____ Call for the Saint; by Leslie Charteris; Macfadden 60-273; c 1947,48 (1st: 1967); $.60 [stories "The King of Beggars" and "The Masked Angel"]

_____ The Saint in Europe; by Leslie Charteris; Macfadden 60-294; c 1936,53 (1st: 1967); $.60 [stories "Paris: The Covetous Headsman," "Amsterdam: The Angel's Eye," "The Rhine: The Rhine Maiden," "Tirol: The Golden Journey," "Lucerne: The Loaded Tourist," "Juan-les-Pins: The Spanish Cow," and "Rome: The Latin Touch"]

_____ The Saint to the Rescue; by Leslie Charteris; Macfadden 60-307; c 1956+ (1st: 1968); $.60 [stories "The Ever-Loving Spouse," "The Fruitful Land," "The Percentage Player," "The Water Merchant," "The Gentle Ladies," and "The Element of Doubt"]

_____ Senor Saint; by Leslie Charteris; Macfadden 60-315; c 1953+ (1st: 1968); $.60 [stories "The Pearls of Peace," "The Revolution Racket," "The Romantic Matron," and "The Golden Frog"]

_____ Thanks to the Saint; by Leslie Charteris; Macfadden 60-365; c 1956,57 (1st: 1968); $.60 [stories "The Bunco Artists," "The Happy Suicide," "The Good Medicine," "The Unescapable Word," "The Perfect Sucker," and "The Careful Terrorist"]

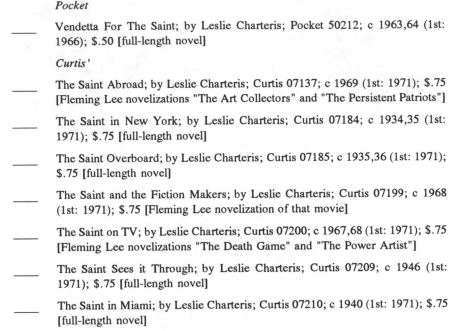

Pocket

____ Vendetta For The Saint; by Leslie Charteris; Pocket 50212; c 1963,64 (1st: 1966); $.50 [full-length novel]

Curtis'

____ The Saint Abroad; by Leslie Charteris; Curtis 07137; c 1969 (1st: 1971); $.75 [Fleming Lee novelizations "The Art Collectors" and "The Persistent Patriots"]

____ The Saint in New York; by Leslie Charteris; Curtis 07184; c 1934,35 (1st: 1971); $.75 [full-length novel]

____ The Saint Overboard; by Leslie Charteris; Curtis 07185; c 1935,36 (1st: 1971); $.75 [full-length novel]

____ The Saint and the Fiction Makers; by Leslie Charteris; Curtis 07199; c 1968 (1st: 1971); $.75 [Fleming Lee novelization of that movie]

____ The Saint on TV; by Leslie Charteris; Curtis 07200; c 1967,68 (1st: 1971); $.75 [Fleming Lee novelizations "The Death Game" and "The Power Artist"]

____ The Saint Sees it Through; by Leslie Charteris; Curtis 07209; c 1946 (1st: 1971); $.75 [full-length novel]

____ The Saint in Miami; by Leslie Charteris; Curtis 07210; c 1940 (1st: 1971); $.75 [full-length novel]

The show was based on the long-running series of mysteries by Leslie Charteris. Charteris created the character in the 1928 book *Meet the Tiger*, and wrote some 60 *Saint* books in all through 1983's *Salvage for the Saint*, thus making Simon Templar the longest running character in detective fiction. The books include full length novels, collections of novelettes and short stories, and omnibus volumes. Charteris died in 1993 at age 85.

The character inspired nine movies--spanning 1938's *The Saint in New York* to 1954's *The Saint's Girl Friday*--a radio series, a syndicated newspaper strip, a comic book series, and *The Saint Detective Magazine* (founded in 1953, it was later renamed *The Saint Mystery Magazine*), all prior to the TV show. The show was produced in England by I.T.C. starting in 1962; it starred Roger Moore and aired in syndication in the United States the following year. Due to the success of the syndicated series, new color episodes were produced and aired on NBC from 1967-69.

With the release of the TV show several publishers re-issued *Saint* books as TV tie-ins. The first American tie-ins were by Fiction, publisher of *The Saint Mystery Magazine*. Fiction issued 14 *Saint* books--spanning K101's *The Saint Steps In* through K114's *The Saint and Mr. Teal*--from November of 1963 to November of 1964, releasing two books apiece at two month intervals. All have Roger Moore photo covers. An additional 16 books were planned--spanning K115's *The Saint Bids Diamonds* to K130's *The Saint Around the World*--and two even had covers made.

Macfadden followed with 13 *Saint* books, beginning with 1966's *The Saint in the Sun*, the only one with a photo cover and show-mention. Its cover states: "Follow the Saint's sensational adventures in Macfadden-Bartell's paperbacks and on NBC's top-rated TV thriller series." The series ran through 1968's *Thanks to the Saint*, with the sequels considered inferred TV tie-ins. The books were re-issued by Manor in the early 1970's, without reference to the show and with models pictured on the covers.

Less prominent *Saint* tie-ins are by Pocket (1966's *Vendetta for the Saint*, with back cover show-mention) and Curtis. The Curtis' include two novelizations (*The Saint Abroad* and *The Saint on TV*, in which Fleming Lee adapts two episodes per book, with Charteris editing); the terrific *The Saint and the Fiction Makers* (which began as a teleplay, was turned into a screenplay [released in 1967 as *The Fiction Makers*], and was subsequently novelized by Lee into a full-length novel, with Charteris editing); and four Saint re-issues (*The Saint in New York*, *The Saint Overboard*, *The Saint Sees it Through*, and *The Saint in Miami*). None of the Curtis' picture Roger Moore, while three (*The Saint Abroad*, *The Saint Sees it Through*, and *The Saint in Miami*) picture professional models. The copyright pages lack issue dates, but cigarette ads tipped into various copies were copyrighted in 1971.

Brief remake series *Return of the Saint* (Ian Ogilvy starred), was produced in England in 1978, and aired in the United States in the winter of 1979-80. Extensive *Saint* paperback series by Charter (later Ace Charter) was then being issued, but bears no connection to the remake show.

SAM BENEDICT
September 15, 1962 - September 7, 1963; NBC

_____ Sam Benedict: Cast the First Stone; by Elsie Lee; Lancer 70-035; c 1963 (1st); $.40 [novelization of the episode "Twenty Aching Years"]

Book's authorship is wrongly attributed to Norman Daniels on the cover and spine (he may have been given the assignment originally); correct author Elsie Lee is credited on the title page.

THE SANDY DUNCAN SHOW
September 17, 1972 - December 31, 1972; CBS

_____ The Sandy Duncan Story; by Rochelle Reed; Pyramid 02934; c 1973 (1st); $.75 [FC Photos: Sandy Duncan]

SANFORD AND SON
January 14, 1972 - September 2, 1977; NBC

_____ Sanford and Son; by Alan Riefe and Dick Harrington; Curtis 09222; c 1973 (1st); $.95 [stills and captions excerpted from the show] [FC Photo: Demond Wilson, Redd Foxx]

SATURDAY NIGHT LIVE
October 11, 1975 -; NBC

_____ Backstage at Saturday Night Live!; by Michael McKenzie; Scholastic Book Services 30919; c 1980 (1st) [FC Photos: Bill Murray, Gilda Radner, John Belushi, Dan Aykroyd; BC Photos: Radner, Jane Curtin, Laraine Newman, Garrett Morris]

With a history of the TV show, individual chapters on the early regulars, and a 1975-79 episode chronology, with guest hosts and musical groups.

SEA HUNT
1957 - 1961; Syndicated

_____ Sea Hunt; by Cole Fannin; Whitman 1541; c 1960 (1st) [FC Illus: Lloyd Bridges]

SEARCH
September 13, 1972 - August 29, 1973; NBC

Bantams

_____ Search; by Robert Weverka; Bantam S7706; c 1973 (1st); $.75 [novelization of the TV-movie pilot "Probe" (Feb-21-1972)] [FC Photo: Hugh O'Brian]

_____ Search: Moonrock; by Robert Weverka; Bantam N8306; c 1973 (1st); $.95 [novelization of the episode "Moonrock"] [FC Photo: O'Brian]

SEARCH FOR TOMORROW
September 3, 1951 - December 26, 1986; CBS/NBC

_____ Search for Tomorrow [old logo version]; by Faith Baldwin; Popular Library 60-8017; c 1966 (1st); $.60 [FC Photo: Mary Stuart]

_____ Search for Tomorrow [new logo version]; by Faith Baldwin; Popular Library 60-2163; c 1966 (1st); $.60 [FC Photo: Stuart]

Various copies were issued as 60-8017, with Popular Library's old pinetree logo on the front cover (as was customary for the publisher until 1966), and as 60-2163, with the new pinetree logo on the front cover and spine (as was customary starting that year). The covers are otherwise identical.

SECRET AGENT
April 3, 1965 - September 10, 1966; CBS

Macfaddens

_____ Secret Agent: Departure Deferred; by W. Howard Baker; Macfadden 50-275; c 1965 (1st: 1966); $.50 [FC Photos: Patrick McGoohan]

_____ Secret Agent: Hell For Tomorrow; by Peter Leslie; Macfadden 50-280; c 1965 (1st: 1966); $.50 [FC Photos: McGoohan]

_____ Secret Agent: Storm Over Rockwall; by W. Howard Baker; Macfadden 50-284; c 1965 (1st: 1966); $.50 [FC Photos: McGoohan]

_____ Secret Agent: No Way Out; by Wilfred McNeilly; Macfadden 50-320; c 1966 (1st); $.50 [FC Photo: McGoohan]

_____ Secret Agent: The Exterminator; by W.A. Ballinger [W. Howard Baker]; Macfadden 50-342; c 1966 (1st: 1967); $.50 [FC Photo: McGoohan]

British import starred Patrick McGoohan as Secret Agent John Drake, in a continuation of the role he introduced in 1961's *Danger Man* and resumed in 1968's *The Prisoner* (see also those shows). The above tie-ins were also published in Britain by Consul, but under the series name "Danger Man." (While the show was released as *Secret Agent* in the United States, it was released as *Danger Man* in Britain, its 1961 title.)

THE SECRET STORM
February 1, 1954 - February 8, 1974; CBS

_____ The Secret Storm: The Unseen; by Joan Hughes; Pocket 75444; c 1970 (1st); $.75 [FC Photo: Joel Crothers, Jada Rowland]

SERGEANT BILKO
See THE PHIL SILVERS SHOW

SERPICO
September 24, 1976 - January 28, 1977; NBC

_____ Serpico; by Peter Maas; Bantam 10265; c 1973 (23rd: 1976); $1.95

The show was based on the 1973 movie, which was in turn based on the 1973 book by Peter Maas. Published extensively since 1973, the show is first mentioned on the otherwise identical 23rd printing.

77 SUNSET STRIP
October 10, 1958 - September 9, 1964; ABC

_____ The Double Take; by Roy Huggins; Pocket 2524; c 1946 (2nd: 1959); $.25 [*]

_____ 77 Sunset Strip; by Roy Huggins; Dell First Edition A176; c 1958 (1st: 1959); $.25 [FC Illus: Efrem Zimbalist, Jr.] [**]

[*] Book introduces Stuart Bailey, the private eye of TV's *77 Sunset Strip*. First issued by Pocket in 1948 (#524), it was re-issued as a TV tie-in with the show. Roy Huggins created and produced the show.

[**] Book includes segments which had appeared as novelettes in the *Saturday Evening Post* in 1946 (under the titles "Appointment With Fear" and "Now You See It") and *Esquire Magazine* in 1952 (under the title "Death and the Skylark"). With the airing of the show the book was issued by Dell as a TV tie-in in the form of a complete novel.

SHAFT
October 9, 1973 - August 20, 1974; CBS

> *Bantams*

_____ Shaft Among the Jews; by Ernest Tidyman; Bantam N7621; c 1972 (1st: 1973); $.95

_____ Shaft Has a Ball; by Ernest Tidyman; Bantam N7699; c 1973 (1st); $.95

_____ Shaft's Carnival of Killers; by Ernest Tidyman; Bantam N8494; c 1974 (1st); $.95

The show was based on the *Shaft* movies and Ernest Tidyman novels. Tidyman created the character of black supersleuth John Shaft in the 1970 book *Shaft*, and co-wrote the screenplay for the 1971 movie the book inspired. Next came 1972's *Shaft's Big Score*, with Tidyman writing that book and screenplay as well. Both books were issued by Bantam with Richard Roundtree covers. A third movie, the Stirling Silliphant-penned *Shaft in Africa*, was released in 1973, but no corresponding book was written. Bantam's three additional *Shaft* books (*Shaft Among the Jews, Shaft Has a Ball*, and *Shaft's Carnival of Killers*) were published from 1973-74, spanning the short-lived run of the show, and while they don't mention the show or picture Roundtree they're considered inferred TV tie-ins. Tidyman's two additional *Shaft* books (1973's *Goodbye, Mr. Shaft* and 1975's *The Last Shaft*) were not published by Bantam.

THE SHARI LEWIS SHOW
October 1, 1960 - September 28, 1963; NBC

_____ The Shari Lewis Show: Fun With the Kids; by Shari Lewis; Macfadden 75-140; c 1960 (1st: 1964); $.75

THE SILENT FORCE
September 21, 1970 - January 11, 1971; ABC

_____ The Silent Force; by Harry Goddard; Popular Library 01418; c 1971 (1st); $.75 [FC Photo: Ed Nelson, Percy Rodriguez, Lynda Day George]

THE SILENT SERVICE
1957 - 1958; Syndicated

_____ The Silent Service; by William C. Chambliss; Signet S1658; c 1959 (1st); $.35 [World War II submarine stories based on the TV show]

SIR LANCELOT
September 24, 1956 - June 24, 1957; NBC

_____ Sir Lancelot; by Dorothy Haas; Whitman Big Little Book 1649; c 1958 (1st) [FC Illus: William Russell]

THE SIX MILLION DOLLAR MAN
October 20, 1973 - March 6, 1978; ABC

Warners

_____ Cyborg; by Martin Caidin; Warner 76-643; c 1972 (2nd: 1974); $1.25 [FC Illus: Lee Majors]

_____ Cyborg [cover-variation]; by Martin Caidin; Warner 88-371; c 1972 (3rd: 1976); $1.50 [FC Illus: Majors]

_____ Cyborg #2: Operation Nuke; by Martin Caidin; Warner 76-061; c 1973 (1st: 1974); $1.25 [original story] [FC Illus: Majors]

_____ The Six Million Dollar Man #1: Wine, Women and War; by Michael Jahn; Warner 76-833; c 1975 (1st); $1.25 [novelization of the episode "Wine, Women, and War"] [FC Illus: Majors]

_____ The Six Million Dollar Man #2: Solid Gold Kidnapping; by Evan Richards [Michael Jahn]; Warner 76-834; c 1975 (1st); $1.25 [novelization of the episode "Solid Gold Kidnapping"] [FC Illus: Majors]

_____ The Six Million Dollar Man #3: High Crystal; by Martin Caidin; Warner 76-408; c 1974 (1st: 1975); $1.25 [original story] [FC Illus: Majors]

_____ The Six Million Dollar Man #4: Pilot Error; by Jay Barbree; Warner 76-835; c 1975 (1st); $1.25 [novelization of the episode "Pilot Error"] [FC Illus: Majors]

_____ The Six Million Dollar Man #5: The Rescue of Athena One; by Michael Jahn; Warner 76-836; c 1975 (1st); $1.25 [novelization of the episodes "The Rescue of Athena One" and "Straight on 'Til Morning"] [FC Illus: Majors]

_____ The Six Million Dollar Man #6: CYBORG IV; by Martin Caidin; Warner 78-655; c 1975 (1st: 1976); $1.50 [original story] [FC Photo: Majors]

Berkleys

_____ The Six Million Dollar Man: The Secret of Bigfoot Pass; by Mike Jahn; Berkley Z3307; c 1976 (1st); $1.25 [novelization of the episode "The Secret of Bigfoot Pass"] [FC Photo: Majors]

_____ The Six Million Dollar Man: International Incidents; by Mike Jahn; Berkley 03331; c 1977 (1st); $1.25 [novelization of the episodes "Double Trouble," "The Deadly Test," and "Love Song for Tanya"] [FC Photo: Majors]

Tempos

_____ The Six Million Dollar Man's Bionic Brain Benders; by Rose Paul; Tempo 12523; c 1975,76 (1st: 1976); $.95 [oversize] [FC Photo: Majors]

_____ The Six Million Dollar Man's Search-A-Word Shape Puzzles; by Dawn Gerger; Tempo 12526; c 1975,76 (1st: 1976); $.95 [oversize] [FC Photo: Majors]

_____ The Six Million Dollar Man's Bionic Eye Rebus Puzzles; by Rose Paul; Tempo 12527; c 1975,76 (1st: 1976); $.95 [oversize] [FC Photo: Majors]

Miscellaneous

____ The Six Million Dollar Man and The Bionic Woman; by Joel H. Cohen; Scholastic Book Services TK3600; c 1976 (1st) [FC Photos: Majors, Lindsay Wagner]

    The show was based on the 1972 book *Cyborg* by Martin Caidin. Caidin, a former military pilot and nuclear warfare technologist, had long been fascinated by the idea of making man and machine one, and had used the theme in two prior works before creating the character of astronaut-turned-Cyborg Steve Austin in 1972. First published by Warner that year (66-986), the book was re-issued twice with the show. Caidin's three additional *Six Million Dollar Man* books (*Operation Nuke, High Crystal,* and *CYBORG IV*) are also original novels; the balance (five books by Michael Jahn and one by Jay Barbree) are novelizations.

    Caidin's friend Barbree, as space correspondent for *NBC-News*, was the only analyst to cover all 100 of America's first manned space missions (May of 1961's flight of the Freedom 7 being the first, June of 1995's flight [and historic docking with the Russian spaceship Mir] of the Space Shuttle Atlantis being the 100th).

    Michael Jahn's *Solid Gold Kidnapping* was written as Evan Richards (the pseudonym was derived from his son Evan Richard Jahn), because reportedly Caidin felt he "was losing Steve Austin to Michael Jahn." Jahn got his start as a science fiction and mystery novelist by way of his TV tie-ins. He'd previously worked as a free lance writer and TV editor at *Cue Magazine*, the weekly entertainment magazine that was later absorbed by *New York Magazine*. When Jahn's Editor Stanley Newman left *Cue* to head the publishing division at MCA/Universal, Jahn went with him. Newman needed someone who knew science, was prolific, and could produce on deadlines, and Jahn's TV tie-ins and subsequent career developed. Jahn has written some 50 books to date, and won an Edgar for 1978's *The Quark Maneuver*.

THE SIXTH SENSE
January 15, 1972 - December 30, 1972; ABC

Tempos

____ The Sixth Sense #1: Witch, Witch, Burning Bright; by John W. Bloch; Tempo 05570; c 1972 (1st); $.95 [shooting script from the episode "Witch, Witch Burning Bright"]

____ The Sixth Sense #2: In the Steps of the Master; by Marion Zimmer Bradley; Tempo 05595; c 1973 (1st); $.95 [original story]

THE $64,000 QUESTION
June 7, 1955 - November 9, 1958; CBS

____ The $64,000 Question Official Quiz Book; by Louis G. Cowan, ed.; Dell First Edition 79; c 1955 (1st); $.25

Producer Louis G. Cowan sold his interest in this, the most popular of the 1950's game shows, soon after the show began, and in 1958 became president of CBS. His post was short-lived, however, for he was forced to resign during the quiz show scandals that followed (the scandals causing the cancellation of *The $64,000 Question*--to which Cowan's name was still associated--and many other game shows). Cowan and his wife died in 1976 when a fire broke out in their Manhattan penthouse, reportedly having originated in their TV set.

THE SMITH FAMILY
January 20, 1971 - June 14, 1972; ABC

_____ The Smith Family #1: Meet the Smiths; by Norman Daniels; Berkley X2127; c 1971 (1st: 1972); $.60 [FC Photo: (top) Henry Fonda, Janet Blair, (middle) Darlene Carr, Ron Howard, (bottom) Michael-James Wixted]

5 original stories: "Personal Affair," "Thank You, Officer Dolan," "Uptown Man," "The Tin Box," and "Pattern of Guilt."

SONS AND DAUGHTERS
September 11, 1974 - November 6, 1974; CBS

_____ Sons and Daughters; by William Johnston; Ballantine 24235; c 1974 (1st); $1.25 [novelization of the TV-movie pilot "Senior Year" (Mar-22-1974)]

SPACE: 1999
1975 - 1977; Syndicated

Pockets

_____ Space: 1999 #1: Breakaway; by E.C. Tubb; Pocket 80184; c 1975 (1st); $1.50 [novelization of the episodes "Breakaway," "Matter of Life and Death," "The Black Sun," and "Ring Around the Moon"] [FC Photo: Barbara Bain, Martin Landau; BC Photos: Landau, Bain, Barry Morse]

_____ Space: 1999 #2: Moon Odyssey; by John Rankine; Pocket 80185; c 1975 (1st); $1.50 [novelization of the episodes "Another Time, Another Place," "Alpha Child," "Voyager's Return," and "The Last Sunset"] [FC Photos: Bain, Landau; BC Photos: Landau, Bain, Morse]

_____ Space: 1999 #3: The Space Guardians; by Brian Ball; Pocket 80198; c 1975 (1st); $1.50 [novelization of the episodes "Force of Life," "Guardian of Piri," and "The Missing Link"] [FC Photo: Morse, Landau, Bain; BC Photos: Landau, Bain, Morse]

_____ Space: 1999 #4: Collision Course; by E.C. Tubb; Pocket 80274; c 1975 (1st: 1976); $1.50 [novelization of the episodes "Collision Course," "End of Eternity," "The Full Circle," and "Death's Other Dominion"] [FC Photo: Landau, Bain; BC Photos: Landau, Bain, Morse]

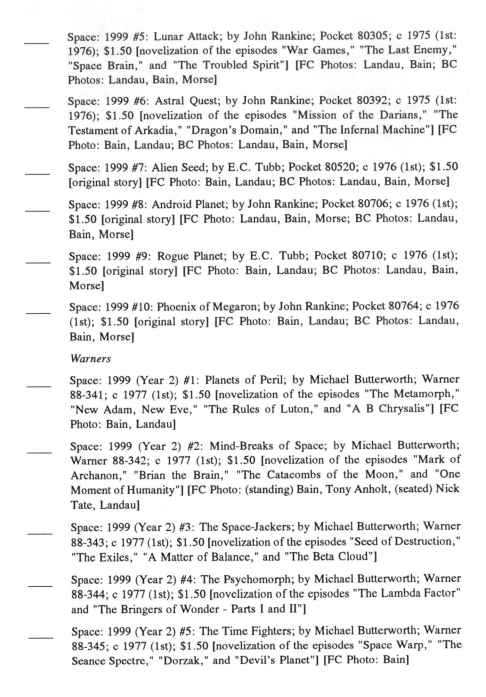

_____ Space: 1999 #5: Lunar Attack; by John Rankine; Pocket 80305; c 1975 (1st: 1976); $1.50 [novelization of the episodes "War Games," "The Last Enemy," "Space Brain," and "The Troubled Spirit"] [FC Photos: Landau, Bain; BC Photos: Landau, Bain, Morse]

_____ Space: 1999 #6: Astral Quest; by John Rankine; Pocket 80392; c 1975 (1st: 1976); $1.50 [novelization of the episodes "Mission of the Darians," "The Testament of Arkadia," "Dragon's Domain," and "The Infernal Machine"] [FC Photo: Bain, Landau; BC Photos: Landau, Bain, Morse]

_____ Space: 1999 #7: Alien Seed; by E.C. Tubb; Pocket 80520; c 1976 (1st); $1.50 [original story] [FC Photo: Bain, Landau; BC Photos: Landau, Bain, Morse]

_____ Space: 1999 #8: Android Planet; by John Rankine; Pocket 80706; c 1976 (1st); $1.50 [original story] [FC Photo: Landau, Bain, Morse; BC Photos: Landau, Bain, Morse]

_____ Space: 1999 #9: Rogue Planet; by E.C. Tubb; Pocket 80710; c 1976 (1st); $1.50 [original story] [FC Photo: Bain, Landau; BC Photos: Landau, Bain, Morse]

_____ Space: 1999 #10: Phoenix of Megaron; by John Rankine; Pocket 80764; c 1976 (1st); $1.50 [original story] [FC Photo: Bain, Landau; BC Photos: Landau, Bain, Morse]

Warners

_____ Space: 1999 (Year 2) #1: Planets of Peril; by Michael Butterworth; Warner 88-341; c 1977 (1st); $1.50 [novelization of the episodes "The Metamorph," "New Adam, New Eve," "The Rules of Luton," and "A B Chrysalis"] [FC Photo: Bain, Landau]

_____ Space: 1999 (Year 2) #2: Mind-Breaks of Space; by Michael Butterworth; Warner 88-342; c 1977 (1st); $1.50 [novelization of the episodes "Mark of Archanon," "Brian the Brain," "The Catacombs of the Moon," and "One Moment of Humanity"] [FC Photo: (standing) Bain, Tony Anholt, (seated) Nick Tate, Landau]

_____ Space: 1999 (Year 2) #3: The Space-Jackers; by Michael Butterworth; Warner 88-343; c 1977 (1st); $1.50 [novelization of the episodes "Seed of Destruction," "The Exiles," "A Matter of Balance," and "The Beta Cloud"]

_____ Space: 1999 (Year 2) #4: The Psychomorph; by Michael Butterworth; Warner 88-344; c 1977 (1st); $1.50 [novelization of the episodes "The Lambda Factor" and "The Bringers of Wonder - Parts I and II"]

_____ Space: 1999 (Year 2) #5: The Time Fighters; by Michael Butterworth; Warner 88-345; c 1977 (1st); $1.50 [novelization of the episodes "Space Warp," "The Seance Spectre," "Dorzak," and "Devil's Planet"] [FC Photo: Bain]

_____ Space: 1999 (Year 2) #6: The Edge of the Infinite; by Michael Butterworth; Warner 88-346; c 1977 (1st); $1.50 [novelization of the episodes "All That Glisters," "Journey to Where," "The Immunity Syndrome," and "The Dorcons"]

Ballantine

_____ The Making of Space: 1999; by Tim Heald; Ballantine 25265; c 1976 (1st); $1.95 [FC Photos: (top) Bain, Landau, (middle) Catherine Schell, Anholt]

The space epic reunited the husband-and-wife team of Martin Landau and Barbara Bain from *Mission: Impossible*, and inspired two sets of TV tie-ins. During its first season Pocket Books released 10 books on the show. The books were also published in Britain by Orbit/Futura, which issued an eleventh book not issued here: E.C. Tubb's original novel *Earthfall*. All of the show's first season episodes but "Earthbound" are novelized in the Pocket series. During its second season Warner Books released six books on the show, as "Space: 1999, Year Two." The books were also published in Britain by Star. All of the show's second season episodes but "The Taybor" are novelized in the Warner series.

SPENSER: FOR HIRE
September 20, 1985 - September 3, 1988; ABC

_____ Spenser: For Hire: Valediction; by Robert B. Parker; Dell 19246; c 1984 (4th: 1986); $3.50

The show was based on the popular *Spenser* books by Robert B. Parker, issued extensively since the early 1970's. With the airing of the TV show in 1985 the above book was issued with front cover show-mention. Other *Spenser* books have been seen with show-mentioning stickers affixed to the covers, but are not included here.

SPIN AND MARTY
See THE MICKEY MOUSE CLUB

STAR TREK
September 8, 1966 - September 2, 1969; NBC

Bantam Novelizations

_____ Star Trek; by James Blish; Bantam F3459; c 1967 (1st); $.50 [FC Illus: William Shatner, Leonard Nimoy] [title becomes "Star Trek 1" upon 21st printing] [novelizations "Charlie's Law" (from the episode "Charlie X"), "Dagger of the Mind," "The Unreal McCoy" (from the pilot episode "The Man Trap"), "Balance of Terror," "The Naked Time," "Miri," and "The Conscience of the King"]

_____ Star Trek 2; by James Blish; Bantam F3439; c 1968 (1st); $.50 [FC Photo: Nimoy, Shatner] [novelizations "Arena," "A Taste of Armageddon," "Tomorrow Is Yesterday," "Errand of Mercy," "Court Martial," "Operation--Annihilate!" "The City on the Edge of Forever," and "Space Seed"]

_____ Star Trek 3; by James Blish; Bantam F4371; c 1969 (1st); $.50 [FC Photo: Shatner, Nimoy, Nichelle Nichols] [novelizations "The Trouble With Tribbles," "The Last Gunfight" (from the episode "Spectre of the Gun"), "The Doomsday Machine," "Assignment: Earth," "Mirror, Mirror," "Friday's Child," and "Amok Time"]

_____ Star Trek 4; by James Blish; Bantam S7009; c 1971 (1st); $.75 [novelizations "All Our Yesterdays," "The Devil in the Dark," "Journey to Babel," "The Menagerie," "The Enterprise Incident," and "A Piece of the Action"]

_____ Star Trek 5; by James Blish; Bantam S7300; c 1972 (1st); $.75 [novelizations "Whom Gods Destroy," "The Tholian Web," "Let That Be Your Last Battlefield," "This Side of Paradise," "Turnabout Intruder," "Requiem for Methuselah," and "The Way to Eden"]

_____ Star Trek 6; by James Blish; Bantam S7364; c 1972 (1st); $.75 [novelizations "The Savage Curtain," "The Lights of Zetar," "The Apple," "By Any Other Name," "The Cloud Minders," and "The Mark of Gideon"]

_____ Star Trek 7; by James Blish; Bantam S7480; c 1972 (1st); $.75 [novelizations "Who Mourns for Adonais?" "The Changeling," "The Paradise Syndrome," "Metamorphosis," "The Deadly Years," and "Elaan of Troyius"]

_____ Star Trek 8; by James Blish; Bantam SP7550; c 1972 (1st); $.75 [novelizations "Spock's Brain," "The Enemy Within," "Catspaw," "Where No Man Has Gone Before," "Wolf in the Fold," and "For the World is Hollow, And I Have Touched the Sky"]

_____ Star Trek 9; by James Blish; Bantam SP7808; c 1973 (1st); $.75 [novelizations "Return to Tomorrow," "The Ultimate Computer," "That Which Survives," "Obsession," "The Return of the Archons," and "The Immunity Syndrome"]

_____ Star Trek 10; by James Blish; Bantam SP8401; c 1974 (1st); $.75 [novelizations "The Alternative Factor," "The Empath," "The Galileo Seven," "Is There in Truth No Beauty?" "A Private Little War," and "The Omega Glory"]

_____ Star Trek 11; by James Blish; Bantam Q8717; c 1975 (1st); $1.25 [novelizations "What Are Little Girls Made of?" "The Squire of Gothos," "Wink of an Eye," "Bread and Circuses," "Day of the Dove" and "Plato's Stepchildren"]

_____ Star Trek 12; by James Blish with J.A. Lawrence; Bantam 11382; c 1977 (1st); $1.75 [novelizations "Patterns of Force," "The Gamesters of Triskelion," "And the Children Shall Lead," "The Carbomite Maneuver," and "Shore Leave"]

_____ Spock Must Die!; by James Blish; Bantam H5515; c 1970 (1st); $.60 [original novel] [FC Photo: Nimoy]

_____ Mudd's Angels; by J.A. Lawrence; Bantam 11802; c 1978 (1st); $1.75 [includes the novelizations "Mudd's Women" and "I, Mudd," and the original story "The Business, as Usual, During Altercations"]

Bantam Fotonovels

___ Star Trek Fotonovel #1: City on the Edge of Forever; Bantam 11345; c 1977 (1st); $1.95 [FC Photo: Shatner, Nimoy] [photo-novelization of the episode "City on the Edge of Forever"]

___ Star Trek Fotonovel #2: Where No Man Has Gone Before; Bantam 11346; c 1965,77 (1st: 1977); $1.95 [FC Photo: Shatner; BC Photo: Shatner, Nimoy] [photo-novelization of the episode "Where No Man Has Gone Before"]

___ Star Trek Fotonovel #3: The Trouble With Tribbles; Bantam 11347; c 1967,77 (1st: 1977); $1.95 [FC Photo: Shatner, Nichols] [photo-novelization of the episode "The Trouble With Tribbles"]

___ Star Trek Fotonovel #4: A Taste of Armageddon; Bantam 11348; c 1967,77 (1st: 1978); $1.95 [FC Photo: Nimoy, Shatner] [photo-novelization of the episode "A Taste of Armageddon"]

___ Star Trek Fotonovel #5: Metamorphosis; Bantam 11349; c 1967,78 (1st: 1978); $1.95 [FC Photo: Nimoy, Shatner, DeForest Kelley] [photo-novelization of the episode "Metamorphosis"]

___ Star Trek Fotonovel #6: All Our Yesterdays; Bantam 11350; c 1969,78 (1st: 1978); $1.95 [FC Photo: Nimoy, Kelley] [photo-novelization of the episode "All Our Yesterdays"]

___ Star Trek Fotonovel #7: The Galileo Seven; Bantam 12041; c 1967,78 (1st: 1978); $2.25 [FC Photo: Kelley, Nimoy] [photo-novelization of the episode "The Galileo Seven"]

___ Star Trek Fotonovel #8: A Piece of the Action; Bantam 12022; c 1968,78 (1st: 1978); $2.25 [FC Photo: Shatner, Nimoy; BC Photo: Nimoy, Kelley] [photo-novelization of the episode "A Piece of the Action"]

___ Star Trek Fotonovel #9: The Devil in the Dark; Bantam 12021; c 1967,78 (1st: 1978); $2.25 [FC Photo: Nimoy; BC Photo: Shatner, Nimoy] [photo-novelization of the episode "The Devil in the Dark"]

___ Star Trek Fotonovel #10: Day of the Dove; Bantam 12017; c 1968,78 (1st: 1978); $2.25 [FC Photo: Shatner] [photo-novelization of the episode "Day of the Dove"]

___ Star Trek Fotonovel #11: The Deadly Years; Bantam 12028; c 1967,78 (1st: 1978); $2.25 [FC Photo: Shatner; BC Photo: Shatner, Nimoy] [photo-novelization of the episode "The Deadly Years"]

___ Star Trek Fotonovel #12: Amok Time; Bantam 12012; c 1967,78 (1st: 1978); $2.25 [FC Photo: Nimoy, Shatner] [photo-novelization of the episode "Amok Time"]

Whitman

___ Star Trek: Mission to Horatius; by Mack Reynolds; Whitman 1549; c 1968 (1st) [FC Illus: Nimoy, Shatner] [original story]

Miscellaneous

_____ The Making of Star Trek; by Stephen E. Whitfield and Gene Roddenberry; Ballantine 73004; c 1968 (1st); $.95 [FC Photo: Shatner, Nimoy] [behind-the-scenes look at the show; Whitfield wrote, Roddenberry credited as co-author]

_____ "The Trouble With Tribbles"; by David Gerrold; Ballantine 23402; c 1973 (1st); $1.50 [FC Photo: Shatner] [about Gerrold's experiences writing for *Star Trek*, contains his famous "Tribbles" script]

_____ The World of Star Trek; by David Gerrold; Ballantine 23403; c 1973 (1st); $1.50 [BC Photo: Nimoy, Kelley, Nichols, Shatner, George Takei, plus extras] [history of the *Star Trek* phenomenon]

_____ Six Science Fiction Plays; by Roger Elwood, ed.; Pocket 48766; c 1976 (1st); $1.95

One of TV's all time favorites, *Star Trek* lasted only three seasons originally, but its legacy seems destined to last forever. The show has spawned four sequels (*Star Trek Animated Series, Star Trek: The Next Generation, Star Trek: Deep Space Nine,* and *Star Trek: Voyager*) and eight movies to date (spanning 1979's *Star Trek: The Motion Picture* to 1996's *Star Trek: First Contact*). In hand with the above has come a vast assortment of *Star Trek* merchandise, a wide and dedicated fan network, and an ever-growing number of books.

While it would be impossible, as well as beyond the scope of this work, to list every *Star Trek* book published, the above books have been included due to their ties to the original run of the show. They include the Bantam novelizations (which adapt all 78 episodes), the Bantam Fotonovels (which, through stills done in cartoon format, novelize 12 episodes), and a few miscellaneous books.

The Bantams include 12 collections of short story novelizations by James Blish, which adapt 76 of the 78 episodes. Blish died before the last stories in *Star Trek 12* were completed; his wife, Judith A. Lawrence, finished them. The series also includes the original Blish novel *Spock Must Die!* and the Judith A. Lawrence book *Mudd's Angels* (it with the remaining two novelizations and the original story "The Business, as Usual, During Altercations"). The books were wildly successful, with many going into dozens of printings, including cover-variation subsequent printings not included here.

The book *Six Science Fiction Plays* includes Harlan Ellison's original version of his famous *Star Trek* script "City on the Edge of Forever." The script won a Writer's Guild Award for its original version, and a Hugo Award for its extensively edited filmed version. (The Writer's Guild Award is the more prestigious of the two, judging the work in its purely written form; the Hugo Award judged the collaborative effort of the filmed product, which Ellison tried to have his name removed from.) The book also includes "Sting!" (an Original Screenplay by Tom Reamy); "Contact Point" (a One-Act Play by Theodore R. Cogswell and George Rae Cogswell); "Stranger With Roses" (a

Science Fiction Entertainment in One Act by John Jakes); "The Mechanical Bride" (an Original Teleplay by Fritz Leiber); and "Let Me Hear You Whisper" (a Play by Paul Zindel).

In the wake of the first *Star Trek* movie in 1979, Pocket Books began a series of highly successful numbered *Star Trek* books. The books (which fall outside this work's scope in being published long after the original run of the show - see the Introductory section of this work for details) include novelizations of the first three *Star Trek* movies (that of the first movie being #1 in the series, that of the second movie being #7, the third being #17) interspersed with original novels. The series branched into the *Star Trek Giant Novel* series in 1986, it containing the subsequent movie novelizations interspersed with original novels in a non-numbered sequence.

STAR TREK ANIMATED SERIES
September 15, 1973 - August 30, 1975; NBC

Ballantines

_____ Star Trek Log One; by Alan Dean Foster; Ballantine 24014; c 1974 (1st); $.95 [novelization of the episodes "Beyond the Farthest Star," "Yesteryear," and "One of Our Planets is Missing"]

_____ Star Trek Log Two; by Alan Dean Foster; Ballantine 24184; c 1974 (1st); $.95 [novelization of the episodes "The Survivor," "The Lorelei Signal," and "The Infinite Vulcan"] [The book opens: "Space is not silent..."]

_____ Star Trek Log Three; by Alan Dean Foster; Ballantine 24260; c 1975 (1st); $1.25 [novelization of the episodes "Once Upon a Planet," "Mudd's Passion," and "The Magicks of Megas-Tu"]

_____ Star Trek Log Four; by Alan Dean Foster; Ballantine 24435; c 1975 (1st); $1.25 [novelization of the episodes "The Terratin Incident," "Time Trap," and "More Tribbles, More Troubles"]

_____ Star Trek Log Five; by Alan Dean Foster; Ballantine 24532; c 1975 (1st); $1.25 [novelization of the episodes "The Ambergris Element," "The Pirates of Orion," and "Jihad"]

_____ Star Trek Log Six; by Alan Dean Foster; Ballantine 24655; c 1976 (1st); $1.50 [novelization of the episodes "Albatross," "The Practical Joker," and "How Sharper Than a Serpent's Tooth"]

_____ Star Trek Log Seven; by Alan Dean Foster; Ballantine 24965; c 1976 (1st); $1.50 [novelization of the episode "The Counter-Clock Incident"]

_____ Star Trek Log Eight; by Alan Dean Foster; Ballantine 25141; c 1976 (1st); $1.50 [novelization of the episode "The Eye of the Beholder"] [FC Illus: William Shatner]

_____ Star Trek Log Nine; by Alan Dean Foster; Ballantine 25557; c 1977 (1st); $1.50 [novelization of the episode "Bem"]

_____ Star Trek Log Ten; by Alan Dean Foster; Ballantine 27212; c 1978 (1st); $1.95 [novelization of the episode "Slaver Weapon"]

Distinguished science fiction author Alan Dean Foster gained his initial reputation in part through his novelizations of several hit science fiction movies (*Star Wars, Alien*, etc.) plus the *Star Trek Animated Series*. All 22 episodes of the show are novelized in the books; books one through six novelize three episodes each, books seven through ten novelize one each. Foster was given carte blanche by the publisher and used the stories as "jumping off points" for his own original *Star Trek* material. In the latter four books in the series about three quarters of the material is his own, including an original unfilmed screenplay novelized in *Log Seven*. The covers of books one through eight include cartoon stills taken from the show; the covers of books 9 and 10, and latter printings of the first eight books, include solid color artwork.

STAR TREK: THE NEXT GENERATION
September 26, 1987 - May 23, 1994; Syndicated

Pocket Books

_____ Star Trek: The Next Generation: Encounter at Farpoint; by David Gerrold; Pocket 65241; c 1987 (1st); $3.95 [novelization of the pilot episode "Encounter at Farpoint"]

_____ Star Trek: The Next Generation #1: Ghost Ship; by Diane Carey; Pocket 66579; c 1988 (1st); $3.95 [FC Illus: Brent Spiner, Jonathan Frakes, LeVar Burton]

_____ Star Trek: The Next Generation #2: The Peacekeepers; by Gene DeWeese; Pocket 66929; c 1988 (1st); $3.95 [FC Illus: Michael Dorn, Patrick Stewart, Marina Sirtis]

_____ Star Trek: The Next Generation #3: The Children of Hamlin; by Carmen Carter; Pocket 67319; c 1988 (1st); $3.95 [FC Illus: Gatès McFadden, Stewart]

_____ Star Trek: The Next Generation #4: Survivors; by Jean Lorrah; Pocket 67438; c 1989 (1st); $3.95 [FC Illus: Denise Crosby, Spiner]

_____ Star Trek: The Next Generation #5: Strike Zone; by Peter David; Pocket 67940; c 1989 (1st); $3.95 [FC Illus: Stewart, Wil Wheaton]

_____ Star Trek: The Next Generation #6: Power Hungry; by Howard Weinstein; Pocket 67714; c 1989 (1st); $3.95 [FC Illus: Sirtis, Frakes]

_____ Star Trek: The Next Generation #7: Masks; by John Vornholt; Pocket 67980; c 1989 (1st); $3.95 [FC Illus: Frakes, Stewart]

_____ Star Trek: The Next Generation #8: The Captains' Honor; by David and Daniel Dvorkin; Pocket 68487; c 1989 (1st); $3.95 [FC Illus: Stewart, Dorn]

_____ Star Trek: The Next Generation #9: A Call to Darkness; by Michael Jan Friedman; Pocket 68708; c 1989 (1st); $3.95 [FC Illus: Diana Muldaur, Dorn, Burton]

_____ Star Trek: The Next Generation #10: A Rock and a Hard Place; by Peter David; Pocket 69364; c 1990 (1st); $3.95 [FC Illus: Sirtis, Frakes]

The slick sequel inspired the long-running series of books by Pocket, including original novels in a numbered sequence (numbers 1 through 10 were published up to 1990, this bibliography's cut-off date), and non-numbered novelizations (including that of the pilot episode "Encounter at Farpoint" - the only pre-1990 entry). The series branched into *The Next Generation Giant Novel* series in 1990.

THE STARLOST
1973 - 1974; Syndicated

_____ The Starlost: Phoenix Without Ashes; by Edward Bryant & Harlan Ellison; Fawcett Gold Medal M3188; c 1975 (1st); $.95 [novelization of the pilot episode "The Starlost"]

Canadian show inspired the above novelization of creator Harlan Ellison's pilot script. While the script won a Writer's Guild Award, the resulting teleplay and series was "turned into a nightmare" in Ellison's words, causing him to bail out early and only 17 episodes to be produced.

STARSKY AND HUTCH
September 10, 1975 - August 21, 1979; ABC

Ballantines

_____ Starsky and Hutch; by Max Franklin [Richard Deming]; Ballantine 24996; c 1975 (1st: 1976); $1.50 [novelization of the TV-movie pilot "Starsky and Hutch" (Apr-30-1975)] [FC Photo: David Soul, Paul Michael Glaser]

_____ Starsky and Hutch #2: Kill Huggy Bear; by Max Franklin [Richard Deming]; Ballantine 25124; c 1976 (1st); $1.50 [novelization of the episode "Kill Huggy Bear"] [FC Photo: Glaser, Soul]

_____ Starsky and Hutch #3: Death Ride; by Max Franklin [Richard Deming]; Ballantine 23921; c 1976 (1st); $1.50 [novelization of the episode "Death Ride"] [FC Photo: Glaser, Soul]

_____ Starsky and Hutch #4: Bounty Hunter; by Max Franklin [Richard Deming]; Ballantine 25669; c 1977 (1st); $1.50 [novelization of the episode "Bounty Hunter"] [FC Photo: Glaser, Soul]

_____ Starsky and Hutch #5: Terror on the Docks; by Max Franklin [Richard Deming]; Ballantine 25709; c 1977 (1st); $1.50 [novelization of the episode "Terror on the Docks"] [FC Photo: Soul, Glaser]

_____ Starsky and Hutch #6: The Psychic; by Max Franklin [Richard Deming];
Ballantine 25710; c 1977 (1st); $1.50 [novelization of the episode "The
Psychic"] [FC Photo: Soul, Glaser]

_____ Starsky and Hutch #7: The Set-Up; by Max Franklin [Richard Deming];
Ballantine 27340; c 1978 (1st); $1.75 [novelization of the episode "The Set-Up"]
[FC Photo: Glaser, Soul]

_____ Starsky and Hutch #8; by Max Franklin [Richard Deming]; Ballantine 27341;
c 1978 (1st); $1.75 [novelization of the episode "Starsky and Hutch on Playboy
Island"] [FC Photo: Soul, Glaser]

Buddy cop show paired the streetwise Starsky with the soft-spoken Hutch
and inspired eight Ballantine novelizations, by Richard Deming as Max
Franklin.

STOREFRONT LAWYERS
September 16, 1970 - September 1, 1971; CBS

_____ Storefront Lawyers; by A.L. Conroy; Bantam S5883; c 1970 (1st); $.75
[novelization of the pilot episode "A Man's Castle"]

STRANGE PARADISE
1969; Syndicated

Paperback Librarys

_____ Strange Paradise #1; by Dorothy Daniels; Paperback Library 63-259; c 1969
(1st); $.60 [FC Photo: Colin Fox]

_____ Strange Paradise #2: Island of Evil; by Dorothy Daniels; Paperback Library
63-321; c 1970 (1st); $.60 [FC Photo: Fox; BC Photo: Kurt Schiegl]

_____ Strange Paradise #3: Raxl, Voodoo Priestess; by Dorothy Daniels; Paperback
Library 63-365; c 1970 (1st); $.60 [FC Photo: Cosette Lee, Schiegl]

A takeoff of *Dark Shadows*, this short-lived soap inspired three books by
prolific Gothic novelist Dorothy Daniels. The books, original stories set during
the first few weeks of the show, were written in collaboration with her husband
Norman Daniels. The two collaborated frequently, under both bylines, in
addition to writing separately.

STRANGE REPORT
January 8, 1971 - September 10, 1971; NBC

_____ Strange Report; by John Burke; Lancer 73219; c 1970 (1st); $.60 [FC Photo:
Anthony Quayle]

SURFSIDE 6
October 3, 1960 - September 24, 1962; ABC

_____ SurfSide 6; by J.M. Flynn; Dell First Edition 8388; c 1962 (1st); $.40 [BC Photo: Margarita Sierra, Troy Donahue, Lee Patterson, Diane McBain, Van Williams]

An additional *SurfSide 6* book was written by Talmage Powell for Whitman Books, but wasn't published due to the cancellation of the show.

SWITCH
September 9, 1975 - September 3, 1978; CBS

Berkleys

_____ Switch; by Mike Jahn; Berkley Z3082; c 1976 (1st); $1.25 [novelization of the TV-movie pilot "Switch" (Mar-21-1975)] [FC Photos: Robert Wagner, Eddie Albert]

_____ Switch #2: Round Up the Usual Suspects; by Mike Jahn; Berkley Z3252; c 1976 (1st); $1.25 [novelization of the episode "Round Up the Usual Suspects"] [FC Photo: Albert, Wagner]

TALES FROM THE DARKSIDE
1984 - 1989; Syndicated

_____ Tales From the Darkside, Vol. 1; by Mitchell Galin and Tom Allen, eds.; Berkley 11095; c 1988 (1st); $3.50

Horror anthology series by the producers of *Night of the Living Dead* inspired the above tie-in. The book includes 5 short story novelizations by Michael McDowell based on teleplays ("The Devil's Advocate," "Inside the Closet," "Halloween Candy," "In the Cards," and "The Odds") interspersed with 11 original stories that became episodes ("The Word Processor of the Gods" [by Stephen King], "A Case of the Stubborns" [Robert Bloch], "Printer's Devil" [Ron Goulart], "Levitation" [Joseph Payne Brennan], "The Satanic Piano" [Carl Jacobi], "Slippage" [Michael P. Kube-McDowell], "The Shrine" [Pamela Sargent], "The Bitterest Pill" [Frederik Pohl], "Hush!" [Zenna Henderson], "The Circus" [Sydney J. Bounds], and "Distant Signals" [Andrew Weiner]).

TALES OF THE UNEXPECTED
See ROALD DAHL'S TALES OF THE UNEXPECTED

TALES OF WELLS FARGO
March 18, 1957 - September 8, 1962; NBC

_____ Wells Fargo and Danger Station; by Sam Allison [Noel Loomis]; Whitman 1588; c 1958 (1st) [FC Illus: Robertson]

_____ Tales of Wells Fargo; by Frank Gruber; Bantam 1726; c 1958 (1st); $.25 [BC Photo: Dale Robertson] [*]

[*] 8 short story novelizations: "Billy the Kid," "The Auction," "Belle Star," "The Vigilantes," "Sam Bass," "The Glory Hole," "John Wesley Hardin," and "Doc Bell."

TAMMY
September 17, 1965 - July 15, 1966; ABC

_____ Tammy Tell Me True; by Cid Ricketts Sumner; Popular Library 50-439; c 1959 (unsp: 1965); $.50 [FC Illus: Sandra Dee]

_____ Tammy in Rome; by Cid Ricketts Sumner; Popular Library SP423; c 1965 (1st); $.50

The show was based on the *Tammy* movies and Cid Ricketts Sumner novels. Sumner created the character in her 1948 book *Tammy Out of Time*; it inspired the 1957 Debbie Reynolds movie *Tammy and the Bachelor*. Next came Sumner's 1959 book *Tammy Tell Me True*; it inspired that 1961 movie and was issued the same year by Popular Library (PC1007). Sandra Dee starred, and is pictured on the cover. A third *Tammy* movie was made in 1963, the Dee-starrer *Tammy and the Doctor*, but no corresponding book was written. The TV show *Tammy* aired from 1965-66, with Popular Library re-issuing *Tammy Tell Me True* as a TV tie-in at the time (the cover still pictures Sandra Dee, though the show starred Debbie Watson). Sumner's third and final Tammy book, *Tammy in Rome*, was also issued at the time, and while it doesn't mention the show it's considered an inferred TV tie-in. It does mention "soon to be a major motion picture" on the cover, but no such movie was made. Followed the show came the fourth and final *Tammy* movie, 1967's *Tammy and the Millionaire*; it starred Debbie Watson from the show, and original episodes were used to produce it.

TARZAN
September 8, 1966 - September 13, 1968; NBC

_____ Tarzan of the Apes; by Edgar Rice Burroughs; Ballantine U2001; c 1912 (3rd: 1966); $.50 [FC Photo: Ron Ely]

_____ The Return of Tarzan; by Edgar Rice Burroughs; Ballantine U2002; c 1913 (3rd: 1967); $.50 [FC Photo: Ely]

The show was the result of a half-century of *Tarzan* movies and Edgar Rice Burroughs novels. Burroughs created the character in the 1912 story "Tarzan of the Apes," which was an overnight success and empire-launcher. He registered Tarzan as a trademark the following year, and wrote four more *Tarzan* books before the character was first brought to film, in 1918's silent movie *Tarzan of the Apes*. The character inspired dozens of additional movies, a comic book series, a newspaper strip, and a radio series all prior to the TV show. (Burroughs died in 1950; much of the Tarzan phenomenon was in his legacy.) In 1963, Ballantine began a series of highly successful Burroughs paperbacks, including the complete *Tarzan* series along with the complete *Mars* science fiction series Burroughs also wrote. The series continued through the run of the TV show, and includes two books with show-mention: *Tarzan of the Apes* and *The Return of Tarzan*. Both have photo covers of Ron Ely and banners mentioning the NBC Friday Night Program. A Canadian issue of *The Return of Tarzan* has the same photo as the American issue, but its banner mentions the CBC Saturday Night Program.

THAT GIRL
September 8, 1966 - September 10, 1971; ABC

_____ That Girl; by Paul W. Fairman; Popular Library 02588; c 1971 (1st); $.60 [FC Photo: Marlo Thomas]

Perky Ann Marie becomes an endangered maiden trapped in a haunted mansion in the windy Maine wilderness in this Gothic *That Girl* novel.

THAT'S INCREDIBLE!
March 3, 1980 - April 30, 1984; ABC

Joves

_____ That's Incredible! Vol. 1; by Wendy Jeffries, ed.; Jove B5807; c 1980 (1st); $2.25

_____ That's Incredible! Vol. 2; by Wendy Jeffries, ed.; Jove B5870; c 1981 (1st); $2.25

_____ That's Incredible! Vol. 3; by Wendy Jeffries, ed.; Jove B5986; c 1981 (1st); $2.25

_____ That's Incredible! Vol. 4; by Wendy Jeffries, ed.; Jove 06171; c 1981 (1st); $2.50

_____ That's Incredible! Vol. 5; by Wendy Jeffries, ed.; Jove 06172; c 1981 (1st); $2.50

_____ That's Incredible! Vol. 6; by Wendy Jeffries, ed.; Jove 06173; c 1981 (1st); $2.50

THEN CAME BRONSON
September 17, 1969 - September 9, 1970; NBC

Pyramids

_____ Then Came Bronson; by William Johnston; Pyramid T-2106; c 1969 (1st); $.75 [FC Photo: Michael Parks]

_____ Then Came Bronson #2: The Ticket; by Chris Stratton [Richard Hubbard]; Pyramid T-2213; c 1970 (1st); $.75 [FC Photo: Parks]

_____ Then Came Bronson #3: Rock!; by Chris Stratton [Richard Hubbard]; Pyramid T2259; c 1970 (1st); $.75 [FC Photo: Parks]

Michael Parks is pictured as drifter Jim Bronson--on his red Harley Sportster--on these three Pyramid tie-ins.

THE THIRD MAN
1959 - 1962; Syndicated

_____   The Third Man; by Graham Greene; Bantam J2427; c 1949,50 (1st new Bantam: 1962); $.40

> The show was based 1949 novel by Graham Greene, which had also inspired the 1949 movie and 1950's radio series. First published by Bantam as a movie tie-in in 1950 (#797), the book was re-issued as a TV tie-in with the show.

THIS MAN DAWSON
1959 - 1960; Syndicated

_____   This Man Dawson; by Henry E. Helseth; Signet S2109; c 1962 (1st); $.35

THUNDER
September 10, 1977 - September 2, 1978; NBC

_____   Thunder: The Mighty Stallion of the Hills; by Mike Jahn; Tempo 14893; c 1978 (1st); $1.25

_____   Thunder: The Mighty Stallion to the Rescue; by Mike Jahn; Tempo 14894; c 1979 (1st); $1.25 [FC Photo: Randi Justin, Melora Hardin]

THE TIME TUNNEL
September 9, 1966 - September 1, 1967; ABC

Pyramids

_____   The Time Tunnel [illustrated cover]; by Murray Leinster [Will F. Jenkins]; Pyramid R-1522; c 1966 (1st: 1967); $.50 [BC Photo: James Darren, Robert Colbert]

_____   The Time Tunnel [photo cover]; by Murray Leinster [Will F. Jenkins]; Pyramid R-1522; c 1966 (1st: 1967); $.50 [FC Photo: Darren; BC Photo: Darren, Colbert]

_____   The Time Tunnel #2: Timeslip!; by Murray Leinster [Will F. Jenkins]; Pyramid R-1680; c 1967 (1st); $.50 [FC Photo: Darren, Colbert, Lee Meriwether]

> Intelligent use of historical detail enlivens Murray Leinster's written versions of the *Time Tunnel* saga. In the books, the captive travelers visit such historical events as the Johnstown Floods, and such personages as Bat Masterson.
> The book *The Time Tunnel's* two cover-variations include the same back cover, book number, and January of 1967 issue dates, but different front covers. The photo cover version includes a photo from the TV show; the illustrated cover version includes the same illustration as found on the cover of an entirely separate *Time Tunnel* book. Published also by Pyramid and written also by Murray Leinster, but simply entitled "Time Tunnel," it, the separate book, was

copyrighted and first printed in 1964, and includes four identical printings (as R-1043) through April of 1967. Its copyright is held by Will F. Jenkins--the real person behind the Murray Leinster pseudonym--while the 1966 copyright of the TV tie-in version is held by Twentieth-Century Fox. Cover artist Jack Gaughan is credited for both covers, even though the one is a photo from the show.

TOMA
October 4, 1973 - September 6, 1974; ABC

Dells

_____ Toma; by David Toma with Michael Brett; Dell 08520; c 1973 (1st: 1974); $1.25

_____ Toma #2: The Airport Affair; by David Toma and Jack Pearl; Dell 04604; c 1975 (1st); $1.25

_____ Toma #3: The Affair of the Unhappy Hooker; by David Toma and Jack Pearl; Dell 05284; c 1976 (1st); $1.50

The show was based on the real-life experiences of David Toma, the Newark Police Detective who mastered the art of disguise. The above books were co-authored by Toma and drawn from his personal experiences.

THE TONIGHT SHOW STARRING JOHNNY CARSON
October 2, 1962 - May 22, 1992; NBC

_____ Happiness is a Dry Martini; by Johnny Carson; Crest T1217; c 1965 (1st: 1968); $.75 [FC Photo: Johnny Carson]

_____ and now... Here's Johnny!; by Nora Ephron; Avon V2251; c 1968 (1st); $.75 [FC Photo: Carson]

_____ Tonight!; by Terry Galanoy; Warner 76-367; c 1972 (1st: 1974); $1.25 [FC Photos: (from top) Johnny Carson, Jack Paar, Steve Allen, Jack Lescoulie]

_____ He-e-e-ere's Johnny; by Robert Lardine; Award AD1425; c 1975 (1st); $1.50 [FC Photo: Carson]

_____ Johnny Tonight!; by Craig Tennis; Pocket 41451; c 1980 (1st); $2.50 [FC Photo: Carson]

_____ Carson: The Unauthorized Biography; by Paul Corkery; Randt 942101; c 1987 (1st); $3.95 [FC Photo: Carson]

_____ King of the Night: The Life of Johnny Carson; by Laurence Leamer; St. Martin's Press 92256; c 1989 (1st: 1990); $5.95 [FC Photo: Carson]

_____ Ed McMahon's Barside Companion; by J.P. Tarcher, ed.; Pocket 77215; c 1969 (1st: 1970); $.95 [FC Photo: Ed McMahon]

_____ Grin and Beer It; by Ed McMahon; Pyramid N4101; c 1976 (1st); $.95 [FC Photo: McMahon]

_____ Here's Ed; by Ed McMahon; Berkley 03592; c 1976 (1st: 1977); $1.95 [FC Photo: McMahon]

Biographies and books of humor were issued during Johnny Carson's 30-year reign as host of *The Tonight Show*, then called *The Tonight Show Starring Johnny Carson*. Carson retired in 1992, giving the keys to Jay Leno. (See also *The Jack Paar Tonight Show*.)

TRIALS OF O'BRIEN
September 18, 1965 - May 18, 1966; CBS

_____ Trials of O'Brien; by Robert L. Fish; Signet D2821; c 1965 (1st); $.50 [FC Photos: Peter Falk]

TWELVE O'CLOCK HIGH
September 18, 1964 - January 13, 1967; ABC

_____ Twelve O'Clock High!; by Beirne Lay, Jr. and Sy Bartlett; Ballantine U5041; c 1948 (1st: 1965); $.60

The show was based on the 1949 movie, which in turn was based on the 1948 book, re-issued by Ballantine as a TV tie-in in 1965. The book was based on the experiences of the co-authors, who served in the U.S. Air Force during World War II.

TWENTY-ONE
September 12, 1956 - October 16, 1958; NBC

_____ Twenty-One; Pyramid G322; c 1957 (1st: 1958); $.35 [FC Photo: Jack Barry] [Introduction by Jack Barry]

This book was issued prior to the infamous quiz show scandals that brought about the show's cancellation. The scandals--which broke when it was revealed that contestants were being provided the answers to the questions by the show's producers--were re-enacted in the 1994 movie *Quiz Show*. Of the scandals, director Robert Redford told *Interview Magazine*: "I see them as the first in a series of downward steps in the loss of [this country's] innocence ... The shocks kept coming: Jack Kennedy's death, Bobby's death, Martin Luther King ... Watergate ... Iran-Contra, S. &. L., ... and now O.J. ... In a historical context, [the quiz show scandals] are very much a big deal."

THE TWILIGHT ZONE
October 2, 1959 - September 18, 1964; CBS

Bantams

_____ Stories From the Twilight Zone; by Rod Serling; Bantam A2046; c 1960 (1st); $.35 [FC Photo: Rod Serling] [novelizations "The Mighty Casey," "Escape Clause," "Walking Distance," "The Fever," "Where is Everybody?" (from the pilot episode), and "The Monsters are Due on Maple Street"]

_____ More Stories From the Twilight Zone; by Rod Serling; Bantam A2227; c 1961 (1st); $.35 [FC Photos: Serling] [novelizations "The Lonely," "Mr. Dingle, the Strong," "A Thing About Machines," "The Big, Tall Wish," "A Stop at Willoughby," "The Odyssey of Flight 33," and "Dust"]

_____ New Stories From the Twilight Zone; by Rod Serling; Bantam A2412; c 1962 (1st); $.35 [FC Photo: Serling] [novelizations "The Whole Truth," "The Shelter," "Showdown with Rance McGrew," "The Night of the Meek," "The Midnight Sun," and "The Rip Van Winkle Caper"]

Tempos

_____ Chilling Stories From Rod Serling's The Twilight Zone; by Walter B. Gibson; Tempo T89; c 1963 (1st: 1965); $.95 [stories "The Ghost of Ticonderoga," "Back There" (N), "Judgment Night" (N), "The Curse of Seven Towers," "The Avenging Ghost," "Return From Oblivion," "The House on the Square," "Death's Masquerade," "The Riddle of the Crypt," and "Dead Man's Chest"]

_____ Rod Serling's Twilight Zone Revisited; by Walter B. Gibson; Tempo T-171; c 1964 (1st: 1967); $.50 [BC Photo: Serling] [stories "Two Live Ghosts," "The Ghost of Dixie Belle," "The Purple Testament" (N), "The Ghost Train," "Beyond the Rim" (N - from the episode "A Hundred Yards Over the Rim"), "The Ghost of Jolly Roger," "The Man in the Bottle" (N), "The Mirror Image" (N), and "The Man Who Dropped By"]

Rod Serling's classic sci-fi anthology inspired the above books. The Bantams are collections of Serling's own short story novelizations of a selection of his teleplays. (He wrote over half the show's teleplays, in addition to producing and narrating it.) The Tempos are collections of short stories by Walter B. Gibson, creator of *The Shadow*. The Gibson stories include six novelizations of Serling-penned episodes (those coded "N" above) and 13 original ghost stories written for the juvenile market.

UFO
1970 - 1972; Syndicated

Warners

_____ UFO-1: Flesh Hunters; by Robert Miall [John Burke]; Warner 75-273; c 1970 (1st: 1973); $.95 [novelization of the episodes "Identified" (pilot), "Exposed," "Close-Up," and "Court Martial"] [FC Photo: Michael Billington; BC Photos: Ed Bishop, Gabrielle Drake, Billington]

_____ UFO-2: Sporting Blood; by Robert Miall [John Burke]; Warner 75-274; c 1971 (1st: 1973); $.95 [novelization of the episodes "The Computer Affair," "The Dalotek Affair," and "Survival"] [BC Photos: Bishop, Drake, Billington]

Underrated British series about aliens--noted for its imaginative stories, ahead-of-its-time special effects, and believable characters both alien and real--remains a popular favorite.

THE UGLIEST GIRL IN TOWN
September 26, 1968 - January 30, 1969; ABC

____   The Ugliest Girl in Town; by Burt Hirschfeld; Popular Library 60-2340; c 1968
(1st); $.60 [FC Photos: (top) Peter Kastner, (bottom) Patricia Brake, Kastner]

Flop about a talent agent who to his own surprise finds himself donning
women's clothing inspired the above book, with star Peter Kastner pictured in
and out of drag on the cover.

THE UNTOUCHABLES
October 15, 1959 - September 10, 1963; ABC

Popular Librarys

____   The Untouchables; by Eliot Ness with Oscar Fraley; Popular Library G403; c
1957 (1st: 1960); $.35

____   The Untouchables [cover-variation]; by Eliot Ness with Oscar Fraley; Popular
Library SP258; c 1957 (unsp: 1964); $.50

____   The Untouchables: 4 Against the Mob; by Oscar Fraley; Popular Library G512;
c 1961 (1st); $.35

____   The Last of the Untouchables; by Oscar Fraley with Paul Robsky; Popular
Library G569; c 1962 (1st); $.35

The show was based on the 1957 book, co-authored by Eliot Ness and
Oscar Fraley and based on Ness' experiences as the Prohibition-era Justice
Department official who battled the Chicago mob with the help of his agents,
"The Untouchables." The book was issued by Popular Library twice with the
show. Fraley also wrote *4 Against the Mob* (about the life of Eliot Ness), and
co-wrote (with Paul Robsky) *The Last of the Untouchables* (in which Robsky,
the last surviving member of The Untouchables, tells "the sensational story Eliot
Ness couldn't reveal"). The books were later re-issued by Award.

V
October 26, 1984 - July 5, 1985; NBC

Pinnacles

____   V; by A.C. Crispin; Pinnacle 42237; c 1984 (1st); $2.95 [novelization of the
two mini-series]

____   V: East Coast Crisis; by Howard Weinstein and A.C. Crispin; Pinnacle 42259;
c 1984 (1st); $2.95

____   V: The Pursuit of Diana; by Allen Wold; Pinnacle 42401; c 1984 (1st); $2.95
[FC Photo: Marc Singer, Jane Badler]

____   V: The Chicago Conversion; by Geo. W. Proctor; Pinnacle 42429; c 1985 (1st);
$2.95

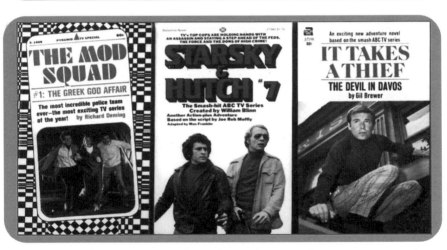

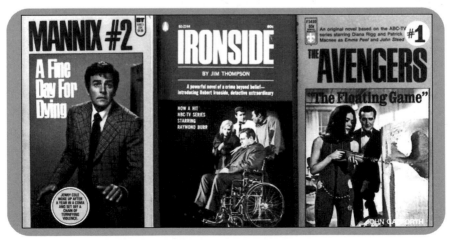

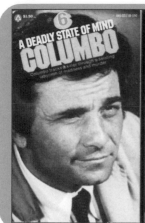

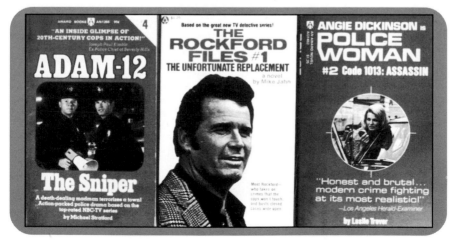

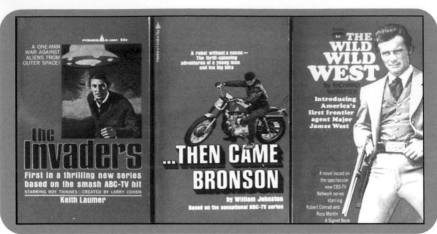

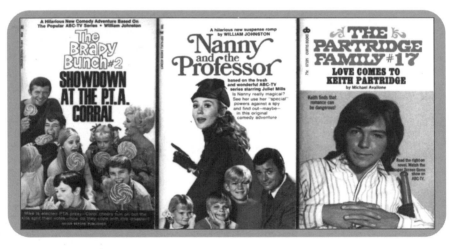

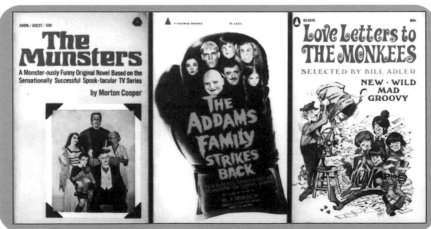

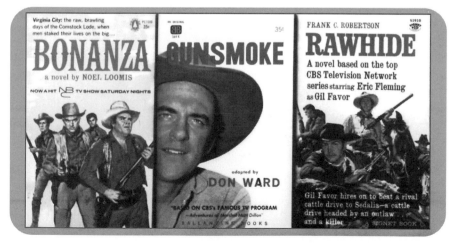

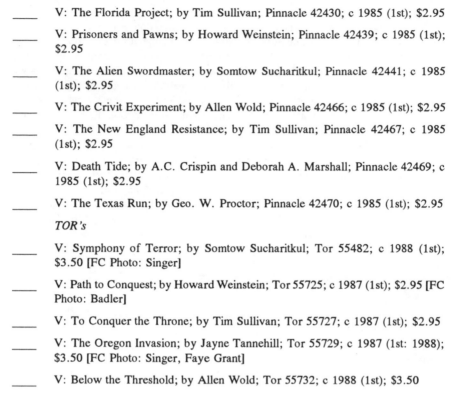

_____ V: The Florida Project; by Tim Sullivan; Pinnacle 42430; c 1985 (1st); $2.95

_____ V: Prisoners and Pawns; by Howard Weinstein; Pinnacle 42439; c 1985 (1st); $2.95

_____ V: The Alien Swordmaster; by Somtow Sucharitkul; Pinnacle 42441; c 1985 (1st); $2.95

_____ V: The Crivit Experiment; by Allen Wold; Pinnacle 42466; c 1985 (1st); $2.95

_____ V: The New England Resistance; by Tim Sullivan; Pinnacle 42467; c 1985 (1st); $2.95

_____ V: Death Tide; by A.C. Crispin and Deborah A. Marshall; Pinnacle 42469; c 1985 (1st); $2.95

_____ V: The Texas Run; by Geo. W. Proctor; Pinnacle 42470; c 1985 (1st); $2.95

TOR's

_____ V: Symphony of Terror; by Somtow Sucharitkul; Tor 55482; c 1988 (1st); $3.50 [FC Photo: Singer]

_____ V: Path to Conquest; by Howard Weinstein; Tor 55725; c 1987 (1st); $2.95 [FC Photo: Badler]

_____ V: To Conquer the Throne; by Tim Sullivan; Tor 55727; c 1987 (1st); $2.95

_____ V: The Oregon Invasion; by Jayne Tannehill; Tor 55729; c 1987 (1st: 1988); $3.50 [FC Photo: Singer, Faye Grant]

_____ V: Below the Threshold; by Allen Wold; Tor 55732; c 1988 (1st); $3.50

The show about alien invaders was introduced in two highly successful mini-series: "V" aired May 1-2, 1983; the sequel "V: The Final Battle" aired May 6-8, 1984. After the first mini-series, Pinnacle Books hired Ann Crispin to write a *V* novelization; the book covered both mini-series and its distribution coincided with the airing of the sequel.

After the success of the sequel, NBC began production on a weekly series, slating it for release in the fall of 1984. Pinnacle signed several authors to write additional *V* books, targeting them for distribution during the show's first season. The books are original stories, using either the characters created for the show or simply using the *V* format--in such settings as Japan and Oregon-- with the author's own characters. The books were released under an odd combination of Pinnacle and TOR, whereby TOR handled the creative and editorial side and Pinnacle the publishing and distribution. After the first eleven books were done, Pinnacle had financial troubles and filed for bankruptcy, which tied things up a couple of years. The rights for the remaining unpublished novels reverted to TOR, and since the writers had already been paid and the books typeset, TOR apparently tried to recoup some of that investment by publishing the books, even though the show had been canceled.

Of *East Coast Crisis*, co-author Howard Weinstein notes: "We were asked to do a sort-of sequel to the two mini-series, but we couldn't step on the toes of the upcoming weekly series. This put us in a somewhat difficult spot--

how to do a story that takes place during the same time period as the two mini-series but without being overly repetitive. So we opted for a parallel tale using a new set of characters on the East Coast, with 'guest appearances' by some of the TV characters. The mini-series had to be largely action-adventure, so we took the opportunity to deal with the 'real-life' aspects of the Visitors' occupation--what went on at the U.N., the White House, the TV networks, etc. We also wove in some real-life characters such as Dan Rather and Isaac Asimov..."

Weinstein adds: "I envisioned the show much like the 60's World War II drama *Combat*, focusing on a small band of heroes fighting the enemy, interacting with other resistance groups as well as civilians on both sides of the front lines. That's what I tried to do with *Path to Conquest*, but by the time I wrote that, it was almost certain the show wouldn't be renewed, so I pulled out all the stops and wrote the kind of broad-scope story I thought the producers should have been doing."

VEGA$
September 20, 1978 - September 16, 1981; ABC

____   Vega$; by Max Franklin [Richard Deming]; Ballantine 28051; c 1978 (1st); $1.75 [novelization of the TV-movie pilot "Vega$" (Apr-25-1978)] [FC Photo: Robert Urich]

THE VIRGINIAN
September 19, 1962 - September 9, 1970; NBC

Paperback Librarys

____   The Virginian; by Owen Wister; Paperback Library 53-190; c 1902 (1st: 1963); $.60 [*]

____   The Virginian; by Owen Wister; Paperback Library 53-908; c 1902 (2nd: 1965); $.60 [*]

   [*] First and second printings are nearly identical, but include different colored title lettering and other cover attributes.

____   The Virginian; by Owen Wister; Paperback Library 64-405; c 1902 (3rd: 1970); $.75

Magnum

____   The Virginian; by Owen Wister; Magnum 14642; c 1902 (1st: 1970); $.75

Owen Wister's landmark novel was "one of America's all time best sellers, a Broadway hit for ten years, a box office smash four times as a movie, [and] now an exciting TV series" - this from the back covers of the above Paperback Library editions of the book. The book was issued extensively since it was first published; the above editions were issued at the time of the show and mention it on the covers. In 1970 the show was renamed *The Men From Shiloh* (see also it), and inspired a Lancer tie-in under that name.

VOYAGE TO THE BOTTOM OF THE SEA
September 14, 1964 - September 15, 1968; ABC

Pyramids

_____ Voyage to the Bottom of the Sea; by Theodore Sturgeon; Pyramid R-1068; c 1961 (2nd: 1964); $.50 [novelization of the 1961 movie] [FC Photo: David Hedison (left), Richard Basehart (right)]

_____ Voyage to the Bottom of the Sea: City Under the Sea; by Paul W. Fairman; Pyramid R-1162; c 1965 (1st); $.50 [original story]

Whitman

_____ Voyage to the Bottom of the Sea; by Raymond F. Jones; Whitman 1517; c 1965 (1st)

The show was based on the 1961 movie, novelized by Theodore Sturgeon in the 1961 book. Published that year by Pyramid as a movie tie-in (G622), it was re-issued as a TV tie-in with the show.

VOYAGERS!
October 3, 1982 - July 31, 1983; NBC

_____ Voyagers!; by Joe Claro; Scholastic Book Services 32740; c 1982 (1st) [novelization of the pilot episode "Voyagers!"] [FC Photo: Meeno Peluce, Jon-Erik Hexum]

Book's cover pictures star John-Erik Hexum, killed in 1984 in a freak accident while filming his subsequent series *Cover-Up*. Apparently to show off, he put a gun loaded with blanks to his head and pulled the trigger; the impact shattered his skull, and a week later he died.

THE WACKIEST SHIP IN THE ARMY
September 19, 1965 - September 4, 1966; NBC

_____ The Wackiest Ship in the Army; by Lee Bergman; Popular Library PC1056; c 1965 (1st); $.50

WAGON TRAIN
September 18, 1957 - September 5, 1965; NBC/ABC

Pockets

_____ Wagon Train: Wagonmaster; by Robert Turner; Pocket 1196; c 1958 (1st); $.25 [FC Illus: Ward Bond]

_____ Wagon Train: The Scout; by Robert Turner; Pocket 1216; c 1958 (1st); $.25 [FC Illus: Robert Horton]

_____ Wagons West!; by Robert Turner; Pocket 1226; c 1959 (1st); $.25 [FC Illus: Horton (left), Bond (right)]

Whitman

____ Wagon Train ["Authorized TV Edition" logo on front cover]; by Troy Nesbit [Franklin Folsom]; Whitman 1567; c 1959 (1st) [FC Illus: Bond, Horton]

____ Wagon Train ["Authorized TV Adventure" logo on spine]; by Troy Nesbit [Franklin Folsom]; Whitman 1567; c 1959 (1st) [FC Illus: Bond, Horton]

Show about the American settlers heading west inspired the above books. The book *Wagonmaster* pictures Ward Bond, who played Major Seth Adams in the TV show until his death in 1960. Bond had also starred--as Elder Wiggs--in the 1950 movie *Wagonmaster*, upon which the show was based.

WALT DISNEY
October 27, 1954 - September 24, 1983; ABC/NBC/CBS

____ The Walt Disney Story of Our Friend the Atom; by Heinz Haber, Ph.D.; Dell First Edition B104; c 1956 (1st); $.35 [re-issued as #LB117]

[Book inspired and was issued in conjunction with the Jan-23-1957 episode "Our Friend the Atom." Foreword by Walt Disney.]

____ The Story of Walt Disney; by Diane Disney Miller as told to Pete Martin; Dell D266; c 1956,57 (1st: 1959); $.35 [FC Illus: Walt Disney]

[Biography of Walt Disney--who "arrived in Hollywood in 1923 with $40 in his pocket"--was co-written by his daughter Diane Disney Miller.]

____ Walt Disney's Andy Burnett on Trial; by Charles I. Coombs; Whitman Big Little Book 1645; c 1958 (1st) [FC Illus: Jerome Courtland]

[Issued in conjunction with Disney's 6-episode "Saga of Andy Burnett" series, which aired during the 1957-58 season.]

____ The Life of Davy Crockett; by Davy Crockett; Signet S1214; c 1955 (1st); $.35

[Issued in conjunction with Disney's 1954-55 season, 5-episode "Davy Crockett" series. Back cover notes: "Everyone ... who has thrilled to Davy Crockett's colorful adventures will marvel at ... the hero's wonderful story as he himself tells it." While the authorship is credited to Crockett--he lived from 1786 to 1836 and kept extensive journals--the Historical Note questions if he was the true author of all the contents.]

____ Legends of Davy Crockett; by Ardis Edwards Burton; Whitman 1619; c 1955 (1st) [FC Illus: Fess Parker]

[Includes 5 stories--"The Creek War," "I Get Into Politics," "The Alamo," "Davy Crockett and Mike Fink," and "Davy Crockett and the Pirates"-- "based on Walt Disney's television films and the motion picture DAVY CROCKETT, KING OF THE WILD FRONTIER with Fess Parker." The show's *Davy Crockett* episodes, adapted into the above stories, provided the basis for two movies: 1955's *Davy Crockett, King of the Wild Frontier* and 1956's *Davy Crockett and the River Pirates*.]

The *Walt Disney* TV show played under several different names (*Disneyland, Walt Disney Presents, Walt Disney's Wonderful World of Color, The Wonderful World of Disney, Disney's Wonderful World,* and *Walt Disney*) and was carried at various times on all three major networks. A series of books by Pyramid in the 1970's, which novelize the Disney feature films, TV-films, and specials, is considered beyond the scope of this work.

THE WALTONS
September 14, 1972 - August 20, 1981; CBS

Earl Hamner Titles

_____ Spencer's Mountain; by Earl Hamner, Jr.; Dell 08180; c 1961 (1st new Dell: 1973); $.95

_____ The Homecoming; by Earl Hamner, Jr.; Avon 15149; c 1970 (1st: 1973); $.95 [FC Photo: Michael Learned, Mary Elizabeth McDonough, Jon Walmsley, Judy Norton, Richard Thomas, Will Geer, Ellen Corby, Kami Cotler, David W. Harper, Eric Scott]

_____ The Homecoming [cover-variation]; by Earl Hamner, Jr.; Avon 15149; c 1970 (3rd: 1973); $.95 [FC Photo: Thomas]

Bantams

_____ The Waltons; by Robert Weverka; Bantam NP6302; c 1974 (1st); $.95 [novelization of the episodes "The Reunion" and "The Love Story"] [FC Illus: (top) Geer, (middle) Corby, Walmsley, McDonough, Cotler, Thomas, Learned, Ralph Waite, (seated in front) Scott, Norton, Harper]

_____ The Waltons: Trouble on the Mountain; by Robert Weverka; Bantam N2280; c 1975 (1st); $.95 [novelization of the episodes "The Typewriter" and "The Separation"] [FC Illus: Learned, Thomas, Waite]

_____ The Waltons: The Easter Story; by Robert Weverka; Bantam Q2411; c 1976 (1st); $1.25 [novelization of the episode "The Crisis" aka "An Easter Story"] [FC Illus: Learned, Waite] [variant 3rd printing has ad for Borden Cheese on the cover]

_____ The Walton Family Cookbook; Sylvia Resnick; Bantam TE2123; c 1975 (1st: 1976); $1.50 [FC Illus: same as on "The Waltons" - NP6302]

Whitmans

_____ The Waltons #1: The Bird Dog; by Dion Henderson; Whitman 1516; c 1975 (1st) [FC Illus: Harper]

_____ The Waltons #2: The Puzzle; by Carl Henry Rathjen; Whitman 1576; c 1975 (1st) [FC Illus: Thomas, Walmsley, McDonough]

_____ The Waltons #3: The Penny Sale; by Gladys Baker Bond; Whitman 1599; c 1975 (1st) [FC Illus: McDonough, Norton, Thomas]

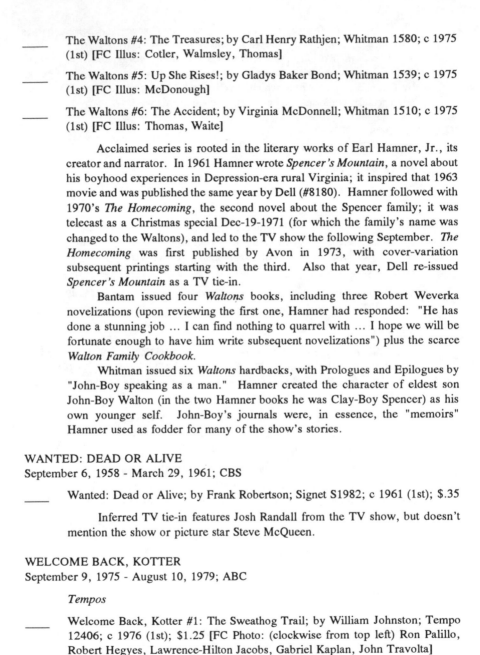

_____ The Waltons #4: The Treasures; by Carl Henry Rathjen; Whitman 1580; c 1975 (1st) [FC Illus: Cotler, Walmsley, Thomas]

_____ The Waltons #5: Up She Rises!; by Gladys Baker Bond; Whitman 1539; c 1975 (1st) [FC Illus: McDonough]

_____ The Waltons #6: The Accident; by Virginia McDonnell; Whitman 1510; c 1975 (1st) [FC Illus: Thomas, Waite]

Acclaimed series is rooted in the literary works of Earl Hamner, Jr., its creator and narrator. In 1961 Hamner wrote *Spencer's Mountain*, a novel about his boyhood experiences in Depression-era rural Virginia; it inspired that 1963 movie and was published the same year by Dell (#8180). Hamner followed with 1970's *The Homecoming*, the second novel about the Spencer family; it was telecast as a Christmas special Dec-19-1971 (for which the family's name was changed to the Waltons), and led to the TV show the following September. *The Homecoming* was first published by Avon in 1973, with cover-variation subsequent printings starting with the third. Also that year, Dell re-issued *Spencer's Mountain* as a TV tie-in.

Bantam issued four *Waltons* books, including three Robert Weverka novelizations (upon reviewing the first one, Hamner had responded: "He has done a stunning job ... I can find nothing to quarrel with ... I hope we will be fortunate enough to have him write subsequent novelizations") plus the scarce *Walton Family Cookbook*.

Whitman issued six *Waltons* hardbacks, with Prologues and Epilogues by "John-Boy speaking as a man." Hamner created the character of eldest son John-Boy Walton (in the two Hamner books he was Clay-Boy Spencer) as his own younger self. John-Boy's journals were, in essence, the "memoirs" Hamner used as fodder for many of the show's stories.

WANTED: DEAD OR ALIVE
September 6, 1958 - March 29, 1961; CBS

_____ Wanted: Dead or Alive; by Frank Robertson; Signet S1982; c 1961 (1st); $.35

Inferred TV tie-in features Josh Randall from the TV show, but doesn't mention the show or picture star Steve McQueen.

WELCOME BACK, KOTTER
September 9, 1975 - August 10, 1979; ABC

Tempos

_____ Welcome Back, Kotter #1: The Sweathog Trail; by William Johnston; Tempo 12406; c 1976 (1st); $1.25 [FC Photo: (clockwise from top left) Ron Palillo, Robert Hegyes, Lawrence-Hilton Jacobs, Gabriel Kaplan, John Travolta]

_____ Welcome Back, Kotter: The Sweathog Trail [cover-variation]; by William Johnston; Ace Tempo Star 79114; c 1976 (1st Tempo Star: 1977); $1.25 [FC Wraparound Photo: Helaine Lembeck, Kaplan, John Sylvester White, Travolta, Hegyes, Jacobs, Palillo]

_____ Welcome Back, Kotter #2: The Sweathog Newshawks; by William Johnston; Tempo 12407; c 1976 (1st); $1.25 [FC Photo: Travolta, Kaplan, Palillo, Hegyes, Jacobs]

_____ Welcome Back, Kotter #3: The Super Sweathogs; by William Johnston; Tempo 12608; c 1976 (1st); $1.25 [FC Photo: (clockwise from top) Travolta, Hegyes, Palillo, Jacobs]

_____ Welcome Back, Kotter #4: 10-4 Sweathogs!; by William Johnston; Tempo 12706; c 1976 (1st); $1.25 [FC Photo: (clockwise from top left) Palillo, Hegyes, Jacobs, Kaplan, Travolta]

_____ Welcome Back, Kotter #5: The Sweathog Sit-In; by William Johnston; Tempo 12944; c 1977 (1st); $1.25 [FC Photo: Jacobs, Travolta, Hegyes, Palillo]

_____ Welcome Back, Kotter #6: Barbarino Drops Out; by William Johnston; Tempo 12945; c 1977 (1st); $1.25 [FC Photo: Travolta]

_____ Meet John Travolta; by Suzanne Munshower; Tempo 12936; c 1976 (1st); $1.25 [FC Photo: Travolta]

_____ John Travolta [adapted from "Meet John Travolta"]; by Suzanne Munshower; Ace Tempo Star 40630; c 1976,78 (1st: 1978); $1.95 [FC Illus: Travolta]

Zebra

_____ The Real John Travolta; by Martin A. Grove; Zebra 89083-227; c 1976 (1st); $1.95 [FC Photo: Travolta]

Show based on the experiences of Gabe Kaplan (as a youth Kaplan attended a school similar to the one he taught at in the show) made a star of John Travolta, pictured as sweathog Vinnie Barbarino on the above books. Featured in such hits then as *Saturday Night Fever* and *Grease*, Travolta resurfaced in 1994 as the Oscar-nominated lead in Quentin Tarantino's *Pulp Fiction*.

WELLS FARGO
See TALES OF WELLS FARGO

WHAT ARE THE ODDS?
1958; Syndicated

_____ What are the Odds?; by Leo Guild; Crest 369; c 1960 (1st); $.25

WHEEL OF FORTUNE
January 6, 1975 -; NBC/CBS/Syndicated

_____   Wheel of Fortune; by David R. Sams and Robert L. Shook; St. Martin's Press
         90833; c 1987 (1st); $3.95 [FC Photo: Vanna White, Pat Sajak]

_____   Vanna White; by Marianne Robin-Tani; St. Martin's Press 90829; c 1987 (1st);
         $2.95 [FC Photo: White] ["the life, the loves, the secrets" of Vanna White]

_____   Vanna Speaks; by Vanna White with Patricia Romanowski; Warner 34668; c
         1987 (1st: 1988); $3.95 [FC Photo: White]

_____   The Official Wheel of Fortune Puzzle Book; by Nancy Jones; Bantam 27204;
         c 1987 (1st); $2.95

THE WILD WILD WEST
September 17, 1965 - September 19, 1969; CBS

_____   The Wild Wild West; by Richard Wormser; Signet D2836; c 1966 (1st); $.50
         [FC Photo: Robert Conrad]

         Original adventures of frontier agent James T. West and his sidekick
Artemus Gordon in this James Bond-western based on the CBS show.

WYATT EARP
September 6, 1955 - September 26, 1961; ABC

_____   Wyatt Earp; by Philip Ketchum; Whitman 1548; c 1956 (1st)

_____   Wyatt Earp; by Davis Lott; Whitman Big Little Book 1644; c 1958 (1st) [FC
         Illus: Hugh O'Brian]

YOU'LL NEVER GET RICH
See THE PHIL SILVERS SHOW

THE YOUNG AND THE RESTLESS
March 26, 1973 -; CBS

         Bantams

_____   The Young and the Restless: The Story of Chris and Snapper; by Deborah
         Sherwood; Bantam Q2556; c 1976 (1st); $1.25 [novelization of several episodes]
         [FC Photos: David Hasselhoff, Trish Stewart]

_____   The Young and the Restless: The Story of Brad and Leslie; by Deborah
         Sherwood; Bantam 10115; c 1976 (1st); $1.25 [novelization of several episodes]
         [FC Photos: Tom Hallick, Janice Lynde]

         Pioneer Communications Networks

_____   The Young and the Restless #1: Unveiled Desires; by Angelica Aimes; Pioneer
         71; c 1986 (1st); $2.50 [novelization of several episodes]

_____ The Young and the Restless #2: Bold Passions; by Angelica Aimes; Pioneer 72; c 1986 (1st); $2.50 [novelization of several episodes]

_____ The Young and the Restless #3: Echoes of Love; by Angelica Aimes; Pioneer 73; c 1986 (1st); $2.50 [novelization of several episodes]

_____ The Young and the Restless #4: A Touch of Paradise; by Angelica Aimes; Pioneer 74; c 1986 (1st); $2.50 [novelization of several episodes]

_____ The Young and the Restless #5: Private Yearnings; by Angelica Aimes; Pioneer 75; c 1986 (1st); $2.50 [novelization of several episodes]

_____ The Young and the Restless #6: Bittersweet Harvest; by Catherine Wheelwright; Pioneer 30; c 1986 (1st); $2.50 [novelization of several episodes]

_____ The Young and the Restless #7: One Shining Moment; by Charlotte Granville; Pioneer 77; c 1986 (1st); $2.50 [novelization of several episodes]

_____ The Young and the Restless #8: Far Side of Love; by Elizabeth Summers; Pioneer 78; c 1986 (1st); $2.50 [novelization of several episodes]

_____ The Young and the Restless #9: The Highest Price; by Angelica Aimes; Pioneer 79; c 1987 (1st); $2.50 [novelization of several episodes]

_____ The Young and the Restless #10: Shining Star; by Erika Bryant; Pioneer 80; c 1987 (1st); $2.50 [novelization of several episodes]

_____ The Young and the Restless #11: Whirlwind; by Erika Bryant; Pioneer 250; c 1987 (1st); $2.50 [novelization of several episodes]

_____ The Young and the Restless #12: Paradise Found; by Erika Bryant; Pioneer 251; c 1987 (1st); $2.50 [novelization of several episodes]

_____ The Young and the Restless #13: Passion's Pride; by Charlotte Granville; Pioneer 252; c 1987 (1st); $2.50 [novelization of several episodes]

_____ The Young and the Restless #14: Free Spirit; by Erika Bryant; Pioneer 253; c 1987 (1st); $2.50 [novelization of several episodes]

YOUNG DR. KILDARE
1972; Syndicated

Beagles

_____ Young Dr. Kildare; by Max Brand; Beagle 95254; c 1938,41 (1st: 1972); $.95 [BC Photo: Gary Merrill, Mark Jenkins]

_____ Dr. Kildare's Trial; by Max Brand; Beagle 95255; c 1941,42 (1st: 1972); $.95 [BC Photo: Merrill, Jenkins]

_____ Dr. Kildare Takes Charge; by Max Brand; Beagle 95256; c 1940,41 (1st: 1972); $.95 [BC Photo: Merrill, Jenkins]

_____ Calling Dr. Kildare; by Max Brand; Beagle 95274; c 1939,40 (1st: 1972); $.95

____ The Secret of Dr. Kildare; by Max Brand; Beagle 95275; c 1939,40 (1st: 1972); $.95

____ Dr. Kildare's Crisis; by Max Brand; Beagle 95276; c 1940,41 (1st: 1972); $.95

____ Dr. Kildare's Search; by Max Brand; Beagle 95277; c 1940+ (1st: 1972); $.95

With the 1972 release of the *Dr. Kildare* remake series *Young Dr. Kildare*, Beagle re-issued the seven original Max Brand novels. (See also *Dr. Kildare*).

THE YOUNG LAWYERS
September 21, 1970 - May 5, 1971; ABC

____ The Young Lawyers: Test Case; by B.D. Ashe; Dell 08629; c 1970 (1st); $.75 [FC Illus: Zalman King, Lee J. Cobb, Judy Pace]

THE YOUNG REBELS
September 20, 1970 - January 3, 1971; ABC

Aces

____ The Young Rebels #1: The Hedgerow Incident; by William Johnston; Ace 32335; c 1970 (1st); $.60 [FC Photo: Alex Hentelhoff, Louis Gossett, Jr., Rick Ely]

____ The Young Rebels #2: The Sea Gold Incident; by William Johnston; Ace 95051; c 1970 (1st); $.60 [FC Photo: Ely; BC Photo: Hentelhoff, Ely, Gossett]

ZORRO
October 10, 1957 - September 24, 1959; ABC

Dell

____ The Mark of Zorro; by Johnston McCulley; Dell D204; c 1924,52 (1st new Dell: 1958); $.35 [FC Illus: Guy Williams]

Whitmans

____ Walt Disney's Zorro [laminated cover]; by Steve Frazee; Whitman 1586; c 1958 (1st)

____ Walt Disney's Zorro [dull cover]; by Steve Frazee; Whitman 1535; c 1958 (1st)

The show was based on the swashbuckling character created by Johnston McCulley in the 1919 story "The Curse of Capistrano." Adapted into the 1920 silent movie *The Mark of Zorro*, the story was then published in book form in 1924 as *The Mark of Zorro*. With the airing of the show in 1957, the book was re-issued by Dell as a TV tie-in. Whitman's *Zorro* was issued under two book numbers; the covers are identical, but #1586 has a laminated cover and #1535 has a dull cover.

TV TIE-INS INDEXED BY AUTHOR

Aarons, Edward S[idney] (1916-1975)
   The Defenders; Gold Medal s1164 [1961]

Ackworth, Robert C[harles] (1923-)
   Dr. Kildare; Lancer 71-308 [1962]
   Dr. Kildare: Assigned to Trouble; Whitman 1547 [1963]

Adams, Don (1926-)

  Co-written with Bill Dana
   Get Smart: Would You Believe?; Bantam 20054 [1982]

Addams, Charles [Samuel] (1912-1988)
   The Addams Family: Drawn and Quartered; Pocket 50058 [1964]
   The Addams Family: Black Maria; Pocket 50059 [1964]
   The Addams Family: Nightcrawlers; Pocket 50060 [1964]
   The Addams Family: Monster Rally; Pocket 50061 [1965]
   The Addams Family: Homebodies; Pocket 50062 [1965]
   The Addams Family: Addams and Evil; Pocket 50063 [1965]
   The Addams Family: Dear Dead Days: A Family Album; Berkley F1175 [1966]

Adler, D.L.
   Knots Landing #13: Dangerous Games; Pioneer 202 [1987]

Adler, William, ed. (Bill Adler) (1929-)
   Funniest Fan Letters to Batman; Signet D2980 [1966]
   Love Letters to the Monkees; Popular Library 60-8049 [1967]
   The Monkees Go Ape; Popular Library 60-8069 [1968]

Aimes, Angelica (1943-)

  as Angelica Aimes
   As the World Turns #7: Now and Forever; Pioneer 47 [1986]
   As the World Turns #8: Shared Moments; Pioneer 48 [1986]
   As the World Turns #13: The Second Time Around; Pioneer 002 [1987]
   Guiding Light #1: So Tender, So True; Pioneer 01 [1986]
   Guiding Light #3: Whispered Secrets, Hidden Hearts; Pioneer 03 [1986]
   Guiding Light #5: Rush to Love; Pioneer 05 [1986]

The Young and the Restless #1: Unveiled Desires; Pioneer 71 [1986]
The Young and the Restless #2: Bold Passions; Pioneer 72 [1986]
The Young and the Restless #3: Echoes of Love; Pioneer 73 [1986]
The Young and the Restless #4: A Touch of Paradise; Pioneer 74 [1986]
The Young and the Restless #5: Private Yearnings; Pioneer 75 [1986]
The Young and the Restless #9: The Highest Price; Pioneer 79 [1987]

as Francesca Evans
Guiding Light #2: Two Lives, Two Loves; Pioneer 02 [1986]

Albert, Marvin H[ubert] (1924-)
Pseudonym: Albert Conroy

Allen, Tom, ed.

Co-edited with Mitchell Galin
Tales From the Darkside, Vol. 1; Berkley 11095 [1988]

Allison, Sam (pseudonym of Noel Loomis, 1905-1969)
Wells Fargo and Danger Station; Whitman 1588 [1958]

Alter, Eric
The Dukes of Hazzard: Gone Racin'; Warner 30324 [1983]

Anderson, James (1936-)
Murder, She Wrote: The Murder of Sherlock Holmes; Avon 89702 [1985]
Murder, She Wrote #2: Horray for Homicide; Avon 89937 [1985]
Murder, She Wrote #3: Lovers and Other Killers; Avon 89938 [1986]

Andrews, Leila (unspecified pseudonym)
Family; Ballantine 25570 [1976]
Family #2: Transitions; Ballantine 25705 [1977]
Family #3: Commitments; Ballantine 25706 [1977]

Anobile, Richard J[oseph] (1947-; surname is pronounced Ah-NO-bee-lay)
Battlestar Galactica: The Photostory; Berkley 04139 [1979]
Mork & Mindy: A Video Novel; Pocket 82754 [1979]

Archer, Ron (pseudonym of Ted White, 1938-)

Co-written with Dave Van Arnam
Lost in Space; Pyramid X-1679 [1967]

Arden, Gwendolynn
One Life to Live #1/#2 [combined]: Moonlight Obsession; Pioneer 400 [1987]

Arneson, D[on] J[on] (1935-)
Mork & Mindy: Code Puzzles From Ork; Cinnamon House 15879 [1979]

Arquette, Cliff (1905-1974)
The Jack Paar Tonight Show: Charley Weaver's Letters from Mamma; Dell D347
[1960]

Arrow, William (house pseudonym for Don Pfeil [-198?] and William Rotsler [1926-])
   Return to the Planet of the Apes #1: Visions from Nowhere; Ballantine 25122
      [1976] (Rotsler)
   Return to the Planet of the Apes #2: Escape from Terror Lagoon; Ballantine 25167
      [1976] (Pfeil)
   Return to the Planet of the Apes #3: Man, the Hunted Animal; Ballantine 25211
      [1976] (Rotsler)

Ashe, B.D.
   The Young Lawyers: Test Case; Dell 08629 [1970]

Avallone, Michael [Angelo, Jr.] (1924-)

   as Michael Avallone
      The Doctors; Popular Library 08115 [1970]
      The Felony Squad; Popular Library 60-8036 [1967]
      The Girl From U.N.C.L.E. #1: The Birds of a Feather Affair; Signet D3012 [1966]
      The Girl From U.N.C.L.E. #2: The Blazing Affair; Signet D3042 [1966]
      Hawaii Five-O; Signet P3622 [1968]
      Hawaii Five-O #2: Terror in the Sun; Signet P3994 [1969]
      The Man From U.N.C.L.E.; Ace G-553 [1965]
      Mannix; Popular Library 60-2256 [1968]
      The Partridge Family; Curtis 05003 [1970]
      The Partridge Family #2: The Haunted Hall; Curtis 05004 [1970]
      The Partridge Family #3: Keith, the Hero; Curtis 05005 [1970]
      The Partridge Family #17: Love Comes to Keith Partridge; Curtis 07335 [1973]

   as Vance Stanton
      The Partridge Family #6: Keith Partridge, Master Spy; Curtis 06150 [1971]
      The Partridge Family #7: The Walking Fingers; Curtis 06162 [1972]
      The Partridge Family #9: The Fat and Skinny Murder Mystery; Curtis 06180 [1972]
      The Partridge Family #11: Who's That Laughing in the Grave?; Curtis 06184
         [1972]

Baker, Pip & Jane (*Doctor Who* scriptwriters)
   Doctor Who #6: Race Against Time; Ballantine 33228 [1986]

Baker, W[illiam Arthur] Howard (1925-1991)

   as W. Howard Baker
      Secret Agent: Departure Deferred; Macfadden 50-275 [1966]
      Secret Agent: Storm Over Rockwall; Macfadden 50-284 [1966]

   as W.A. Ballinger
      Secret Agent: The Exterminator; Macfadden 50-342 [1967]

Baldwin, Faith (1893-1978)
   Search for Tomorrow; Popular Library 60-8017 [1966]

Ball, Brian [Neville] (1932-)
   Space: 1999 #3: The Space Guardians; Pocket 80198 [1975]

Ballard, W[illis] T[odhunter] (1903-1980)
Pseudonym: Brian Fox

Ballinger, W.A. (pseudonym of W. Howard Baker, 1925-1991)
  Secret Agent: The Exterminator; Macfadden 50-342 [1967]

Bancroft, Bob
  As the World Turns #1: Magic of Love; Pioneer 41 [1986]

Barbour, John A.

  Co-written with Maria Pruetzel
    Chico and the Man: The Freddie Prinze Story; Master's Press 89251 [1978]

Barbree, Jay (1933-)
  The Six Million Dollar Man #4: Pilot Error; Warner 76-835 [1975]

Bard, Daniel
  The Aquanauts; Popular Library G516 [1961]

Bartlett, Sy (1903-)

  Co-written with Beirne Lay, Jr.
    Twelve O'Clock High!; Ballantine U5041 [1965]

Bashe, Patricia Ann Romanowski (1956-)
Pseudonym: Patricia Romanowski

Bauer, Steven (1948-)
  Steven Spielberg's Amazing Stories; Charter 01906 [1986]
  Steven Spielberg's Amazing Stories Volume II; Charter 01912 [1986]

Bennett, Kacia
  As the World Turns #9: In the Name of Love; Pioneer 49 [1987]
  As the World Turns #10: This Precious Moment; Pioneer 50 [1987]
  As the World Turns #14: Always and Forever; Pioneer 003 [1987]
  Guiding Light #13: Love's Fragile Web; Pioneer 13 [1987]
  Guiding Light #14: Choices; Pioneer 14 [1987]

Bensen, Don[ald R.] (1927-)

  as Jackson Flynn
    Gunsmoke #1: The Renegades; Award AN1283 [1974]
    Gunsmoke #3: Duel at Dodge City; Award AN1328 [1974]
    Gunsmoke #4: Cheyenne Vengeance; Award AN1403 [1975]

Benton, Lewis R[obert], Ph.D., ed. (1920-)
  The Beverly Hillbillies Book of Country Humor; Dell 0553 [1964]

Bergman, Lee (1928-)
  The Wackiest Ship in the Army; Popular Library PC1056 [1965]

Berman, Connie (1949-)
    Charlie's Angels: Farrah & Lee; Tempo 14275 [1977]
    The Hardy Boys: The Shaun Cassidy Scrapbook; Tempo 14738 [1978]
    Laverne and Shirley: Penny Marshall & Cindy Williams; Tempo 12937 [1977]

Bernard, Joel
    The Man From U.N.C.L.E. #21: The Thinking Machine Affair; Ace 51704 [1970]

Bernard, Rafe
    The Invaders #3: Army of the Undead; Pyramid R-1711 [1967]

Bertling, Paul [R.]
    M*A*S*H: The Official 4077 Quiz Manual; Signet AE4135 [1986]

Betancourt, John Gregory (1963-)
    Amazing Stories Book 5: Starskimmer; TSR 74353 [1986]

Blish, James [Benjamin] (1921-1975)
    Star Trek; Bantam F3459 [1967]
    Star Trek 2; Bantam F3439 [1968]
    Star Trek 3; Bantam F4371 [1969]
    Star Trek: Spock Must Die!; Bantam H5515 [1970]
    Star Trek 4; Bantam S7009 [1971]
    Star Trek 5; Bantam S7300 [1972]
    Star Trek 6; Bantam S7364 [1972]
    Star Trek 7; Bantam S7480 [1972]
    Star Trek 8; Bantam SP7550 [1972]
    Star Trek 9; Bantam SP7808 [1973]
    Star Trek 10; Bantam SP8401 [1974]
    Star Trek 11; Bantam Q8717 [1975]

  Co-written with J.A. Lawrence
    Star Trek 12; Bantam 11382 [1977]

Bloch, John W.
    The Sixth Sense #1: Witch, Witch, Burning Bright; Tempo 05570 [1972]

Block, Lawrence (1938-)
    Markham: The Case of the Pornographic Photos; Belmont 236 [1961]

Boe, Eugene, ed. (1922-1992)
    The Wit and Wisdom of Archie Bunker; Popular Library 08194 [1971]
    Edith Bunker's All in the Family Cookbook; Popular Library 08195 [1971]

Bond, Gladys Baker (1912-)
    Family Affair: Buffy Finds a Star; Whitman 1567 [1970]
    The Waltons #3: The Penny Sale; Whitman 1599 [1975]
    The Waltons #5: Up She Rises!; Whitman 1539 [1975]

Bonderoff, Jason [Dennis] (1946-)
    The Official Dallas Trivia Book; Signet AE3504 [1985]
    Magnum, P.I.: Tom Selleck: An Unauthorized Biography; Signet AE2063 [1983]

Bonham, B.L., ed.
  Bonanza: Heroes of the Wild West; Whitman 1569 [1970]

Bowen, Robert Sidney (1900-1977)
  Hawaii Five-O: Top Secret; Whitman 1511 [1969]

Bowles, Jerry
  The Gong Show Book; Ace Tempo Star 29814 [1977]

Boyd, Frank (pseudonym of Frank Kane, 1912-1968)
  Johnny Staccato; Gold Medal 980 [1960]

Boyd, Johanna
  As the World Turns #3: Lovers Who Dare; Pioneer 43 [1986]

Boyd, John
  As the World Turns #4: Horizons of the Heart; Pioneer 44 [1986]

Boyington, Col. Gregory "Pappy" (1912-1988)
  Baa Baa Black Sheep; Bantam 10790 [1977]

Bracco, Edgar Jean
  Boots and Saddles; Berkley G-180 [1958]
  Flight; Berkley G291 [1959]

Braden, Tom [Thomas Wardell Braden] (1918-)
  Eight is Enough; Crest 23002 [1977]

Bradley, Marion [Eleanor] Zimmer (1930-)
  The Sixth Sense #2: In the Steps of the Master; Tempo 05595 [1973]

Brand, Max (pseudonym of Frederick Faust, 1892-1944)
  Young Dr. Kildare; Avon F-133 [1962]
  Calling Dr. Kildare; Dell R123 [1961]
  Dr. Kildare's Trial; Dell R125 [1962]
  The Secret of Dr. Kildare; Dell 7712 [1962]
  Dr. Kildare's Crisis; Dell 1980 [1962]
  Dr. Kildare's Search; Dell 1981 [1962]
  Dr. Kildare Takes Charge; Dell 1983 [1962]

Brett, Michael (1921-)

  Co-written with David Toma
    Toma; Dell 08520 [1974]

Brewer, Gil (1922-1983)
  It Takes a Thief #1: The Devil in Davos; Ace 37598 [1969]
  It Takes a Thief #2: Mediterranean Caper; Ace 37599 [1969]
  It Takes a Thief #3: Appointment in Cairo; Ace 37600 [1970]

Brewster, Dennis
  I Dream of Jeannie; Pocket 10130 [1966]

Brodhead, James E[aston] (1932-)
  Rowan & Martin's Laugh-In #3: Inside Laugh-In; Signet T4059 [1969]

Brooks, Nicole
  Days of Our Lives #8: The Summer Wind; Pioneer 58 [1986]
  Days of Our Lives #9: Friends and Lovers; Pioneer 59 [1987]
  Days of Our Lives #13: Crimes of the Heart; Pioneer 152 [1987]
  General Hospital #1/#2 [combined]: Forever and a Day; Pioneer 300 [1987] [Brooks
    wrote #1 of set only]
  General Hospital #3: Winds of Change; Pioneer 301 [1987]

Brooks, Walter [Rollin] (1886-1958)
  The Original Mr. Ed; Bantam J2530 [1963]

Brosnan, Kate
  Mary Hartman, Mary Hartman: Louise Lasser, Louise Lasser; Belmont Tower
    50992 [1976]

Brown, Joe David (1915-1976)
  Paper Moon [orig. title "Addie Pray"]; Signet W6409 [1974]

Brownley, Margaret
  As the World Turns #11: Full Circle; Pioneer 000 [1987]
  As the World Turns #12: Storm Warnings; Pioneer 001 [1987]

Bryant, Edward [Winslow, Jr.] (1945-)

  Co-written with Harlan Ellison
    The Starlost: Phoenix Without Ashes; Fawcett Gold Medal M3188 [1975]

Bryant, Erika

  The Young and the Restless #10: Shining Star; Pioneer 80 [1987]
  The Young and the Restless #11: Whirlwind; Pioneer 250 [1987]
  The Young and the Restless #12: Paradise Found; Pioneer 251 [1987]
  The Young and the Restless #14: Free Spirit; Pioneer 253 [1987]

Bryars, Chris[topher]
  The Real Mary Tyler Moore; Pinnacle 230988 [1977]

Burke, Cordelia
  Another World #8: Haunted by the Past; Pioneer 38 [1986]
  Another World #13: Schemes and Dreams; Pioneer 052 [1987]

Burke, John [Frederick] (1922-)

  as John Burke
    Strange Report; Lancer 73219 [1970]

  as Robert Miall
    UFO-1: Flesh Hunters; Warner 75-273 [1973]
    UFO-2: Sporting Blood; Warner 75-274 [1973]

Burnett, W[illiam] R[iley] (1899-1982)
  The Asphalt Jungle; Pocket 6078 [1961]

Burroughs, Edgar Rice (1875-1950)
    Tarzan of the Apes; Ballantine U2001 [1966]
    The Return of Tarzan; Ballantine U2002 [1967]

Burstein, Patricia [Ann] (1945-)
    Charlie's Angels: Farrah: An Unauthorized Biography of Farrah Fawcett-Majors;
        Signet W7723 [1977]

Burton, Ardis Edwards (1903?-)
    Walt Disney: Legends of Davy Crockett; Whitman 1619 [1955]

Butterworth, Michael (1947-)
    Space: 1999 (Year 2) #1: Planets of Peril; Warner 88-341 [1977]
    Space: 1999 (Year 2) #3: The Space-Jackers; Warner 88-343 [1977]
    Space: 1999 (Year 2) #4: The Psychomorph; Warner 88-344 [1977]
    Space: 1999 (Year 2) #5: The Time Fighters; Warner 88-345 [1977]
    Space: 1999 (Year 2) #6: The Edge of the Infinite; Warner 88-346 [1977]

  Co-written with Jeff Jones (Jones uncredited)
    Space: 1999 (Year 2) #2: Mind-Breaks of Space; Warner 88-342 [1977]

Butterworth, William E[dmund III] (1929-)

  Co-written with Richard Hooker
    M*A*S*H Goes to New Orleans; Pocket 78490 [1975]
    M*A*S*H Goes to Paris; Pocket 78491 [1975]
    M*A*S*H Goes to London; Pocket 78941 [1975]
    M*A*S*H Goes to Morocco; Pocket 80264 [1976]
    M*A*S*H Goes to Las Vegas; Pocket 80265 [1976]
    M*A*S*H Goes to Hollywood; Pocket 80408 [1976]
    M*A*S*H Goes to Vienna; Pocket 80458 [1976]
    M*A*S*H Goes to Miami; Pocket 80705 [1976]
    M*A*S*H Goes to San Francisco; Pocket 80786 [1976]
    M*A*S*H Goes to Texas; Pocket 80892 [1977]
    M*A*S*H Goes to Montreal; Pocket 80910 [1977]
    M*A*S*H Goes to Moscow; Pocket 80911 [1977]

Caidin, Martin (1927-)
    Cyborg; Warner 76-643 [1974]
    Cyborg #2: Operation Nuke; Warner 76-061 [1974]
    The Six Million Dollar Man #3: High Crystal; Warner 76-408 [1975]
    The Six Million Dollar Man #6: CYBORG IV; Warner 78-655 [1976]

Calin, Harold [Jason] (-1987?)
    Combat; Lancer 70-042 [1963]
    Combat: Men, Not Heroes; Lancer 70-060 [1963]
    Combat: No Rest for Heroes; Lancer 72-910 [1965]

Cameron, Jody
    Family Affair: Buffy's Cookbook; Berkley W2092 [1971]

  See also: Jody Cameron Malis

Cameron, Lou (1924-)

  as Lou Cameron
    How the West Was Won; Ballantine 27401 [1978]
    The Outsider; Popular Library 60-2373 [1969]

  as Howard Lee
    Kung Fu #4: A Praying Mantis Kills; Warner 76-467 [1974]

Campbell, Julie
    Rin Tin Tin's Rinty; Whitman 1542 [1954]

Carey, Diane [L.] (1954-)
    Star Trek: The Next Generation #1: Ghost Ship; Pocket 66579 [1988]

Carpozi, George, Jr. (1920-)
    Vince Edwards: A Biography of Television's "Dr. Ben Casey"; Belmont L92-556
    [1962]

Carr, William H[enry] A[lexander] (1924-)
    Jack Paar Tonight Show: What is Jack Paar Really Like?; Lancer 70-005 [1962]

Carson, Johnny (1925-)
    The Tonight Show: Happiness is a Dry Martini; Crest T1217 [1968]

Carter, Carmen [Cecilia] (1954-)
    Star Trek: The Next Generation #3: The Children of Hamlin; Pocket 67319 [1988]

Carter, James
    The Little People: Debbie Preston Teenage Reporter in the Michael Gray Hawaiian
    Mystery; Tiger Beat XQ2024 [1973]

Carter, John
    The New Avengers #2: The Eagle's Nest; Berkley 03994 [1978]

Carter, Mary
    Prisoner: Cell Block H #6: Trials of Erica; Pinnacle 41404 [1981]

Cassiday, Bruce [Bingham] (1920-)

  as Bruce Cassiday
    The Bold Ones: The Surrogate Womb; Manor 95260 [1973]
    The Bold Ones #2: A Quality of Fear; Manor 95296 [1973]
    The Bold Ones #3: To Get Along With the Beautiful Girls; Manor 12215 [1974]
    General Hospital #2: Surgeon's Crisis; Award AS1024 [1972]
    General Hospital #3: In the Name of Love; Award AN1238 [1974]
    Code Name: Jericho - Operation Goldkill; Award A211F K [1967]
    Marcus Welby, M.D.: Rock a Cradle Empty; Ace 51938 [1970]
    Marcus Welby, M.D. #2: The Acid Test; Ace 51939 [1970]
    Marcus Welby, M.D. #3: The Fire's Center; Ace 51941 [1971]

as Michael Stratford
  Adam-12 #4: The Sniper; Award AN1266 [1974]

Castle, Frank [E.]
  Hawaiian Eye; Dell First Edition K112 [1962]

Catalano, Grace [A.] (1961-)
  Growing Pains: Kirk Cameron: Dream Guy; Bantam 27135 [1987]

Cavaliere, Anne
  Knots Landing #3: Love Unbound; Pioneer 63 [1986]
  Knots Landing #9: A House Divided; Pioneer 69 [1987]

Cave, Peter [Leslie] (1940-)
  The New Avengers #1: House of Cards; Berkley 03993 [1978]

Chambliss, William C. (1908?-1975)
  The Silent Service; Signet S1658 [1959]

Chandler, C.K.
  Lucan; Ballantine 27402 [1978]

Charteris, Leslie (1907-1993; surname [legally adopted in 1926 from Leslie Charles
Bowyer Yin birthname] is pronounced TCHAR-ter-iss)
  The Saint Steps In; Fiction K101 [1963]
  The Saint Sees it Through; Fiction K102 [1963]
  The Saint Closes the Case; Fiction K103 [1964]
  The Avenging Saint; Fiction K104 [1964]
  The Saint's Getaway; Fiction K105 [1964]
  The Saint in New York; Fiction K106 [1964]
  Enter the Saint; Fiction K107 [1964]
  The Saint Meets His Match; Fiction K108 [1964]
  Featuring the Saint; Fiction K109 [1964]
  Alias the Saint; Fiction K110 [1964]
  The Saint Overboard; Fiction K111 [1964]
  The Saint - The Brighter Buccaneer; Fiction K112 [1964]
  The Saint vs The Scotland Yard; Fiction K113 [1964]
  The Saint and Mr. Teal; Fiction K114 [1964]
  The Saint in the Sun; Macfadden 60-238 [1966]
  The Saint Goes West; Macfadden 60-246 [1966]
  Saint Errant; Macfadden 60-247 [1966]
  The Saint on the Spanish Main; Macfadden 60-252 [1966]
  Trust the Saint; Macfadden 60-253 [1966]
  The Saint Around the World; Macfadden 60-260 [1966]
  The Saint Intervenes; Macfadden 60-262 [1966]
  The Saint Goes On; Macfadden 60-265 [1966]
  Call for the Saint; Macfadden 60-273 [1967]
  The Saint in Europe; Macfadden 60-294 [1967]
  The Saint to the Rescue; Macfadden 60-307 [1968]

Senor Saint; Macfadden 60-315 [1968]
Thanks to the Saint; Macfadden 60-365 [1968]
Vendetta For The Saint; Pocket 50212 [1966]
The Saint Abroad; Curtis 07137 [1971] *
The Saint in New York; Curtis 07184 [1971]
The Saint Overboard; Curtis 07185 [1971]
The Saint and the Fiction Makers; Curtis 07199 [1971] *
The Saint on TV; Curtis 07200 [1971] *
The Saint Sees it Through; Curtis 07209 [1971]
The Saint in Miami; Curtis 07210 [1971]

* Fleming Lee wrote, Charteris edited

Chunovic, Louis

  as Charles Heath
    The A-Team 6: Operation Desert Sun: The Untold Story; Dell 10039 [1984]

Church, Ralph
    Mork & Mindy; Pocket 82729 [1979]

Clark, Dick (1929-)
    American Bandstand: Your Happiest Years; Cardinal GC-96 [1961]

Claro, Joe [Joseph Claro]
    Family Ties: Alex Gets the Business; Avon 75235 [1986]
    Voyagers!; Scholastic Book Services 32740 [1982]

Cleary, Beverly [Atlee Bunn] (1916-)
    Leave it to Beaver; Berkley G406 [1960]
    Leave it to Beaver: Here's Beaver; Berkley G497 [1961]
    Leave it to Beaver: Beaver and Wally; Berkley G557 [1961]

Clement, Henry (pseudonym of Edward Fenton, 1917-1994)
    Beacon Hill; Popular Library 08397 [1975]
    Beacon Hill #2: The Colonel and Fawn; Popular Library 08427 [1975]
    Columbo #3: Any Old Port in a Storm; Popular Library 00317 [1975]
    Columbo #4: By Dawn's Early Light; Popular Library 00326 [1975]
    Prisoner: Cell Block H #2: The Franky Doyle Story; Pinnacle 41175 [1981]

Cohen, Joel H[ugh]
    Good Times: Jimmie Walker: The Dyn-O-Mite Kid; Scholastic Book Services
      TX3442 [1976]
    Here's Lucy: Laugh With Lucy: The Story of Lucille Ball; Scholastic Book Services
      TX2544 [1974]
    I Spy: Cool Cos: The Story of Bill Cosby; Scholastic Book Services TX1388 [1969]
    The Six Million Dollar Man and The Bionic Woman; Scholastic Book Services
      TK3600 [1976]

Conroy, A.L.
    Storefront Lawyers; Bantam S5883 [1970]

Conroy, Albert (pseudonym of Marvin H. Albert, 1924-)
Mr. Lucky; Dell First Edition B165 [1960]

Coombs, Charles I[ra] (1914-)
Maverick; Whitman 1566 [1959]
Walt Disney's Andy Burnett on Trial; Whitman Big Little Book 1645 [1958]

Cooper, Mary Ann (American author)
Knots Landing #1: Secrets of Knots Landing; Pioneer 61 [1986]

Cooper, Morton (1925-)
The Munsters; Avon G1237 [1964]

Cooper, Sonni
As the World Turns #5: Forbidden Passions; Pioneer 45 [1986]
As the World Turns #6: Love Trap; Pioneer 46 [1986]

Corkery, Paul (1946-)
The Tonight Show: Carson: The Unauthorized Biography; Randt 942101 [1987]

Costigan, Lee (pseudonym of Hank Searls, 1922-)
The New Breed; Gold Medal s1186 [1962]

Coulson, Robert [Stratton] (1928-)

Co-written with Gene DeWeese
Amazing Stories Book 4: Nightmare Universe; TSR 74817 [1985]

Co-written with Gene DeWeese, jointly as Thomas Stratton
The Man From U.N.C.L.E. #11: The Invisibility Affair; Ace G-645 [1967]
The Man From U.N.C.L.E. #12: The Mind-Twisters Affair; Ace G-663 [1967]

Cowan, Louis G., ed. (-1976)
The $64,000 Question: Official Quiz Book; Dell First Edition 79 [1955]

Cox, William R[obert] (1901-1988)
Bonanza #2: Black Silver; Media M102 [1967]

Creed, Marlene
Another World #7: Tangled Web; Pioneer 37 [1986]
Guiding Light #8: Restless Hearts; Pioneer 08 [1986]
Guiding Light #9: Playing With Fire; Pioneer 09 [1987]
Guiding Light #10: Swept Away; Pioneer 10 [1987]
Guiding Light #12: Tender Loving Care; Pioneer 12 [1987]

Crispin, A[nn] C[arol] (1950-)
V; Pinnacle 42237 [1984]

Co-written with Deborah A. Marshall
V: Death Tide; Pinnacle 42469 [1985]

Co-written with Howard Weinstein
V: East Coast Crisis; Pinnacle 42259 [1984]

Crockett, Davy (1786-1836)
    Walt Disney: The Life of Davy Crockett; Signet S1214 [1955]

Crume, Vic (female author)
    The Partridge Family #5: Terror by Night; Curtis 06148 [1971]
    The Partridge Family #10: Marked for Terror; Curtis 06182 [1972]
    The Partridge Family #14: Thirteen at Killer Gorge; Curtis 06190 [1973]

Cudlippe, Edythe (1929-)
  Pseudonym: Jane Horatio

Cummings, J. Hoyt
    Poker According to Maverick; Dell First Edition B142 [1959]

Cunningham, Cathy (pseudonym of Chet Cunningham, 1928-)
    As the World Turns #2: Ruling Passions; Pioneer 42 [1986]
    Capitol #3: Forbidden Tomorrows; Pioneer 93 [1986]
    Capitol #4: Passion's Masterpiece; Pioneer 94 [1986]

Cunningham, Chet (1928-)
  Pseudonym: Cathy Cunningham

Cunningham, Scott
    Knots Landing #4: Misguided Hearts; Pioneer 64 [1986]
    Knots Landing #7: Tell Me No Lies; Pioneer 67 [1986]

Dahl, Roald (1916-1990)
    Roald Dahl's Tales of the Unexpected; Vintage 74081 [1979]

Daly, Marsha [H.]
    Kojak: Telly Savalas: TV's Golden Greek; Berkley Z3021 [1975]

Dana, Bill (1924-)

  Co-written with Don Adams
    Get Smart: Would You Believe?; Bantam 20054 [1982]

Daniels, Dorothy (1915-; born Dorothy Smith, married Norman Daniels in 1937)
    Strange Paradise #1; Paperback Library 63-259 [1969]
    Strange Paradise #2: Island of Evil; Paperback Library 63-321 [1970]
    Strange Paradise #3: Raxl, Voodoo Priestess; Paperback Library 63-365 [1970]

Daniels, Norman [A.] (1905-; born Norman A. Danberg)
    Arrest and Trial; Lancer 72-696 [1963]
    Arrest and Trial: The Missing Witness; Lancer 72-723 [1964]
    The Avengers #8: "The Magnetic Man"; Berkley X1637 [1968]
    The Avengers #9: "Moon Express"; Berkley X1658 [1969]
    Ben Casey: A Rage for Justice; Lancer 70-011 [1962]
    Ben Casey: The Fire Within; Lancer 70-045 [1963]
    Chase; Berkley 02553 [1974]
    The Detectives; Lancer 71-316 [1962]
    Dr. Kildare's Secret Romance; Lancer 70-007 [1962]
    Dr. Kildare's Finest Hour; Lancer 70-032 [1963]

Maya #1: The Forbidden City; Berkley F1538 [1967]
The Rat Patrol; Paperback Library 53-387 [1966]
The Smith Family #1: Meet the Smiths; Berkley X2127 [1971]

Dann, Victoria
Knots Landing #8: Once in a Lifetime; Pioneer 68 [1986]

Dannay, Frederic (1905-1982; born Daniel Nathan, name legally changed)
Pseudonym: Ellery Queen

David, Peter [Allen] (1956-)
Star Trek: The Next Generation #5: Strike Zone; Pocket 67940 [1989]
Star Trek: The Next Generation #10: A Rock and a Hard Place; Pocket 69364
[1990]

Davidson, Avram (1923-1993)

as Ellery Queen
Ellery Queen: The House of Brass; Signet Y6958 [1975]

Davidson, Ben
Happy Days: The Official Fonzie Scrapbook; Tempo 14044 [1976]

Davies, Fredric (joint pseudonym for Ron Ellik [1938-1968] and Fredric Langley)
The Man From U.N.C.L.E. #14: The Cross of Gold Affair; Ace G-689 [1968]

Davis, Franklin M[ilton], Jr. (1918-1981)
Combat: The Counterattack; Whitman 1520 [1964]

De Rosso, H[enry] A[ndrew] (1917-1960)
The Rebel; Whitman 1548 [1961]

Dean, Monica
Dallas #13: A Cry in the Night; Pioneer 102 [1987]

Deck, Carol (editor at *Flip Magazine*)
The Partridge Family: The David Cassidy Story; Curtis 06154 [1972]

Delbourgo, Joelle, ed.

Co-written with Diane J. Perlberg
Dallas: The Quotations of J. R. Ewing; Bantam 14440 [1980]

Deming, Richard (1915-1983)

as Richard Deming
Dragnet: The Case of the Courteous Killer; Pocket 1198 [1958]
Dragnet: The Case of the Crime King; Pocket 1214 [1959]
Dragnet: Case histories from the popular television series; Whitman 1527 [1957]
The Mod Squad #1: The Greek God Affair; Pyramid X-1888 [1968]
The Mod Squad #2: A Groovy Way to Die; Pyramid X-1908 [1968]
The Mod Squad #3: The Sock-it-to-Em Murders; Pyramid X-1922 [1968]
The Mod Squad #4: Spy-In; Pyramid X-1986 [1969]
The Mod Squad #5: The Hit; Pyramid X-2214 [1970]

Diller, Phyllis (1917-)
  Phyllis Diller's Housekeeping Hints; Crest R1082 [1968]
  Phyllis Diller's Marriage Manual; Crest R1245 [1969]

Disch, Thomas M[ichael] (1940-)
  The Prisoner; Ace 67900 [1969]

Doherty, Linda
  Happy Days: Fonzie's Scrambled Word Find Puzzles; Tempo 12645 [1976]
  Hardy Boys Super Sleuth Word Finds; Tempo 14514 [1977]
  Nancy Drew Secret Scrambled Word Finds; Tempo 14512 [1977]

Doty, Roy (1922-)
  Rowan & Martin's Laugh-In #2: Mod, Mod World; Signet T3845 [1969]

Downs, Hugh [Malcolm] (1921-)
  The Jack Paar Tonight Show: Yours Truly, Hugh Downs; Avon F-106 [1960]

Dresser, Davis (1904-1977)
  Pseudonym: Brett Halliday

Duncan, Deidre
  Days of Our Lives #11: Fantasies; Pioneer 150 [1987]

Dvorkin, David (1943-) and Daniel (1969-) (father and son)
  Star Trek: The Next Generation #8: The Captains' Honor; Pocket 68487 [1989]

Edmonds, I[vy] G[ordon] (1917-)
  Lassie: The Wild Mountain Trail; Whitman 1513 [1966]
  The Rat Patrol: The Iron Monster Raid; Whitman 1547 [1968]

Effinger, George Alec (1947-)
  Planet of the Apes #1: Man the Fugitive; Award AN1373 [1974]
  Planet of the Apes #2: Escape to Tomorrow; Award AN1407 [1975]
  Planet of the Apes #3: Journey Into Terror; Award AN1436 [1975]
  Planet of the Apes #4: Lord of the Apes; Award AN1488 [1976]

Einstein, Charles (1926-)
  The Naked City; Dell First Edition A180 [1959] (Cover and spine attribute
    authorship to Stirling Silliphant, who wrote the teleplays upon which the stories
    in the book were based.)
  Playhouse 90: No Time At All; Dell D224 [1958]

Elkin, Sam
  Ben Casey: The Strength of his Hands; Lancer 70-037 [1963]

Ellik, Ron[ald Davis] (1938-1968)

  Co-written with Fredric Langley, jointly as Fredric Davies
    The Man From U.N.C.L.E. #14: The Cross of Gold Affair; Ace G-689 [1968]

Elliot, John [Herbert] (1918-)

  Co-written with Fred Hoyle
    A For Andromeda; Crest d773 [1964]
    Andromeda Breakthrough; Crest R1080 [1967]

Elliott, David (pseudonym of David Elliott Pedneau, 1947-1990)
    Private Eye #2: Blue Movie; Ivy 0270 [1988]

Ellis, Leo R[oy] (1909-)
    Hawaii Five-O: The Octopus Caper; Whitman 1553 [1971]

Ellison, Harlan [Jay] (1934-)

  Co-written with Edward Bryant
    The Starlost: Phoenix Without Ashes; Fawcett Gold Medal M3188 [1975]

Elman, Richard (1934-)
  Pseudonym: Richard Alan Simmons

Elrick, George S[eefurth] (1921-)
    Batman and Robin in the Cheetah Caper; Whitman Big Little Book 2031 [1969]
    Bonanza: The Bubble Gum Kid; Whitman Big Little Book 2002 [1967]
    Daktari: Night of Terror; Whitman Big Little Book 2018 [1968]
    "flipper": Killer Whale Trouble; Whitman Big Little Book 2003 [1967]
    "flipper": Deep-Sea Photographer; Whitman Big Little Book 2032 [1969]
    Lassie: Adventure in Alaska; Whitman Big Little Book 2004 [1967]
    Lassie and the Shabby Sheik; Whitman Big Little Book 2027 [1968]
    The Man From U.N.C.L.E.: The Calcutta Affair; Whitman Big Little Book 2011
      [1967]

Elton, Packer
    Roy Rogers on the Trail of the Zeroes; Whitman 2361 [1954]

Elwood, Roger [P.] (1943-)
    Fantasy Island; Weekly Reader F435 [1981]
    Joanie Loves Chachi; Weekly Reader F536 [1982]

  as Editor
    Star Trek: Six Science Fiction Plays; Pocket 48766 [1976]

Emerson, Ru (1944-; female author)
    Beauty and the Beast: Masques; Avon 76194 [1990]

Emery, Clayton (1953-)

  Co-written with Earl Wajenberg
    Amazing Stories Book 1: The 4-D Funhouse; TSR 74176 [1985]

Emms, William (*Doctor Who* scriptwriter)
    Doctor Who #4: Mission to Venus; Ballantine 33229 [1986]

Enderlin, Lee (1951-)
    Amazing Stories Book 6: Day of the Mayfly; TSR 74352 [1986]

Ephron, Nora (1941-)
 The Tonight Show: and now... Here's Johnny!; Avon V2251 [1968]

Evans, Francesca (pseudonym of Angelica Aimes, 1943-)
 Guiding Light #2: Two Lives, Two Loves; Pioneer 02 [1986]

Fairman, Paul W. (1916-1977)
 Bridget Loves Bernie; Lancer 74795 [1972]
 The Girl With Something Extra; Lancer 75491 [1973]
 Lancer; Popular Library 60-2349 [1968]
 Love, American Style; Pinnacle P047-N [1971]
 Love, American Style, 2; Pinnacle P081-N [1972]
 One Step Beyond: The World Grabbers; Monarch 471 [1964]
 The Partridge Family #4: The Ghost of Graveyard Hill; Curtis 06147 [1971]
 The Partridge Family #8: The Treasure of Ghost Mountain; Curtis 06164 [1972]
 That Girl; Popular Library 02588 [1971]
 Voyage to the Bottom of the Sea: City Under the Sea; Pyramid R-1162 [1965]

Fannin, Cole
 Gene Autry and the Golden Stallion; Whitman 1511 [1954]
 Leave it to Beaver; Whitman 1526 [1962]
 The Lucy Show: Lucy and the Madcap Mystery; Whitman 1505 [1963]
 The Real McCoys and Danger at the Ranch; Whitman 1577 [1961]
 The Rifleman; Whitman 1569 [1959]
 Rin Tin Tin and The Ghost Wagon Train; Whitman 1579 [1958]
 Roy Rogers and The Brasada Bandits; Whitman 1500 [1955]
 Roy Rogers: King of the Cowboys; Whitman 1503 [1956]
 Roy Rogers and Dale Evans in River of Peril; Whitman 1504 [1957]
 Sea Hunt; Whitman 1541 [1960]

Faucher, Elizabeth
 Charles in Charge; Scholastic Book Services 33550 [1984]
 Charles in Charge, Again; Scholastic Book Services 41008 [1987]

Faust, Frederick (1892-1944)
 Pseudonym: Max Brand

Fawcette, Gene (cartoonist)

 Co-written with Howard Liss
 The Monkees; Popular Library 50-8026 [1966]

Fay, Jerry
 The Clampetts of Beverly Hills; Avon G1203 [1964]
 The Beverly Hillbillies Live it Up!; Avon G1250 [1965]

Fenton, Edward (1917-1994)

 as Edward Fenton
 The Partridge Family #13: The Mystery of the Mad Millionairess; Curtis 06186 [1973]

as Henry Clement
   Beacon Hill; Popular Library 08397 [1975]
   Beacon Hill #2: The Colonel and Fawn; Popular Library 08427 [1975]
   Columbo #3: Any Old Port in a Storm; Popular Library 00317 [1975]
   Columbo #4: By Dawn's Early Light; Popular Library 00326 [1975]
   Prisoner: Cell Block H #2: The Franky Doyle Story; Pinnacle 41175 [1981]

Fenton, William
   Fury and the Lone Pine Mystery; Whitman 1537 [1957]

Fickling, G.G. (joint pseudonym for Forrest E. "Skip" [1925-] and Gloria Gautraud
Fickling, husband and wife)
   Honey West: Bombshell; Pyramid R-1106 [1964]
   Honey West: This Girl for Hire; Pyramid R-1151 [1965]
   Honey West: A Gun for Honey; Pyramid R-1167 [1965]
   Honey West: Honey in the Flesh; Pyramid R-1179 [1965]
   Honey West: Girl on the Prowl; Pyramid R-1339 [1965]
   Honey West: Blood and Honey; Pyramid R-1340 [1965]
   Honey West: Dig a Dead Doll; Pyramid R-1355 [1965]
   Honey West: Girl on the Loose; Pyramid R-1356 [1965]
   Honey West: Kiss for a Killer; Pyramid R-1357 [1965]
   Honey West: Honey on Her Tail; Pyramid T2410 [1971]
   Honey West: Stiff as a Broad; Pyramid T2494 [1971]

Fish, Robert L[loyd] (1912-1981)
   Trials of O'Brien; Signet D2821 [1965]

Flint, Stella
   Days of Our Lives #7: Red Sky at Dawn; Pioneer 57 [1986]

Flynn, J.M. (1927-1985)
   SurfSide 6; Dell First Edition 8388 [1962]

Flynn, Jackson (house pseud. for Don Bensen [1927-] and Gordon D. Shirreffs [1914-])
   Gunsmoke #1: The Renegades; Award AN1283 [1974] (Bensen)
   Gunsmoke #2: Shootout; Award AN1284 [1974] (Shirreffs)
   Gunsmoke #3: Duel at Dodge City; Award AN1328 [1974] (Bensen)
   Gunsmoke #4: Cheyenne Vengeance; Award AN1403 [1975] (Bensen)

Folsom, Franklin [Brewster] (1907-)
   Pseudonym: Troy Nesbit

Forbes, Frances
   Days of Our Lives; Popular Library 60-2397 [1969]

Forbes, Kathryn (pseudonym of Kathryn McLean, 1909-1966)
   Mama's Bank Account; Bantam 1513 [1956]

Foster, Alan Dean (1946-)
   Star Trek Log One; Ballantine 24014 [1974]
   Star Trek Log Two; Ballantine 24184 [1974]
   Star Trek Log Three; Ballantine 24260 [1975]

Star Trek Log Four; Ballantine 24435 [1975]
Star Trek Log Five; Ballantine 24532 [1975]
Star Trek Log Six; Ballantine 24655 [1976]
Star Trek Log Seven; Ballantine 24965 [1976]
Star Trek Log Eight; Ballantine 25141 [1976]
Star Trek Log Nine; Ballantine 25557 [1977]
Star Trek Log Ten; Ballantine 27212 [1978]

Fox, Brian (pseudonym of W.T. Ballard, 1903-1980)
Alias Smith and Jones: Dead Ringer; Award A896S [1971]
Alias Smith and Jones: The Outlaw Trail; Award AS1006 [1972]

Fraley, Oscar [B.] (1914-)
The Untouchables: 4 Against the Mob; Popular Library G512 [1961]

Co-written with Eliot Ness
The Untouchables; Popular Library G403 [1960]

Co-written with Paul Robsky
The Last of the Untouchables; Popular Library G569 [1962]

Franklin, Edwina
Another World #1: Let's Love Again; Pioneer 31 [1986]

Franklin, Max (pseudonym of Richard Deming, 1915-1983)
Charlie's Angels; Ballantine 25665 [1977]
Charlie's Angels #2: The Killing Kind; Ballantine 25707 [1977]
Charlie's Angels #3: Angels on a String; Ballantine 25691 [1977]
Charlie's Angels #4: Angels in Chains; Ballantine 27182 [1977]
Charlie's Angels #5: Angels on Ice; Ballantine 27342 [1978]
Starsky and Hutch; Ballantine 24996 [1976]
Starsky and Hutch #2: Kill Huggy Bear; Ballantine 25124 [1976]
Starsky and Hutch #3: Death Ride; Ballantine 23921 [1976]
Starsky and Hutch #4: Bounty Hunter; Ballantine 25669 [1977]
Starsky and Hutch #5: Terror on the Docks; Ballantine 25709 [1977]
Starsky and Hutch #6: The Psychic; Ballantine 25710 [1977]
Starsky and Hutch #7: The Set-Up; Ballantine 27340 [1978]
Starsky and Hutch #8; Ballantine 27341 [1978]
Vega$; Ballantine 28051 [1978]

Frazee, [Charles] Steve (1909-1992)
Bonanza: Killer Lion; Whitman 1568 [1966]
Cheyenne and the Lost Gold of Lion Park; Whitman 1587 [1958]
The High Chaparral: Apache Way; Whitman 1519 [1969]
Lassie: The Mystery of Bristlecone Pine; Whitman 1505 [1967]
Lassie: The Secret of the Smelters' Cave; Whitman 1514 [1968]
Lassie: Lost in the Snow; Whitman 1504 [1969]
Lassie: Trouble at Panter's Lake; Whitman 1515 [1972]
The Outcasts; Popular Library 60-2345 [1968]
Walt Disney's Zorro; Whitman 1586 [1958]

Frid, Jonathan, ed. (1924-)
  Dark Shadows: Barnabas Collins: A Personal Picture Album; Paperback Library 62-210 [1969]

Friedman, Michael Jan (1955-)
  Star Trek: The Next Generation #9: A Call to Darkness; Pocket 68708 [1989]

Friend, Ed (pseudonym of Richard Wormser, 1908-1977)
  The Green Hornet in the Infernal Light; Dell 3231 [1966]
  The High Chaparral: Coyote Gold; Tempo 05302 [1969]
  The Most Deadly Game #1: The Corpse in the Castle; Lancer 73200 [1970]

Fuller, Roger (pseudonym of Don Tracy, 1905-1976)
  Burke's Law: Who Killed Beau Sparrow?; Perma M-4310 [1964]
  Burke's Law: Who Killed Madcap Millicent?; Pocket 50030 [1964]
  The Defenders: All the Silent Voices; Pocket 50056 [1964]
  The Defenders: Ordeal; Pocket 50107 [1964]
  The Defenders: Eve of Judgment; Pocket 50190 [1965]
  The Fugitive: Fear in a Desert Town; Pocket 35012 [1964]
  Again Peyton Place; Pocket 75196 [1967]
  Carnival in Peyton Place; Pocket 75250 [1967]
  Pleasures of Peyton Place; Pocket 75267 [1968]
  Secrets of Peyton Place; Pocket 75285 [1968]
  The Evils of Peyton Place; Pocket 75334 [1969]
  Hero in Peyton Place; Pocket 75367 [1969]
  The Temptations of Peyton Place; Pocket 75423 [1970]
  Thrills of Peyton Place; Pocket 75457 [1969]
  Nice Girl from Peyton Place; Pocket 75470 [1970]

Gaddis, R[oscoe] V[ernon] "Gadabout" (1896-1986)

  Co-written with George Sullivan
  Gadabout Gaddis: The Flying Fisherman; Pocket 75224 [1967]

Galanoy, Terry (1927-)
  The Tonight Show: Tonight!; Warner 76-367 [1974]

Galin, Mitchell, ed.

  Co-edited with Tom Allen
  Tales From the Darkside, Vol. 1; Berkley 11095 [1988]

Gallagher, Richard [Farrington] (1926-)
  Cannon #1: Murder By Gemini; Lancer 74783 [1971]
  Cannon #2: The Stewardess Strangler; Lancer 75260 [1971]
  The Most Deadly Game #2: The One-Armed Murder; Lancer 73216 [1971]

Gardner, Erle Stanley (1889-1970)
  Perry Mason: The Case of the Fan-Dancer's Horse; Pocket 886 [1957]
  Perry Mason: The Case of the Gilded Lady; Cardinal C-337 [1959]
  Perry Mason: The Case of the Dubious Bridegroom; Cardinal C-376 [1959]
  Perry Mason: The Case of the Screaming Woman; Cardinal C-377 [1959]

Perry Mason: The Case of the Perjured Parrot; Cardinal C-379 [1959]
Perry Mason: The Case of the Hesitant Hostess; Cardinal C-381 [1959]
Perry Mason: The Case of the Daring Decoy; Pocket 6001 [1960]
Perry Mason: The Case of the Lonely Heiress; Pocket 6027 [1960]
Perry Mason: The Case of the Calendar Girl; Pocket 6040 [1960]
Perry Mason: The Case of the Fiery Fingers; Pocket 6044 [1960]

Garforth, John
The Avengers #1: "The Floating Game"; Berkley F1410 [1967]
The Avengers #2: "The Laugh Was On Lazarus"; Berkley F1411 [1967]
The Avengers #3: "The Passing of Gloria Munday"; Berkley F1431 [1967]
The Avengers #4: "Heil Harris!"; Berkley F1445 [1967]

Garth, Ed (pseudonym of William Johnston, 1924-)
Matt Lincoln #1: The Revolutionist; Lancer 73201 [1970]
Matt Lincoln #2: The Hostage; Lancer 73211 [1971]

Gelles-Cole, Sandi (1949-)
Pseudonym: Samantha Phillips

Gerger, Dawn
Hardy Boys Baffling Word Webs; Tempo 14515 [1977]
Nancy Drew Clever Crosswords; Tempo 14513 [1977]
The Six Million Dollar Man's Search-A-Word Shape Puzzles; Tempo 12526 [1976]

Gerrold, David (1944-; born Jarrold David Friedman)
Star Trek: "The Trouble With Tribbles"; Ballantine 23402 [1973]
The World of Star Trek; Ballantine 23403 [1973]
Star Trek: The Next Generation: Encounter at Farpoint; Pocket 65241 [1987]

Gibson, Walter B[rown] (1897-1985)
Chilling Stories From Rod Serling's The Twilight Zone; Tempo T89 [1965]
Rod Serling's Twilight Zone Revisited; Tempo T-171 [1967]

Glidden, Frederick D[illey] (1908-1975)
Pseudonym: Luke Short

Goddard, Harry
The Silent Force; Popular Library 01418 [1971]

Goldman, Lawrence Louis (1907-)
Judd for the Defense; Paperback Library 53-625 [1968]
Judd for the Defense #2: The Secret Listeners; Paperback Library 53-721 [1968]

Goodgold, Ed[win] (1944-)
I Spy: Robert Culp & Bill Cosby; Grosset & Dunlap 1097 [1967]

Gorham, Gilian
Days of Our Lives #1: Love's Shattered Dreams; Pioneer 51 [1986]
Days of Our Lives #2: Hearts Past Reason; Pioneer 52 [1986]
Days of Our Lives #3: Search for Love; Pioneer 53 [1986]
Days of Our Lives #4: Sentimental Longings; Pioneer 54 [1986]

Goulart, Ron[ald Joseph] (1933-)

as Ron Goulart, co-written with Glen A. Larson [Goulart wrote, Larson given co-author credit]
Battlestar Galactica 8: Greetings From Earth; Berkley 06047 [1983]
Battlestar Galactica 9: Experiment in Terra; Berkley 06418 [1984]
Battlestar Galactica 10: The Long Patrol; Berkley 07105 [1984]

as Howard Lee
Kung Fu #2: Chains; Warner 76-465 [1973]
Kung Fu #3: Superstition; Warner 76-466 [1973]

as Con Steffanson
Laverne and Shirley #1: Teamwork; Warner 88-294 [1976]
Laverne and Shirley #2: Easy Money; Warner 88-295 [1976]
Laverne and Shirley #3: Gold Rush; Warner 88-296 [1976]

as Joseph Silva, co-written with Len Wein and Marv Wolfman
The Incredible Hulk in Stalker From the Stars; Pocket 82084 [1978]

Grace, Virginia
Another World #6: Forgive and Forget; Pioneer 36 [1986]

Granville, Charlotte
The Young and the Restless #7: One Shining Moment; Pioneer 77 [1986]
The Young and the Restless #13: Passion's Pride; Pioneer 252 [1987]

Grave, Stephen (pseudonym of David J. Schow, 1955-)
Miami Vice #1: The Florida Burn; Avon 89930 [1985]
Miami Vice #2: The Vengeance Game; Avon 89931 [1985]

Greene, Graham (1904-1991)
The Third Man; Bantam J2427 [1962]

Gregory, James
The Partridge Family: David, David, David; Curtis 06167 [1972]

Grove, Martin A.
Happy Days: fonzie!; Zebra 89083-228 [1976]
Welcome Back, Kotter: The Real John Travolta; Zebra 89083-227 [1976]

Gruber, Frank (1904-1969)
Tales of Wells Fargo; Bantam 1726 [1958]

Guild, Leo
What are the Odds?; Crest 369 [1960]

Gunn, James E[dwin] (1923-)
The Immortal; Bantam S5924 [1970]

Haas, Ben[jamin Leopold] (1926-1977)
Pseudonym: Richard Meade

Haas, Dorothy [F.]
Sir Lancelot; Whitman Big Little Book 1649 [1958]

Haber, Heinz, Ph.D. (1913-)
The Walt Disney Story of Our Friend the Atom; Dell First Edition B104 [1956]

Halacy, D[aniel] S[tephen], Jr. (1919-)
Ripcord; Whitman 1522 [1962]

Hale, Helen (pseudonym of Lucille Burnett Mulcahy)
The Roy Rogers Show: Dale Evans and Danger in Crooked Canyon; Whitman 1506 [1958]

Hall, Monty (1923-)

Co-written with Bill Libby
Let's Make a Deal: Emcee Monty Hall; Ballantine 24370 [1975]

Halliday, Brett (pseudonym of Davis Dresser [1904-1977]; later house pseudonym for Ryerson Johnson [1901-], Robert Terrall [1914-], and others)
Michael Shayne: Murder Takes No Holiday; Dell D379 [1961] (Terrall)
Michael Shayne: The Corpse Came Calling; Dell D401 [1961] (Dresser)
Michael Shayne's Long Chance; Dell D416 [1961] (Dresser)
Michael Shayne: Death Has Three Lives; Dell D423 [1961] (Dresser)
Michael Shayne: Dolls Are Deadly; Dell D424 [1961] (Johnson)
Michael Shayne: Stranger in Town; Dell D425 [1961] (Dresser)
Michael Shayne: The Homicidal Virgin; Dell D437 [1961] (Dresser)
Michael Shayne: Killers From the Keys; Dell 4476 [1962] (Johnson)

Hambly, Barbara [Joan] (1951-)
Beauty and the Beast; Avon 75795 [1989]
Beauty and the Beast: Song of Orpheus; Avon 75798 [1990]

Hamner, Earl [Henry], Jr. (1923-)
The Waltons: Spencer's Mountain; Dell 08180 [1973]
The Waltons: The Homecoming; Avon 15149 [1973]

Hardwick, Richard [Holmes, Jr.] (1923-)
"flipper": The Mystery of the Black Schooner; Whitman 2324 [1966]
Hawk; Belmont B50-741 [1966]

Harrington, Dick

Co-written with Alan Riefe
Sanford and Son; Curtis 09222 [1973]

Harris, Eleanor
I Love Lucy: The Real Story of Lucille Ball; Ballantine 78 [1954]

Harris, Walter (1925-)
The New Avengers #3: To Catch a Rat; Berkley 03995 [1978]

Henderson, Dion [Winslow] (1921-1984)
   The Waltons #1: The Bird Dog; Whitman 1516 [1975]

Hershkovits, David (1947-)
   Miami Vice: Don Johnson; St. Martin's Press 90165 [1986]

Herz, Peggy (1936-; born Peggy Dilts, married James A. Hudson in 1966 and wrote as
Peggy Hudson until 1972 divorce; married Edgar L. Herz in 1972 and wrote as Peggy
Herz)

   as Peggy Herz
      Happy Days: The Truth About Fonzie; Scholastic Book Services TK3571 [1976]
      Nancy Drew and The Hardy Boys; Scholastic Book Services TX4103 [1977]
      The Hardy Boys and Nancy Drew; Scholastic Book Services TX4496 [1978]
      All About "M*A*S*H"; Scholastic Book Services TK3237 [1975]
      The Mork & Mindy Story; Scholastic Book Services TX4757 [1979]
      All About "Rhoda"; Scholastic Book Services TK3121 [1975]

Heyman, Evan Lee (American author)
      Cain's Hundred; Popular Library PC1010 [1961]
      Miami Undercover; Popular Library G554 [1961]

Hickok, Will (pseudonym of C. William Harrison, 1913-)
      The Restless Gun; Signet 1541 [1958]
      Trail of the Restless Gun; Signet 1675 [1959]

Hiken, Nat (1914-1968)
      The Phil Silvers Show: Sergeant Bilko; Ballantine 229 [1957]

Hill, John
      The Man From U.N.C.L.E.'s ABC of Espionage; Signet D3045 [1966]

Hill, Roger (1951-)

   Co-written with Glen A. Larson [Hill wrote, Larson given co-author credit]
      Knight Rider; Pinnacle 42170 [1983]
      Knight Rider #2: Trust Doesn't Rust; Pinnacle 42181 [1984]
      Knight Rider #3: Hearts of Stone; Pinnacle 42182 [1984]

Hinchcliffe, Philip (*Doctor Who* producer)
      Doctor Who #8 and the Masque of Mandragora; Pinnacle 40640 [1979]
      Doctor Who #10 and the Seeds of Doom; Pinnacle 40639 [1980]

Hine, Al[fred Blakelee] (1915-1974)

   as Al Hine
      Bewitched; Dell 0551 [1965]

   as Bradford Street
      Primus; Bantam S7262 [1971]

Hirschfeld, Burt (1923-)
    The Ewings of Dallas; Bantam 14439 [1980]
    The Women of Dallas; Bantam 14497 [1981]
    The Men of Dallas; Bantam 20390 [1981]
    General Hospital; Lancer 70-055 [1963]
    General Hospital: Emergency Entrance; Lancer 72-917 [1965]
    The Ugliest Girl in Town; Popular Library 60-2340 [1968]

Hitchcock, Alfred [Joseph], ed. (1899-1980)
    Alfred Hitchcock Presents: 12 Stories They Wouldn't Let Me Do On TV; Dell
        D231 [1958]
    Alfred Hitchcock Presents: 13 More Stories They Wouldn't Let Me Do On TV;
        Dell D281 [1959]

Hoffman, Betty Hannah (1918-)

  Co-written with Kathryn Murray
    My Husband, Arthur Murray; Avon T510 [1960]

Holly, J[oan Carol] Hunter (1932-1982)
    The Man From U.N.C.L.E. #10: The Assassination Affair; Ace G-636 [1967]

Holt, Michael (pseudonym of David Martin, 1935-)
    Doctor Who #2: Crisis in Space; Ballantine 33225 [1986]

Honig, Donald (1931-)
    The Americans; Popular Library PC1006 [1961]

Hooker, Richard (pseudonym of H. Richard Hornberger, 1924-)
    M*A*S*H; Pocket 77232 [1973]
    M*A*S*H Mania; Pocket 82178 [1979]

  Co-written with William E. Butterworth
    M*A*S*H Goes to New Orleans; Pocket 78490 [1975]
    M*A*S*H Goes to Paris; Pocket 78491 [1975]
    M*A*S*H Goes to London; Pocket 78941 [1975]
    M*A*S*H Goes to Morocco; Pocket 80264 [1976]
    M*A*S*H Goes to Las Vegas; Pocket 80265 [1976]
    M*A*S*H Goes to Hollywood; Pocket 80408 [1976]
    M*A*S*H Goes to Vienna; Pocket 80458 [1976]
    M*A*S*H Goes to Miami; Pocket 80705 [1976]
    M*A*S*H Goes to San Francisco; Pocket 80786 [1976]
    M*A*S*H Goes to Texas; Pocket 80892 [1977]
    M*A*S*H Goes to Montreal; Pocket 80910 [1977]
    M*A*S*H Goes to Moscow; Pocket 80911 [1977]

Hooton, Barbara [C.]

  Co-written with "Patrick Dennis" [Edward Everett Tanner III]
    Guestward Ho!; Popular Library SP71 [1960]

Horatio, Jane (pseudonym of Edythe Cudlippe, 1929-)
    General Hospital: A Matter of Life and Death; Award A858S [1971]

Hornberger, H. Richard (1924-)
  Pseudonym: Richard Hooker

Hoskins, Robert (1933-1993)

  as Michael Kerr
    Prisoner: Cell Block H #4: The Frustrations of Vera; Pinnacle 41215 [1981]

Houston, David (1938-)
    Lindsay Wagner: Superstar of The Bionic Woman; Belmont Tower 50979 [1976]

Hoyle, Fred (1915-)

  Co-written with John Elliot
    A For Andromeda; Crest d773 [1964]
    Andromeda Breakthrough; Crest R1080 [1967]

Hoyle, Trevor (1940-)
    Terry Nation's Blake's 7: Their First Adventure; Citadel Press 1103 [1988]
    Terry Nation's Blake's 7: Scorpio Attack; Citadel Press 1082 [1988]
    Terry Nation's Blake's 7: Project Avalon; Citadel Press 1102 [1988]

Hubbard, Richard (-1974)
  Pseudonym: Chris Stratton

Hudson, James A[lbert] (1924-)
    Flip Wilson Close-Up; Avon V2459 [1972]
    The Partridge Family: Young Mr. Cassidy; Scholastic Book Services TK2070
      [1972]
    The Partridge Family: Meet David Cassidy ["Young Mr. Cassidy" abridged];
      Scholastic Book Services TX2123 [1972]

Huggins, Roy (1914-)
    77 Sunset Strip: The Double Take; Pocket 2524 [1959]
    77 Sunset Strip; Dell First Edition A176 [1959]

Hughes, Joan
    Love of Life: The Perilous Summer; Pocket 75445 [1970]
    The Secret Storm: The Unseen; Pocket 75444 [1970]

Hulke, Malcolm (1924-1979)
    Doctor Who #2 and the Doomsday Weapon; Pinnacle 40566 [1979]
    Doctor Who #3 and the Dinosaur Invasion; Pinnacle 40606 [1979]

Hunt, Gerry

  Co-written with Marcia Rosen
    The Cheers Bartending Guide; Avon 70189 [1986]

Hunter, Evan (1926-)
  Pseudonym: Ed McBain

Hutchinson, W.H.
   Gene Autry and the Big Valley Grab; Whitman 2302 [1952]

Jahn, Joseph Michael (1943-)

   as Michael Jahn
      The Black Sheep Squadron: The Hawk Flies on Sunday; Bantam 13645 [1980]
      The Invisible Man; Fawcett Gold Medal P3460 [1975]
      The Six Million Dollar Man #1: Wine, Women and War; Warner 76-833 [1975]
      The Six Million Dollar Man #5: The Rescue of Athena One; Warner 76-836 [1975]

   as Mike Jahn
      The Black Sheep Squadron: Devil in the Slot; Bantam 11938 [1978]
      The Rockford Files #1: The Unfortunate Replacement; Popular Library 00318
         [1975]
      The Rockford Files #2: The Deadliest Game; Popular Library 00354 [1976]
      The Six Million Dollar Man: The Secret of Bigfoot Pass; Berkley Z3307 [1976]
      The Six Million Dollar Man: International Incidents; Berkley 03331 [1977]
      Switch; Berkley Z3082 [1976]
      Switch #2: Round Up the Usual Suspects; Berkley Z3252 [1976]
      Thunder: The Mighty Stallion of the Hills; Tempo 14893 [1978]
      Thunder: The Mighty Stallion to the Rescue; Tempo 14894 [1979]

   as Evan Richards
      The Six Million Dollar Man #2: Solid Gold Kidnapping; Warner 76-834 [1975]

Janeshutz, Trish (1947-; born Patricia Marie Janeshutz and married Rob MacGregor in
1983; has written as Trish Janeshutz and T.J. MacGregor)

   as Trish Janeshutz, co-written with Rob MacGregor
      The Making of Miami Vice; Ballantine 33669 [1986]

Jeffries, Wendy, ed.
      That's Incredible! Vol. 1; Jove B5807 [1980]
      That's Incredible! Vol. 2; Jove B5870 [1981]
      That's Incredible! Vol. 3; Jove B5986 [1981]
      That's Incredible! Vol. 4; Jove 06171 [1981]
      That's Incredible! Vol. 5; Jove 06172 [1981]
      That's Incredible! Vol. 6; Jove 06173 [1981]

Jenkins, Will[iam] F[itzgerald] (1896-1975)
   Pseudonym: Murray Leinster

Jennings, Dean [Southern] (1905-1969)

   Co-written with Art Linkletter
      Art Linkletter's House Party: Confessions of a Happy Man; Cardinal GC-124
         [1962]

Jessup, Richard (1925-1982)
   Pseudonym: Richard Telfair

Johnson, George (1917-)
  The Jack Paar Tonight Show: The Real Jack Paar; Gold Medal s1263 [1962]

Johnson, [Walter] Ryerson (1901-)

  as Brett Halliday
    Michael Shayne: Dolls Are Deadly; Dell D424 [1961]
    Michael Shayne: Killers From the Keys; Dell 4476 [1962]

Johnston, William (1924-)

  as William Johnston
    Banyon; Paperback Library 64-669 [1971]
    Ben Casey; Lancer 70-006 [1962]
    Bewitched: The Opposite Uncle; Whitman 1572 [1970]
    The Brady Bunch; Lancer 73-849 [1969]
    The Brady Bunch #2: Showdown at the P.T.A. Corral; Lancer 73-864 [1969]
    The Brady Bunch #3: Count Up to Blast-Down!; Lancer 73872 [1970]
    The Brady Bunch #4: The Bumbler Strikes Again; Lancer 73891 [1970]
    The Brady Bunch #5: The Quarterback Who Came to Dinner; Lancer 73206 [1970]
    Captain Nice; Tempo T-155 [1967]
    Dr. Kildare: The Heart Has an Answer; Lancer 70-043 [1963]
    Dr. Kildare: The Faces of Love; Lancer 70-049 [1963]
    Dr. Kildare: The Magic Key; Whitman 1519 [1964]
    F Troop: The Great Indian Uprising; Whitman 1544 [1967]
    The Flying Nun: Miracle At San Tanco; Ace G-702 [1968]
    The Flying Nun: The Littlest Rebels; Ace G-725 [1968]
    The Flying Nun #3: Mother of Invention; Ace 24300 [1969]
    The Flying Nun #4: The Little Green Men; Ace 24301 [1969]
    The Flying Nun #5: The Underground Picnic; Ace 24302 [1970]
    Get Smart!; Tempo T-103 [1965]
    Get Smart: Sorry, Chief...; Tempo T-119 [1966]
    Get Smart Once Again!; Tempo T-121 [1966]
    Get Smart #4: Max Smart and the Perilous Pellets; Tempo T-140 [1966]
    Get Smart #5: Missed It By That Much!; Tempo T-154 [1967]
    Get Smart #6: And Loving It!; Tempo T-159 [1967]
    Get Smart #7: Max Smart - The Spy Who Went Out to the Cold; Tempo T-174
      [1968]
    Get Smart #8: Max Smart Loses Control; Tempo T-191 [1968]
    Get Smart #9: Max Smart and the Ghastly Ghost Affair; Tempo 05326 [1969]
    Gilligan's Island; Whitman 1566 [1966]
    Happy Days 1: Ready To Go Steady; Tempo 05794 [1974]
    Happy Days 2: Fonzie Drops In; Tempo 07452 [1974]
    Happy Days 3: The Invaders; Tempo 12267 [1975]
    Happy Days 4: Fonzie, Fonzie, Superstar; Tempo 12414 [1976]
    Happy Days 5: The Fonz & La Zonga; Tempo 12607 [1976]
    Happy Days 6: The Bike Tycoon; Tempo 12609 [1976]
    Happy Days 7: Dear Fonzie...; Tempo 12946 [1977]

Happy Days 8: Fonzie Goes to College; Tempo 14034 [1977]
The Iron Horse; Popular Library 60-2156 [1967]
Ironside: The Picture Frame Frame-Up; Whitman 1521 [1969]
Medical Story #2: Kill Me, Please...; Signet W6802 [1976]
Mod Squad: Home is Where the Quick Is; Pinnacle P027-N [1971]
The Monkees in Who's Got the Button?; Whitman 1539 [1968]
The Munsters and the Great Camera Caper; Whitman 1510 [1965]
The Munsters: The Last Resort; Whitman 1567 [1966]
My Friend Tony; Lancer 73-838 [1969]
Nanny and the Professor; Lancer 73876 [1970]
Nanny and the Professor #2: What Hath Nanny Wrought?; Lancer 73889 [1970]
Nanny and the Professor #3: The Bloop Box; Lancer 73205 [1970]
The Nurses; Bantam F2497 [1963]
Room 222: What Ever Happened to Mavis Rooster?; Tempo 05339 [1970]
Room 222 #2: Monday Morning Father; Tempo 05342 [1970]
Room 222 #3: Love is a Three Letter Word; Tempo 05358 [1970]
Room 222 #4: Bomb in the Classroom; Tempo 05372 [1971]
Room 222 #5: A Little Grass on the Side; Tempo 05414 [1971]
Room 222 #6: Have You Heard About Kelly?; Tempo 05594 [1973]
Sons and Daughters; Ballantine 24235 [1974]
Then Came Bronson; Pyramid T-2106 [1969]
Welcome Back, Kotter #1: The Sweathog Trail; Tempo 12406 [1976]
Welcome Back, Kotter #2: The Sweathog Newshawks; Tempo 12407 [1976]
Welcome Back, Kotter #3: The Super Sweathogs; Tempo 12608 [1976]
Welcome Back, Kotter #4: 10-4 Sweathogs!; Tempo 12706 [1976]
Welcome Back, Kotter #5: The Sweathog Sit-In; Tempo 12944 [1977]
Welcome Back, Kotter #6: Barbarino Drops Out; Tempo 12945 [1977]
The Young Rebels #1: The Hedgerow Incident; Ace 32335 [1970]
The Young Rebels #2: The Sea Gold Incident; Ace 95051 [1970]

as Ed Garth
Matt Lincoln #1: The Revolutionist; Lancer 73201 [1970]
Matt Lincoln #2: The Hostage; Lancer 73211 [1971]

as Alex Steele
The New People: They Came From the Sea; Tempo 05308 [1969]

Jones, [J.] Jeff

Co-written with Michael Butterworth (Jones uncredited)
Space: 1999 (Year 2) #2: Mind-Breaks of Space; Warner 88-342 [1977]

Jones, Nancy
The Official Wheel of Fortune Puzzle Book; Bantam 27204 [1987]

Jones, Raymond F. (1915-)
Voyage to the Bottom of the Sea; Whitman 1517 [1965]

Kane, Bob (1916-)
    Batman; Signet D2939 [1966]
    Batman vs. The Joker; Signet D2969 [1966]
    Batman vs. The Penguin; Signet D2970 [1966]

Kane, Frank (1912-1968)

  as Frank Kane
    The Lineup; Dell First Edition B125 [1959]

  as Frank Boyd
    Johnny Staccato; Gold Medal 980 [1960]

Kane, Henry (1918-)
    Peter Gunn; Dell First Edition B155 [1960]

Katz, Susan (1944?-1982)
    CHiPs: The Erik Estrada Scrapbook; Tempo 17209 [1980]

Keith, Brandon
    The Greet Hornet: The Case of the Disappearing Doctor; Whitman 1570 [1966]
    I Spy: Message From Moscow; Whitman 1542 [1966]
    The Man From U.N.C.L.E. and the Affair of the Gentle Saboteur; Whitman 1541
        [1966]
    The Man From U.N.C.L.E. and the Affair of the Gunrunners' Gold; Whitman 1543
        [1967]

Kendrick, Baynard [Hardwick] (1894-1977)
    Longstreet: The Last Express; Lancer 74779 [1971]
    Longstreet: Reservations For Death; Lancer 74784 [1971]
    Longstreet: Blind Man's Bluff; Lancer 74788 [1971]
    Longstreet: Out of Control; Lancer 75287 [1972]
    Longstreet: You Die Today!; Lancer 75305 [1972]

Kerr, Jean (1923-)
    Please Don't Eat the Daisies; Crest d834 [1965]

Kerr, Michael (pseudonym of Robert Hoskins, 1933-1993)
    Prisoner: Cell Block H #4: The Frustrations of Vera; Pinnacle 41215 [1981]

Kerrigan, Kate Lowe (pseudonym of Frances Rickett, 1921-)
    Another World; Ballantine 25859 [1978]
    Another World II; Ballantine 25860 [1978]
    Guiding Light #6: Secret Passions; Pioneer 06 [1986]
    Guiding Light #7: That Special Feeling; Pioneer 07 [1986]

Kersten, Mary Clare
    Dallas #11: Reality Strikes; Pioneer 100 [1987]
    Dallas #14: Family Secrets; Pioneer 103 [1987]

Ketchum, Philip [L.] (1902-1969)
    Wyatt Earp; Whitman 1548 [1956]

Key, Ted [Theodore Key] (1912-)
All Hazel; Bantam A2411 [1962]
Hazel Time; Bantam J2990 [1965]
Life With Hazel; Bantam F3325 [1967]

King, David (pseudonym of Howard Pehrson, 1914-1994)
The Rat Patrol #2 in Desert Danger; Paperback Library 53-411 [1967]
The Rat Patrol #3 in The Trojan Tank Affair; Paperback Library 53-477 [1967]
The Rat Patrol #4 in Two-Faced Enemy; Paperback Library 53-566 [1967]
The Rat Patrol #5 in Target for Tonight; Paperback Library 53-628 [1968]
The Rat Patrol #6 in Desert Masquerade; Paperback Library 53-696 [1968]

Kirchoff, Mary [Lynn] (1959-)
Amazing Stories Book 3: Portrait in Blood; TSR 74186 [1985]

Kitzes, Esther
See: E. Kitzes Knox

Kleinbaum, N.H.
Growing Pains; Bantam 26881 [1987]

Knight, David (pseudonym of Richard S. Prather, 1921-)
Dragnet: Case No. 561; Pocket 1120 [1956]

Knox, E. Kitzes (joint pseudonym for Esther Kitzes and Helen Knox)
Gomer Pyle, U.S.M.C.; Pyramid R-1267 [1965]

Knox, Helen
See: E. Kitzes Knox

Kohner, Frederick (1905-1986)
Gidget in Love; Dell 2872 [1965]
Gidget Goes Parisienne; Dell 2874 [1966]
Gidget Goes New York; Dell 2897 [1968]

Koziakin, Vladimir
Hardy Boys Mystery Mazes; Tempo 14508 [1977]
Nancy Drew Mystery Mazes; Tempo 14504 [1977]

Kupperberg, Paul [Howard] (1955-)
The Hulk and Spider-Man in Murdermoon; Pocket 82094 [1979]

Landon, Margaret [Dorothea Mortenson] (1903-1993)
Anna and the King of Siam; Pocket 77653 [1972]

Landsburg, Alan [William] (1933-)
In Search of Lost Civilizations (#1); Bantam 10582 [1976]
In Search of Extraterrestrials (#2); Bantam 10722 [1977]
In Search of Magic and Witchcraft (#3); Bantam 10851 [1977]
In Search of Strange Phenomena; Bantam 10855 [1977]
In Search of Myths and Monsters; Bantam 11137 [1977]
In Search of Missing Persons; Bantam 11459 [1978]

Langley, Fredric

  Co-written with Ron Ellik, jointly as Fredric Davies
    The Man From U.N.C.L.E. #14: The Cross of Gold Affair; Ace G-689 [1968]

Lardine, Robert
    The Tonight Show: He-e-e-ere's Johnny; Award AD1425 [1975]

Larson, Glen A. (1937-)

  Co-written with Ron Goulart
    Battlestar Galactica 8: Greetings From Earth; Berkley 06047 [1983]
    Battlestar Galactica 9: Experiment in Terra; Berkley 06418 [1984]
    Battlestar Galactica 10: The Long Patrol; Berkley 07105 [1984]

  Co-written with Roger Hill
    Knight Rider; Pinnacle 42170 [1983]
    Knight Rider #2: Trust Doesn't Rust; Pinnacle 42181 [1984]
    Knight Rider #3: Hearts of Stone; Pinnacle 42182 [1984]

  Co-written with Michael Resnick
    Battlestar Galactica 5: Galactica Discovers Earth; Berkley 04744 [1980]

  Co-written with Robert Thurston
    Battlestar Galactica; Berkley 03958 [1978]
    Battlestar Galactica 2: The Cylon Death Machine; Berkley 04080 [1979]
    Battlestar Galactica 3: The Tombs of Kobol; Berkley 04267 [1979]
    Battlestar Galactica 4: The Young Warriors; Berkley 04655 [1980]
    Battlestar Galactica 11: The Nightmare Machine; Berkley 08618 [1985]
    Battlestar Galactica 12: "Die, Chameleon!"; Berkley 09095 [1986]
    Battlestar Galactica 13: Apollo's War; Berkley 09476 [1987]
    Battlestar Galactica 14: Surrender the Galactica; Ace Tempo Star 05104 [1988]

  Co-written with Nicholas Yermakov
    Battlestar Galactica 6: The Living Legend; Berkley 05249 [1982]
    Battlestar Galactica 7: War of the Gods; Berkley 05660 [1982]

Books were written by Goulart, Hill, Resnick, etc.; Larson, creator and executive producer of *Battlestar Galactica* and *Knight Rider*, was given co-author credit but wasn't involved in the writing.

Lasker, Michael (composite gangster figure)

  Co-written with "Richard Alan Simmons" [Richard Elman]
    The Gangster Chronicles; Jove K5808 [1981]

Latham, Caroline [S.] (1940-)
    Miami Vice: Miami Magic; Zebra 8217-1800 [1985]

Laumer, [John] Keith (1925-1993; surname is pronounced LAW-mer)
    The Avengers #5: "The Afrit Affair"; Berkley X1547 [1968]
    The Avengers #6: "The Drowned Queen"; Berkley X1565 [1968]
    The Avengers #7: "The Gold Bomb"; Berkley X1592 [1968]

The Invaders #1; Pyramid R-1664 [1967]
The Invaders #2: Enemies From Beyond; Pyramid X-1689 [1967]

Lawrence, Alfred
Cade's County; Popular Library 08184 [1972]
Columbo; Popular Library 01524 [1972]
Columbo #2: The Dean's Death; Popular Library 00265 [1975]

Lawrence, J[udith] A. (Mrs. James Blish)
Star Trek: Mudd's Angels; Bantam 11802 [1978]

  Co-written with James Blish
Star Trek 12; Bantam 11382 [1977]

Lawrence, Marcia
All My Children #1/#2 [combined]: Once and Always; Pioneer 350 [1987]
    [Lawrence wrote #1 of set only]
Days of Our Lives #10: Promises and Lies; Pioneer 60 [1987]
Days of Our Lives #12: Past Loves and Lies; Pioneer 151 [1987]
Days of Our Lives #14: Obsessions; Pioneer 153 [1987]
General Hospital #1/#2 [combined]: Forever and a Day; Pioneer 300 [1987]
    [Lawrence wrote #2 of set only]
Knots Landing #10: Family Affairs; Pioneer 70 [1987]

Lay, Beirne, Jr. (1909-1982)

  Co-written with Sy Bartlett
Twelve O'Clock High!; Ballantine U5041 [1965]

Leamer, Laurence [Allen] (1941-)
The Tonight Show: King of the Night: The Life of Johnny Carson; St. Martin's
    Press 92256 [1990]

Lee, Elsie (1912-1987)
Sam Benedict: Cast the First Stone; Lancer 70-035 [1963]

Lee, Fleming (1933-)
The Saint Abroad; Curtis 07137 [1971]
The Saint and the Fiction Makers; Curtis 07199 [1971]
The Saint on TV; Curtis 07200 [1971]

Lee, Howard (house pseudonym for Lou Cameron [1924-], Ron Goulart [1933-], and
Barry N. Malzberg [1939-])
Kung Fu #1: The Way of the Tiger, the Sign of the Dragon; Warner 76-464 [1973]
    (Malzberg)
Kung Fu #2: Chains; Warner 76-465 [1973] (Goulart)
Kung Fu #3: Superstition; Warner 76-466 [1973] (Goulart)
Kung Fu #4: A Praying Mantis Kills; Warner 76-467 [1974] (Cameron)

Lee, Manfred B[ennington] (1905-1971; born Manford Lepofsky, name legally changed)
Pseudonym: Ellery Queen

Lee, Stan (1922-; born Stanley Martin Lieber, name legally changed)
Stan Lee Presents The Incredible Hulk; Pocket 81446 [1978]
Stan Lee Presents The Incredible Hulk #2; Pocket 82559 [1979]

Co-written with Larry Lieber
The Incredible Hulk; Tempo 17179 [1980]
The Incredible Hulk Volume 2; Tempo 17314 [1981]

Lee, Tara
Days of Our Lives #6: Forsaken Dreams; Pioneer 56 [1986]

Lee, Wayne C[yril] (1917-)
Bat Masterson; Whitman 1550 [1960]

Lehman, Ernest [Paul] (1915-)
Playhouse 90: The Comedian and Other Stories; Signet 1446 [1957]

Leighton, Frances Spatz (female author)
The Patty Duke Show: Patty goes to Washington; Ace F-278 [1964]

Leinster, Murray (pseudonym of Will F. Jenkins, 1896-1975)
Land of the Giants; Pyramid X-1846 [1968]
Land of the Giants #2: The Hot Spot; Pyramid X-1921 [1969]
Land of the Giants #3: Unknown Danger; Pyramid X-2105 [1969]
Men Into Space; Berkley G461 [1960]
The Time Tunnel; Pyramid R-1522 [1967]
The Time Tunnel #2: Timeslip!; Pyramid R-1680 [1967]

Leslie, Josephine [Aimee Campbell] (1898-1979)
The Ghost and Mrs. Muir; Pocket 77761 [1974] [previously published under the
author's pseudonym of R.A. Dick]

Leslie, Peter (1922-)
The Man From U.N.C.L.E. #7: The Radioactive Camel Affair; Ace G-600 [1966]
The Man From U.N.C.L.E. #9: The Diving Dames Affair; Ace G-617 [1967]
The Man From U.N.C.L.E. #16: The Splintered Sunglasses Affair; Ace G-752
[1968]
The Man From U.N.C.L.E. #18: The Unfair Fare Affair; Ace 51701 [1969]
The Man From U.N.C.L.E. #23: The Finger in the Sky Affair; Ace 51706 [1971]
Secret Agent: Hell For Tomorrow; Macfadden 50-280 [1966]

Levinson, Bill [William A. Levinson]

Co-written with Dewey "Pigmeat" Markham
Laugh-In: Here Come the Judge!; Popular Library 60-8080 [1969]

Levy, Elizabeth (1942-)
Father Murphy's First Miracle; Random House 85810 [1983]

Lewis, Mary Beth
Mork & Mindy Puzzlers; Cinnamon House 15880 [1979]

Lewis, Shari (1934-)
The Shari Lewis Show: Fun With the Kids; Macfadden 75-140 [1964]

Libby, Bill [William M. Libby] (1927-1984)

Co-written with Monty Hall
Let's Make a Deal: Emcee Monty Hall; Ballantine 24370 [1975]

Lieber, Larry

Co-written with Stan Lee
The Incredible Hulk; Tempo 17179 [1980]
The Incredible Hulk Volume 2; Tempo 17314 [1981]

Linkletter, Art[hur Gordan] (1912-)
Kids Say the Darndest Things!; Cardinal C-330 [1959]
The Secret World of Kids; Cardinal GC-92 [1960]
Kids Still Say the Darndest Things!; Cardinal GC-157 [1962]
Kids Sure Rite Funny!; Crest k646 [1963]
A Child's Garden of Misinformation; Crest d949 [1966]
Oops! Or, Life's Awful Moments; Pocket 75179 [1968]
I Wish I'd Said That!; Pocket 75412 [1969]
People Are Funny; Cardinal C-384 [1960]

Co-written with Dean Jennings
Confessions of a Happy Man; Cardinal GC-124 [1962]

All but *People Are Funny* are based on the show *Art Linkletter's House Party*.

Liss, Howard (1922-)

Co-written with Gene Fawcette
The Monkees; Popular Library 50-8026 [1966]

Lockhart, Max (pseudonym of Doris R. Meredith, 1944-)
Private Eye #4: Nobody Dies in Chinatown; Ivy 0272 [1988]

Lockwood, Daniel
The Mary Hartman Story; Bolder 9098 [1976]

London, John Griffith (Jack London) (1876-1916)
Adventures of Captain David Grief; Popular Library PC300 [1957]

Loomis, Noel [Miller] (1905-1969)

as Noel Loomis
Bonanza; Popular Library PC1000 [1960]
Have Gun, Will Travel; Dell First Edition B156 [1960]

as Sam Allison
Wells Fargo and Danger Station; Whitman 1588 [1958]

Lorrah, Jean (194?-)
Star Trek: The Next Generation #4: Survivors; Pocket 67438 [1989]

Lott, Davis [Newton] (1913-)
    Wyatt Earp; Whitman Big Little Book 1644 [1958]

Lottman, Eileen [Shurb] (1927-)

    as Eileen Lottman
        The Bionic Woman: Welcome Home, Jaime; Berkley Z3230 [1976]
        The Bionic Woman: Extracurricular Activities; Berkley O3326 [1977]
        Dynasty; Bantam 23352 [1983]
        Dynasty: Alexis Returns; Bantam 24431 [1984]

    as Maud Willis
        Doctor's Hospital #1: One of Our Own; Pocket 80231 [1975]

Lupoff, Richard A[llen] (1935-)
    Pseudonym: Addison E. Steele

Lynds, Dennis (1924-)
    S.W.A.T. #1: Crossfire!; Pocket 80241 [1975]

Lyon, Winston (pseudonym of William Woolfolk, 1917-)
    Batman vs. Three Villains of Doom; Signet D2940 [1966]
    Batman vs. The Fearsome Foursome; Signet D2995 [1966]

McBain, Ed (pseudonym of Evan Hunter, 1926-)
        87th Precinct: Lady, Lady, I did it!; Perma M-4253 [1962]
        87th Precinct: The Con Man; Perma M-4264 [1962]
        87th Precinct: Killer's Payoff; Perma M-4265 [1962]
        87th Precinct: The Mugger; Perma M-4266 [1962]
        87th Precinct: Killer's Choice; Perma M-4267 [1962]
        87th Precinct: Cop Hater; Perma M-4268 [1962]

McCall, Judson
    Getting Together; Curtis 07173 [1971]

MacCargo, J.T. (house pseudonym for Peter Rabe [1921-1990] and ?)
        Mannix #1: The Faces of Murder; Belmont Tower 50793 [1975] (?)
        Mannix #2: A Fine Day For Dying; Belmont Tower 50823 [1975] (Rabe)
        Mannix #3: A Walk on the Blind Side; Belmont Tower 50825 [1975] (?)
        Mannix #4: Round Trip to Nowhere; Belmont Tower 50834 [1975] (Rabe)

McCulley, Johnston (1883-1958)
    The Mark of Zorro; Dell D204 [1958]

McDaniel, David [Edward] (1939-1977)
        The Man From U.N.C.L.E. #4: The Dagger Affair; Ace G-571 [1966]
        The Man From U.N.C.L.E. #6: The Vampire Affair; Ace G-590 [1966]
        The Man From U.N.C.L.E. #8: The Monster Wheel Affair; Ace G-613 [1967]
        The Man From U.N.C.L.E. #13: The Rainbow Affair; Ace G-670 [1967]
        The Man From U.N.C.L.E. #15: The Utopia Affair; Ace G-729 [1968]
        The Man From U.N.C.L.E. #17: The Hollow Crown Affair; Ace 51700 [1969]
        The Prisoner #2: Number Two; Ace 67901 [1969]

McDonnell, Virginia [Bleecker] (1917-)
   Guiding Light #11; Hidden Fears; Pioneer 11 [1987]
   The Waltons #6: The Accident; Whitman 1510 [1975]

McGaughy, Dudley Dean (-1986)
   Pseudonym: Dean Owen

MacGregor, Rob[ert]

   as Rob MacGregor, co-written with wife Trish Janeshutz
   The Making of Miami Vice; Ballantine 33669 [1986]

   as T.N. Robb
   Private Eye #1; Ivy 0269 [1988]
   Private Eye #3: Flip Side; Ivy 0271 [1988]

McKenzie, Michael (1954-)
   Backstage at Saturday Night Live!; Scholastic Book Services 30919 [1980]

McKenzie, Roger
   Stan Lee Presents: Battlestar Galactica; Ace Tempo Star 04876 [1978]
   Stan Lee Presents: Battlestar Galactica Volume II; Ace Tempo Star 04877 [1979]

McLean, Kathryn [Anderson] (1909-1966)
   Pseudonym: Kathryn Forbes

McMahon, Ed (1923-)
   The Tonight Show: Grin and Beer It; Pyramid N4101 [1976]
   The Tonight Show: Here's Ed; Berkley 03592 [1977]

McNeilly, Wilfred [Glassford] (1921-1983)
   Secret Agent: No Way Out; Macfadden 50-320 [1966]

Maas, Peter (1929-)
   Serpico; Bantam 10265 [1976]

Malis, Jody Cameron

   as Jody Cameron Malis
   The Dark Shadows Cookbook; Ace 13810 [1970]
   "The Newlywed Game" Cookbook; Pocket 75652 [1971]

   as Jody Cameron
   Family Affair: Buffy's Cookbook; Berkley W2092 [1971]

Malzberg, Barry N[athaniel] (1939-)

   as Howard Lee
   Kung Fu #1: The Way of the Tiger, the Sign of the Dragon; Warner 76-464 [1973]

Mann, Abby (1927-; born Abraham Goodman)
   Medical Story; Signet W6785 [1975]

Mann, Patrick (pseudonym of Leslie Waller, 1923-)
   Falcon Crest; Dell 12437 [1984]

Manners, Margaret (1914-1974; i.e., Margaret Manners Lippman)
Love of Life; Dell First Edition B183 [1961]

Mantell, Paul
Co-written with Avery Hart

Dallas #1: Love Conquers Fear; Pioneer 81 [1986]
Dallas #2: Ardent Memories; Pioneer 82 [1986]
Dallas #3: Love's Challenge; Pioneer 83 [1986]
Dallas #4: The Power of Passion; Pioneer 84 [1986]
Dallas #5: Dangerous Desire; Pioneer 85 [1986]
Dallas #6: Double Dealing; Pioneer 86 [1986]
Dallas #7: Hostage Heart; Pioneer 87 [1986]
Dallas #8: This Cherished Land; Pioneer 88 [1986]
Dallas #9: Power Play; Pioneer 89 [1987]
Dallas #10: Winner Take All; Pioneer 90 [1987]

Malloy, Dylan
Another World #9: Suspicions; Pioneer 39 [1986]

Markham, Dewey "Pigmeat" (1904-1981)

Co-written with Bill Levinson
Laugh-In: Here Come the Judge!; Popular Library 60-8080 [1969]

Marsh, Spencer (1931-)
All in the Family: God, Man and Archie Bunker; Bantam T7913 [1976]
All in the Family: Edith the Good; Harper & Row RD 214 [1977]

Marshall, Deborah A.

Co-written with A.C. Crispin
V: Death Tide; Pinnacle 42469 [1985]

Marston, William Moulton (1893-1947)
Pseudonym: Charles Moulton

Martin, David (1935-)

as David Martin
Doctor Who #1: Search for the Doctor; Ballantine 33224 [1986]
Doctor Who #3: Garden of Evil; Ballantine 33226 [1986]

as Michael Holt
Doctor Who #2: Crisis in Space; Ballantine 33225 [1986]

Martin, Pete (1901-1980)

Co-written with Diane Disney Miller
The Story of Walt Disney; Dell D266 [1959]

Martin, Philip
   Doctor Who #5: Invasion of the Ormazoids; Ballantine 33231 [1986]

Mason, Douglas R[ankine] (1918-)
   Pseudonym: John Rankine

Matcha, Jack (1919-)
   The Brady Bunch in "The Treasure of Mystery Island"; Tiger Beat XQ2011 [1972]
   The Brady Bunch in the New York Mystery; Tiger Beat XQ2014 [1972]
   The Brady Bunch in Adventure on the High Seas; Tiger Beat XQ2017 [1973]

Matthews, Dick

   Co-written with JoAnne Worley
      Rowan & Martin's Laugh-In #4: JoAnne Worley's Chicken Joke Book; Signet
      T4060 [1969]

Meade, Richard (pseudonym of Ben Haas, 1926-1977)
   Cimmaron Strip; Popular Library 60-2245 [1967]

Meredith, D[oris] R. (1944-)
   Pseudonym: Max Lockhart

Metalious, George (1924?-)

   Co-written with June O'Shea
      The Girl From "Peyton Place"; Dell 2888 [1965]

Metalious, Grace [de Repentigny] (1924-1964)
   Peyton Place; Pocket 75087 [1965]

Meyers, Barlow (1902-; female author)
   Have Gun, Will Travel; Whitman 1568 [1959]
   The Lawrence Welk Show: Janet Lennon: Adventure at Two Rivers; Whitman 1536
      [1961]
   The Lawrence Welk Show: Janet Lennon at Camp Calamity; Whitman 1539 [1962]
   The Lawrence Welk Show: Janet Lennon and the Angels; Whitman 1583 [1963]
   The Mickey Mouse Club: Walt Disney's Annette: Mystery at Medicine Wheel;
      Whitman 1512 [1964]
   The Restless Gun; Whitman 1559 [1959]

Meyers, Richard S. (1953-)
   The Incredible Hulk in Cry of the Beast; Pocket 82085 [1979]

Miall, Robert (pseudonym of John Burke, 1922-)
   UFO-1: Flesh Hunters; Warner 75-273 [1973]
   UFO-2: Sporting Blood; Warner 75-274 [1973]

Michael, Marjorie (Mrs. George Michael)
   The Michaels in Africa: I Married a Hunter; Pyramid PR 14 [1958]

Michaels, Angela
   Prisoner: Cell Block H #5: The Reign of Queen Bea; Pinnacle 41403 [1981]

Miksch, W[illiam] F.
The Addams Family Strikes Back; Pyramid R-1257 [1965]

Millard, Joe [Joseph John Millard] (1908-1989)
Hec Ramsey #2: The Hunted; Award AN1232 [1974]

Miller, Albert G[riffith] (1905-1982)
Fury: Stallion of Broken Wheel Ranch; Tempo T14 [1962]

Miller, Diane Disney (1933-)

Co-written with Pete Martin
The Story of Walt Disney; Dell D266 [1959]

Miller, Snowden
Gene Autry and the Badmen of Broken Bow; Whitman 2355 [1951]
Roy Rogers and the Rimrod Renegades; Whitman 2305 [1952]

Miller, Victor B[rooke] (1940-)
Kojak #1: Siege; Pocket 78487 [1974]
Kojak #2: Requiem for a Cop; Pocket 78488 [1974]
Kojak #3: Girl in the River; Pocket 78817 [1975]
Kojak #4: Therapy in Dynamite; Pocket 78865 [1975]
Kojak #5: Death Is Not a Passing Grade; Pocket 78912 [1975]
Kojak #6: A Very Deadly Game; Pocket 78960 [1975]
Kojak #7: Take-over; Pocket 78996 [1975]
Kojak #8: Gun Business; Pocket 78998 [1975]
Kojak #9: The Trade-off; Pocket 80045 [1975]

Miner, Mae (American author)
Capitol #1: Unspoken Desires; Pioneer 91 [1986]

Moore, Mary Ellen
Mork & Mindy: The Robin Williams Scrapbook; Ace Tempo Star 73200 [1979]

Morey, Walt[er Nelson] (1907-1992)
Gentle Ben; Tempo T-166 [1967]

Morley, Evan [Sherman] (female publishing exec.)
Hardy Boys Secret Codes; Tempo 14505 [1977]
Nancy Drew Secret Codes; Tempo 14509 [1977]

Mulcahy, Lucille Burnett
Pseudonym: Helen Hale

Munshower, Suzanne (1945-)
Happy Days: Hollywood's Newest Superstar: Henry Winkler; Berkley Z3231 [1976]
Miami Vice: Don Johnson: An Unauthorized Biography; Signet AE4345 [1986]
Welcome Back, Kotter: Meet John Travolta; Tempo 12936 [1976]

Murray, Kathryn [Hazel] (1906-)

  Co-written with Betty Hannah Hoffman
    My Husband, Arthur Murray; Avon T510 [1960]

Nesbit, Troy (pseudonym of Franklin Folsom, 1907-)
    Wagon Train; Whitman 1567 [1959]
    Fury and the Mystery at Trappers' Hole; Whitman 1557 [1959]

Ness, Eliot (1903-1957)

  Co-written with Oscar Fraley
    The Untouchables; Popular Library G403 [1960]

Newman, Paul S. (1924-; comic book writer)
    Gentle Ben: Mystery in the Everglades; Whitman Big Little Book 2035 [1969]
    Gunsmoke: Showdown on Front Street; Whitman 1520 [1969]
    The Invaders: Alien Missile Threat; Whitman Big Little Book 2012 [1967]

Nixon, Agnes [Eckhardt] (1927-)
    The Guiding Light; Popular Library 60-8034 [1967]

Norbom, Mary Ann
    Richard Dawson and Family Feud; Signet J9773 [1981]

O'Connor, Patrick (1925-; born Robert O'Connor)
    The Monkees Go Mod; Popular Library 60-8046 [1967]

O'Connor, Richard (1915-1975)
    Bat Masterson; Bantam A1888 [1958]

O'Shea, June [L.]

  Co-written with George Metalious
    The Girl From "Peyton Place"; Dell 2888 [1965]

O'Shell, Maggie
    Prisoner: Cell Block H #3: The Karen Travers Story; Pinnacle 41176 [1981]

Oram, John (pseudonym of John Oram Thomas)
    The Man From U.N.C.L.E. #3: The Copenhagen Affair; Ace G-564 [1965]
    The Man From U.N.C.L.E. #22: The Stone-Cold Dead in the Market Affair; Ace
      51705 [1970]

Osborn, John Jay, Jr. (1945-)
    The Associates; Popular Library 04530 [1979]
    The Paper Chase; Popular Library 04357 [1978]

Owen, Dean (pseudonym of Dudley Dean McGaughy, -1986)
    Bonanza #1: Winter Grass; Paperback Library 52-726 [1968]
    Bonanza #2: Ponderosa Kill; Paperback Library 52-757 [1968]
    Hec Ramsey; Award AN1169 [1973]
    The Men From Shiloh #1: Lone Trail for the Virginian; Lancer 74775 [1971]
    Rebel of Broken Wheel; Monarch 218 [1961]

Owen, Jim M. (1903-1972)
  Jim Owen's Hillbilly Humor; Pocket 75623 [1970]

Paar, Jack (1918-)
  The Jack Paar Tonight Show: I Kid You Not; Cardinal GC-103 [1961]
  The Jack Paar Tonight Show: My Saber is Bent; Cardinal GC-148 [1962]

Parker, Claire
  The Rookies; Bantam N7703 [1973]

Parker, Robert B[rown] (1932-)
  Spenser: For Hire: Valediction [1986]

Patrick, Andrew
  Baretta: Beyond the Law; Berkley 03515 [1977]

Patten, Lewis B[yford] (1915-1981)
  Gene Autry and the Ghost Riders; Whitman 1510 [1955]
  Gene Autry and Arapaho War Drums; Whitman 1512 [1957]
  The Adventures of Jim Bowie; Whitman Big Little Book 1648 [1958]

Paul, Rose
  The Six Million Dollar Man's Bionic Brain Benders; Tempo 12523 [1976]
  The Six Million Dollar Man's Bionic Eye Rebus Puzzles; Tempo 12527 [1976]
  The Bionic Woman's Brain Teasers; Tempo 12528 [1976]

Pearl, Jack [Jacques Bain Pearl] (1923-)
  Divorce Court #1: Gilchrist vs. Gilchrist: A Question of Adultery; Pocket 75667
    [1971]
  Divorce Court #2: Lazer vs. Lazer: The Black Widow; Pocket 75668 [1971]
  Garrison's Gorillas; Dell 2798 [1967]
  Garrison's Gorillas and the Fear Formula; Whitman 1548 [1968]
  The Invaders: Dam of Death; Whitman 1545 [1967]
  Nancy; Pyramid T2339 [1970]

  Co-written with David Toma
  Toma #2: The Airport Affair; Dell 04604 [1975]
  Toma #3: The Affair of the Unhappy Hooker; Dell 05284 [1976]

Pedneau, Dave [David Elliott Pedneau] (1947-1990)
  Pseudonym: David Elliott

Pehrson, Howard [Virgil] (1914-1994)
  Pseudonym: David King

Perkins, Amanda
  Another World #12: Love Play; Pioneer 051 [1987]
  Another World #14: The Art of Love; Pioneer 053 [1987]

Perlberg, Diane J., ed.

  Co-written with Joelle Delbourgo
  Dallas: The Quotations of J. R. Ewing; Bantam 14440 [1980]

Pfeffer, Susan Beth (1948-)
Head of the Class; Bantam 28190 [1989]
Paper Dolls; Dell 96777 [1984]

Pfeil, Don[ald J.] (-198?; surname is pronounced "File")

as William Arrow
Return to the Planet of the Apes #2: Escape from Terror Lagoon; Ballantine 25167
[1976]

Phillifent, John T[homas] (1916-1976)
The Man From U.N.C.L.E. #5: The Mad Scientist Affair; Ace G-581 [1966]
The Man From U.N.C.L.E. #19: The Power Cube Affair; Ace 51702 [1969]
The Man From U.N.C.L.E. #20: The Corfu Affair; Ace 51703 [1970]

Phillips, Samantha (pseudonym of Sandi Gelles-Cole, 1949-)
Knots Landing #2: Uncharted Love; Pioneer 62 [1986]
Knots Landing #5: Mothers and Daughters; Pioneer 65 [1986]

Pike, Charles E.
Happy Days: The Fonz: The Henry Winkler Story; Pocket 80746 [1976]

Posner, Richard (1944-)
Lucas Tanner: A Question of Guilt; Pyramid V3777 [1975]
Lucas Tanner #2: A Matter of Love; Pyramid V3928 [1975]
Lucas Tanner #3: For Her to Decide; Pyramid V4042 [1976]

Powell, Talmage (1920-)
Mission: Impossible: The Priceless Particle; Whitman 1515 [1969]
Mission: Impossible: The Money Explosion; Whitman 1512 [1970]

Prather, Richard S[cott] (1921-)
Pseudonym: David Knight

Preble, Amanda
Knots Landing #11: A Second Chance; Pioneer 200 [1987]

Proctor, Geo[rge] W[yatt] (1946-)
V: The Chicago Conversion; Pinnacle 42429 [1985]
V: The Texas Run; Pinnacle 42470 [1985]

Pruetzel, Maria (mother of Freddie Prinze)

Co-written with John A. Barbour
Chico and the Man: The Freddie Prinze Story; Master's Press 89251 [1978]

Queen, Ellery (joint pseudonym for Frederic Dannay [1905-1982] and Manfred B. Lee
[1905-1971]; later house pseudonym for Jack Vance [1916-], Avram Davidson [1923-
1993], and others)
Ellery Queen: The Madman Theory; Signet Y6715 [1975] (Vance)
Ellery Queen: The Finishing Stroke; Signet Y6819 [1975] (Dannay/Lee)
Ellery Queen: Face to Face; Signet Y6872 [1975] (Dannay/Lee)
Ellery Queen: The House of Brass; Signet Y6958 [1975] (Davidson)

Ellery Queen: Cop Out; Signet Y6996 [1975] (Dannay/Lee)
Ellery Queen: The Last Woman in His Life; Signet Y7123 [1975] (Dannay/Lee)
Ellery Queen: The Vanishing Corpse; Pyramid V4094 [1976] (?)

Rabe, Peter (1921-1990)

as J.T. MacCargo
Mannix #2: A Fine Day For Dying; Belmont Tower 50823 [1975]
Mannix #4: Round Trip to Nowhere; Belmont Tower 50834 [1975]

Racina, Thom (pseudonym of Thomas Frank Raucina, 1946-)
Baretta: Sweet Revenge; Berkley 03559 [1977]
Kojak in San Francisco; Berkley Z3237 [1976]
Quincy, M.E.; Ace 69945 [1977]
Quincy, M.E. #2; Ace 69946 [1977]

Raintree, Lee (pseudonym of Con Sellers, 1922-1992)
Dallas; Dell 11752 [1978]

Rankine, John (pseudonym of Douglas R. Mason, 1918-)
Space: 1999 #2: Moon Odyssey; Pocket 80185 [1975]
Space: 1999 #5: Lunar Attack; Pocket 80305 [1976]
Space: 1999 #6: Astral Quest; Pocket 80392 [1976]
Space: 1999 #8: Android Planet; Pocket 80706 [1976]
Space: 1999 #10: Phoenix of Megaron; Pocket 80764 [1976]

Rathjen, Carl Henry (1909-1984)
Land of the Giants: Flight of Fear; Whitman 1516 [1969]
The Waltons #2: The Puzzle; Whitman 1576 [1975]
The Waltons #4: The Treasures; Whitman 1580 [1975]

Raucina, Thomas Frank (1946-)
Pseudonym: Thom Racina

Reed, Rochelle
The Sandy Duncan Show: The Sandy Duncan Story; Pyramid 02934 [1973]

Co-written with Susan Dey
The Partridge Family: For Girls Only; Tiger Beat XQ2001 [1972]

Reeder, Russell Potter, Jr. (Colonel Red Reeder) (1902-)
Mackenzie's Raiders: The Mackenzie Raid; Ballantine 460K [1960]

Renauld, Ron[ald Gerard]

as Charles Heath
The A-Team; Dell 10009 [1984]
The A-Team 2: Small But Deadly Wars; Dell 10020 [1984]
The A-Team 3: When You Comin' Back, Range Rider?; Dell 10027 [1984]
The A-Team 4: Old Scores to Settle; Dell 10034 [1984]
The A-Team 5: Ten Percent of Trouble; Dell 10037 [1984]

Resnick, Michael [Diamond] (1942-)

  Co-written with Glen A. Larson [Resnick wrote, Larson given co-author credit]
    Battlestar Galactica 5: Galactica Discovers Earth; Berkley 04744 [1980]

Resnick, Sylvia [Safran] (1927-)
    The Partridge Family Cookbook; Curtis 09219 [1973]
    The Walton Family Cookbook; Bantam TE2123 [1976]

Reynolds, Mack [Dallas McCord Reynolds] (1917-)
    Star Trek: Mission to Horatius; Whitman 1549 [1968]

Rice, Jeff (1944-)
    The Night Stalker; Pocket 78343 [1973]
    The Night Strangler; Pocket 78352 [1974]

Richards, Evan (pseudonym of Joseph Michael Jahn, 1943-)
    The Six Million Dollar Man #2: Solid Gold Kidnapping; Warner 76-834 [1975]

Richmond, Roe [Roaldus Frederick Richmond] (1910-)
    The Deputy; Dell First Edition B172 [1960]

Rickett, Frances (1921-)

  as Kate Lowe Kerrigan
    Another World; Ballantine 25859 [1978]
    Another World II; Ballantine 25860 [1978]
    Guiding Light #6: Secret Passions; Pioneer 06 [1986]
    Guiding Light #7: That Special Feeling; Pioneer 07 [1986]

  as Martha Winslow
    Another World #2: Love's Destiny; Pioneer 32 [1986]
    Another World #3: Affairs of the Moment; Pioneer 33 [1986]
    Another World #4: Love's Encore; Pioneer 34 [1986]
    Another World #5: Caress From the Past; Pioneer 35 [1986]
    Another World #10: Deceptions; Pioneer 40 [1987]

Riefe, Alan (1925-)

  Co-written with Dick Harrington
    Sanford and Son; Curtis 09222 [1973]

Rios, Tere (pseudonym of Marie Teresa Rios Versace, 1917-)
    The Flying Nun: The Fifteenth Pelican; Avon ZS130 [1967]

Rivers, Jim
    Roy Rogers and the Enchanted Canyon; Whitman 1502 [also Whitman 2373] [1954]

Robb, T.N. (pseudonym of Rob MacGregor)
    Private Eye #1; Ivy 0269 [1988]
    Private Eye #3: Flip Side; Ivy 0271 [1988]

Robertson, Frank C[hester] (1890-1969)
Have Gun, Will Travel: A Man Called Paladin; Macfadden 60-191 [1964]
Rawhide; Signet S1910 [1961]
Wanted: Dead or Alive; Signet S1982 [1961]

Robin-Tani, Marianne
Wheel of Fortune: Vanna White; St. Martin's Press 90829 [1987]

Robinson, Richard (1945-)
Kung Fu: The Peaceful Way; Pyramid 03315 [1974]

Robsky, Paul (-1973)

Co-written with Oscar Fraley
The Last of the Untouchables; Popular Library G569 [1962]

Roddenberry, Gene (1921-1991)

Co-written with Stephen E. Whitfield [Whitfield wrote, Roddenberry given co-author credit]
The Making of Star Trek; Ballantine 73004 [1968]

Roeburt, John (1909?-1972)
The Roaring 20's: Sing Out Sweet Homicide; Dell First Edition K105 [1961]

Romano, Deane [Louis] (1927-)
Banacek; Bantam N7881 [1973]

Romanowski, Patricia (pseudonym of Patricia Ann Romanowski Bashe, 1956-)

Co-written with Vanna White
Wheel of Fortune: Vanna Speaks; Warner 34668 [1988]

Rosen, Marcia

Co-written with Gerry Hunt
The Cheers Bartending Guide; Avon 70189 [1986]

Ross, Marilyn (pseudonym of Dan Ross, 1912-1995)
Dark Shadows #1; Paperback Library 52-386 [1966]
Dark Shadows #2: Victoria Winters; Paperback Library 52-421 [1967]
Dark Shadows #3: Strangers at Collins House; Paperback Library 52-543 [1967]
Dark Shadows #4: The Mystery of Collinwood; Paperback Library 52-610 [1968]
Dark Shadows #5: The Curse of Collinwood; Paperback Library 52-608 [1968]
Dark Shadows #6: Barnabas Collins; Paperback Library 62-001 [1968]
Dark Shadows #7: The Secret of Barnabas Collins; Paperback Library 62-039 [1969]
Dark Shadows #8: The Demon of Barnabas Collins; Paperback Library 62-084 [1969]
Dark Shadows #9: The Foe of Barnabas Collins; Paperback Library 62-135 [1969]
Dark Shadows #10: The Phantom and Barnabas Collins; Paperback Library 62-195 [1969]

Dark Shadows #11: Barnabas Collins versus the Warlock; Paperback Library 62-212 [1969]

Dark Shadows #12: The Peril of Barnabas Collins; Paperback Library 62-244 [1969]

Dark Shadows #13: Barnabas Collins and the Mysterious Ghost; Paperback Library 63-258 [1970]

Dark Shadows #14: Barnabas Collins and Quentin's Demon; Paperback Library 63-275 [1970]

Dark Shadows #15: Barnabas Collins and the Gypsy Witch; Paperback Library 63-296 [1970]

Dark Shadows #16: Barnabas, Quentin and the Mummy's Curse; Paperback Library 63-318 [1970]

Dark Shadows #17: Barnabas, Quentin and the Avenging Ghost; Paperback Library 63-338 [1970]

Dark Shadows #18: Barnabas, Quentin and the Nightmare Assassin; Paperback Library 63-363 [1970]

Dark Shadows #19: Barnabas, Quentin and the Crystal Coffin; Paperback Library 63-385 [1970]

Dark Shadows #20: Barnabas, Quentin and the Witch's Curse; Paperback Library 63-402 [1970]

Dark Shadows #21: Barnabas, Quentin and the Haunted Cave; Paperback Library 63-427 [1970]

Dark Shadows #22: Barnabas, Quentin and the Frightened Bride; Paperback Library 63-446 [1970]

Dark Shadows #23: Barnabas, Quentin and the Scorpio Curse; Paperback Library 63-468 [1970]

Dark Shadows #24: Barnabas, Quentin and the Serpent; Paperback Library 63-491 [1970]

Dark Shadows #25: Barnabas, Quentin and the Magic Potion; Paperback Library 63-515 [1971]

Dark Shadows #26: Barnabas, Quentin and the Body Snatchers; Paperback Library 63-534 [1971]

Dark Shadows #27: Barnabas, Quentin and Dr. Jekyll's Son; Paperback Library 63-554 [1971]

Dark Shadows #28: Barnabas, Quentin and the Grave Robbers; Paperback Library 63-585 [1971]

Dark Shadows #29: Barnabas, Quentin and the Sea Ghost; Paperback Library 64-663 [1971]

Dark Shadows #30: Barnabas, Quentin and the Mad Magician; Paperback Library 64-714 [1971]

Dark Shadows #31: Barnabas, Quentin and the Hidden Tomb; Paperback Library 64-772 [1971]

Dark Shadows #32: Barnabas, Quentin and the Vampire Beauty; Paperback Library 64-824 [1972]

House of Dark Shadows; Paperback Library 64-537 [1970]

Ross, Dan [William Edward Daniel Ross] (1912-1995)
Pseudonym: Marilyn Ross

Rotsler, William (1926-)

  as William Rotsler
    The A-Team #1: Defense Against Terror; Wanderer 49608 [1983]
    The A-Team #2: The Danger Maze; Wanderer 52761 [1984]
    It's Your Move; Archway 54716 [1984]
    Joanie Loves Chachi #1: Secrets; Wanderer 46010 [1982]
    Joanie Loves Chachi #2: A Test of Hearts; Wanderer 46011 [1982]
    The Love Boat #1: Voyage of Love; Wanderer 49802 [1983]
    Magnum, P.I. #1: Maui Mystery; Wanderer 49607 [1983]
    Mr. Merlin Episode 1; Wanderer 44479 [1981]
    Mr. Merlin Episode 2; Wanderer 44480 [1981]

  as William Arrow
    Return to the Planet of the Apes #1: Visions from Nowhere; Ballantine 25122
      [1976]
    Return to the Planet of the Apes #3: Man, the Hunted Animal; Ballantine 25211
      [1976]

St. John, George
    M*A*S*H Trivia: The Unofficial Quiz Book; Warner 32000 [1983]

Sams, David R. (1958-)

  Co-written with Robert L. Shook
    Wheel of Fortune; St. Martin's Press 90833 [1987]

Sankey, Alice [Ann-Susan] (1910-)
    The Buccaneers; Whitman Big Little Book 1646 [1958]

Santini, Rosemarie (American author)
    Agnes Nixon's All My Children Book I: Tara & Philip; Jove B4892 [1980]
    Agnes Nixon's All My Children Book II: Erica; Jove B4895 [1980]
    Agnes Nixon's All My Children Book III: The Lovers; Jove K4896 [1981]

Saunders, David (pseudonym of Daniel Sontup, 1922-)
    M Squad: The Case of the Chicago Cop-Killer; Belmont 91-254 [1962]

Saunders, Jeraldine (cruise ship director)
    The Love Boats; Pinnacle 240698 [1976]

Schow, David J. (1955-)
  Pseudonym: Stephen Grave

Schroeder, Doris
    Annie Oakley in Danger at Diablo; Whitman 1540 [1955]
    Annie Oakley in the Ghost Town Secret; Whitman 1538 [1957]
    Annie Oakley in Double Trouble; Whitman 1538 [1958]
    The Beverly Hillbillies: The Saga of Wildcat Creek; Whitman 1572 [1963]
    Gunsmoke; Whitman Big Little Book 1647 [1958]
    Lassie: Forbidden Valley; Whitman 1508 [1959]

The Lawrence Welk Show: The Lennon Sisters: The Secret of Holiday Island; Whitman 1544 [1960]

The Mickey Mouse Club: Walt Disney's Spin and Marty: Trouble at Triple-R; Whitman 1577 [1958]

The Mickey Mouse Club: Walt Disney's Annette: Sierra Summer; Whitman 1585 [1960]

The Mickey Mouse Club: Walt Disney's Annette: The Desert Inn Mystery; Whitman 1546 [1961]

The Mickey Mouse Club: Walt Disney's Annette and the Mystery at Moonstone Bay; Whitman 1537 [1962]

The Mickey Mouse Club: Walt Disney's Annette and the Mystery at Smugglers' Cove; Whitman 1574 [1963]

Patty Duke and Mystery Mansion; Whitman 1514 [1964]

Patty Duke and the Adventure of the Chinese Junk; Whitman 2334 [1966]

Rin Tin Tin and Call to Danger; Whitman 1539 [1957]

Searls, Hank [Henry Hunt Searls, Jr.] (1922-)
  Pseudonym: Lee Costigan

Segall, Lee (1905-)
  The Dr. I.Q. Quiz Book; Ace 15700 [1971]

Seid, Chloe
  Another World #11: Whispers From the Past; Pioneer 050 [1987]

Sellers, Con[nie Leslie, Jr.] (1922-1992)
  Pseudonym: Lee Raintree

Sellier, Charles E., Jr. (1925?-)
  The Life and Times of Grizzly Adams; Schick Sunn 917214 [1977]

Serling, [Edward] Rod[man] (1924-1975)
  Kraft Television Theater: Patterns; Bantam F1832 [1958]
  Night Gallery; Bantam S7160 [1971]
  Night Gallery 2; Bantam SP7203 [1972]
  Stories From the Twilight Zone; Bantam A2046 [1960]
  More Stories From the Twilight Zone; Bantam A2227 [1961]
  New Stories From the Twilight Zone; Bantam A2412 [1962]

Seskin, Jane [R.]
  Fantasy Island #1; Ballantine 27939 [1978]
  Fantasy Island #2; Ballantine 27940 [1979]

Shakespeare, Henry (American angler)
  Gadabout Gaddis: Secrets of Successful Fishing; Dell First Edition M102 [1964]

Sharkey, Jack [John Michael Sharkey] (1931-1992)
  The Addams Family; Pyramid R-1229 [1965]

Shelton, [Austin] Jess[e, Jr.] (1926-)
  Daktari; Ace G-604 [1966]

Sherwood, Deborah (American author)
    The Young and the Restless: The Story of Chris and Snapper; Bantam Q2556
    [1976]
    The Young and the Restless: The Story of Brad and Leslie; Bantam 10115 [1976]

Shirreffs, Gordon D[onald] (1914-)

  as Jackson Flynn
    Gunsmoke #2: Shootout; Award AN1284 [1974]

Shook, Robert L. (1938-)

  Co-written with David R. Sams
    Wheel of Fortune; St. Martin's Press 90833 [1987]

Short, Luke, ed. (pseudonym of Frederick D. Glidden, 1908-1975)
    Frontier: 150 Years of the West; Bantam A1401 [1955]

Shulman, Max (1919-1988)
    The Many Loves of Dobie Gillis; Bantam F2041 [1960]

Sicilia, Gail, ed.
    Zingers From The Hollywood Squares; Popular Library 00221 [1974]
    More Zingers From The Hollywood Squares; Popular Library 04113 [1978]

Silliphant, Stirling [Dale] (1918-1996)
    See: Charles Einstein

Silva, Joseph (pseudonym of Ron Goulart, 1933-)

  Co-written with Len Wein and Marv Wolfman
    The Incredible Hulk in Stalker From the Stars; Pocket 82084 [1978]

Simmons, Richard Alan (pseudonym of Richard Elman, 1934-)

  Co-written with "Michael Lasker"
    The Gangster Chronicles; Jove K5808 [1981]

Simon, Morris
    Amazing Stories Book 2: Jaguar!; TSR 74177 [1985]

Sinclair, Murray [M.] (1950-)
    Prisoner: Cell Block H; Pinnacle 41113 [1980]

Slesar, Henry (1927-)
    Alfred Hitchcock Presents Clean Crimes and Neat Murders; Avon T-485 [1960]
    Alfred Hitchcock Introduces A Crime For Mothers and Others; Avon F-121 [1962]
    The Edge of Night #1: The Seventh Mask; Ace 18785 [1969]

Smith, April (TV producer)
    James at 15; Dell 14389 [1977]
    James at 15: Friends; Dell 12666 [1978]

Smith, Frederick E[screet] (1922-)
    The Persuaders Book One: The Heart-Shaped Birthmark; Ballantine 02630 [1972]
    The Persuaders Book Two: Five Miles to Midnight; Ballantine 02633 [1972]

Snow, Dorothea J[ohnston] (1909-)
    Circus Boy: Under the Big Top; Whitman 1549 [1957]
    Circus Boy: War on Wheels; Whitman 1578 [1958]
    Lassie and the Mystery at Blackberry Bog; Whitman 1536 [1956]
    Lassie and the Secret of Summer; Whitman 1589 [1958]

Solomon, Louis (1911-1981)
    All in the Family: TV's First Family; Scholastic Book Services TK2297 [1973]

Sontup, Daniel (1922-)
    Pseudonym: David Saunders

Sotona, Wayne [Richard]
    The High Chaparral: Hell and High Water; Tempo 05319 [1969]

Stanton, Vance (pseudonym of Michael Avallone, 1924-)
    The Partridge Family #6: Keith Partridge, Master Spy; Curtis 06150 [1971]
    The Partridge Family #7: The Walking Fingers; Curtis 06162 [1972]
    The Partridge Family #9: The Fat and Skinny Murder Mystery; Curtis 06180 [1972]
    The Partridge Family #11: Who's That Laughing in the Grave?; Curtis 06184 [1972]

Steele, Addison E. (pseudonym of Richard A. Lupoff, 1935-)
    Buck Rogers in the 25th Century; Dell 10843 [1978]
    Buck Rogers #2: That Man on Beta; Dell 10948 [1979]

Steele, Alex (pseudonym of William Johnston, 1924-)
    The New People: They Came From the Sea; Tempo 05308 [1969]

Steffanson, Con (pseudonym of Ron Goulart, 1933-)
    Laverne and Shirley #1: Teamwork; Warner 88-294 [1976]
    Laverne and Shirley #2: Easy Money; Warner 88-295 [1976]
    Laverne and Shirley #3: Gold Rush; Warner 88-296 [1976]

Stevens, Serita Deborah (1949-)
    Cagney & Lacey; Dell 11050 [1985]
    Days of Our Lives #5: Passion's Lure; Pioneer 55 [1986]

Stewart, Linda
    Pseudonym: Sam Stewart

Stewart, Sam (pseudonym of Linda Stewart)
    McCoy; Dell 05293 [1976]

Stine, Hank [Henry Eugene Stine] (1945-)
    The Prisoner #3: A Day in the Life; Ace 67902 [1970]

Stratford, Michael (pseudonym of Bruce Cassiday, 1920-)
    Adam-12 #4: The Sniper; Award AN1266 [1974]

Stratton, Chris (pseudonym of Richard Hubbard, -1974)
  Adam-12: The Runaway; Award AN1002 [1972]
  Adam-12: Dead On Arrival; Award AN1027 [1972]
  Adam-12: The Hostages; Award AN1174 [1974]
  The Bugaloos and the Vile Vibes; Curtis 07131 [1971]
  The Bugaloos #2: Rock City Rebels; Curtis 07132 [1971]
  The Bugaloos #3: Benita's Platter Pollution; Curtis 07136 [1971]
  Emergency!; Popular Library 08198 [1972]
  Getting Together #2: Bobby: Superstar; Curtis 07180 [1971]
  Gunsmoke; Popular Library 08146 [1970]
  Here Come the Brides; Curtis 06062 [1969]
  Medical Center; Popular Library 01336 [1970]
  Then Came Bronson #2: The Ticket; Pyramid T-2213 [1970]
  Then Came Bronson #3: Rock!; Pyramid T2259 [1970]

Stratton, Thomas (joint pseudonym for Robert Coulson [1928-] and Gene DeWeese
[1934-])
  The Man From U.N.C.L.E. #11: The Invisibility Affair; Ace G-645 [1967]
  The Man From U.N.C.L.E. #12: The Mind-Twisters Affair; Ace G-663 [1967]

Street, Bradford (pseudonym of Al Hine, 1915-1974)
  Primus; Bantam S7262 [1971]

Streeter, Edward (1891-1976)
  Father of the Bride; Popular Library SP162 [1962]

Strong, Charles S[tanley] (1906-1962)
  Lassie: Treasure Hunter; Whitman 1552 [1960]

Sturgeon, Theodore [Hamilton] (1918-1985; born Edward Hamilton Waldo)
  Voyage to the Bottom of the Sea; Pyramid R-1068 [1964]

Sucharitkul, Somtow (1950-)
  V: The Alien Swordmaster; Pinnacle 42441 [1985]
  V: Symphony of Terror; Tor 55482 [1988]

Sullivan, George (sports columnist)

  Co-written with R.V. "Gadabout" Gaddis
    Gadabout Gaddis: The Flying Fisherman; Pocket 75224 [1967]

Sullivan, Tim[othy Robert] (1948-)
  V: The Florida Project; Pinnacle 42430 [1985]
  V: The New England Resistance; Pinnacle 42467 [1985]
  V: To Conquer the Throne; Tor 55727 [1987]

Summers, Elizabeth
  The Young and the Restless #8: Far Side of Love; Pioneer 78 [1986]

Sumner, Cid Ricketts (1890-1970; female author)
  Tammy Tell Me True; Popular Library 50-439 [1965]
  Tammy in Rome; Popular Library SP423 [1965]

Susans, Claire
    Charlie's Angels: Farrah's World; Dell 12922 [1977]

T, Mr. (1952-)
    The A-Team: Mr. T: The Man With the Gold; St. Martin's Press 90274 [1984]

Tabler, Madeline (American author)
    Capitol #2: Intimate Glimpses; Pioneer 92 [1986]

Tannehill, Jayne
    V: The Oregon Invasion; Tor 55729 [1988]

Tanner, Edward Everett III (1921-1976)
    Pseudonym: Patrick Dennis

Tarcher, J[eremy] P[hilip], ed. (1932-)
    The Tonight Show: Ed McMahon's Barside Companion; Pocket 77215 [1970]

Taylor, Laura
    Dallas #12: Shattered Dreams; Pioneer 101 [1987]

Telfair, Richard (pseudonym of Richard Jessup, 1925-1982)
    Danger Man: Target for Tonight; Dell First Edition K111 [1962]
    Hotel de Paree: Sundance; Gold Medal 999 [1960]

Tennis, Craig (1942-)
    The Tonight Show: Johnny Tonight!; Pocket 41451 [1980]

Terrall, Robert (1914-)

  as Brett Halliday
    Michael Shayne: Murder Takes No Holiday; Dell D379 [1961]

Thomas, John Oram
    Pseudonym: John Oram

Thomas, Roy, ed. (1940-)
    Stan Lee Presents The Incredible Hulk: A Video Novel; Pocket 82827 [1979]

Thompson, Jim [James Myers Thompson] (1906-1976)
    Ironside; Popular Library 60-2244 [1967]

Thompson, Thomas (1913-1993)
    Bonanza: One Man with Courage; Media M101 [1966]

Thurston, Robert [Donald] (1936-)

  Co-written with Glen A. Larson [Thurston wrote, Larson given co-author credit]
    Battlestar Galactica; Berkley 03958 [1978]
    Battlestar Galactica 2: The Cylon Death Machine; Berkley 04080 [1979]
    Battlestar Galactica 3: The Tombs of Kobol; Berkley 04267 [1979]
    Battlestar Galactica 4: The Young Warriors; Berkley 04655 [1980]
    Battlestar Galactica 11: The Nightmare Machine; Berkley 08618 [1985]
    Battlestar Galactica 12: "Die, Chameleon!"; Berkley 09095 [1986]

Battlestar Galactica 13: Apollo's War; Berkley 09476 [1987]
Battlestar Galactica 14: Surrender the Galactica; Ace Tempo Star 05104 [1988]

Tidyman, Ernest (1928-1984)
Shaft Among the Jews; Bantam N7621 [1973]
Shaft Has a Ball; Bantam N7699 [1973]
Shaft's Carnival of Killers; Bantam N8494 [1974]

Tiger, John (pseudonym of Walter H. Wager, 1924-)
I Spy; Popular Library SP400 [1965]
I Spy #2: Masterstroke; Popular Library 60-2127 [1966]
I Spy #3: Superkill; Popular Library 60-2157 [1967]
I Spy #4: Wipeout; Popular Library 60-2180 [1967]
I Spy #5: Countertrap; Popular Library 60-2206 [1967]
I Spy #6: Doomdate; Popular Library 60-2237 [1967]
I Spy #7: Death-Twist; Popular Library 60-2311 [1968]
Mission: Impossible; Popular Library 60-8042 [1967]
Mission: Impossible #4: Code Name: Little Ivan; Popular Library 60-2464 [1969]

Toma, David (1933-)

Co-written with Michael Brett
Toma; Dell 08520 [1974]

Co-written with Jack Pearl
Toma #2: The Airport Affair; Dell 04604 [1975]
Toma #3: The Affair of the Unhappy Hooker; Dell 05284 [1976]

Tracy, Don[ald Fiske] (1905-1976)
Pseudonym: Roger Fuller

Travers, Peter (movie critic for *Rolling Stone*)
Charlie's Angels: Peter Travers' Favorite TV Angels; Xerox N 104 [1978]

Trevor, Leslie
Police Woman #1: The Rape; Award AQ1438 [1975]
Police Woman #2: Code 1013: Assassin; Award AQ1452 [1975]
Police Woman #3: Death of a Call Girl; Award AQ1487 [1975]

Tubb, E[dwin] C[harles] (1919-)
Space: 1999 #1: Breakaway; Pocket 80184 [1975]
Space: 1999 #4: Collision Course; Pocket 80274 [1976]
Space: 1999 #7: Alien Seed; Pocket 80520 [1976]
Space: 1999 #9: Rogue Planet; Pocket 80710 [1976]

Turner, Robert [Harry] (1915-)
Gunsmoke; Whitman 1587 [1958]
Wagon Train: Wagonmaster; Pocket 1196 [1958]
Wagon Train: The Scout; Pocket 1216 [1958]
Wagon Train: Wagons West!; Pocket 1226 [1959]

Van Arnam, Dave [David G. Van Arnam]

  Co-written with "Ron Archer" [Ted White]
    Lost in Space; Pyramid X-1679 [1967]

Vance, Jack [John Holbrook Vance] (1916-)

  as Ellery Queen
    Ellery Queen: The Madman Theory; Signet Y6715 [1975]

Versace, Marie Teresa Rios (1917-)
  Pseudonym: Tere Rios

Vornholt, John [Blair] (1951-)
  Star Trek: The Next Generation #7: Masks; Pocket 67980 [1989]

Vowell, David H[enry]
  Dragnet 1968; Popular Library 60-8045 [1968]

Wager, Walter H[erman] (1924-)
  Pseudonym: John Tiger

Wagner, Robin S.
  Mork & Mindy 2: The Incredible Shrinking Mork; Pocket 83677 [1980]

Wajenberg, Earl (1953-)

  Co-written with Clayton Emery
    Amazing Stories Book 1: The 4-D Funhouse; TSR 74176 [1985]

Walker, Max
  Mission: Impossible #2: Code Name: Judas; Popular Library 60-2261 [1968]
  Mission: Impossible #3: Code Name: Rapier; Popular Library 60-2325 [1968]

Waller, Leslie (1923-)
  Pseudonym: Patrick Mann

Ward, Don[ald G.] (1911-)
  Gunsmoke; Ballantine 236 [1957]

Ward, Teresa
  All My Children #1/#2 [combined]: Once and Always; Pioneer 350 [1987] [Ward wrote #2 of set only]

Watkin, Lawrence Edward (1901-1981)
  The Mickey Mouse Club: Walt Disney's Spin and Marty [orig. title "Marty Markham"]; Whitman 1535 [1956]

Webb, Jack [Randolph] (1920-1982)
  Dragnet: The Badge; Crest s341 [1959]

Webb, Jean Francis
  Guiding Light #4: Revenge of the Heart; Pioneer 04 [1986]

Wein, Len (cartoonist)

Co-written with Marv Wolfman and "Joseph Silva" [Ron Goulart]
The Incredible Hulk in Stalker From the Stars; Pocket 82084 [1978]

Weinberg, Larry [Lawrence E. Weinberg]
Father Murphy's Promise; Random House 85318 [1982]

Weinstein, Howard (1954-)
Star Trek: The Next Generation #6: Power Hungry; Pocket 67714 [1989]
V: Prisoners and Pawns; Pinnacle 42439 [1985]
V: Path to Conquest; Tor 55725 [1987]

Co-written with A.C. Crispin
V: East Coast Crisis; Pinnacle 42259 [1984]

Weverka, Robert (1926-)
Apple's Way; Bantam 9848 [1975]
Griff; Bantam N8339 [1973]
Search; Bantam S7706 [1973]
Search: Moonrock; Bantam N8306 [1973]
The Waltons; Bantam NP6302 [1974]
The Waltons: Trouble on the Mountain; Bantam N2280 [1975]
The Waltons: The Easter Story; Bantam Q2411 [1976]

Wheelwright, Catherine
The Young and the Restless #6: Bittersweet Harvest; Pioneer 30 [1986]

Whitaker, David (1930-1980)
Doctor Who in an Exciting Adventure with the Daleks; Avon G1322 [1967]

White, Ted [Theodore Edward White] (1938-)
Pseudonym: Ron Archer

White, Vanna (1957-)

Co-written with Patricia Romanowski
Wheel of Fortune: Vanna Speaks; Warner 34668 [1988]

Whitfield, Stephen E[dward]

Co-written with Gene Roddenberry [Whitfield wrote, Roddenberry given co-author credit]
The Making of Star Trek; Ballantine 73004 [1968]

Whittington, Harry [Benjamin] (1915-1989)
Bonanza: Treachery Trail; Whitman 1571 [1968]
The Man From U.N.C.L.E. #2: The Doomsday Affair; Ace G-560 [1965]

Wilcox, Collin (1924-)
McCloud #1; Award AN1203 [1973]
McCloud #2: The New Mexico Connection; Award AN1259 [1974]

Wilder, Laura [Elizabeth] Ingalls (1867-1957)
  Little House on the Prairie; Perennial Library P357 [1975]

Williams, Roy (1907-1976)
  The Mickey Mouse Club: The Secret World of Roy Williams; Bantam 1697 [1957]

Williams, Wayne
  Hardy Boys Puzzle Mysteries; Tempo 14507 [1977]
  Hardy Boys Detective Logic Puzzles; Tempo 14510 [1977]
  Nancy Drew Detective Logic Puzzles; Tempo 14506 [1977]
  Nancy Drew Mystery Puzzles; Tempo 14511 [1977]

Willis, Maud (pseudonym of Eileen Lottman, 1927-)
  Doctor's Hospital #1: One of Our Own; Pocket 80231 [1975]

Wilson, David
  McCloud #3: The Killing; Award AN1281 [1974]
  McCloud #4: The Corpse-Maker; Award AN1365 [1974]
  McCloud #5: A Dangerous Place to Die; Award AN1368 [1975]
  McCloud #6: Park Avenue Executioner; Award AQ1463 [1975]

Winslow, Martha (pseudonym of Frances Rickett, 1921-)
  Another World #2: Love's Destiny; Pioneer 32 [1986]
  Another World #3: Affairs of the Moment; Pioneer 33 [1986]
  Another World #4: Love's Encore; Pioneer 34 [1986]
  Another World #5: Caress From the Past; Pioneer 35 [1986]
  Another World #10: Deceptions; Pioneer 40 [1987]

Winston, Daoma (1922-)
  Bracken's World #1; Paperback Library 64-237 [1969]
  Bracken's World #2: The High Country; Paperback Library 64-279 [1970]
  Bracken's World #3: Sound Stage; Paperback Library 64-364 [1970]

Wister, Owen (1860-1938)
  The Virginian; Paperback Library 53-190 [1963]

Wohl, Burton (American author)
  All in the Family; Bantam Q2566 [1976]

Wold, Allen [L.] (1943-)
  V: The Pursuit of Diana; Pinnacle 42401 [1984]
  V: The Crivit Experiment; Pinnacle 42466 [1985]
  V: Below the Threshold; Tor 55732 [1988]

Wolff, Brian
  Knots Landing #6: Mothers and Daughters; Pioneer 66 [1986]

Wolfman, Marv (cartoonist)

  Co-written with Len Wein and "Joseph Silva" [Ron Goulart]
    The Incredible Hulk in Stalker From the Stars; Pocket 82084 [1978]

Woodley, Richard [Allen] (1937-)
    Man From Atlantis #1; Dell 15368 [1977]
    Man From Atlantis #2: Death Scouts; Dell 15369 [1977]
    Man From Atlantis #3: Killer Spores; Dell 15926 [1978]
    Man From Atlantis #4: Ark of Doom; Dell 15927 [1978]

Woolfolk, William (1917-)
  Pseudonym: Winston Lyon

Worley, JoAnne (1942-)

  Co-written with Dick Matthews
    Rowan & Martin's Laugh-In #4: JoAnne Worley's Chicken Joke Book; Signet
      T4060 [1969]

Wormser, Richard [Edward] (1908-1977)

  as Richard Wormser
    The Wild Wild West; Signet D2836 [1966]

  as Ed Friend
    The Green Hornet in the Infernal Light; Dell 3231 [1966]
    The High Chaparral: Coyote Gold; Tempo 05302 [1969]
    The Most Deadly Game #1: The Corpse in the Castle; Lancer 73200 [1970]

Wylie, Philip [Gordon] (1902-1971)
    Name of the Game: Los Angeles: A.D. 2017; Popular Library 00272 [1971]

Yermakov, Nicholas (1951-)

  Co-written with Glen A. Larson [Yermakov wrote, Larson given co-author credit]
    Battlestar Galactica 6: The Living Legend; Berkley 05249 [1982]
    Battlestar Galactica 7: War of the Gods; Berkley 05660 [1982]

Young, Chic [Murat Bernard Young] (1901-1973)
    Blondie #1; Signet P3710 [1968]
    Blondie #2; Signet P3711 [1968]

TV TIE-INS INDEXED BY PUBLISHER

ACE BOOKS (Ace Books, Inc.)

Ace Letter Series

F-278	The Patty Duke Show: Patty goes to Washington; Frances Spatz Leighton [1964]
G-553	The Man From U.N.C.L.E.; Michael Avallone [1965]
G-560	The Man From U.N.C.L.E. #2: The Doomsday Affair; Harry Whittington [1965]
G-564	The Man From U.N.C.L.E. #3: The Copenhagen Affair; John Oram [1965]
G-571	The Man From U.N.C.L.E. #4: The Dagger Affair; David McDaniel [1966]
G-581	The Man From U.N.C.L.E. #5: The Mad Scientist Affair; John T. Phillifent [1966]
G-590	The Man From U.N.C.L.E. #6: The Vampire Affair; David McDaniel [1966]
G-600	The Man From U.N.C.L.E. #7: The Radioactive Camel Affair; Peter Leslie [1966]
G-604	Daktari; Jess Shelton [1966]
G-613	The Man From U.N.C.L.E. #8: The Monster Wheel Affair; David McDaniel [1967]
G-617	The Man From U.N.C.L.E. #9: The Diving Dames Affair; Peter Leslie [1967]
G-636	The Man From U.N.C.L.E. #10: The Assassination Affair; J. Hunter Holly [1967]
G-645	The Man From U.N.C.L.E. #11: The Invisibility Affair; Thomas Stratton [1967]

The following "Ace G" books also include the 020- prefix.

G-663	The Man From U.N.C.L.E. #12: The Mind-Twisters Affair; Thomas Stratton [1967]
G-670	The Man From U.N.C.L.E. #13: The Rainbow Affair; David McDaniel [1967]

G-689	The Man From U.N.C.L.E. #14: The Cross of Gold Affair; Fredric Davies [1968]
G-702	The Flying Nun: Miracle At San Tanco; William Johnston [1968]
G-725	The Flying Nun: The Littlest Rebels; William Johnston [1968]
G-729	The Man From U.N.C.L.E. #15: The Utopia Affair; David McDaniel [1968]
G-752	The Man From U.N.C.L.E. #16: The Splintered Sunglasses Affair; Peter Leslie [1968]

Ace Numbered Series (Prefix 441- and 020-; 020's are coded "*")

05104	Battlestar Galactica 14: Surrender the Galactica; Glen A. Larson and Robert Thurston [1988]
13810	The Dark Shadows Cookbook; Jody Cameron Malis [1970]
15700	The Dr. I.Q. Quiz Book; Lee Segall [1971]
18785	The Edge of Night #1: The Seventh Mask; Henry Slesar [1969]
24300*	The Flying Nun #3: Mother of Invention; William Johnston [1969]
24301*	The Flying Nun #4: The Little Green Men; William Johnston [1969]
24302	The Flying Nun #5: The Underground Picnic; William Johnston [1970]
32335	The Young Rebels #1: The Hedgerow Incident; William Johnston [1970]
37598*	It Takes a Thief #1: The Devil in Davos; Gil Brewer [1969]
37599	It Takes a Thief #2: Mediterranean Caper; Gil Brewer [1969]
37600	It Takes a Thief #3: Appointment in Cairo; Gil Brewer [1970]
51700*	The Man From U.N.C.L.E. #17: The Hollow Crown Affair; David McDaniel [1969]
51701*	The Man From U.N.C.L.E. #18: The Unfair Fare Affair; Peter Leslie [1969]
51702	The Man From U.N.C.L.E. #19: The Power Cube Affair; John T. Phillifent [1969]
51703	The Man From U.N.C.L.E. #20: The Corfu Affair; John T. Phillifent [1970]
51704	The Man From U.N.C.L.E. #21: The Thinking Machine Affair; Joel Bernard [1970]
51705	The Man From U.N.C.L.E. #22: The Stone-Cold Dead in the Market Affair; John Oram [1970]
51706	The Man From U.N.C.L.E. #23: The Finger in the Sky Affair; Peter Leslie [1971]
51938	Marcus Welby, M.D.: Rock a Cradle Empty; Bruce Cassiday [1970]
51939	Marcus Welby, M.D. #2: The Acid Test; Bruce Cassiday [1970]
51941	Marcus Welby, M.D. #3: The Fire's Center; Bruce Cassiday [1971]
67900*	The Prisoner; Thomas M. Disch [1969]
67901	The Prisoner #2: Number Two; David McDaniel [1969]
67902	The Prisoner #3: A Day in the Life; Hank Stine [1970]
69945	Quincy, M.E.; Thom Racina [1977]
69946	Quincy, M.E. #2; Thom Racina [1977]
95051	The Young Rebels #2: The Sea Gold Incident; William Johnston [1970]

ACE TEMPO STARS (Grosset & Dunlap)

The Grosset & Dunlap imprint of Tempo Books branched into the "Tempo Star" line in the late 1970's, which Ace Books, as a Grosset & Dunlap subsidiary, distributed. (Prefix 441-)

04876	Stan Lee Presents: Battlestar Galactica; Roger McKenzie [1978]
04877	Stan Lee Presents: Battlestar Galactica Volume II; Roger McKenzie [1979]
24005	Fish Strikes Out; T.J. Hemmings [1977]
24515	Happy Days: Fonzie Drops In; William Johnston [1977]
29814	The Gong Show Book; Jerry Bowles [1977]
40630	Welcome Back, Kotter: John Travolta [adapted from Meet John Travolta]; Suzanne Munshower [1978]
73200	Mork & Mindy: The Robin Williams Scrapbook; Mary Ellen Moore [1979]
79114	Welcome Back, Kotter: The Sweathog Trail; William Johnston [1977]

ARCHWAY PAPERBACKS (Pocket Books, Inc.)

Prefix 671-

54716	It's Your Move; William Rotsler [1984]

AVON BOOKS (The Hearst Corporation)

Avon Letter Prefix Series

F-106	The Jack Paar Tonight Show: Yours Truly, Hugh Downs; Hugh Downs [1960]
F-121	Alfred Hitchcock Introduces A Crime For Mothers and Others; Henry Slesar [1962]
F-133	Young Dr. Kildare; Max Brand [1962]
T-485	Alfred Hitchcock Presents Clean Crimes and Neat Murders; Henry Slesar [1960]
T510	My Husband, Arthur Murray; Kathryn Murray with Betty Hannah Hoffman [1960]
G1203	The Clampetts of Beverly Hills; Jerry Fay [1964]
G1237	The Munsters; Morton Cooper [1964]
G1250	The Beverly Hillbillies Live it Up!; Jerry Fay [1965]
ZS130	The Flying Nun: The Fifteenth Pelican; Tere Rios [1967]
G1322	Doctor Who in an Exciting Adventure with the Daleks; David Whitaker [1967]
V2251	The Tonight Show: and now... Here's Johnny!; Nora Ephron [1968]

Avon Numbered Series (Prefix 380-)

V2459	Flip Wilson Close-Up; James A. Hudson [1972]
15149	The Waltons: The Homecoming; Earl Hamner, Jr. [1973]

70189	The Cheers Bartending Guide; Marcia Rosen and Gerry Hunt [1986]
75235	Family Ties: Alex Gets the Business; Joe Claro [1986]
75795	Beauty and the Beast; Barbara Hambly [1989]
75798	Beauty and the Beast: Song of Orpheus; Barbara Hambly [1990]
76194	Beauty and the Beast: Masques; Ru Emerson [1990]
89702	Murder, She Wrote: The Murder of Sherlock Holmes; James Anderson [1985]
89930	Miami Vice #1: The Florida Burn; Stephen Grave [1985]
89931	Miami Vice #2: The Vengeance Game; Stephen Grave [1985]
89937	Murder, She Wrote #2: Horray for Homicide; James Anderson [1985]
89938	Murder, She Wrote #3: Lovers and Other Killers; James Anderson [1986]

AWARD BOOKS (Universal Publishing & Distributing Corp.)

A211F K	Code Name: Jericho - Operation Goldkill; Bruce Cassiday [1967]
A858S	General Hospital: A Matter of Life and Death; Jane Horatio [1971] (has "426" on spine)
A896S	Alias Smith and Jones: Dead Ringer; Brian Fox [1971]
AN1002	Adam-12: The Runaway; Chris Stratton [1972]
AS1006	Alias Smith and Jones: The Outlaw Trail; Brian Fox [1972]
AS1024	General Hospital #2: Surgeon's Crisis; Bruce Cassiday [1972]
AN1027	Adam-12: Dead On Arrival; Chris Stratton [1972]
AN1169	Hec Ramsey; Dean Owen [1973]
AN1174	Adam-12: The Hostages; Chris Stratton [1974]
AN1203	McCloud #1; Collin Wilcox [1973]
AN1232	Hec Ramsey #2: The Hunted; Joe Millard [1974]
AN1238	General Hospital #3: In the Name of Love; Bruce Cassiday [1974]
AN1259	McCloud #2: The New Mexico Connection; Collin Wilcox [1974]
AN1266	Adam-12 #4: The Sniper; Michael Stratford [1974]
AN1281	McCloud #3: The Killing; David Wilson [1974]

Prefix 426-

AN1283	Gunsmoke #1: The Renegades; Jackson Flynn [1974]
AN1284	Gunsmoke #2: Shootout; Jackson Flynn [1974]
AN1328	Gunsmoke #3: Duel at Dodge City; Jackson Flynn [1974]
AN1365	McCloud #4: The Corpse-Maker; David Wilson [1974]
AN1368	McCloud #5: A Dangerous Place to Die; David Wilson [1975]
AN1373	Planet of the Apes #1: Man the Fugitive; George Alec Effinger [1974]
AN1403	Gunsmoke #4: Cheyenne Vengeance; Jackson Flynn [1975]
AN1407	Planet of the Apes #2: Escape to Tomorrow; George Alec Effinger [1975]
AD1425	The Tonight Show: He-e-e-ere's Johnny; Robert Lardine [1975]
AN1436	Planet of the Apes #3: Journey Into Terror; George Alec Effinger [1975]
AQ1438	Police Woman #1: The Rape; Leslie Trevor [1975]
AQ1452	Police Woman #2: Code 1013: Assassin; Leslie Trevor [1975]
AQ1463	McCloud #6: Park Avenue Executioner; David Wilson [1975]

AQ1487   Police Woman #3: Death of a Call Girl; Leslie Trevor [1975]
AN1488   Planet of the Apes #4: Lord of the Apes; George Alec Effinger [1976]

BALLANTINE BOOKS (Ballantine Books, Inc.)

78   I Love Lucy: The Real Story of Lucille Ball; Eleanor Harris [1954]
229   The Phil Silvers Show: Sergeant Bilko; Nat Hiken [1957]
236   Gunsmoke; Don Ward [1957]
289K   The Phil Silvers Show: Sgt. Bilko Joke Book [1959]
364K   Gunsmoke; Don Ward [1960]
460K   Mackenzie's Raiders: The Mackenzie Raid; Colonel Red Reeder [1960]
U2001   Tarzan of the Apes; Edgar Rice Burroughs [1966]
U2002   The Return of Tarzan; Edgar Rice Burroughs [1967]
U5041   Twelve O'Clock High!; Beirne Lay, Jr. and Sy Bartlett [1965]
73004   The Making of Star Trek; Stephen E. Whitfield and Gene Roddenberry
          [1968]

Prefix 345-

02630   The Persuaders Book One: The Heart-Shaped Birthmark; Frederick E. Smith
          [1972]
02633   The Persuaders Book Two: Five Miles to Midnight; Frederick E. Smith
          [1972]
23402   Star Trek: "The Trouble With Tribbles"; David Gerrold [1973]
23403   The World of Star Trek; David Gerrold [1973]
23921   Starsky and Hutch #3: Death Ride; Max Franklin [1976]
24014   Star Trek Log One; Alan Dean Foster [1974]
24184   Star Trek Log Two; Alan Dean Foster [1974]
24235   Sons and Daughters; William Johnston [1974]
24260   Star Trek Log Three; Alan Dean Foster [1975]
24370   Let's Make a Deal: Emcee Monty Hall; Monty Hall and Bill Libby [1975]
24435   Star Trek Log Four; Alan Dean Foster [1975]
24532   Star Trek Log Five; Alan Dean Foster [1975]
24655   Star Trek Log Six; Alan Dean Foster [1976]
24965   Star Trek Log Seven; Alan Dean Foster [1976]
24996   Starsky and Hutch; Max Franklin [1976]
25122   Return to the Planet of the Apes #1: Visions from Nowhere; William Arrow
          [1976]
25124   Starsky and Hutch #2: Kill Huggy Bear; Max Franklin [1976]
25141   Star Trek Log Eight; Alan Dean Foster [1976]
25167   Return to the Planet of the Apes #2: Escape from Terror Lagoon; William
          Arrow [1976]
25211   Return to the Planet of the Apes #3: Man, the Hunted Animal; William
          Arrow [1976]
25265   The Making of Space: 1999; Tim Heald [1976]
25557   Star Trek Log Nine; Alan Dean Foster [1977]
25570   Family; Leila Andrews [1976]

25665	Charlie's Angels; Max Franklin [1977]
25669	Starsky and Hutch #4: Bounty Hunter; Max Franklin [1977]
25691	Charlie's Angels #3: Angels on a String; Max Franklin [1977]
25705	Family #2: Transitions; Leila Andrews [1977]
25706	Family #3: Commitments; Leila Andrews [1977]
25707	Charlie's Angels #2: The Killing Kind; Max Franklin [1977]
25709	Starsky and Hutch #5: Terror on the Docks; Max Franklin [1977]
25710	Starsky and Hutch #6: The Psychic; Max Franklin [1977]
25859	Another World; Kate Lowe Kerrigan [1978]
25860	Another World II; Kate Lowe Kerrigan [1978]
27182	Charlie's Angels #4: Angels in Chains; Max Franklin [1977]
27212	Star Trek Log Ten; Alan Dean Foster [1978]
27340	Starsky and Hutch #7: The Set-Up; Max Franklin [1978]
27341	Starsky and Hutch #8; Max Franklin [1978]
27342	Charlie's Angels #5: Angels on Ice; Max Franklin [1978]
27401	How the West Was Won; Lou Cameron [1978]
27402	Lucan; C.K. Chandler [1978]
27939	Fantasy Island #1; Jane Seskin [1978]
27940	Fantasy Island #2; Jane Seskin [1979]
28051	Vega$; Max Franklin [1978]
28127	Another World II; Kate Lowe Kerrigan [1978]
33224	Doctor Who #1: Search for the Doctor; David Martin [1986]
33225	Doctor Who #2: Crisis in Space; Michael Holt [1986]
33226	Doctor Who #3: Garden of Evil; David Martin [1986]
33228	Doctor Who #6: Race Against Time; Pip & Jane Baker [1986]
33229	Doctor Who #4: Mission to Venus; William Emms [1986]
33231	Doctor Who #5: Invasion of the Ormazoids; Philip Martin [1986]
33669	The Making of Miami Vice; Trish Janeshutz and Rob MacGregor [1986]

BANTAM BOOKS (Bantam Books, Inc.)

A1401	Frontier: 150 Years of the West; Luke Short, ed. [1955]
1513	Mama's Bank Account; Kathryn Forbes [1956]
1697	The Mickey Mouse Club: The Secret World of Roy Williams; Roy Williams [1957]
1726	Tales of Wells Fargo; Frank Gruber [1958]
F1832	Kraft Television Theater: Patterns; Rod Serling [1958]
A1888	Bat Masterson; Richard O'Connor [1958]
F2041	The Many Loves of Dobie Gillis; Max Shulman [1960]
A2046	Stories From the Twilight Zone; Rod Serling [1960]
A2227	More Stories From the Twilight Zone; Rod Serling [1961]
A2411	All Hazel; Ted Key [1962]
A2412	New Stories From the Twilight Zone; Rod Serling [1962]
J2427	The Third Man; Graham Greene [1962]
F2497	The Nurses; William Johnston [1963]
J2530	The Original Mr. Ed; Walter Brooks [1963]

J2990   Hazel Time; Ted Key [1965]
J2991   All Hazel; Ted Key [1965]
F3325   Life With Hazel; Ted Key [1967]
F3439   Star Trek 2; James Blish [1968]
F3459   Star Trek; James Blish [1967]
F4371   Star Trek 3; James Blish [1969]

Prefix 553-

TE2123   The Walton Family Cookbook; Sylvia Resnick [1976]
N2280   The Waltons: Trouble on the Mountain; Robert Weverka [1975]
Q2411   The Waltons: The Easter Story; Robert Weverka [1976]
Q2556   The Young and the Restless: The Story of Chris and Snapper; Deborah
          Sherwood [1976]
Q2566   All in the Family; Burton Wohl [1976]
H5515   Star Trek: Spock Must Die!; James Blish [1970]
S5883   Storefront Lawyers; A.L. Conroy [1970]
S5924   The Immortal; James E. Gunn [1970]
NP6302   The Waltons; Robert Weverka [1974]
N6316   Apple's Way; Robert Weverka [1975]
S7009   Star Trek 4; James Blish [1971]
S7160   Night Gallery; Rod Serling [1971]
SP7203   Night Gallery 2; Rod Serling [1972]
S7262   Primus; Bradford Street [1971]
S7300   Star Trek 5; James Blish [1972]
S7364   Star Trek 6; James Blish [1972]
S7480   Star Trek 7; James Blish [1972]
SP7550   Star Trek 8; James Blish [1972]
N7621   Shaft Among the Jews; Ernest Tidyman [1973]
N7699   Shaft Has a Ball; Ernest Tidyman [1973]
N7703   The Rookies; Claire Parker [1973]
S7706   Search; Robert Weverka [1973]
SP7808   Star Trek 9; James Blish [1973]
N7881   Banacek; Deane Romano [1973]
T7913   All in the Family: God, Man and Archie Bunker; Spencer Marsh [1976]
N8306   Search: Moonrock; Robert Weverka [1973]
N8339   Griff; Robert Weverka [1973]
SP8401   Star Trek 10; James Blish [1974]
N8494   Shaft's Carnival of Killers; Ernest Tidyman [1974]
Q8717   Star Trek 11; James Blish [1975]
9848   Apple's Way; Robert Weverka [1975]
10115   The Young and the Restless: The Story of Brad and Leslie; Deborah
          Sherwood [1976]
10265   Serpico; Peter Maas [1976]
10582   In Search of Lost Civilizations (#1); Alan Landsburg [1976]
10722   In Search of Extraterrestrials (#2); Alan Landsburg [1977]
10790   Baa Baa Black Sheep; Col. Gregory "Pappy" Boyington [1977]

10851	In Search of Magic and Witchcraft (#3); Alan Landsburg [1977]
10855	In Search of Strange Phenomena; Alan Landsburg [1977]
11137	In Search of Myths and Monsters; Alan Landsburg [1977]
11345	Star Trek Fotonovel #1: City on the Edge of Forever [1977]
11346	Star Trek Fotonovel #2: Where No Man Has Gone Before [1977]
11347	Star Trek Fotonovel #3: The Trouble With Tribbles [1977]
11348	Star Trek Fotonovel #4: A Taste of Armageddon [1978]
11349	Star Trek Fotonovel #5: Metamorphosis [1978]
11350	Star Trek Fotonovel #6: All Our Yesterdays [1978]
11382	Star Trek 12; James Blish with J.A. Lawrence [1977]
11459	In Search of Missing Persons; Alan Landsburg [1978]
11802	Star Trek: Mudd's Angels; J.A. Lawrence [1978]
11938	The Black Sheep Squadron: Devil in the Slot; Mike Jahn [1978]
12012	Star Trek Fotonovel #12: Amok Time [1978]
12017	Star Trek Fotonovel #10: Day of the Dove [1978]
12021	Star Trek Fotonovel #9: The Devil in the Dark [1978]
12022	Star Trek Fotonovel #8: A Piece of the Action [1978]
12028	Star Trek Fotonovel #11: The Deadly Years [1978]
12041	Star Trek Fotonovel #7: The Galileo Seven [1978]
13645	The Black Sheep Squadron: The Hawk Flies on Sunday; Michael Jahn [1980]
14439	The Ewings of Dallas; Burt Hirschfeld [1980]
14440	Dallas: The Quotations of J. R. Ewing; Diane J. Perlberg [1980]
14497	The Women of Dallas; Burt Hirschfeld [1981]
20054	Get Smart: Would You Believe?; Don Adams & Bill Dana [1982]
20390	The Men of Dallas; Burt Hirschfeld [1981]
23352	Dynasty; Eileen Lottman [1983]
24431	Dynasty: Alexis Returns; Eileen Lottman [1984]
26881	Growing Pains; N.H. Kleinbaum [1987]
27135	Growing Pains: Kirk Cameron: Dream Guy; Grace Catalano [1987]
27204	The Official Wheel of Fortune Puzzle Book; Nancy Jones [1987]
28190	Head of the Class; Susan Beth Pfeffer [1989]

BEAGLE BOOKS (Beagle Books, Inc.)

Prefix 8441-

95254	Young Dr. Kildare; Max Brand [1972]
95255	Dr. Kildare's Trial; Max Brand [1972]
95256	Dr. Kildare Takes Charge; Max Brand [1972]
95274	Calling Dr. Kildare; Max Brand [1972]
95275	The Secret of Dr. Kildare; Max Brand [1972]
95276	Dr. Kildare's Crisis; Max Brand [1972]
95277	Dr. Kildare's Search; Max Brand [1972]

BELMONT BOOKS (Belmont Productions, Inc.)

236	Markham: The Case of the Pornographic Photos; Lawrence Block [1961]
91-254	M Squad: The Case of the Chicago Cop-Killer; David Saunders [1962]
L92-556	Vince Edwards: A Biography of Television's "Dr. Ben Casey"; George Carpozi, Jr. [1962]
B50-741	Hawk; Richard Hardwick [1966]

BELMONT TOWER BOOKS (Tower Publications, Inc.)

50793	Mannix #1: The Faces of Murder; J.T. MacCargo [1975]
50823	Mannix #2: A Fine Day For Dying; J.T. MacCargo [1975]
50825	Mannix #3: A Walk on the Blind Side; J.T. MacCargo [1975]
50834	Mannix #4: Round Trip to Nowhere; J.T. MacCargo [1975]
50979	Lindsay Wagner: Superstar of The Bionic Woman; David Houston [1976]
50992	Mary Hartman, Mary Hartman: Louise Lasser, Louise Lasser; Kate Brosnan [1976]

BERKLEY BOOKS (Berkley Publishing Corporation; later MCA, Inc.)

Berkley Letter Prefix Series

G180	Boots and Saddles; Edgar Jean Bracco [1958]
G291	Flight; Edgar Jean Bracco [1959]
G406	Leave it to Beaver (Berkley Medallion); Beverly Cleary [1960]
G461	Men Into Space; Murray Leinster [1960]
G497	Leave it to Beaver: Here's Beaver (Berkley Medallion); Beverly Cleary [1961]
G557	Leave it to Beaver: Beaver and Wally (Berkley Medallion); Beverly Cleary [1961]
F1175	The Addams Family: Dear Dead Days: A Family Album; Chas Addams [1966]
F1331	Leave it to Beaver (Berkley Highland); Beverly Cleary [1966]
F1332	Leave it to Beaver: Here's Beaver (Berkley Highland); Beverly Cleary [1966]
F1333	Leave it to Beaver: Beaver and Wally (Berkley Highland); Beverly Cleary [1966]
F1410	The Avengers #1: "The Floating Game" (1st pr); John Garforth [1967]
F1411	The Avengers #2: "The Laugh Was On Lazarus" (1st pr); John Garforth [1967]
F1431	The Avengers #3: "The Passing of Gloria Munday" (1st pr); John Garforth [1967]
F1445	The Avengers #4: "Heil Harris!" (1st pr); John Garforth [1967]
F1538	Maya #1: The Forbidden City; Norman Daniels [1967]
X1547	The Avengers #5: "The Afrit Affair"; Keith Laumer [1968]
X1565	The Avengers #6: "The Drowned Queen"; Keith Laumer [1968]
X1592	The Avengers #7: "The Gold Bomb"; Keith Laumer [1968]

X1637   The Avengers #8: "The Magnetic Man"; Norman Daniels [1968]
X1658   The Avengers #9: "Moon Express"; Norman Daniels [1969]
X1666   The Avengers #1: "The Floating Game" (2nd pr); John Garforth [1969]
X1667   The Avengers #2: "The Laugh Was On Lazarus" (2nd pr); John Garforth
          [1969]
X1668   The Avengers #3: "The Passing of Gloria Munday" (2nd pr); John Garforth
          [1969]
X1669   The Avengers #4: "Heil Harris!" (2nd pr); John Garforth [1969]

Berkley Numbered Series (Prefix 425-)

W2092   Family Affair: Buffy's Cookbook; Jody Cameron [1971]
X2127   The Smith Family #1: Meet the Smiths; Norman Daniels [1971]
02553   Chase; Norman Daniels [1974]
Z3021   Kojak: Telly Savalas: TV's Golden Greek; Marsha Daly [1975]
Z3082   Switch; Mike Jahn [1976]
Z3230   The Bionic Woman: Welcome Home, Jaime; Eileen Lottman [1976]
Z3231   Happy Days: Hollywood's Newest Superstar: Henry Winkler; Suzanne
          Munshower [1976]
Z3237   Kojak in San Francisco; Thom Racina [1976]
Z3252   Switch #2: Round Up the Usual Suspects; Mike Jahn [1976]
Z3307   The Six Million Dollar Man: The Secret of Bigfoot Pass; Mike Jahn [1976]
O3326   The Bionic Woman: Extracurricular Activities; Eileen Lottman [1977]
03331   The Six Million Dollar Man: International Incidents; Mike Jahn [1977]
03515   Baretta: Beyond the Law; Andrew Patrick [1977]
03559   Baretta: Sweet Revenge; Thom Racina [1977]
03592   The Tonight Show: Here's Ed; Ed McMahon [1977]
03958   Battlestar Galactica; Glen A. Larson and Robert Thurston [1978]
03993   The New Avengers #1: House of Cards; Peter Cave [1978]
03994   The New Avengers #2: The Eagle's Nest; John Carter [1978]
03995   The New Avengers #3: To Catch a Rat; Walter Harris [1978]
04080   Battlestar Galactica 2: The Cylon Death Machine; Glen A. Larson and
          Robert Thurston [1979]
04139   Battlestar Galactica: The Photostory; Richard J. Anobile [1979]
04267   Battlestar Galactica 3: The Tombs of Kobol; Glen A. Larson and Robert
          Thurston [1979]
04655   Battlestar Galactica 4: The Young Warriors; Glen A. Larson and Robert
          Thurston [1980]
04744   Battlestar Galactica 5: Galactica Discovers Earth; Glen A. Larson and
          Michael Resnick [1980]
05249   Battlestar Galactica 6: The Living Legend; Glen A. Larson and Nicholas
          Yermakov [1982]
05660   Battlestar Galactica 7: War of the Gods; Glen A. Larson and Nicholas
          Yermakov [1982]
06047   Battlestar Galactica 8: Greetings From Earth; Glen A. Larson and Ron
          Goulart [1983]

06418   Battlestar Galactica 9: Experiment in Terra; Glen A. Larson and Ron Goulart [1984]

07105   Battlestar Galactica 10: The Long Patrol; Glen A. Larson and Ron Goulart [1984]

08618   Battlestar Galactica 11: The Nightmare Machine; Glen A. Larson and Robert Thurston [1985]

09095   Battlestar Galactica 12: "Die, Chameleon!"; Glen A. Larson and Robert Thurston [1986]

09476   Battlestar Galactica 13: Apollo's War; Glen A. Larson and Robert Thurston [1987]

11095   Tales From the Darkside, Vol. 1; Mitchell Galin and Tom Allen, eds. [1988]

BOLDER BOOKS (Hampstead Hall Publishers)

9098   The Mary Hartman Story; Daniel Lockwood [1976]

CARDINAL EDITIONS (Pocket Books, Inc.)

Cardinal "C" Series

C-330   Art Linkletter's House Party: Kids Say the Darndest Things!; Art Linkletter [1959]

C-337   Perry Mason: The Case of the Gilded Lady; Erle Stanley Gardner [1959]

C-376   Perry Mason: The Case of the Dubious Bridegroom; Erle Stanley Gardner [1959]

C-377   Perry Mason: The Case of the Screaming Woman; Erle Stanley Gardner [1959]

C-379   Perry Mason: The Case of the Perjured Parrot; Erle Stanley Gardner [1959]

C-381   Perry Mason: The Case of the Hesitant Hostess; Erle Stanley Gardner [1959]

C-384   People Are Funny; Art Linkletter [1960]

Cardinal "GC" Series

GC-92   Art Linkletter's House Party: The Secret World of Kids; Art Linkletter [1960]

GC-96   American Bandstand: Your Happiest Years; Dick Clark [1961]

GC-103   The Jack Paar Tonight Show: I Kid You Not; Jack Paar [1961]

GC-124   Art Linkletter's House Party: Confessions of a Happy Man; Art Linkletter with Dean Jennings [1962]

GC-148   The Jack Paar Tonight Show: My Saber is Bent; Jack Paar [1962]

GC-157   Art Linkletter's House Party: Kids Still Say the Darndest Things!; Art Linkletter [1962]

CHARTER BOOKS (The Berkley Publishing Group)

Prefix 441-

01906   Steven Spielberg's Amazing Stories; Steven Bauer [1986]
01912   Steven Spielberg's Amazing Stories Volume II; Steven Bauer [1986]

CINNAMON HOUSE (Grosset & Dunlap)

15879   Mork & Mindy: Code Puzzles From Ork; D.J. Arneson [1979]
15880   Mork & Mindy Puzzlers; Mary Beth Lewis [1979]

CITADEL PRESS (Lyle Stuart, Inc.)

1082   Terry Nation's Blake's 7: Scorpio Attack; Trevor Hoyle [1988]
1102   Terry Nation's Blake's 7: Project Avalon; Trevor Hoyle [1988]
1103   Terry Nation's Blake's 7: Their First Adventure; Trevor Hoyle [1988]

CREST (Fawcett Publications, Inc.)

s341   Dragnet: The Badge; Jack Webb [1959]
369   What are the Odds?; Leo Guild [1960]
k646   Art Linkletter's House Party: Kids Sure Rite Funny!; Art Linkletter [1963]
d773   A For Andromeda; Fred Hoyle and John Elliot [1964]
d834   Please Don't Eat the Daisies; Jean Kerr [1965]
d949   Art Linkletter's House Party: A Child's Garden of Misinformation; Art Linkletter [1966]
k997   Art Linkletter's House Party: Kids Sure Rite Funny!; Art Linkletter [1965]

Prefix 232-

R1080   Andromeda Breakthrough; Fred Hoyle and John Elliot [1967]
R1082   Phyllis Diller's Housekeeping Hints; Phyllis Diller [1968]
T1217   The Tonight Show: Happiness is a Dry Martini; Johnny Carson [1968]
R1245   Phyllis Diller's Marriage Manual; Phyllis Diller [1969]

Prefix 449-

T2027   Phyllis Diller's Housekeeping Hints; Phyllis Diller [1969]
23002   Eight is Enough; Tom Braden [1977]

CURTIS BOOKS (Popular Library, Inc.)

Prefix 123-

06062   Here Come the Brides; Chris Stratton [1969]

Prefix 502-

05003   The Partridge Family; Michael Avallone [1970]
05004   The Partridge Family #2: The Haunted Hall; Michael Avallone [1970]
05005   The Partridge Family #3: Keith, the Hero; Michael Avallone [1970]
06147   The Partridge Family #4: The Ghost of Graveyard Hill; Paul W. Fairman [1971]
06148   The Partridge Family #5: Terror by Night; Vic Crume [1971]
06150   The Partridge Family #6: Keith Partridge, Master Spy; Vance Stanton [1971]
06154   The Partridge Family: The David Cassidy Story; Carol Deck [1972]
06162   The Partridge Family #7: The Walking Fingers; Vance Stanton [1972]
06164   The Partridge Family #8: The Treasure of Ghost Mountain; Paul W. Fairman [1972]
06167   The Partridge Family: David, David, David; James Gregory [1972]
06180   The Partridge Family #9: The Fat and Skinny Murder Mystery; Vance Stanton [1972]
06182   The Partridge Family #10: Marked for Terror; Vic Crume [1972]
06184   The Partridge Family #11: Who's That Laughing in the Grave?; Vance Stanton [1972]
06186   The Partridge Family #13: The Mystery of the Mad Millionairess; Edward Fenton [1973]
06189   The Partridge Family #12: Phantom of the Rock Concert; Lee Hays [1973]
06190   The Partridge Family #14: Thirteen at Killer Gorge; Vic Crume [1973]
06191   The Partridge Family #15: The Disappearing Professor; Lee Hays [1973]
07131   The Bugaloos and the Vile Vibes; Chris Stratton [1971]
07132   The Bugaloos #2: Rock City Rebels; Chris Stratton [1971]
07136   The Bugaloos #3: Benita's Platter Pollution; Chris Stratton [1971]
07137   The Saint Abroad; Leslie Charteris [1971]
07173   Getting Together; Judson McCall [1971]
07180   Getting Together #2: Bobby: Superstar; Chris Stratton [1971]
07184   The Saint in New York; Leslie Charteris [1971]
07185   The Saint Overboard; Leslie Charteris [1971]
07199   The Saint and the Fiction Makers; Leslie Charteris [1971]
07200   The Saint on TV; Leslie Charteris [1971]
07209   The Saint Sees it Through; Leslie Charteris [1971]
07210   The Saint in Miami; Leslie Charteris [1971]
07321   The Partridge Family #16: The Stolen Necklace; Lee Hays [1973]
07335   The Partridge Family #17: Love Comes to Keith Partridge; Michael Avallone [1973]
09219   The Partridge Family Cookbook; Sylvia Resnick [1973]
09222   Sanford and Son; Alan Riefe and Dick Harrington [1973]

DELL BOOKS (Dell Publishing Co.)

Dell Letter Prefix Series

D204	The Mark of Zorro; Johnston McCulley [1958]
D224	Playhouse 90: No Time At All; Charles Einstein [1958]
D231	Alfred Hitchcock Presents: 12 Stories They Wouldn't Let Me Do On TV; Alfred Hitchcock, ed. [1958]
D266	The Story of Walt Disney; Diane Disney Miller and Pete Martin [1959]
D281	Alfred Hitchcock Presents: 13 More Stories They Wouldn't Let Me Do On TV; Alfred Hitchcock, ed. [1959]
D347	The Jack Paar Tonight Show: Charley Weaver's Letters from Mamma; Cliff Arquette [1960]
D379	Michael Shayne: Murder Takes No Holiday; Brett Halliday [1961]
D401	Michael Shayne: The Corpse Came Calling; Brett Halliday [1961]
D416	Michael Shayne's Long Chance; Brett Halliday [1961]
D423	Michael Shayne: Death Has Three Lives; Brett Halliday [1961]
D424	Michael Shayne: Dolls Are Deadly; Brett Halliday [1961]
D425	Michael Shayne: Stranger in Town; Brett Halliday [1961]
D437	Michael Shayne: The Homicidal Virgin; Brett Halliday [1961]
R123	Calling Dr. Kildare; Max Brand [1961]
R125	Dr. Kildare's Trial; Max Brand [1962]

Dell Numbered Series (no prefixes)

0551	Bewitched; Al Hine [1965]
0553	The Beverly Hillbillies Book of Country Humor; Lewis R. Benton, Ph.D., ed. [1964]
1980	Dr. Kildare's Crisis; Max Brand [1962]
1981	Dr. Kildare's Search; Max Brand [1962]
1983	Dr. Kildare Takes Charge; Max Brand [1962]
2798	Garrison's Gorillas; Jack Pearl [1967]
2872	Gidget in Love; Frederick Kohner [1965]
2874	Gidget Goes Parisienne; Frederick Kohner [1966]
2888	The Girl From "Peyton Place"; George Metalious and June O'Shea [1965]
2897	Gidget Goes New York; Frederick Kohner [1968]
3231	The Green Hornet in the Infernal Light; Ed Friend [1966]
4476	Michael Shayne: Killers From the Keys; Brett Halliday [1962]
7712	The Secret of Dr. Kildare; Max Brand [1962]

Dell Numbered Series (Prefix 440-)

04604	Toma #2: The Airport Affair; David Toma and Jack Pearl [1975]
05284	Toma #3: The Affair of the Unhappy Hooker; David Toma and Jack Pearl [1976]
05293	McCoy; Sam Stewart [1976]

08180	The Waltons: Spencer's Mountain; Earl Hamner, Jr. [1973]
08520	Toma; David Toma with Michael Brett [1974]
08629	The Young Lawyers: Test Case; B.D. Ashe [1970]
10009	The A-Team; Charles Heath [1984]
10020	The A-Team 2: Small But Deadly Wars; Charles Heath [1984]
10027	The A-Team 3: When You Comin' Back, Range Rider?; Charles Heath [1984]
10034	The A-Team 4: Old Scores to Settle; Charles Heath [1984]
10037	The A-Team 5: Ten Percent of Trouble; Charles Heath [1984]
10039	The A-Team 6: Operation Desert Sun: The Untold Story; Charles Heath [1984]
10843	Buck Rogers in the 25th Century; Addison E. Steele [1978]
10948	Buck Rogers #2: That Man on Beta; Addison E. Steele [1979]
11050	Cagney & Lacey; Serita Deborah Stevens [1985]
11752	Dallas [white cover]; Lee Raintree [1978]
11752	Dallas [red cover]; Lee Raintree [1980]
12437	Falcon Crest; Patrick Mann [1984]
12666	James at 15: Friends; April Smith [1978]
12922	Charlie's Angels: Farrah's World; Claire Susans [1977]
14389	James at 15; April Smith [1977]
15368	Man From Atlantis #1; Richard Woodley [1977]
15369	Man From Atlantis #2: Death Scouts; Richard Woodley [1977]
15926	Man From Atlantis #3: Killer Spores; Richard Woodley [1978]
15927	Man From Atlantis #4: Ark of Doom; Richard Woodley [1978]
19246	Spenser: For Hire: Valediction; Robert B. Parker [1986]
92666	James at 15: Friends; April Smith [1980]
94389	James at 15; April Smith [1980]
96777	Paper Dolls; Susan Beth Pfeffer [1984]

DELL FIRST EDITIONS (Dell Publishing Co.)

79	The $64,000 Question: Official Quiz Book; Louis G. Cowan, ed. [1955]
A176	77 Sunset Strip; Roy Huggins [1959]
A180	The Naked City; Charles Einstein [1959]
B104	The Walt Disney Story of Our Friend the Atom; Heinz Haber, Ph.D. [1956]
B125	The Lineup; Frank Kane [1959]
B142	Poker According to Maverick; J. Hoyt Cummings [1959]
B155	Peter Gunn; Henry Kane [1960]
B156	Have Gun, Will Travel; Noel Loomis [1960]
B165	Mr. Lucky; Albert Conroy [1960]
B172	The Deputy; Roe Richmond [1960]
B183	Love of Life; Margaret Manners [1961]
K105	The Roaring 20's: Sing Out Sweet Homicide; John Roeburt [1961]
K111	Danger Man: Target for Tonight; Richard Telfair [1962]
K112	Hawaiian Eye; Frank Castle [1962]
M102	Gadabout Gaddis: Secrets of Successful Fishing; Henry Shakespeare [1964]
8388	SurfSide 6; J.M. Flynn [1962]

FAWCETT GOLD MEDAL
see **GOLD MEDAL**

FICTION BOOKS (Fiction Publishing Company)

K101	The Saint Steps In; Leslie Charteris [1963]
K102	The Saint Sees it Through; Leslie Charteris [1963]
K103	The Saint Closes the Case; Leslie Charteris [1964]
K104	The Avenging Saint; Leslie Charteris [1964]
K105	The Saint's Getaway; Leslie Charteris [1964]
K106	The Saint in New York; Leslie Charteris [1964]
K107	Enter the Saint; Leslie Charteris [1964]
K108	The Saint Meets His Match; Leslie Charteris [1964]
K109	Featuring the Saint; Leslie Charteris [1964]
K110	Alias the Saint; Leslie Charteris [1964]
K111	The Saint Overboard; Leslie Charteris [1964]
K112	The Saint - The Brighter Buccaneer; Leslie Charteris [1964]
K113	The Saint vs The Scotland Yard; Leslie Charteris [1964]
K114	The Saint and Mr. Teal; Leslie Charteris [1964]

GOLD MEDAL (Fawcett Publications, Inc.)

980	Johnny Staccato; Frank Boyd [1960]
999	Hotel de Paree: Sundance; Richard Telfair [1960]
s1164	The Defenders; Edward S. Aarons [1961]
s1186	The New Breed; Lee Costigan [1962]
s1263	The Jack Paar Tonight Show: The Real Jack Paar; George Johnson [1962]

Prefix 449- (Fawcett Gold Medals)

M3188	The Starlost: Phoenix Without Ashes; Edward Bryant & Harlan Ellison [1975]
P3460	The Invisible Man; Michael Jahn [1975]

GOLDEN APPLE PUBLISHERS (MCA, Inc.)

Prefix 553-

19746	The Black Sheep Squadron: The Hawk Flies on Sunday; Michael Jahn [1984]

IVY BOOKS (Ballantine Books, Inc.)

Prefix 8041-

0269	Private Eye #1; T.N. Robb [1988]
0270	Private Eye #2: Blue Movie; David Elliott [1988]
0271	Private Eye #3: Flip Side; T.N. Robb [1988]
0272	Private Eye #4: Nobody Dies in Chinatown; Max Lockhart [1988]

JOVE BOOKS (Jove Publications, Inc.)

Prefix 515-

B4892	Agnes Nixon's All My Children Book I: Tara & Philip; Rosemarie Santini [1980]
B4895	Agnes Nixon's All My Children Book II: Erica; Rosemarie Santini [1980]
K4896	Agnes Nixon's All My Children Book III: The Lovers; Rosemarie Santini [1981]
B5807	That's Incredible! Vol. 1; Wendy Jeffries, ed. [1980]
K5808	The Gangster Chronicles; Michael Lasker and Richard Alan Simmons [1981]
B5870	That's Incredible! Vol. 2; Wendy Jeffries, ed. [1981]
B5986	That's Incredible! Vol. 3; Wendy Jeffries, ed. [1981]
06171	That's Incredible! Vol. 4; Wendy Jeffries, ed. [1981]
06172	That's Incredible! Vol. 5; Wendy Jeffries, ed. [1981]
06173	That's Incredible! Vol. 6; Wendy Jeffries, ed. [1981]

LANCER BOOKS (Lancer Books, Inc.)

70-005	The Jack Paar Tonight Show: What is Jack Paar Really Like?; William H.A. Carr [1962]
70-006	Ben Casey; William Johnston [1962]
70-007	Dr. Kildare's Secret Romance; Norman Daniels [1962]
70-011	Ben Casey: A Rage for Justice; Norman Daniels [1962]
70-032	Dr. Kildare's Finest Hour; Norman Daniels [1963]
70-035	Sam Benedict: Cast the First Stone; Elsie Lee [1963]
70-037	Ben Casey: The Strength of his Hands; Sam Elkin [1963]
70-042	Combat; Harold Calin [1963]
70-043	Dr. Kildare: The Heart Has an Answer; William Johnston [1963]
70-045	Ben Casey: The Fire Within; Norman Daniels [1963]
70-049	Dr. Kildare: The Faces of Love; William Johnston [1963]
70-055	General Hospital; Burt Hirschfeld [1963]
70-060	Combat: Men, Not Heroes; Harold Calin [1963]
71-308	Dr. Kildare; Robert C. Ackworth [1962]
71-316	The Detectives; Norman Daniels [1962]
72-696	Arrest and Trial; Norman Daniels [1963]
72-723	Arrest and Trial: The Missing Witness; Norman Daniels [1964]
72-910	Combat: No Rest for Heroes; Harold Calin [1965]

72-917	General Hospital: Emergency Entrance; Burt Hirschfeld [1965]
73-838	My Friend Tony; William Johnston [1969]
73-849	The Brady Bunch; William Johnston [1969]
73-864	The Brady Bunch #2: Showdown at the P.T.A. Corral; William Johnston [1969]

Prefix 447-

73200	The Most Deadly Game #1: The Corpse in the Castle; Ed Friend [1970]
73201	Matt Lincoln #1: The Revolutionist; Ed Garth [1970]
73205	Nanny and the Professor #3: The Bloop Box; William Johnston [1970]
73206	The Brady Bunch #5: The Quarterback Who Came to Dinner; William Johnston [1970]
73211	Matt Lincoln #2: The Hostage; Ed Garth [1971]
73216	The Most Deadly Game #2: The One-Armed Murder; Richard Gallagher [1971]
73219	Strange Report; John Burke [1970]
73872	The Brady Bunch #3: Count Up to Blast-Down!; William Johnston [1970]
73876	Nanny and the Professor; William Johnston [1970]
73889	Nanny and the Professor #2: What Hath Nanny Wrought?; William Johnston [1970]
73891	The Brady Bunch #4: The Bumbler Strikes Again; William Johnston [1970]
74775	The Men From Shiloh #1: Lone Trail for the Virginian; Dean Owen [1971]
74779	Longstreet: The Last Express; Baynard Kendrick [1971]
74783	Cannon #1: Murder By Gemini; Richard Gallagher [1971]
74784	Longstreet: Reservations For Death; Baynard Kendrick [1971]
74788	Longstreet: Blind Man's Bluff; Baynard Kendrick [1971]
74795	Bridget Loves Bernie; Paul Fairman [1972]
75260	Cannon #2: The Stewardess Strangler; Richard Gallagher [1971]
75287	Longstreet: Out of Control; Baynard Kendrick [1972]
75305	Longstreet: You Die Today!; Baynard Kendrick [1972]
75491	The Girl With Something Extra; Paul W. Fairman [1973]

MACFADDEN BOOKS (Macfadden-Bartell Corporation)

75-140	The Shari Lewis Show: Fun With the Kids; Shari Lewis [1964]
50-275	Secret Agent: Departure Deferred; W. Howard Baker [1966]
50-280	Secret Agent: Hell For Tomorrow; Peter Leslie [1966]
50-284	Secret Agent: Storm Over Rockwall; W. Howard Baker [1966]
50-320	Secret Agent: No Way Out; Wilfred McNeilly [1966]
50-342	Secret Agent: The Exterminator; W.A. Ballinger [1967]
60-191	Have Gun, Will Travel: A Man Called Paladin; Frank C. Robertson [1964]
60-238	The Saint in the Sun; Leslie Charteris [1966]
60-246	The Saint Goes West; Leslie Charteris [1966]
60-247	Saint Errant; Leslie Charteris [1966]
60-252	The Saint on the Spanish Main; Leslie Charteris [1966]

60-253	Trust the Saint; Leslie Charteris [1966]
60-260	The Saint Around the World; Leslie Charteris [1966]
60-262	The Saint Intervenes; Leslie Charteris [1966]
60-265	The Saint Goes On; Leslie Charteris [1966]
60-273	Call for the Saint; Leslie Charteris [1967]
60-294	The Saint in Europe; Leslie Charteris [1967]
60-307	The Saint to the Rescue; Leslie Charteris [1968]

Prefix 520-

60-315	Senor Saint; Leslie Charteris [1968]
60-365	Thanks to the Saint; Leslie Charteris [1968]

MAGNUM BOOKS

14642	The Virginian; Owen Wister [1970]
74783	Cannon: Murder By Gemini; Richard Gallagher [1976]

MANOR BOOKS (Manor Books, Inc.)

Prefix 532-

95260	The Bold Ones: The Surrogate Womb; Bruce Cassiday [1973]
95296	The Bold Ones #2: A Quality of Fear; Bruce Cassiday [1973]
12215	The Bold Ones #3: To Get Along With the Beautiful Girls; Bruce Cassiday [1974]

MASTER'S PRESS, INC. (Merchant's Publishing Co.)

89251	Chico and the Man: The Freddie Prinze Story; Maria Pruetzel and John A. Barbour [1978]

MEDIA BOOKS (Profit Press, Inc.)

M101	Bonanza: One Man with Courage; Thomas Thompson [1966]
M102	Bonanza #2: Black Silver; William R. Cox [1967]

MONARCH BOOKS (Monarch Books, Inc.)

218	Rebel of Broken Wheel; Dean Owen [1961]
471	One Step Beyond: The World Grabbers; Paul W. Fairman [1964]

PAPERBACK LIBRARY (Paperback Library, Inc.)

The following books include no prefixes.

53-190	The Virginian (1st pr); Owen Wister [1963]
53-908	The Virginian (2nd pr); Owen Wister [1965]
52-386	Dark Shadows #1; Marilyn Ross [1966]
53-387	The Rat Patrol; Norman Daniels [1966]
53-411	The Rat Patrol #2 in Desert Danger; David King [1967]
52-421	Dark Shadows #2: Victoria Winters; Marilyn Ross [1967]
53-477	The Rat Patrol #3 in The Trojan Tank Affair; David King [1967]
52-543	Dark Shadows #3: Strangers at Collins House; Marilyn Ross [1967]

The following books include the 610- prefix.

53-566	The Rat Patrol #4 in Two-Faced Enemy; David King [1967]
52-608	Dark Shadows #5: The Curse of Collinwood; Marilyn Ross [1968]
52-610	Dark Shadows #4: The Mystery of Collinwood; Marilyn Ross [1968]
53-625	Judd for the Defense; Lawrence Louis Goldman [1968]
53-628	The Rat Patrol #5 in Target for Tonight; David King [1968]
53-696	The Rat Patrol #6 in Desert Masquerade; David King [1968]
53-721	Judd for the Defense #2: The Secret Listeners; Lawrence Louis Goldman [1968]
52-726	Bonanza #1: Winter Grass; Dean Owen [1968]
52-757	Bonanza #2: Ponderosa Kill; Dean Owen [1968]
62-001	Dark Shadows #6: Barnabas Collins; Marilyn Ross [1968]
62-039	Dark Shadows #7: The Secret of Barnabas Collins; Marilyn Ross [1969]
62-062	Dark Shadows: Barnabas Collins in a Funny Vein [1969]
62-084	Dark Shadows #8: The Demon of Barnabas Collins; Marilyn Ross [1969]
62-135	Dark Shadows #9: The Foe of Barnabas Collins; Marilyn Ross [1969]

The following books include no prefixes.

62-195	Dark Shadows #10: The Phantom and Barnabas Collins; Marilyn Ross [1969]
62-210	Dark Shadows: Barnabas Collins: A Personal Picture Album; Jonathan Frid, ed. [1969]
62-212	Dark Shadows #11: Barnabas Collins vs the Warlock; Marilyn Ross [1969]
64-237	Bracken's World #1; Daoma Winston [1969]
62-244	Dark Shadows #12: The Peril of Barnabas Collins; Marilyn Ross [1969]
63-258	Dark Shadows #13: Barnabas Collins and the Mysterious Ghost; Marilyn Ross [1970]
63-259	Strange Paradise #1; Dorothy Daniels [1969]
63-275	Dark Shadows #14: Barnabas Collins and Quentin's Demon; Marilyn Ross [1970]
64-279	Bracken's World #2: The High Country; Daoma Winston [1970]

63-296   Dark Shadows #15: Barnabas Collins and the Gypsy Witch; Marilyn Ross [1970]

63-318   Dark Shadows #16: Barnabas, Quentin and the Mummy's Curse; Marilyn Ross [1970]

63-321   Strange Paradise #2: Island of Evil; Dorothy Daniels [1970]

63-338   Dark Shadows #17: Barnabas, Quentin and the Avenging Ghost; Marilyn Ross [1970]

63-363   Dark Shadows #18: Barnabas, Quentin and the Nightmare Assassin; Marilyn Ross [1970]

64-364   Bracken's World #3: Sound Stage; Daoma Winston [1970]

63-365   Strange Paradise #3: Raxl, Voodoo Priestess; Dorothy Daniels [1970]

63-385   Dark Shadows #19: Barnabas, Quentin and the Crystal Coffin; Marilyn Ross [1970]

63-402   Dark Shadows #20: Barnabas, Quentin and the Witch's Curse; Marilyn Ross [1970]

64-405   The Virginian (3rd pr); Owen Wister [1970]

63-419   The Dark Shadows Book of Vampires and Werewolves; Barnabas and Quentin Collins, eds. [1970]

63-427   Dark Shadows #21: Barnabas, Quentin and the Haunted Cave; Marilyn Ross [1970]

63-446   Dark Shadows #22: Barnabas, Quentin and the Frightened Bride; Marilyn Ross [1970]

63-468   Dark Shadows #23: Barnabas, Quentin and the Scorpio Curse; Marilyn Ross [1970]

63-491   Dark Shadows #24: Barnabas, Quentin and the Serpent; Marilyn Ross [1970]

63-515   Dark Shadows #25: Barnabas, Quentin and the Magic Potion; Marilyn Ross [1971]

63-534   Dark Shadows #26: Barnabas, Quentin and the Body Snatchers; Marilyn Ross [1971]

64-537   House of Dark Shadows; Marilyn Ross [1970]

63-554   Dark Shadows #27: Barnabas, Quentin and Dr. Jekyll's Son; Marilyn Ross [1971]

63-585   Dark Shadows #28: Barnabas, Quentin and the Grave Robbers; Marilyn Ross [1971]

The following books include the 446- prefix.

64-663   Dark Shadows #29: Barnabas, Quentin and the Sea Ghost; Marilyn Ross [1971]

64-669   Banyon; William Johnston [1971]

64-714   Dark Shadows #30: Barnabas, Quentin and the Mad Magician; Marilyn Ross [1971]

64-772   Dark Shadows #31: Barnabas, Quentin and the Hidden Tomb; Marilyn Ross [1971]

64-824   Dark Shadows #32: Barnabas, Quentin and the Vampire Beauty; Marilyn Ross [1972]

PERENNIAL LIBRARY (Harper & Row)

P357   Little House on the Prairie; Laura Ingalls Wilder [1975]

PERMABOOKS (Pocket Books, Inc.)

M-4253   87th Precinct: Lady, Lady, I did it!; Ed McBain [1962]
M-4264   87th Precinct: The Con Man; Ed McBain [1962]
M-4265   87th Precinct: Killer's Payoff; Ed McBain [1962]
M-4266   87th Precinct: The Mugger; Ed McBain [1962]
M-4267   87th Precinct: Killer's Choice; Ed McBain [1962]
M-4268   87th Precinct: Cop Hater; Ed McBain [1962]
M-4310   Burke's Law: Who Killed Beau Sparrow?; Roger Fuller [1964]

PINNACLE BOOKS (Pinnacle Books, Inc.)

Prefix 523-

P027-N   Mod Squad: Home is Where the Quick Is; William Johnston [1971]
P047-N   Love, American Style; Paul Fairman [1971]
P081-N   Love, American Style, 2; Paul Fairman [1972]
230988   The Real Mary Tyler Moore; Chris Bryars [1977]
240698   The Love Boats; Jeraldine Saunders [1976]
40565   Doctor Who #1 and the Day of the Daleks; Terrance Dicks [1979]
40566   Doctor Who #2 and the Doomsday Weapon; Malcolm Hulke [1979]
40606   Doctor Who #3 and the Dinosaur Invasion; Malcolm Hulke [1979]
40608   Doctor Who #4 and the Genesis of the Daleks; Terrance Dicks [1979]
40609   Doctor Who #6 and the Loch Ness Monster; Terrance Dicks [1979]
40611   Doctor Who #5 and the Revenge of the Cybermen; Terrance Dicks [1979]
40638   Doctor Who #7 and the Talons of Weng-Chiang; Terrance Dicks [1979]
40639   Doctor Who #10 and the Seeds of Doom; Philip Hinchcliffe [1980]
40640   Doctor Who #8 and the Masque of Mandragora; Philip Hinchcliffe [1979]
40641   Doctor Who #9 and the Android Invasion; Terrance Dicks [1980]
41113   Prisoner: Cell Block H; Murray Sinclair [1980]
41175   Prisoner: Cell Block H #2: The Franky Doyle Story; Henry Clement [1981]
41176   Prisoner: Cell Block H #3: The Karen Travers Story; Maggie O'Shell [1981]
41215   Prisoner: Cell Block H #4: The Frustrations of Vera; Michael Kerr [1981]
41403   Prisoner: Cell Block H #5: The Reign of Queen Bea; Angela Michaels
              [1981]
41404   Prisoner: Cell Block H #6: Trials of Erica; Mary Carter [1981]
42170   Knight Rider; Glen A. Larson and Roger Hill [1983]
42181   Knight Rider #2: Trust Doesn't Rust; Glen A. Larson and Roger Hill [1984]
42182   Knight Rider #3: Hearts of Stone; Glen A. Larson and Roger Hill [1984]
42237   V; A.C. Crispin [1984]
42259   V: East Coast Crisis; Howard Weinstein and A.C. Crispin [1984]
42401   V: The Pursuit of Diana; Allen Wold [1984]

PIONEER COMMUNICATIONS NETWORK ("Soaps & Serials")

Prefix 916217-

48	As the World Turns #8: Shared Moments; Angelica Aimes [1986]
49	As the World Turns #9: In the Name of Love; Kacia Bennett [1987]
50	As the World Turns #10: This Precious Moment; Kacia Bennett [1987]
51	Days of Our Lives #1: Love's Shattered Dreams; Gilian Gorham [1986]
52	Days of Our Lives #2: Hearts Past Reason; Gilian Gorham [1986]
53	Days of Our Lives #3: Search for Love; Gilian Gorham [1986]
54	Days of Our Lives #4: Sentimental Longings; Gilian Gorham [1986]
55	Days of Our Lives #5: Passion's Lure; Serita Deborah Stevens [1986]
56	Days of Our Lives #6: Forsaken Dreams; Tara Lee [1986]
57	Days of Our Lives #7: Red Sky at Dawn; Stella Flint [1986]
58	Days of Our Lives #8: The Summer Wind; Nicole Brooks [1986]
59	Days of Our Lives #9: Friends and Lovers; Nicole Brooks [1987]
60	Days of Our Lives #10: Promises and Lies; Marcia Lawrence [1987]
61	Knots Landing #1: Secrets of Knots Landing; Mary Ann Cooper [1986]
62	Knots Landing #2: Uncharted Love; Samantha Phillips [1986]
63	Knots Landing #3: Love Unbound; Anne Cavaliere [1986]
64	Knots Landing #4: Misguided Hearts; Scott Cunningham [1986]
65	Knots Landing #5: Mothers and Daughters; Samantha Phillips [1986]
66	Knots Landing #6: Starting Over; Brian Wolff [1986]
67	Knots Landing #7: Tell Me No Lies; Scott Cunningham [1986]
68	Knots Landing #8: Once in a Lifetime; Victoria Dann [1986]
69	Knots Landing #9: A House Divided; Anne Cavaliere [1987]
70	Knots Landing #10: Family Affairs; Marcia Lawrence [1987]
71	The Young and the Restless #1: Unveiled Desires; Angelica Aimes [1986]
72	The Young and the Restless #2: Bold Passions; Angelica Aimes [1986]
73	The Young and the Restless #3: Echoes of Love; Angelica Aimes [1986]
74	The Young and the Restless #4: A Touch of Paradise; Angelica Aimes [1986]
75	The Young and the Restless #5: Private Yearnings; Angelica Aimes [1986]
77	The Young and the Restless #7: One Shining Moment; Charlotte Granville [1986]
78	The Young and the Restless #8: Far Side of Love; Elizabeth Summers [1986]
79	The Young and the Restless #9: The Highest Price; Angelica Aimes [1987]
80	The Young and the Restless #10: Shining Star; Erika Bryant [1987]
81	Dallas #1: Love Conquers Fear; Paul Mantell & Avery Hart [1986]
82	Dallas #2: Ardent Memories; Paul Mantell & Avery Hart [1986]
83	Dallas #3: Love's Challenge; Paul Mantell & Avery Hart [1986]
84	Dallas #4: The Power of Passion; Paul Mantell & Avery Hart [1986]
85	Dallas #5: Dangerous Desire; Paul Mantell & Avery Hart [1986]
86	Dallas #6: Double Dealing; Paul Mantell & Avery Hart [1986]
87	Dallas #7: Hostage Heart; Paul Mantell & Avery Hart [1986]
88	Dallas #8: This Cherished Land; Paul Mantell & Avery Hart [1986]
89	Dallas #9: Power Play; Paul Mantell & Avery Hart [1987]
90	Dallas #10: Winner Take All; Paul Mantell & Avery Hart [1987]
91	Capitol #1: Unspoken Desires; Mae Miner [1986]

92	Capitol #2: Intimate Glimpses; Madeline Tabler [1986]
93	Capitol #3: Forbidden Tomorrows; Cathy Cunningham [1986]
94	Capitol #4: Passion's Masterpiece; Cathy Cunningham [1986]
000	As the World Turns #11: Full Circle; Margaret Brownley [1987]
001	As the World Turns #12: Storm Warnings; Margaret Brownley [1987]
002	As the World Turns #13: The Second Time Around; Angelica Aimes [1987]
003	As the World Turns #14: Always and Forever; Kacia Bennett [1987]
050	Another World #11: Whispers From the Past; Chloe Seid [1987]
051	Another World #12: Love Play; Amanda Perkins [1987]
052	Another World #13: Schemes and Dreams; Cordelia Burke [1987]
053	Another World #14: The Art of Love; Amanda Perkins [1987]
100	Dallas #11: Reality Strikes; Mary Clare Kersten [1987]
101	Dallas #12: Shattered Dreams; Laura Taylor [1987]
102	Dallas #13: A Cry in the Night; Monica Dean [1987]
103	Dallas #14: Family Secrets; by Mary Clare Kersten [1987]
150	Days of Our Lives #11: Fantasies; Deidre Duncan [1987]
151	Days of Our Lives #12: Past Loves and Lies; Marcia Lawrence [1987]
152	Days of Our Lives #13: Crimes of the Heart; Nicole Brooks [1987]
153	Days of Our Lives #14: Obsessions; Marcia Lawrence [1987]
200	Knots Landing #11: A Second Chance; Amanda Preble [1987]
201	Knots Landing #12: _____ ; by _____ [1987]
202	Knots Landing #13: Dangerous Games; D.L. Adler [1987]
250	The Young and the Restless #11: Whirlwind; Erika Bryant [1987]
251	The Young and the Restless #12: Paradise Found; Erika Bryant [1987]
252	The Young and the Restless #13: Passion's Pride; Charlotte Granville [1987]
253	The Young and the Restless #14: Free Spirit; Erika Bryant [1987]
300	General Hospital #1/#2 [combined]: Forever and a Day; Nicole Brooks (#1) and Marcia Lawrence (#2) [1987]
301	General Hospital #3: Winds of Change; Nicole Brooks [1987]
350	All My Children #1/#2 [combined]: Once and Always; Marcia Lawrence (#1) and Teresa Ward (#2) [1987]
400	One Life to Live #1/#2 [combined]: Moonlight Obsession; Gwendolynn Arden [1987]

POCKET BOOKS (Pocket Books, Inc.)

886	Perry Mason: The Case of the Fan-Dancer's Horse; Erle Stanley Gardner [1957]
1120	Dragnet: Case No. 561; David Knight [1956]
1196	Wagon Train: Wagonmaster; Robert Turner [1958]
1198	Dragnet: The Case of the Courteous Killer; Richard Deming [1958]
1214	Dragnet: The Case of the Crime King; Richard Deming [1959]
1216	Wagon Train: The Scout; Robert Turner [1958]
1226	Wagon Train: Wagons West!; Robert Turner [1959]
2524	77 Sunset Strip: The Double Take; Roy Huggins [1959]
6001	Perry Mason: The Case of the Daring Decoy; Erle Stanley Gardner [1960]
6027	Perry Mason: The Case of the Lonely Heiress; Erle Stanley Gardner [1960]

6040	Perry Mason: The Case of the Calendar Girl; Erle Stanley Gardner [1960]
6044	Perry Mason: The Case of the Fiery Fingers; Erle Stanley Gardner [1960]
6078	The Asphalt Jungle; W.R. Burnett [1961]
10130	I Dream of Jeannie; Dennis Brewster [1966]
35012	The Fugitive: Fear in a Desert Town; Roger Fuller [1964]
48766	Star Trek: Six Science Fiction Plays; Roger Elwood, ed. [1976]
50030	Burke's Law: Who Killed Madcap Millicent?; Roger Fuller [1964]
50056	The Defenders: All the Silent Voices; Roger Fuller [1964]
50058	The Addams Family: Drawn and Quartered; Chas Addams [1964]
50059	The Addams Family: Black Maria; Chas Addams [1964]
50060	The Addams Family: Nightcrawlers; Chas Addams [1964]
50061	The Addams Family: Monster Rally; Chas Addams [1965]
50062	The Addams Family: Homebodies; Chas Addams [1965]
50063	The Addams Family: Addams and Evil; Chas Addams [1965]
50107	The Defenders: Ordeal; Roger Fuller [1964]
50190	The Defenders: Eve of Judgment; Roger Fuller [1965]
50212	Vendetta For The Saint; Leslie Charteris [1966]
75087	Peyton Place; Grace Metalious [1965]
75179	Art Linkletter's House Party: Oops! Or, Life's Awful Moments; Art Linkletter [1968]
75196	Again Peyton Place; Roger Fuller [1967]
75224	Gadabout Gaddis: The Flying Fisherman; R.V. "Gadabout" Gaddis as told to George Sullivan [1967]
75250	Carnival in Peyton Place; Roger Fuller [1967]
75267	Pleasures of Peyton Place; Roger Fuller [1968]
75278	Art Linkletter's House Party: Kids Say the Darndest Things!; Art Linkletter [1968]
75285	Secrets of Peyton Place; Roger Fuller [1968]

Prefix 671-

41451	The Tonight Show: Johnny Tonight!; Craig Tennis [1980]
65241	Star Trek: The Next Generation: Encounter at Farpoint; David Gerrold [1987]
66579	Star Trek: The Next Generation #1: Ghost Ship; Diane Carey [1988]
66929	Star Trek: The Next Generation #2: The Peacekeepers; Gene DeWeese [1988]
67319	Star Trek: The Next Generation #3: The Children of Hamlin; Carmen Carter [1988]
67438	Star Trek: The Next Generation #4: Survivors; Jean Lorrah [1989]
67714	Star Trek: The Next Generation #6: Power Hungry; Howard Weinstein [1989]
67940	Star Trek: The Next Generation #5: Strike Zone; Peter David [1989]
67980	Star Trek: The Next Generation #7: Masks; John Vornholt [1989]
68487	Star Trek: The Next Generation #8: The Captains' Honor; David and Daniel Dvorkin [1989]

80264	M*A*S*H Goes to Morocco; Richard Hooker and William E. Butterworth [1976]
80265	M*A*S*H Goes to Las Vegas; Richard Hooker and William E. Butterworth [1976]
80274	Space: 1999 #4: Collision Course; E.C. Tubb [1976]
80305	Space: 1999 #5: Lunar Attack; John Rankine [1976]
80392	Space: 1999 #6: Astral Quest; John Rankine [1976]
80408	M*A*S*H Goes to Hollywood; Richard Hooker and William E. Butterworth [1976]
80458	M*A*S*H Goes to Vienna; Richard Hooker and William E. Butterworth [1976]
80520	Space: 1999 #7: Alien Seed; E.C. Tubb [1976]
80705	M*A*S*H Goes to Miami; Richard Hooker and William E. Butterworth [1976]
80706	Space: 1999 #8: Android Planet; John Rankine [1976]
80710	Space: 1999 #9: Rogue Planet; E.C. Tubb [1976]
80746	Happy Days: The Fonz: The Henry Winkler Story; Charles E. Pike [1976]
80764	Space: 1999 #10: Phoenix of Megaron; John Rankine [1976]
80786	M*A*S*H Goes to San Francisco; Richard Hooker and William E. Butterworth [1976]
80892	M*A*S*H Goes to Texas; Richard Hooker and William E. Butterworth [1977]
80910	M*A*S*H Goes to Montreal; Richard Hooker and William E. Butterworth [1977]
80911	M*A*S*H Goes to Moscow; Richard Hooker and William E. Butterworth [1977]
81446	Stan Lee Presents The Incredible Hulk; Stan Lee [1978]
82084	The Incredible Hulk in Stalker From the Stars; Len Wein, Marv Wolfman, and Joseph Silva [1978]
82085	The Incredible Hulk in Cry of the Beast; Richard S. Meyers [1979]
82094	The Hulk and Spider-Man in Murdermoon; Paul Kupperberg [1979]
82178	M*A*S*H Mania; Richard Hooker [1979]
82559	Stan Lee Presents The Incredible Hulk #2; Stan Lee [1979]
82729	Mork & Mindy; Ralph Church [1979]
82754	Mork & Mindy: A Video Novel; Richard J. Anobile [1979]
82827	Stan Lee Presents The Incredible Hulk: A Video Novel; Roy Thomas, ed. [1979]
83677	Mork & Mindy #2: The Incredible Shrinking Mork; Robin S. Wagner [1980]

POPULAR LIBRARY (Popular Library, Inc.)

Popular Library Letter Prefix Series

G403	The Untouchables; Eliot Ness with Oscar Fraley [1960]
G512	The Untouchables: 4 Against the Mob; Oscar Fraley [1961]
G516	The Aquanauts; Daniel Bard [1961]

G554   Miami Undercover; Evan Lee Heyman [1961]
G569   The Last of the Untouchables; Oscar Fraley with Paul Robsky [1962]
PC300   Adventures of Captain David Grief; Jack London [1957]
PC1000   Bonanza; Noel Loomis [1960]
PC1006   The Americans; Donald Honig [1961]
PC1010   Cain's Hundred; Evan Lee Heyman [1961]
PC1056   The Wackiest Ship in the Army; Lee Bergman [1965]
SP71   Guestward Ho!; Barbara Hooton and Patrick Dennis [1960]
SP162   Father of the Bride; Edward Streeter [1962]
SP258   The Untouchables; Eliot Ness with Oscar Fraley [1964]
SP400   I Spy; John Tiger [1965]
SP423   Tammy in Rome; Cid Ricketts Sumner [1965]

Popular Library 50- and 60- Series

50-439   Tammy Tell Me True; Cid Ricketts Sumner [1965]
50-8026   The Monkees; Gene Fawcette and Howard Liss [1966]
60-2127   I Spy #2: Masterstroke; John Tiger [1966]
60-2156   The Iron Horse; William Johnston [1967]
60-2157   I Spy #3: Superkill; John Tiger [1967]
60-2163   Search for Tomorrow [new logo]; Faith Baldwin [1966]
60-2180   I Spy #4: Wipeout; John Tiger [1967]
60-2206   I Spy #5: Countertrap; John Tiger [1967]
60-2237   I Spy #6: Doomdate; John Tiger [1967]
60-2244   Ironside; Jim Thompson [1967]
60-2245   Cimmaron Strip; Richard Meade [1967]
60-2256   Mannix; Michael Avallone [1968]
60-2261   Mission: Impossible #2: Code Name: Judas; Max Walker [1968]
60-2311   I Spy #7: Death-Twist; John Tiger [1968]
60-2325   Mission: Impossible #3: Code Name: Rapier; Max Walker [1968]
60-2340   The Ugliest Girl in Town; Burt Hirschfeld [1968]
60-2345   The Outcasts; Steve Frazee [1968]
60-2348   The Ghost and Mrs. Muir; Alice Denham [1968]
60-2349   Lancer; Paul W. Fairman [1968]
60-2373   The Outsider; Lou Cameron [1969]
60-2397   Days of Our Lives; Frances Forbes [1969]
60-2464   Mission: Impossible #4: Code Name: Little Ivan; John Tiger [1969]
60-8017   Search for Tomorrow [old logo]; Faith Baldwin [1966]
60-8034   The Guiding Light; Agnes Nixon [1967]
60-8036   The Felony Squad; Michael Avallone [1967]
60-8042   Mission: Impossible; John Tiger [1967]
60-8045   Dragnet 1968; David H. Vowell [1968]
60-8046   The Monkees Go Mod; Patrick O'Connor [1967]
60-8049   Love Letters to the Monkees; Bill Adler, ed. [1967]
60-8069   The Monkees Go Ape; Bill Adler, ed. [1968]
60-8080   Laugh-In: Here Come the Judge!; Dewey "Pigmeat" Markham with Bill
            Levinson [1969]

Popular Library Numbered Series (Prefix 445-)

00221	Zingers From The Hollywood Squares; Gail Sicilia, ed. [1974]
00265	Columbo #2: The Dean's Death; Alfred Lawrence [1975]
00269	Harry O #1; Lee Hays [1975]
00272	Name of the Game: Los Angeles: A.D. 2017; Philip Wylie [1971]
00317	Columbo #3: Any Old Port in a Storm; Henry Clement [1975]
00318	The Rockford Files #1: The Unfortunate Replacement; Mike Jahn [1975]
00326	Columbo #4: By Dawn's Early Light; Henry Clement [1975]
00337	Harry O #2: The High Cost of Living; Lee Hays [1976]
00354	The Rockford Files #2: The Deadliest Game; Mike Jahn [1976]
01336	Medical Center; Chris Stratton [1970]
01418	The Silent Force; Harry Goddard [1971]
01524	Columbo; Alfred Lawrence [1972]
02588	That Girl; Paul W. Fairman [1971]
03109	Columbo #5: Murder by the Book; Lee Hays [1976]
03118	Columbo #6: A Deadly State of Mind; Lee Hays [1976]
04113	More Zingers From The Hollywood Squares; Gail Sicilia, ed. [1978]
04357	The Paper Chase; John Jay Osborn, Jr. [1978]
04530	The Associates; John Jay Osborn, Jr. [1979]
08115	The Doctors; Michael Avallone [1970]
08146	Gunsmoke; Chris Stratton [1970]
08184	Cade's County; Alfred Lawrence [1972]
08194	All in the Family: The Wit and Wisdom of Archie Bunker; Eugene Boe, ed. [1971]
08195	Edith Bunker's All in the Family Cookbook; Eugene Boe [1971]
08198	Emergency!; Chris Stratton [1972]
08216	All in the Family: Archie Bunker's Family Album [1973]
08325	Nakia; Lee Hays [1975]
08382	Columbo #1; Alfred Lawrence [1975]
08397	Beacon Hill; Henry Clement [1975]
08427	Beacon Hill #2: The Colonel and Fawn; Henry Clement [1975]
08578	Executive Suite; Cameron Hawley [1977]

PYRAMID BOOKS (Pyramid Publications, Inc.)

G322	Twenty-One [1958]
R-1068	Voyage to the Bottom of the Sea; Theodore Sturgeon [1964]
R-1106	Honey West: Bombshell; G.G. Fickling [1964]
R-1151	Honey West: This Girl for Hire; G.G. Fickling [1965]
R-1162	Voyage to the Bottom of the Sea: City Under the Sea; Paul W. Fairman [1965]
R-1167	Honey West: A Gun for Honey; G.G. Fickling [1965]
R-1179	Honey West: Honey in the Flesh; G.G. Fickling [1965]
R-1229	The Addams Family; Jack Sharkey [1965]
R-1257	The Addams Family Strikes Back; W.F. Miksch [1965]

Pyramid "Royal" Series

PR 14   The Michaels in Africa: I Married a Hunter; Marjorie Michael [1958]

RANDOM HOUSE

Oversize Paperbacks; Prefix 394-

85318   Father Murphy's Promise; Larry Weinberg [1982]
85810   Father Murphy's First Miracle; Elizabeth Levy [1983]

ST. MARTIN'S PRESS

Prefix 312-

90165   Miami Vice: Don Johnson; David Hershkovits [1986]
90274   The A-Team: Mr. T: The Man With the Gold; Mr. T [1984]
90829   Wheel of Fortune: Vanna White; Marianne Robin-Tani [1987]
90833   Wheel of Fortune; David R. Sams and Robert L. Shook [1987]
92256   The Tonight Show: King of the Night: The Life of Johnny Carson; Laurence
           Leamer [1990]

SCHICK SUNN CLASSIC BOOKS

917214   The Life and Times of Grizzly Adams; Charles E. Sellier, Jr. [1977]

SCHOLASTIC BOOK SERVICES (Scholastic Magazines, Inc.)

SBS "TK" series (regular-size)

TK1084   Gentle Ben; Walt Morey [1967]
TK2070   The Partridge Family: Young Mr. Cassidy; James A. Hudson [1972]
TK2297   All in the Family: TV's First Family; Louis Solomon [1973]
TK3121   All About "Rhoda"; Peggy Herz [1975]
TK3237   All About "M*A*S*H"; Peggy Herz [1975]
TK3571   Happy Days: The Truth About Fonzie; Peggy Herz [1976]
TK3600   The Six Million Dollar Man and The Bionic Woman; Joel H. Cohen [1976]

SBS "TX" series (oversize)

TX1388   I Spy: Cool Cos: The Story of Bill Cosby; Joel H. Cohen [1969]
TX1933   Flip Wilson Close-Up; James A. Hudson [1971]
TX2030   Flip [orig. title "Flip Wilson Close-Up"]; James A. Hudson [1971]
TX2123   The Partridge Family: Meet David Cassidy ["Young Mr. Cassidy"
           abridged]; James A. Hudson [1972]

TX2544   Here's Lucy: Laugh With Lucy: The Story of Lucille Ball; Joel H. Cohen
         [1974]
TX3442   Good Times: Jimmie Walker: The Dyn-O-Mite Kid; Joel H. Cohen [1976]
TX4103   Nancy Drew and The Hardy Boys; Peggy Herz; [1977]
TX4496   The Hardy Boys and Nancy Drew; Peggy Herz [1978]
TX4757   The Mork & Mindy Story; Peggy Herz [1979]

SBS Numbered Series (Prefix 590-; regular-size)

30919   Backstage at Saturday Night Live!; Michael McKenzie [1980]
32740   Voyagers!; Joe Claro [1982]
33550   Charles in Charge; Elizabeth Faucher [1984]
41008   Charles in Charge, Again; Elizabeth Faucher [1987]

SIGNET BOOKS (New American Library)

S1214   Walt Disney: The Life of Davy Crockett; Davy Crockett [1955]
1446   Playhouse 90: The Comedian and Other Stories; Ernest Lehman [1957]
1541   The Restless Gun; Will Hickok [1958]
S1658   The Silent Service; William C. Chambliss [1959]
1675   Trail of the Restless Gun; Will Hickok [1959]
S1910   Rawhide; Frank C. Robertson [1961]
S1973   The Brothers Brannagan; Henry E. Helseth [1961]
S1982   Wanted: Dead or Alive; Frank C. Robertson [1961]
S2109   This Man Dawson; Henry E. Helseth [1962]
D2821   Trials of O'Brien; Robert L. Fish [1965]
D2836   The Wild Wild West; Richard Wormser [1966]
D2939   Batman; Bob Kane [1966]
D2940   Batman vs. Three Villains of Doom; Winston Lyon [1966]
D2969   Batman vs. The Joker; Bob Kane [1966]
D2970   Batman vs. The Penguin; Bob Kane [1966]
D2980   Funniest Fan Letters to Batman; Bill Adler, ed. [1966]
D2995   Batman vs. The Fearsome Foursome; Winston Lyon [1966]
D3012   The Girl From U.N.C.L.E. #1: The Birds of a Feather Affair; Michael
         Avallone [1966]
D3042   The Girl From U.N.C.L.E. #2: The Blazing Affair; Michael Avallone
         [1966]
D3045   The Man From U.N.C.L.E.'s ABC of Espionage; John Hill [1966]
P3622   Hawaii Five-O; Michael Avallone [1968]
P3710   Blondie #1; Chic Young [1968]
P3711   Blondie #2; Chic Young [1968]
P3994   Hawaii Five-O #2: Terror in the Sun; Michael Avallone [1969]

Prefix 451-

T3844   Rowan & Martin's Laugh-In #1; Morgul the Friendly Drelb [1969]
T3845   Rowan & Martin's Laugh-In #2: Mod, Mod World; Roy Doty [1969]

T4059	Rowan & Martin's Laugh-In #3: Inside Laugh-In; James E. Brodhead [1969]
T4060	Rowan & Martin's Laugh-In #4: JoAnne Worley's Chicken Joke Book; JoAnne Worley with Dick Matthews [1969]
T5817	Hawaii Five-O; Michael Avallone [1970]
T5818	Hawaii Five-O #2: Terror in the Sun; Michael Avallone [1970]
W6409	Paper Moon [orig. title "Addie Pray"]; Joe David Brown [1974]
Y6715	Ellery Queen: The Madman Theory; Ellery Queen [1975]
W6785	Medical Story; Abby Mann [1975]
W6802	Medical Story #2: Kill Me, Please...; William Johnston [1976]
Y6819	Ellery Queen: The Finishing Stroke; Ellery Queen [1975]
Y6872	Ellery Queen: Face to Face; Ellery Queen [1975]
Y6958	Ellery Queen: The House of Brass; Ellery Queen [1975]
Y6996	Ellery Queen: Cop Out; Ellery Queen [1975]
Y7123	Ellery Queen: The Last Woman in His Life; Ellery Queen [1975]
W7723	Charlie's Angels: Farrah: An Unauthorized Biography of Farrah Fawcett-Majors; Patricia Burstein [1977]
J9773	Richard Dawson and Family Feud; Mary Ann Norbom [1981]

Note: "AE" indicates a five-digit book number (AE1419 = 11419).

AE2063	Magnum, P.I.: Tom Selleck: An Unauthorized Biography; Jason Bonderoff [1983]
AE2212	Ripley's Believe It or Not! #31 [1982]
AE2213	Ripley's Believe It or Not! #32 [1982]
AE2214	Ripley's Believe It or Not! #33 [1982]
AE2215	Ripley's Believe It or Not! #34 [1982]
AE3504	The Official Dallas Trivia Book; Jason Bonderoff [1985]
AE4135	M*A*S*H: The Official 4077 Quiz Manual; Paul Bertling [1986]
AE4345	Miami Vice: Don Johnson: An Unauthorized Biography; Suzanne Munshower [1986]

TEMPO BOOKS (Grosset & Dunlap)

Tempo "T" Series
  2-digit numbers: T = 47 (T14 = 4714)
  3-digit numbers: T = 48 (T-103 = 4803)

T-14	Fury: Stallion of Broken Wheel Ranch; Albert G. Miller [1962]
T-89	Chilling Stories From Rod Serling's Twilight Zone; Walter B. Gibson [1965]
T-103	Get Smart!; William Johnston [1965]
T-119	Get Smart: Sorry, Chief...; William Johnston [1966]
T-121	Get Smart Once Again!; William Johnston [1966]
T-140	Get Smart #4: Max Smart and the Perilous Pellets; William Johnston [1966]
T-154	Get Smart #5: Missed It By That Much!; William Johnston [1967]
T-155	Captain Nice; William Johnston [1967]
T-159	Get Smart #6: And Loving It!; William Johnston [1967]

T-166   Gentle Ben; Walt Morey [1967j
T-171   Rod Serling's Twilight Zone Revisited; Walter B. Gibson [1967]
T-174   Get Smart #7: Max Smart - The Spy Who Went Out to the Cold; William
           Johnston [1968]
T-191   Get Smart #8: Max Smart Loses Control; William Johnston [1968]

Tempo Numbered Series (Prefix 448- on all but *Coyote Gold*)

05302   The High Chaparral: Coyote Gold; Ed Friend [1969]
05308   The New People: They Came From the Sea; Alex Steele [1969]
05319   The High Chaparral: Hell and High Water; Wayne Sotona [1969]
05326   Get Smart #9: Max Smart and the Ghastly Ghost Affair; William Johnston
           [1969]
05339   Room 222: Whatever Happened to Mavis Rooster?; William Johnston [1970]
05342   Room 222 #2: Monday Morning Father; William Johnston [1970]
05358   Room 222 #3: Love is a Three Letter Word; William Johnston [1970]
05365   Can You Top This?; Panelists and Guest Stars [1971]
05372   Room 222 #4: Bomb in the Classroom; William Johnston [1971]
05414   Room 222 #5: A Little Grass On The Side; William Johnston [1971]
05570   The Sixth Sense #1: Witch, Witch, Burning Bright; John W. Bloch [1972]
05594   Room 222 #6: Have you heard about Kelly?; William Johnston [1973]
05595   The Sixth Sense #2: In the Steps of the Master; Marion Zimmer Bradley
           [1973]
05794   Happy Days 1: Ready to Go Steady; William Johnston [1974]
07452   Happy Days 2: Fonzie Drops In; William Johnston [1974]
12267   Happy Days 3: The Invaders; William Johnston [1975]
12406   Welcome Back, Kotter #1: The Sweathog Trail; William Johnston [1976]
12407   Welcome Back, Kotter #2: The Sweathog Newshawks; William Johnston
           [1976]
12414   Happy Days 4: Fonzie, Fonzie, Superstar; William Johnston [1976]
12523   The Six Million Dollar Man's Bionic Brain Benders; Rose Paul [1976]
12526   The Six Million Dollar Man's Search-A-Word Shape Puzzles; Dawn Gerger
           [1976]
12527   The Six Million Dollar Man's Bionic Eye Rebus Puzzles; Rose Paul [1976]
12528   The Bionic Woman's Brain Teasers; Rose Paul [1976]
12607   Happy Days 5: The Fonz & La Zonga; William Johnston [1976]
12608   Welcome Back, Kotter #3: The Super Sweathogs; William Johnston [1976]
12609   Happy Days 6: The Bike Tycoon; William Johnston [1976]
12645   Happy Days: Fonzie's Scrambled Word Find Puzzles; Linda Doherty [1976]
12706   Welcome Back, Kotter #4: 10-4 Sweathogs!; William Johnston [1976]
12936   Welcome Back, Kotter: Meet John Travolta; Suzanne Munshower [1976]
12937   Laverne and Shirley: Penny Marshall & Cindy Williams; Connie Berman
           [1977]
12944   Welcome Back, Kotter #5: The Sweathog Sit-In; William Johnston [1977]
12945   Welcome Back, Kotter #6: Barbarino Drops Out; William Johnston [1977]
12946   Happy Days 7: Dear Fonzie...; William Johnston [1977]
14034   Happy Days 8: Fonzie Goes to College; William Johnston [1977]

14044	Happy Days: The Official Fonzie Scrapbook; Ben Davidson [1976]
14275	Charlie's Angels: Farrah & Lee; Connie Berman [1977]
14504	Nancy Drew Mystery Mazes; Vladimir Koziakin [1977]
14505	Hardy Boys Secret Codes; Evan Morley [1977]
14506	Nancy Drew Detective Logic Puzzles; Wayne Williams [1977]
14507	Hardy Boys Puzzle Mysteries; Wayne Williams [1977]
14508	Hardy Boys Mystery Mazes; Vladimir Koziakin [1977]
14509	Nancy Drew Secret Codes; Evan Morley [1977]
14510	Hardy Boys Detective Logic Puzzles; Wayne Williams [1977]
14511	Nancy Drew Mystery Puzzles; Wayne Williams [1977]
14512	Nancy Drew Secret Scrambled Word Finds; Linda Doherty [1977]
14513	Nancy Drew Clever Crosswords; Dawn Gerger [1977]
14514	Hardy Boys Super Sleuth Word Finds; Linda Doherty [1977]
14515	Hardy Boys Baffling Word Webs; Dawn Gerger [1977]
14738	The Hardy Boys: The Shaun Cassidy Scrapbook; Connie Berman [1978]
14893	Thunder: The Mighty Stallion of the Hills; Mike Jahn [1978]
14894	Thunder: The Mighty Stallion to the Rescue; Mike Jahn [1979]
17179	The Incredible Hulk; Stan Lee and Larry Lieber [1980]
17209	CHiPs: The Erik Estrada Scrapbook; Susan Katz [1980]
17314	The Incredible Hulk Volume 2; Stan Lee and Larry Lieber [1981]

See also ACE TEMPO STAR.

TIGER BEAT (New American Library, Inc.)

Prefix 451-

XQ2001	The Partridge Family: For Girls Only; Susan Dey and Rochelle Reed [1972]
XQ2011	The Brady Bunch in "The Treasure of Mystery Island"; Jack Matcha [1972]
XQ2014	The Brady Bunch in the New York Mystery; Jack Matcha [1972]
XQ2017	The Brady Bunch in Adventure on the High Seas; Jack Matcha [1973]
XQ2024	The Little People: Debbie Preston Teenage Reporter in The Michael Gray Hawaiian Mystery; James Carter [1973]
LAU 1	The Partridge Family: Susan Dey's Secrets On Boys, Beauty & Popularity [orig. title "For Girls Only"]; Susan Dey and Rochelle Reed [1972]

TOR BOOKS (Tom Doherty Associates, Inc.)

Prefix 812-

55482	V: Symphony of Terror; Somtow Sucharitkul [1988]
55725	V: Path to Conquest; Howard Weinstein [1987]
55727	V: To Conquer the Throne; Tim Sullivan [1987]
55729	V: The Oregon Invasion; Jayne Tannehill [1988]
55732	V: Below the Threshold; Allen Wold [1988]

TSR (Random House)

Prefix 394-

74176	Amazing Stories Book 1: The 4-D Funhouse; Clayton Emery and Earl Wajenberg [1985]
74177	Amazing Stories Book 2: Jaguar!; Morris Simon [1985]
74186	Amazing Stories Book 3: Portrait in Blood; Mary Kirchoff [1985]
74352	Amazing Stories Book 6: Day of the Mayfly; Lee Enderlin [1986]
74353	Amazing Stories Book 5: Starskimmer; John Gregory Betancourt [1986]
74817	Amazing Stories Book 4: Nightmare Universe; Gene DeWeese and Robert Coulson [1985]

VINTAGE BOOKS (Random House)

Prefix 394-

74081	Roald Dahl's Tales of the Unexpected; Roald Dahl [1979]

WANDERER BOOKS (Simon & Shuster)

Oversize Paperbacks; Prefix 671-

44479	Mr. Merlin Episode 1; William Rotsler [1981]
44480	Mr. Merlin Episode 2; William Rotsler [1981]
46010	Joanie Loves Chachi #1: Secrets; William Rotsler [1982]
46011	Joanie Loves Chachi #2: A Test of Hearts; William Rotsler [1982]
49607	Magnum, P.I. #1: Maui Mystery; William Rotsler [1983]
49608	The A-Team #1: Defense Against Terror; William Rotsler [1983]
49802	The Love Boat #1: Voyage of Love; William Rotsler [1983]
52761	The A-Team #2: The Danger Maze; William Rotsler [1984]

WARNER BOOKS (Warner Books, Inc.)

Prefix 446-

Warner Books bought Paperback Library in 1972, continuing Paperback Library's 446-prefix. The first Warners, including *Banyon,* were issued as "Warner Paperback Library" editions, and include the Paperback Library logo.

74-285	Banyon; William Johnston [1972]
75-273	UFO-1: Flesh Hunters; Robert Miall [1973]
75-274	UFO-2: Sporting Blood; Robert Miall [1973]
76-061	The Six Million Dollar Man: Cyborg #2: Operation Nuke; Martin Caidin [1974]
76-367	The Tonight Show: Tonight!; Terry Galanoy [1974]
76-408	The Six Million Dollar Man #3: High Crystal; Martin Caidin [1975]

76-464	Kung Fu #1: The Way of the Tiger, the Sign of the Dragon; Howard Lee [1973]
76-465	Kung Fu #2: Chains; Howard Lee [1973]
76-466	Kung Fu #3: Superstition; Howard Lee [1973]
76-467	Kung Fu #4: A Praying Mantis Kills; Howard Lee [1974]
76-643	The Six Million Dollar Man: Cyborg; Martin Caidin [1974]
76-833	The Six Million Dollar Man #1: Wine, Women and War; Michael Jahn [1975]
76-834	The Six Million Dollar Man #2: Solid Gold Kidnapping; Evan Richards [1975]
76-835	The Six Million Dollar Man #4: Pilot Error; Jay Barbree [1975]
76-836	The Six Million Dollar Man #5: The Rescue of Athena One; Michael Jahn [1975]
78-655	The Six Million Dollar Man #6: CYBORG IV; Martin Caidin [1976]
88-294	Laverne and Shirley #1: Teamwork; Con Steffanson [1976]
88-295	Laverne and Shirley #2: Easy Money; Con Steffanson [1976]
88-296	Laverne and Shirley #3: Gold Rush; Con Steffanson [1976]
88-341	Space: 1999 (Year 2) #1: Planets of Peril; Michael Butterworth [1977]
88-342	Space: 1999 (Year 2) #2: Mind-Breaks of Space; Michael Butterworth with Jeff Jones [1977]
88-343	Space: 1999 (Year 2) #3: The Space-Jackers; Michael Butterworth [1977]
88-344	Space: 1999 (Year 2) #4: The Psychomorph; Michael Butterworth [1977]
88-345	Space: 1999 (Year 2) #5: The Time Fighters; Michael Butterworth [1977]
88-346	Space: 1999 (Year 2) #6: The Edge of the Infinite; Michael Butterworth [1977]
88-371	The Six Million Dollar Man: Cyborg; Martin Caidin [1976]

Later Warners

30324	The Dukes of Hazzard: Gone Racin'; Eric Alter [1983]
31141	The Paper Chase; John Jay Osborn, Jr. [1983]
32000	M*A*S*H Trivia: The Unofficial Quiz Book; George St. John [1983]
34668	Wheel of Fortune: Vanna Speaks with Patricia Romanowski; Vanna White [1988]

WEEKLY READER BOOKS

| F435 | Fantasy Island; Roger Elwood [1981] |
| F536 | Joanie Loves Chachi; Roger Elwood [1982] |

WHITMAN PUBLISHING COMPANY (Western Publishing Co.)

Whitman Book Company expanded their standard-size line of children's hardbacks to include TV tie-ins in the early 1950's. Early tie-ins were based on Westerns, with detective shows, adventure shows, and sitcoms soon becoming popular. The first tie-ins, based on the *Roy Rogers* and *Gene Autry* TV shows, were a continuation of those series the publisher had already started (based on the *Roy Rogers* and *Gene Autry* radio series and movies) in the 1940's. Dustjackets were used initially, but were discontinued when the publisher turned to laminated covers (termed "glossies" or "wraparounds") in 1953. Laminated covers were used until the mid-1960's, when a cheaper but more durable cloth cover was used.

Titles issued through the late 1960's include illustrated endpapers and drawings interspersed throughout the text. Titles issued subsequently include plain endpapers and lack drawings. All but two of the TV tie-ins are 7-3/4 inches tall: *Patty Duke and the Adventure of the Chinese Junk* and *"flipper": The Mystery of the Black Schooner* are 8-1/2 inches tall.

Most Whitman TV tie-ins issued through 1960 have "Authorized TV Edition" logos on the front covers. Most issued from 1960-72 have "Authorized TV Adventure" logos on the spines. Certain books (like *The Rifleman*) were issued in both formats, with identical covers and book numbers between the formats. There are two groups of exceptions to the preceding:

(1) The *Gene Autry* books, the *Roy Rogers* books, the *Annie Oakley* books *Ghost Town Secret* and *Danger at Diablo*, and the *Rin Tin Tin* book *Rinty*, lack the TV logos but say "Authorized Edition" on the spines.

(2) The *Annette* books, the *Spin and Marty* books, and the book *Legends of Davy Crockett* (books from the Disney shows *The Mickey Mouse Club* and *Walt Disney*), lack the TV logos but include the words "Walt Disney" and "Authorized Edition" on the covers or spines.

Whitman TV tie-ins issued since 1972 lack the TV logos but include the new Whitman logo (a "W" inside a box) on the spines and front covers, along with the statement "A Whitman Book" on the front covers. Such books include the *Waltons* books and the *Lassie* book *Trouble at Panter's Lake*.

The Whitmans generally lacked cover prices, with store stickers bearing prices affixed to many of the covers instead. Alternatively, the covers of certain early titles include the number "49" (signifying a 49 cent cover price), separated from the main book number by a colon.

Because the Whitman book numbers were not assigned sequentially, and because many book numbers (1500, 1504, etc.) are shared by more than one title, the Whitmans are listed twice, first by book number, then by title.

In addition to the following standard-size titles, Whitman issued TV tie-ins in two separate "Big Little Book" series, which are listed subsequently.

Whitmans By Book Number

1500	Roy Rogers and The Brasada Bandits; Cole Fannin [1955]
1500	Lassie and the Secret of Summer; Dorothea J. Snow [1964]
1502	Roy Rogers and the Enchanted Canyon; Jim Rivers [1954]

1503	Roy Rogers: King of the Cowboys; Cole Fannin [1956]
1504	Roy Rogers and Dale Evans in River of Peril; Cole Fannin [1957]
1504	Lassie: Lost in the Snow; Steve Frazee [1969]
1505	The Lucy Show: Lucy and the Madcap Mystery; Cole Fannin [1963]
1505	Lassie: The Mystery of Bristlecone Pine; Steve Frazee [1967]
1506	The Roy Rogers Show: Dale Evans and Danger in Crooked Canyon; Helen Hale [1958]
1508	Lassie: Forbidden Valley; Doris Schroeder [1959]
1509	Lassie and the Mystery at Blackberry Bog; Dorothea J. Snow [1966]
1510	Gene Autry and the Ghost Riders; Lewis B. Patten [1955]
1510	Dragnet: Case histories from the popular television series; Richard Deming [1970]
1510	The Munsters and the Great Camera Caper; William Johnston [1965]
1510	The Waltons #6: The Accident; Virginia McDonnell [1975]
1511	Gene Autry and the Golden Stallion; Cole Fannin [1954]
1511	Hawaii Five-O: Top Secret; Robert Sidney Bowen [1969]
1512	Gene Autry and Arapaho War Drums; Lewis B. Patten [1957]
1512	The Mickey Mouse Club: Walt Disney's Annette: Mystery at Medicine Wheel; Barlow Meyers [1964]
1512	Mission: Impossible: The Money Explosion; Talmage Powell [1970]
1513	Lassie: The Wild Mountain Trail; I.G. Edmonds [1966]
1514	Patty Duke and Mystery Mansion; Doris Schroeder [1964]
1514	Lassie: The Secret of the Smelters' Cave; Steve Frazee [1968]
1515	Mission: Impossible: The Priceless Particle; Talmage Powell [1969]
1515	Lassie: Trouble at Panter's Lake; Steve Frazee [1972]
1516	Land of the Giants: Flight of Fear; Carl Henry Rathjen [1969]
1516	The Waltons #1: The Bird Dog; Dion Henderson [1975]
1517	Voyage to the Bottom of the Sea; Raymond F. Jones [1965]
1517	The Mod Squad: Assignment: The Hideout; Richard Deming [1970]
1519	Dr. Kildare: The Magic Key; William Johnston [1964]
1519	The High Chaparral: Apache Way; Steve Frazee [1969]
1520	Combat: The Counterattack; Franklin M. Davis, Jr. [1964]
1520	Gunsmoke: Showdown on Front Street; Paul S. Newman [1969]
1521	Ironside: The Picture Frame Frame-Up; William Johnston [1969]
1522	Ripcord; D.S. Halacy, Jr. [1962]
1526	Leave it to Beaver; Cole Fannin [1962]
1527	Dragnet: Case histories from the popular television series; Richard Deming [1957]
1535	The Mickey Mouse Club: Walt Disney's Spin and Marty [orig. title "Marty Markham"]; Lawrence Edward Watkin [1956]
1535	Walt Disney's Zorro [dull cover]; Steve Frazee [1958]
1536	Lassie and the Mystery at Blackberry Bog; Dorothea J. Snow [1956]
1536	The Lawrence Welk Show: Janet Lennon: Adventure at Two Rivers; Barlow Meyers [1961]
1537	Fury and the Lone Pine Mystery; William Fenton [1957]

1537   The Mickey Mouse Club: Walt Disney's Annette and the Mystery at Moonstone Bay; Doris Schroeder [1962]

1538   Annie Oakley in the Ghost Town Secret; Doris Schroeder [1957]

1538   Annie Oakley in Double Trouble; Doris Schroeder [1958]

1538   The Mod Squad: Assignment: The Arranger; Richard Deming [1969]

1539   Rin Tin Tin and Call to Danger; Doris Schroeder [1957]

1539   The Lawrence Welk Show: Janet Lennon at Camp Calamity; Barlow Meyers [1962]

1539   The Monkees in Who's Got the Button?; William Johnston [1968]

1539   The Waltons #5: Up She Rises!; Gladys Baker Bond [1975]

1540   Annie Oakley in Danger at Diablo; Doris Schroeder [1955]

1541   Sea Hunt; Cole Fannin [1960]

1541   The Man From U.N.C.L.E. and the Affair of the Gentle Saboteur; Brandon Keith [1966]

1542   Rin Tin Tin's Rinty; Julie Campbell [1954]

1542   I Spy: Message From Moscow; Brandon Keith [1966]

1543   The Man From U.N.C.L.E. and the Affair of the Gunrunners' Gold; Brandon Keith [1967]

1544   The Lawrence Welk Show: The Lennon Sisters: The Secret of Holiday Island; Doris Schroeder [1960]

1544   F Troop: The Great Indian Uprising; William Johnston [1967]

1545   The Invaders: Dam of Death; Jack Pearl [1967]

1546   The Mickey Mouse Club: Walt Disney's Annette: The Desert Inn Mystery; Doris Schroeder [1961]

1547   Dr. Kildare: Assigned to Trouble; Robert C. Ackworth [1963]

1547   The Rat Patrol: The Iron Monster Raid; I.G. Edmonds [1968]

1548   Wyatt Earp; Philip Ketchum [1956]

1548   The Rebel; H.A. De Rosso [1961]

1548   Garrison's Gorillas and the Fear Formula; Jack Pearl [1968]

1549   Circus Boy: Under the Big Top; Dorothea J. Snow [1957]

1549   Star Trek: Mission to Horatius; Mack Reynolds [1968]

1550   Bat Masterson; Wayne C. Lee [1960]

1552   Lassie: Treasure Hunter; Charles S. Strong [1960]

1553   Hawaii Five-O: The Octopus Caper; Leo R. Ellis [1971]

1557   Fury and the Mystery at Trappers' Hole; Troy Nesbit [1959]

1559   The Restless Gun; Barlow Meyers [1959]

1566   Maverick; Charles I. Coombs [1959]

1566   Gilligan's Island; William Johnston [1966]

1567   Wagon Train; Troy Nesbit [1959]

1567   The Munsters: The Last Resort; William Johnston [1966]

1567   Family Affair: Buffy Finds a Star; Gladys Baker Bond [1970]

1568   Have Gun, Will Travel; Barlow Meyers [1959]

1568   Bonanza: Killer Lion; Steve Frazee [1966]

1569   The Rifleman; Cole Fannin [1959]

1569   The Big Valley; Charles Heckelmann [1966]

1569   Bonanza: Heroes of the Wild West; B.L. Bonham, ed. [1970]

1570	The Greet Hornet: The Case of the Disappearing Doctor; Brandon Keith [1966]
1571	Bonanza: Treachery Trail; Harry Whittington [1968]
1572	The Beverly Hillbillies: The Saga of Wildcat Creek; Doris Schroeder [1963]
1572	Bewitched: The Opposite Uncle; William Johnston [1970]
1574	The Mickey Mouse Club: Walt Disney's Annette and the Mystery at Smugglers' Cove; Doris Schroeder [1963]
1576	The Waltons #2: The Puzzle; Carl Henry Rathjen [1975]
1577	The Mickey Mouse Club: Walt Disney's Spin and Marty: Trouble at Triple-R; Doris Schroeder [1958]
1577	The Real McCoys and Danger at the Ranch; Cole Fannin [1961]
1578	Circus Boy: War on Wheels; Dorothea J. Snow [1958]
1579	Rin Tin Tin and The Ghost Wagon Train; Cole Fannin [1958]
1580	The Waltons #4: The Treasures; Carl Henry Rathjen [1975]
1583	The Lawrence Welk Show: Janet Lennon and the Angels; Barlow Meyers [1963]
1585	The Mickey Mouse Club: Walt Disney's Annette: Sierra Summer; Doris Schroeder [1960]
1586	Walt Disney's Zorro [laminated cover]; Steve Frazee [1958]
1587	Cheyenne and the Lost Gold of Lion Park; Steve Frazee [1958]
1587	Gunsmoke; Robert Turner [1958]
1588	Wells Fargo and Danger Station; Sam Allison [1958]
1589	Lassie and the Secret of Summer; Dorothea J. Snow [1958]
1599	The Waltons #3: The Penny Sale; Gladys Baker Bond [1975]
1619	Walt Disney: Legends of Davy Crockett; Ardis Edwards Burton [1955]
2302	Gene Autry and the Big Valley Grab [dustjacket]; W.H. Hutchinson [1952]
2302	Gene Autry and the Big Valley Grab [laminated cover]; W.H. Hutchinson [1954]
2305	Roy Rogers and the Rimrod Renegades [dustjacket]; Snowden Miller [1952]
2305	Roy Rogers and the Rimrod Renegades [laminated cover]; Snowden Miller [1954]
2324	"flipper": The Mystery of the Black Schooner; Richard Hardwick [1966]
2334	Patty Duke and the Adventure of the Chinese Junk; Doris Schroeder [1966]
2355	Gene Autry and the Badmen of Broken Bow [dustjacket]; Snowden Miller [1951]
2361	Roy Rogers on the Trail of the Zeroes; Packer Elton [1954]
2373	Roy Rogers and the Enchanted Canyon; Jim Rivers [1954]

Whitmans By Title

Annie Oakley in Danger at Diablo; Doris Schroeder; Whitman 1540 [1955]
Annie Oakley in the Ghost Town Secret; Doris Schroeder; Whitman 1538 [1957]
Annie Oakley in Double Trouble; Doris Schroeder; Whitman 1538 [1958]
Bat Masterson; Wayne C. Lee; Whitman 1550 [1960]
The Beverly Hillbillies: The Saga of Wildcat Creek; Doris Schroeder; Whitman 1572 [1963]

Bewitched: The Opposite Uncle; William Johnston; Whitman 1572 [1970]
The Big Valley; Charles Heckelmann; Whitman 1569 [1966]
Bonanza: Killer Lion; Steve Frazee; Whitman 1568 [1966]
Bonanza: Treachery Trail; Harry Whittington; Whitman 1571 [1968]
Bonanza: Heroes of the Wild West; B.L. Bonham, ed.; Whitman 1569 [1970]
Cheyenne and the Lost Gold of Lion Park; Steve Frazee; Whitman 1587 [1958]
Circus Boy: Under the Big Top; Dorothea J. Snow; Whitman 1549 [1957]
Circus Boy: War on Wheels; Dorothea J. Snow; Whitman 1578 [1958]
Combat: The Counterattack; Franklin M. Davis, Jr.; Whitman 1520 [1964]
Dr. Kildare: Assigned to Trouble; Robert C. Ackworth; Whitman 1547 [1963]
Dr. Kildare: The Magic Key; William Johnston; Whitman 1519 [1964]
Dragnet: Case histories from the popular television series; Richard Deming; Whitman
     1527 [1957]
Dragnet: Case histories from the popular television series (cover-variation); Richard
     Deming; Whitman 1510 [1970]
F Troop: The Great Indian Uprising; William Johnston; Whitman 1544 [1967]
Family Affair: Buffy Finds a Star; Gladys Baker Bond; Whitman 1567 [1970]
"flipper": The Mystery of the Black Schooner; Richard Hardwick; Whitman 2324 [1966]
Fury and the Lone Pine Mystery; William Fenton; Whitman 1537 [1957]
Fury and the Mystery at Trappers' Hole; Troy Nesbit; Whitman 1557 [1959]
Garrison's Gorillas and the Fear Formula; Jack Pearl; Whitman 1548 [1968]
Gene Autry and the Badmen of Broken Bow [dustjacket]; Snowden Miller; Whitman
     2355 [1951]
Gene Autry and the Big Valley Grab [dustjacket]; W.H. Hutchinson; Whitman 2302
     [1952]
Gene Autry and the Big Valley Grab [laminated cover]; W.H. Hutchinson; Whitman
     2302 [1954]
Gene Autry and the Golden Stallion; Cole Fannin; Whitman 1511 [1954]
Gene Autry and the Ghost Riders; Lewis B. Patten; Whitman 1510 [1955]
Gene Autry and Arapaho War Drums; Lewis B. Patten; Whitman 1512 [1957]
Gilligan's Island; William Johnston; Whitman 1566 [1966]
The Greet Hornet: The Case of the Disappearing Doctor; Brandon Keith; Whitman 1570
     [1966]
Gunsmoke; Robert Turner; Whitman 1587 [1958]
Gunsmoke: Showdown on Front Street; Paul S. Newman; Whitman 1520 [1969]
Have Gun, Will Travel; Barlow Meyers; Whitman 1568 [1959]
Hawaii Five-O: Top Secret; Robert Sidney Bowen; Whitman 1511 [1969]
Hawaii Five-O: The Octopus Caper; Leo R. Ellis; Whitman 1553 [1971]
The High Chaparral: Apache Way; Steve Frazee; Whitman 1519 [1969]
I Spy: Message From Moscow; Brandon Keith; Whitman 1542 [1966]
The Invaders: Dam of Death; Jack Pearl; Whitman 1545 [1967]
Ironside: The Picture Frame Frame-Up; William Johnston; Whitman 1521 [1969]
Land of the Giants: Flight of Fear; Carl Henry Rathjen; Whitman 1516 [1969]
Lassie and the Mystery at Blackberry Bog; Dorothea J. Snow; Whitman 1536 [1956]
Lassie and the Mystery at Blackberry Bog (cover-variation); Dorothea J. Snow; Whitman
     1509 [1966]
Lassie and the Secret of Summer; Dorothea J. Snow; Whitman 1589 [1958]

Lassie and the Secret of Summer (cover-variation); Dorothea J. Snow; Whitman 1500 [1964]

Lassie: Forbidden Valley; Doris Schroeder; Whitman 1508 [1959]

Lassie: Treasure Hunter; Charles S. Strong; Whitman 1552 [1960]

Lassie: The Wild Mountain Trail; I.G. Edmonds; Whitman 1513 [1966]

Lassie: The Mystery of Bristlecone Pine; Steve Frazee; Whitman 1505 [1967]

Lassie: The Secret of the Smelters' Cave; Steve Frazee; Whitman 1514 [1968]

Lassie: Lost in the Snow; Steve Frazee; Whitman 1504 [1969]

Lassie: Trouble at Panter's Lake; Steve Frazee; Whitman 1515 [1972]

The Lawrence Welk Show: The Lennon Sisters: The Secret of Holiday Island; Doris Schroeder; Whitman 1544 [1960]

The Lawrence Welk Show: Janet Lennon: Adventure at Two Rivers; Barlow Meyers; Whitman 1536 [1961]

The Lawrence Welk Show: Janet Lennon at Camp Calamity; Barlow Meyers; Whitman 1539 [1962]

The Lawrence Welk Show: Janet Lennon and the Angels; Barlow Meyers; Whitman 1583 [1963]

Leave it to Beaver; Cole Fannin; Whitman 1526 [1962]

The Lucy Show: Lucy and the Madcap Mystery; Cole Fannin; Whitman 1505 [1963]

The Man From U.N.C.L.E. and the Affair of the Gentle Saboteur; Brandon Keith; Whitman 1541 [1966]

The Man From U.N.C.L.E. and the Affair of the Gunrunners' Gold; Brandon Keith; Whitman 1543 [1967]

Maverick; Charles I. Coombs; Whitman 1566 [1959]

The Mickey Mouse Club: Walt Disney's Annette: Sierra Summer; Doris Schroeder; Whitman 1585 [1960]

The Mickey Mouse Club: Walt Disney's Annette: The Desert Inn Mystery; Doris Schroeder; Whitman 1546 [1961]

The Mickey Mouse Club: Walt Disney's Annette and the Mystery at Moonstone Bay; Doris Schroeder; Whitman 1537 [1962]

The Mickey Mouse Club: Walt Disney's Annette and the Mystery at Smugglers' Cove; Doris Schroeder; Whitman 1574 [1963]

The Mickey Mouse Club: Walt Disney's Annette: Mystery at Medicine Wheel; Barlow Meyers; Whitman 1512 [1964]

The Mickey Mouse Club: Walt Disney's Spin and Marty [orig. title "Marty Markham"]; Lawrence Edward Watkin; Whitman 1535 [1956]

The Mickey Mouse Club: Walt Disney's Spin and Marty: Trouble at Triple-R; Doris Schroeder; Whitman 1577 [1958]

Mission: Impossible: The Priceless Particle; Talmage Powell; Whitman 1515 [1969]

Mission: Impossible: The Money Explosion; Talmage Powell; Whitman 1512 [1970]

The Mod Squad: Assignment: The Arranger; Richard Deming; Whitman 1538 [1969]

The Mod Squad: Assignment: The Hideout; Richard Deming; Whitman 1517 [1970]

The Monkees in Who's Got the Button?; William Johnston; Whitman 1539 [1968]

The Munsters and the Great Camera Caper; William Johnston; Whitman 1510 [1965]

The Munsters: The Last Resort; William Johnston; Whitman 1657 [1966]

Patty Duke and Mystery Mansion; Doris Schroeder; Whitman 1514 [1964]

Patty Duke and the Adventure of the Chinese Junk; Doris Schroeder; Whitman 2334 [1966]

The Rat Patrol: The Iron Monster Raid; I.G. Edmonds; Whitman 1547 [1968]

The Real McCoys and Danger at the Ranch; Cole Fannin; Whitman 1577 [1961]

The Rebel; H.A. De Rosso; Whitman 1548 [1961]

The Restless Gun; Barlow Meyers; Whitman 1559 [1959]

The Rifleman; Cole Fannin; Whitman 1569 [1959]

Rin Tin Tin's Rinty; Julie Campbell; Whitman 1542 [1954]

Rin Tin Tin and Call to Danger; Doris Schroeder; Whitman 1539 [1957]

Rin Tin Tin and The Ghost Wagon Train; Cole Fannin; Whitman 1579 [1958]

Ripcord; D.S. Halacy, Jr.; Whitman 1522 [1962]

Roy Rogers and the Rimrod Renegades [dustjacket]; Snowden Miller; Whitman 2305 [1952]

Roy Rogers and the Rimrod Renegades [laminated cover]; Snowden Miller; Whitman 2305 [1954]

Roy Rogers and the Enchanted Canyon; Jim Rivers; Whitman 1502 [also Whitman 2373] [1954]

Roy Rogers: The Trail of the Zeroes; Packer Elton; Whitman 2361 [1954]

Roy Rogers and The Brasada Bandits; Cole Fannin; Whitman 1500 [1955]

Roy Rogers: King of the Cowboys; Cole Fannin; Whitman 1503 [1956]

Roy Rogers and Dale Evans in River of Peril; Cole Fannin; Whitman 1504 [1957]

The Roy Rogers Show: Dale Evans and Danger in Crooked Canyon; Helen Hale; Whitman 1506 [1958]

Sea Hunt; Cole Fannin; Whitman 1541 [1960]

Star Trek: Mission to Horatius; Mack Reynolds; Whitman 1549 [1968]

Voyage to the Bottom of the Sea; Raymond F. Jones; Whitman 1517 [1965]

Wagon Train; Troy Nesbit; Whitman 1567 [1959]

Walt Disney: Legends of Davy Crockett; Ardis Edwards Burton; Whitman 1619 [1955]

The Waltons #1: The Bird Dog; Dion Henderson; Whitman 1516 [1975]

The Waltons #2: The Puzzle; Carl Henry Rathjen; Whitman 1576 [1975]

The Waltons #3: The Penny Sale; Gladys Baker Bond; Whitman 1599 [1975]

The Waltons #4: The Treasures; Carl Henry Rathjen; Whitman 1580 [1975]

The Waltons #5: Up She Rises!; Gladys Baker Bond; Whitman 1539 [1975]

The Waltons #6: The Accident; Virginia McDonnell; Whitman 1510 [1975]

Wells Fargo and Danger Station; Sam Allison; Whitman 1588 [1958]

Wyatt Earp; Philip Ketchum; Whitman 1548 [1956]

Zorro [laminated cover]; Steve Frazee; Whitman 1586 [1958]

Zorro [dull cover]; Steve Frazee; Whitman 1535 [1958]

WHITMAN BIG LITTLE BOOK TV SERIES

Whitman issued a series of six Big Little Books in 1958, all based on TV shows featuring fictional and real-life historical figures. The books, numbers 1644 to 1649, include the trademark "The Big Little Book TV Series" on the front cover logos and endpapers. The books are laminated hardbacks with wraparound covers, and stand 5-3/4 inches tall. Illustrated facing pages alternate with text pages throughout the stories.

1644	Wyatt Earp; Davis Lott [1958]
1645	Walt Disney's Andy Burnett on Trial; Charles I. Coombs [1958]
1646	The Buccaneers; Alice Sankey [1958]
1647	Gunsmoke; Doris Schroeder [1958]
1648	The Adventures of Jim Bowie; Lewis B. Patten [1958]
1649	Sir Lancelot; Dorothy Haas [1958]

WHITMAN - A BIG LITTLE BOOK

Whitman began a new series of Big Little Books in 1967, this time using the logo "A Big Little Book" on the spines and endpapers. A total of 35 titles were issued (numbers 2001 through 2035), all based on TV shows, cartoons, and comic characters. The ten titles based on TV shows are identified below. Also known as the "2000 Series," the books are dull-cover hardbacks and stand 5 inches tall. Illustrated facing pages alternate with text pages throughout the stories.

The first 12 titles were issued in 1967, then re-issued twice in 1968, for a total of three printings apiece. The first printings are identified by blue endpapers with white logos, the second printings by white endpapers with gray logos, the third printings by plain white endpapers. The remaining 23 titles were issued following the third printing of the first 12 titles, and include one printing each, with plain white endpapers. The series ran through 1969.

Nearly all of the books in the series have $.39 cover prices stamped on the upper right hand corner of the front covers. Certain books, including certain copies of "flipper": Deep-Sea Photographer, lack them.

Beginning in 1973, certain titles were re-issued in a limpbound "5700" Series, with identical covers to the corresponding titles in the 2000 series.

2002	Bonanza: The Bubble Gum Kid; George S. Elrick [1967]
2003	"flipper": Killer Whale Trouble; George S. Elrick [1967]
2004	Lassie: Adventure in Alaska; George S. Elrick [1967]
2011	The Man From U.N.C.L.E.: The Calcutta Affair; George S. Elrick [1967]
2012	The Invaders: Alien Missile Threat; Paul S. Newman [1967]
2018	Daktari: Night of Terror; George S. Elrick [1968]
2027	Lassie and the Shabby Sheik; George S. Elrick [1968]
2031	Batman and Robin in the Cheetah Caper; George S. Elrick [1969]
2032	"flipper": Deep-Sea Photographer; George S. Elrick [1969]
2035	Gentle Ben: Mystery in the Everglades; Paul S. Newman [1969]

XEROX EDUCATION PUBLICATIONS (Xerox Corporation)

"Discovering Paperbacks"

N 104   Charlie's Angels: Peter Travers' Favorite TV Angels; Peter Travers [1978]

ZEBRA BOOKS (Kensington Publishing Corp.)

89083-227 Welcome Back, Kotter: The Real John Travolta; Martin A. Grove [1976]
89083-228 Happy Days: fonzie!; Martin A. Grove [1976]
8217-1800 Miami Vice: Miami Magic; Caroline Latham [1985]

ACTORS PICTURED LIST

Aaker, Lee (1943-)
  Rin Tin Tin .... Rusty
Aames, Willie (1960-)
  Charles in Charge .... Buddy Lembeck
  Eight is Enough .... Tommy Bradford
Adams, Don (1926-)
  Get Smart .... Maxwell Smart (Agent 86 for Control)
Adams, Nick (1931-1968)
  The Rebel .... Johnny Yuma
Albert, Eddie (1908-)
  Switch .... Frank McBride
Albertson, Jack (1907-1981)
  Chico and the Man .... Ed Brown (The Man)
Albright, Lola (1925-)
  Peter Gunn .... Edie Hart
Alda, Alan (1936-)
  M*A*S*H .... Capt. Benjamin Franklin (Hawkeye) Pierce
Alexander, Ben (1911-1969)
  Dragnet .... Off. Frank Smith
Alicia, Ana (1956-)
  Falcon Crest .... Melissa Agretti Cumson
Allen, Elizabeth (1934-)
  Bracken's World .... Laura Deane
Allen, Marty (1922-)
  The Hollywood Squares .... Himself
Allen, Steve (1921-)
  The Tonight Show .... Himself
Ames, Rachel
  General Hospital .... Nurse Audrey March
Anderson, Barbara (1945-)
  Ironside .... Eve Whitfield
Anderson, Melissa Sue (1962-)
  Little House on the Prairie .... Mary Ingalls Kendall
Anderson, Warner (1911-1976)
  The Lineup .... Det. Lt. Ben Guthrie
Andrews, Tige (1923-)
  The Detectives .... Lt. John Russo
  The Mod Squad .... Capt. Adam Greer

301

Anholt, Tony
  Space: 1999 . . . . First Off. Tony Verdeschi
Armstrong, Kerry
  Prisoner: Cell Block H . . . . Lynn Warner
Arness, James (1923-)
  Gunsmoke . . . . Marshal Matt Dillon
  How the West Was Won . . . . Zeb Macahan
Arngrim, Stefan (1955-)
  Land of the Giants . . . . Barry Lockridge
Arquette, Cliff (1905-1974)
  The Hollywood Squares . . . . Charley Weaver
  The Jack Paar Tonight Show . . . . Charley Weaver
Astin, John (1930-)
  The Addams Family . . . . Gomez Addams
Atterbury, Malcolm (1907-)
  Apple's Way . . . . Grandfather Aldon
Autry, Gene (1907-)
  The Gene Autry Show . . . . Himself
Aykroyd, Dan (1952-)
  Saturday Night Live . . . . Himself
Bach, Catherine (1954-)
  The Dukes of Hazzard . . . . Daisy Duke
Backus, Henny
  Blondie . . . . Cora Dithers
Backus, Jim (1913-1989)
  Blondie . . . . J.C. Dithers
Badler, Jane
  V . . . . Diana
Baer, Max, Jr. (1937-)
  The Beverly Hillbillies . . . . Jethro Bodine
Bain, Barbara (1931-)
  Mission: Impossible . . . . Cinnamon Carter
  Space: 1999 . . . . Dr. Helena Russell
Baio, Scott (1961-)
  Charles in Charge . . . . Charles
  Joanie Loves Chachi . . . . Chachi Arcola
Baker, Colin
  Doctor Who . . . . The Doctor
Baker, Tom (1934-)
  Doctor Who . . . . The Doctor
Ball, Lucille (1911-1989)
  Here's Lucy . . . . Lucy Carter
  I Love Lucy . . . . Lucy Ricardo
  The Lucy Show . . . . Lucy Carmichael
Bari, Lenny
  Fish . . . . Mike
Barrett, Nancy
  Dark Shadows . . . . Carolyn Stoddard/Charity Trask
Barris, Chuck (1928-)
  The Gong Show . . . . Himself

Barry, Gene (1921-)
   Bat Masterson .... Bat Masterson
   Burke's Law .... Capt. Amos Burke
   The Name of the Game .... Glenn Howard
Barry, Jack (1918-1984)
   Twenty-One .... Himself
Basehart, Richard (1914-1984)
   Voyage to the Bottom of the Sea .... Adm. Harriman Nelson
Bateman, Jason (1969-)
   It's Your Move .... Matthew Burton
Bateman, Justine (1966-)
   Family Ties .... Mallory Keaton
Baur, Elizabeth (1948-)
   Lancer .... Teresa O'Brien
Baxter-Birney, Meredith (1947-)
   Bridget Loves Bernie .... Bridget Fitzgerald Steinberg
   Family .... Nancy Lawrence Maitland
   Family Ties .... Elyse Keaton
Bel Geddes, Barbara (1922-)
   Dallas .... Eleanor Southworth (Miss Ellie) Ewing
Bellamy, Ralph (1904-1991)
   The Most Deadly Game .... Ethan Arcane
Belushi, John (1949-1982)
   Saturday Night Live .... Himself
Benedict, Dirk (1944-)
   The A-Team .... Lt. Templeton "Face" Peck
   Battlestar Galactica .... Lt. Starbuck
Bennett, Joan (1910-1990)
   Dark Shadows .... Elizabeth Collins Stoddard/Judith Collins
Beradino, John (1917-1996)
   General Hospital .... Dr. Steve Hardy
   The New Breed .... Sgt. Vince Cavelli
Berry, Ken (1930-)
   F Troop .... Capt. Wilton Parmenter
Berthrong, Deirdre
   James at Fifteen .... Kathy Hunter
Bethune, Zina (1946-)
   The Nurses .... Gail Lucas
Betz, Carl (1920-1978)
   Judd for the Defense .... Clinton Judd
Billington, Michael (1941-)
   UFO .... Col. Paul Foster
Birney, David (1939-)
   Bridget Loves Bernie .... Bernie Steinberg
Bishop, Ed (1933-)
   UFO .... Cmdr. Edward Straker
Blair, Janet (1921-)
   The Smith Family .... Betty Smith
Blake, Robert (1934-)
   Baretta .... Det. Tony Baretta
Blocker, Dan (1932-1972)
   Bonanza .... Hoss Cartwright

Blossom, Rock (1896-1978)
The Addams Family . . . . Grandmama Addams
Bolling, Tiffany
The New People . . . . Susan Bradley
Bonaduce, Danny (1959-)
The Partridge Family . . . . Danny Partridge
Bond, Ward (1903-1960)
Wagon Train . . . . Major Seth Adams
Booke, Sorrell (1930-1994)
The Dukes of Hazzard . . . . Jefferson Davis "Boss" Hogg
Boone, Brendon
Garrison's Gorillas . . . . Chief
Boone, Randy (1942-)
Cimmaron Strip . . . . Francis Wilde
Boone, Richard (1910-1981)
Have Gun, Will Travel . . . . Paladin
Hec Ramsey . . . . Hec Ramsey
Bowman, Lee (1914-1979)
Miami Undercover . . . . Jeff Thompson
Braddock, Mickey (see Mickey Dolenz)
Brake, Patricia (1942-)
The Ugliest Girl in Town . . . . Julie Renfield
Brandon, Clark (1958-)
Mr. Merlin . . . . Zachary Rogers
Bray, Robert (1917-1983)
Lassie . . . . Corey Stuart
Breck, Peter (1929-)
The Big Valley . . . . Nick Barkley
Brennan, Walter (1894-1974)
The Real McCoys . . . . Grandpa Amos McCoy
Bridges, Beau (1941-)
Medical Story . . . . Steve Ducker
Bridges, Lloyd (1913-)
Sea Hunt . . . . Mike Nelson
Bridges, Todd (1966-)
Fish . . . . Loomis
Broderick, James (1930-1982)
Family . . . . Doug Lawrence
Brolin, James (1940-)
Marcus Welby, M.D. . . . . Dr. Steven Kiley
Brolin, Josh
Private Eye . . . . Johnny Betts
Brophy, Kevin
Lucan . . . . Lucan
Brown, Chelsea
Laugh-In . . . . Herself
Brown, Georg Stanford (1943-)
The Rookies . . . . Off. Terry Webster
Brown, Robert (1927-)
Here Come the Brides . . . . Jason Bolt
Primus . . . . Carter Primus

Cassidy, David (1950-)
  The Partridge Family . . . . Keith Partridge
Cassidy, Shaun (1958-)
  The Hardy Boys/Nancy Drew Mysteries . . . . Joe Hardy
Cassidy, Ted (1932-1979)
  The Addams Family . . . . Lurch
Cassisi, John
  Fish . . . . Victor Kreutzer
Cerusico, Enzo (1943-)
  My Friend Tony . . . . Tony Novello
Chamberlain, Richard (1935-)
  Dr. Kildare . . . . Dr. James Kildare
Cherry, Byron
  The Dukes of Hazzard . . . . Coy Duke
Chiles, Linden
  James at Fifteen . . . . Dr. Paul Hunter
Christopher, William (1932-)
  M*A*S*H . . . . Father Francis Mulcahy
Clark, Dick (1929-)
  American Bandstand . . . . Himself
Clarke, John
  The New Breed . . . . Off. Joe Huddleston
Cobb, Julie
  Charles in Charge . . . . Jill Pembroke
Cobb, Lee J. (1911-1976)
  The Young Lawyers . . . . Atty. David Barrett
Cohoon, Patti (1959-)
  Apple's Way . . . . Cathy Apple
Colbert, Robert
  The Time Tunnel . . . . Dr. Doug Phillips
Cole, Dennis (1940-)
  Bracken's World . . . . Davey Evans
  The Felony Squad . . . . Det. Jim Briggs
Cole, Michael (1945-)
  The Mod Squad . . . . Pete Cochran
Coleman, Jack (1958-)
  Dynasty . . . . Steven Carrington
Collins, Joan (1933-)
  Dynasty . . . . Alexis Carrington Colby
Connelley, Christopher (1941-1988)
  Paper Moon . . . . Moses "Moze" Pray
Connors, Chuck (1921-)
  Arrest and Trial . . . . Atty. John Egan
  The Rifleman . . . . Lucas McCain
Connors, Mike (1925-)
  Mannix . . . . Joe Mannix
Conrad, Robert (1935-)
  Hawaiian Eye . . . . Tom Lopaka
  The Wild Wild West . . . . James T. West
Conrad, William (1920-1994)
  Cannon . . . . Frank Cannon

Danova, Cesare (1926-)
Garrison's Gorillas .... Actor
Danson, Ted (1947-)
Cheers .... Sam Malone
Darren, James (1936-)
The Time Tunnel .... Dr. Tony Newman
Darrow, Henry (1933-)
The High Chaparral .... Manolito Montoya
Davalos, Dick (1935-)
The Americans .... Jeff Canfield
David, Thayer (-1978)
Dark Shadows .... Prof. Elliot Stokes/Sandor the Gypsy
Davidson, John (1941-)
The Girl With Something Extra .... John Burton
Davis, Gail (1925-)
Annie Oakley .... Annie Oakley
Davis, Jim (1915-1981)
Dallas .... John Ross "Jock" Ewing
Davis, Josie
Charles in Charge .... Sarah Powell
Davis, Roger
Alias Smith and Jones .... Hannibal Heyes (alias Joshua Smith)
Dark Shadows .... Jeff Clark/Charles Delaware Tate
Dawber, Pam (1951-)
Mork & Mindy .... Mindy Beth McConnell
Dawson, Richard (1932-)
Family Feud .... Himself
DeCarlo, Yvonne (1922-)
The Munsters .... Lily Munster
Dee, Sandra (1942-)
Tammy .... Tammy Tarleton (from the Tammy movies)
Denning, Richard (1914-)
Michael Shayne .... Michael Shayne
Denver, Bob (1935-)
Gilligan's Island .... Gilligan
Dey, Susan (1952-)
The Partridge Family .... Laurie Partridge
Dickinson, Angie (1932-)
Police Woman .... Sgt. Suzanne "Pepper" Anderson
Diller, Phyllis (1917-)
Phyllis Diller .... Herself
Disney, Walt (1901-1966)
Walt Disney .... Himself
Dolenz, Mickey (1945-)
Circus Boy (under the stage name Mickey Braddock) .... Corky
The Monkees .... Himself
Donahue, Troy (1936-)
SurfSide 6 .... Sandy Winfield, II
Doremus, David (1958-)
Nanny and the Professor .... Hal Everett

Ellis, Carolyn
   The Bugaloos . . . . Joy
Ely, Rick
   The Young Rebels . . . . Jeremy Larkin
Ely, Ron (1938-)
   Tarzan . . . . Tarzan
Erickson, Leif (1911-1986)
   The High Chaparral . . . . Big John Cannon
Estrada, Erik (1949-)
   CHiPs . . . . Off. Frank "Ponch" Poncherello
Eubanks, Bob
   The Newlywed Game . . . . Himself
Evans, Dale (1912-)
   The Roy Rogers Show . . . . Herself
Evans, Linda (1942-)
   The Big Valley . . . . Audra Barkley
   Dynasty . . . . Krystle Jennings Carrington
Everett, Chad (1936-)
   Medical Center . . . . Dr. Joe Gannon
Falk, Peter (1927-)
   Columbo . . . . Lt. Columbo
   Trials of O'Brien . . . . Daniel J. O'Brien
Fargo, Donna
   The Hollywood Squares . . . . Herself
Farr, Jamie (1934-)
   M*A*S*H . . . . Cpl. Maxwell Klinger
Farr, Lee
   The Detectives . . . . Lt. James Conway
Farrell, Mike (1939-)
   M*A*S*H . . . . Capt. B.J. Hunnicut
Fawcett-Majors, Farrah (1947-)
   Charlie's Angels . . . . Jill Munroe
Feldon, Barbara (1939-)
   Get Smart . . . . Agent 99
Ferdin, Pamelyn (1959-)
   Blondie . . . . Cookie Bumstead
Ferrer, Jose (1912-)
   Medical Story . . . . Dr. Knowland
Ferrer, Mel (1917-)
   Falcon Crest . . . . Phillip Erikson
Ferrigno, Lou (1952-)
   The Incredible Hulk . . . . The Incredible Hulk
Field, Sally (1946-)
   The Flying Nun . . . . Sister Bertrille
   The Girl With Something Extra . . . . Sally Burton
Fink, John
   Nancy . . . . Dr. Adam Hudson
Fleming, Eric (1925-1966)
   Rawhide . . . . Gil Favor
Flood, Ann
   The Edge of Night . . . . Nancy Karr

Fonda, Henry (1905-1982)
   The Deputy . . . . Marshal Simon Fry
   The Smith Family . . . . Det. Sgt. Chad Smith
Forbes, Scott (1921-)
   Jim Bowie . . . . Jim Bowie
Ford, Glenn (1916-)
   Cade's County . . . . Sheriff Sam Cade
Ford, Paul (1901-1976)
   The Phil Silvers Show . . . . Col. John Hall
Forrest, Steve (1924-)
   S.W.A.T. . . . . Lt. Dan "Hondo" Harrelson
Forster, Brian (1960-)
   The Partridge Family . . . . Christopher Partridge
Forster, Robert (1941-)
   Banyon . . . . Miles C. Banyon
   Nakia . . . . Dep. Nakia Parker
Forsythe, John (1918-)
   Dynasty . . . . Blake Carrington
Foster, Jodie (1962-)
   Paper Moon . . . . Addie Pray
Fox, Colin
   Strange Paradise . . . . Jean Paul Desmond
Fox, Michael J. (1961-)
   Family Ties . . . . Alex Keaton
Foxworth, Robert (1941-)
   Falcon Crest . . . . Chase Gioberti
Foxx, Redd (1922-1991)
   Sanford and Son . . . . Fred Sanford
Frakes, Jonathan
   Star Trek: The Next Generation . . . . Cmdr. William Riker
Francis, Anne (1930-)
   Honey West . . . . Honey West
Franciscus, James (1934-1991)
   The Naked City . . . . Det. Jim Halloran
Francks, Don (1932-)
   Jericho . . . . Franklin Sheppard
Frank, Gary (1950-)
   Family . . . . Willie Lawrence
Frid, Jonathan (1924-)
   Dark Shadows . . . . Barnabas Collins
Fuller, Robert (1933-)
   Emergency! . . . . Dr. Kelly Brackett
Funicello, Annette (1942-)
   The Mickey Mouse Club . . . . Annette
Gaddis, R.V. "Gadabout" (1896-1986)
   Gadabout Gaddis . . . . Himself
Galloway, Don (1937-)
   Ironside . . . . Det. Sgt. Ed Brown
Garner, James (1928-)
   Maverick . . . . Bret Maverick
   The Rockford Files . . . . Jim Rockford

Garrett, Jimmy
   The Lucy Show . . . . Jerry Carmichael
Garrison, David
   It's Your Move . . . . Norman Lamb
Garver, Kathy (1948-)
   Family Affair . . . . Catherine "Cissy" Davis
Gazzara, Ben (1930-)
   Arrest and Trial . . . . Det. Sgt. Nick Anderson
Geer, Will (1902-1978)
   The Waltons . . . . Zeb (Grandpa) Walton
Gelbwaks, Jeremy (1963-)
   The Partridge Family . . . . Christopher Partridge
George, Christopher (1929-1983)
   The Immortal . . . . Ben Richards
   The Rat Patrol . . . . Sgt. Sam Troy
George, Lynda Day (1944-)
   The Silent Force . . . . Amelia Cole
Gerard, Gil (1943-)
   Buck Rogers in the 25th Century . . . . Capt. William "Buck" Rogers
Gibson, Henry (1935-)
   Laugh-In . . . . Himself
Gilbert, Melissa (1964-)
   Little House on the Prairie . . . . Laura Ingalls Wilder
Givens, Robin (1964-)
   Head of the Class . . . . Darlene Merriman
Glaser, Paul Michael (1943-)
   Starsky and Hutch . . . . Det. Dave Starsky
Gless, Sharon (1943-)
   Cagney & Lacey . . . . Det. Chris Cagney
Gobel, George (1920-1991)
   The Hollywood Squares . . . . Himself
Gold, Tracey (1969-)
   Growing Pains . . . . Carol Seaver
Goodeve, Grant (1952-)
   Eight is Enough . . . . David Bradford
Goodman, Dody (1929-)
   Mary Hartman, Mary Hartman . . . . Martha Shumway
Gordon, Barry (1948-)
   Fish . . . . Charlie Harrison
Gordon, Gerald
   The Doctors . . . . Dr. Nick Bellini
Gorshin, Frank (1935-)
   Batman . . . . The Riddler
Gosfield, Maurice (1913-1964)
   The Phil Silvers Show . . . . Pvt. Duane Doberman
Gossett, Louis, Jr. (1936-)
   The Young Rebels . . . . Isak Poole
Grammer, Kelsey (1955-)
   Cheers . . . . Dr. Frasier Crane
Grandy, Fred (1948-)
   The Love Boat . . . . Yeoman-Purser Burl "Gopher" Smith

Grant, Bernie
   The Guiding Light .... Dr. Paul Fletcher
Grant, Faye
   V .... Dr. Julie Parrish
Grassle, Karen (1944-)
   Little House on the Prairie .... Caroline Ingalls
Graves, Peter (1925-)
   Mission: Impossible .... James Phelps
Gray, Erin (1952-)
   Buck Rogers in the 25th Century .... Col. Wilma Deering
Gray, Linda (1940-)
   Dallas .... Sue Ellen Ewing
Gray, Michael (1951-)
   The Little People .... Ronnie Collins
Graziano, Rocky (1921-1990)
   Miami Undercover .... Rocky
Greenbush, Lindsay/Sidney (twins, 1970-)
   Little House on the Prairie .... Carrie Ingalls
Greene, Lorne (1915-1987)
   Battlestar Galactica .... Cmdr. Adama
   Bonanza .... Ben Cartwright
   Griff .... Wade "Griff" Griffin
Groh, David (1939-)
   Rhoda .... Joe Gerard
Gross, Michael (1947-)
   Family Ties .... Steve Keaton
Gwynne, Fred (1926-1993)
   The Munsters .... Herman Munster
Haggerty, Dan (1941-)
   The Life and Times of Grizzly Adams .... James "Grizzly" Adams
Hagman, Larry (1931-)
   Dallas .... John Ross "J.R." Ewing, Jr.
Hall, Grayson (-1985)
   Dark Shadows .... Dr. Julia Hoffman/Magda the Gypsy
Hall, Monty (1923-)
   Let's Make a Deal .... Himself
Hall, Zooey
   The New People .... Bob Lee
Hallick, Tom (1941-)
   The Young and the Restless .... Brad Eliot
Halpin, Luke
   Flipper .... Sandy Ricks
Hamilton, Linda (1957-)
   Beauty and the Beast .... Catherine Chandler
Hanley, Bridget (1941-)
   Here Come the Brides .... Candy Pruitt
Hannah, Daryl (1961-)
   Paper Dolls .... Taryn Blake (from the TV-movie)
Hardin, Melora (1967-)
   Thunder .... Cindy
Harper, David W. (1961-)
   The Waltons .... Jim-Bob Walton

Harper, Ron (1935-)
   Garrison's Gorillas . . . . Lt. Craig Garrison
   Planet of the Apes . . . . Alan Virdon
Harper, Valerie (1940-)
   Rhoda . . . . Rhoda Morgenstern Gerard
Harrelson, Woody (1961-)
   Cheers . . . . Woody Boyd
Harrison, Linda (1945-)
   Bracken's World . . . . Paulette Douglas
Harrison, Noel (1936-)
   The Girl From U.N.C.L.E. . . . . Mark Slate
Hartman, David (1935-)
   The Bold Ones . . . . Dr. Paul Hunter
   Lucas Tanner . . . . Lucas Tanner
Harty, Patricia (1941-)
   Blondie . . . . Blondie Bumstead
Haskell, Peter (1934-)
   Bracken's World . . . . Kevin Grant
Hasselhoff, David (1952-)
   Knight Rider . . . . Michael Knight
   The Young and the Restless . . . . Dr. Snapper Foster
Hatch, Richard (1947-)
   Battlestar Galactica . . . . Capt. Apollo
Hathaway, Noah
   Battlestar Galactica . . . . Boxey
Hawn, Goldie (1945-)
   Laugh-In . . . . Herself
Haynes, Lloyd (1934-1986)
   Room 222 . . . . Pete Dixon
Hedison, David (1929-)
   Voyage to the Bottom of the Sea . . . . Capt. Lee Crane
Hegyes, Robert (1951-)
   Welcome Back, Kotter . . . . Juan Epstein
Henderson, Florence (1934-)
   The Brady Bunch . . . . Carol Brady
Henesy, David (1956-)
   Dark Shadows . . . . David Collins/Jamison Collins
Hensley, Pamela (1950-)
   Buck Rogers in the 25th Century . . . . Princess Ardala
Hentelhoff, Alex
   The Young Rebels . . . . Henry Abington
Herbert, Percy (1925-)
   Cimmaron Strip . . . . Mac Gregor
Hexum, Jon-Erik (1957-1984)
   Voyagers! . . . . Phineas Bogg
Hickman, Darryl (1931-)
   The Americans . . . . Ben Canfield
Hill, Steven (1922-)
   Mission: Impossible . . . . Daniel Briggs
Hitchcock, Alfred (1899-1980)
   Alfred Hitchcock Presents . . . . Himself

Holliman, Earl (1928-)
  Hotel de Paree .... Sundance
Horton, Robert (1924-)
  Wagon Train .... Flint McCullough
Houseman, John (1902-1988)
  The Paper Chase .... Prof. Charles W. Kingsfield, Jr.
Howard, Ron (1954-)
  Happy Days .... Richie Cunningham
  The Smith Family .... Bob Smith
Howard, Susan (1946-)
  Dallas .... Donna Culver Krebbs
Hubbard, David
  James at Fifteen .... Sly Hazeltine
Hubbard, Elizabeth
  The Doctors .... Dr. Althea Davis
Hughes, Barnard (1915-)
  Mr. Merlin .... Max Merlin
Hugo, Larry
  The Edge of Night .... Mike Karr
Hunt, Gareth (1943-)
  The New Avengers .... Mike Gambit
Hutchins, Will (1932-)
  Blondie .... Dagwood Bumstead
Hyde-White, Wilfred (1903-1991)
  The Associates .... Emerson Marshall
Jackson, Kate (1948-)
  Charlie's Angels .... Sabrina Duncan
  The Rookies .... Jill Danko
Jacobs, Lawrence-Hilton (1953-)
  Welcome Back, Kotter .... Freddie "Boom Boom" Washington
Jaffe, Sam (1891-1984)
  Ben Casey .... Dr. David Zorba
James, John (1956-)
  Dynasty .... Jeff Colby
Janssen, David (1930-1980)
  The Fugitive .... Dr. Richard Kimble
  Harry O .... Harry Orwell
Jaress, Jill
  The New People .... Ginny Loomis
Jarrett, Renne (1946-)
  Nancy .... Nancy Smith
Jarvis, Graham (1930-)
  Mary Hartman, Mary Hartman .... Charlie Haggers
Jason, Rick (1926-)
  Combat .... Lt. Gil Hanley
Jefferson, Herbert, Jr. (1946-)
  Battlestar Galactica .... Lt. Boomer
Jenkins, Mark
  Young Dr. Kildare .... Dr. James Kildare
Jensen, Karen
  Bracken's World .... Rachel Holt

Jensen, Maren (1956-)
  Battlestar Galactica . . . . Athena
Johnson, Arch (1923-)
  The Asphalt Jungle . . . . Capt. Gus Honochek
Johnson, Arte (1934-)
  Laugh-In . . . . Himself
Johnson, Don (1949-)
  Miami Vice . . . . Det. James "Sonny" Crockett
Johnson, Janet Louise (1958-)
  The Hardy Boys/Nancy Drew Mysteries . . . . Nancy Drew
Jones, Anissa (1958-1976)
  Family Affair . . . . Buffy Davis
Jones, Carolyn (1929-1983)
  The Addams Family . . . . Morticia Addams
Jones, Davy (1946-)
  The Monkees . . . . Himself
Jones, Shirley (1934-)
  The Partridge Family . . . . Shirley Partridge
Joyce, Elaine (1945-)
  Mr. Merlin . . . . Alexandria
Kanaly, Steve (1946-)
  Dallas . . . . Ray Krebbs
Kaplan, Gabriel (1945-)
  Welcome Back, Kotter . . . . Gabe Kotter
Kastner, Peter (1944-)
  The Ugliest Girl in Town . . . . Timothy Blair (aka "Timmy")
Kasznar, Kurt (1913-1979)
  Land of the Giants . . . . Cmdr. Alexander Fitzhugh
Kavner, Julie (1951-)
  Rhoda . . . . Brenda Morgenstern
Kaye, Caren (1951-)
  It's Your Move . . . . Eileen Burton
Keane, Teri
  The Edge of Night . . . . Martha Marceau
Keith, Brian (1921-)
  Family Affair . . . . Bill Davis
Kelley, DeForest (1920-)
  Star Trek . . . . Dr. Leonard "Bones" McKoy
Kelly, Jack (1927-)
  Maverick . . . . Bart Maverick
Kercheval, Ken (1935-)
  Dallas . . . . Cliff Barnes
Kerns, Joanna (1953-)
  Growing Pains . . . . Maggie Seaver
Kerns, Sandra
  Charles in Charge . . . . Ellen Powell
Kerwin, Lance (1960-)
  James at Fifteen . . . . James Hunter
Key, Dianne (1955-)
  Eight is Enough . . . . Nancy Bradford

Lennon, Dianne (1939-)
    The Lawrence Welk Show . . . . Herself
Lennon, Janet (1946-)
    The Lawrence Welk Show . . . . Herself
Lennon, Kathy (1942-)
    The Lawrence Welk Show . . . . Herself
Lennon, Peggy (1941-)
    The Lawrence Welk Show . . . . Herself
Lerman, April (1969-)
    Charles in Charge . . . . Lila Pembroke
Lescoulie, Jack (1917-)
    The Tonight Show . . . . Himself
Lewis, Al (1923-)
    The Munsters . . . . Grandpa Munster
Leyton, John (1939-)
    Jericho . . . . Nicholas Gage
Linden, Hal (1931-)
    The Hollywood Squares . . . . Himself
Linkletter, Art (1912-)
    Art Linkletter's House Party . . . . Himself
    People Are Funny . . . . Himself
Linville, Larry (1939-)
    M*A*S*H . . . . Maj. Frank Burns
Lipton, Peggy (1948-)
    The Mod Squad . . . . Julie Barnes
London, Julie (1926-)
    Emergency! . . . . Nurse Dixie McCall
Long, Richard (1927-1974)
    The Big Valley . . . . Jarrod Barkley
    Nanny and the Professor . . . . Prof. Harold Everett
Long, Shelley (1949-)
    Cheers . . . . Diane Chambers
Lookinland, Michael (1960-)
    The Brady Bunch . . . . Bobby Brady
Lord, Jack (1930-)
    Hawaii Five-O . . . . Steve McGarrett
Loring, Lisa (1958-)
    The Addams Family . . . . Wednesday Thursday Addams
Lumley, Joanna (1946-)
    The New Avengers . . . . Purdey
Lund, Deanna
    Land of the Giants . . . . Valerie Scott
Lundigan, William (1914-1975)
    Men Into Space . . . . Col. Edward McCauley
Lupus, Peter (1937-)
    Mission: Impossible . . . . Willy Armitage
Lynde, Janice
    The Young and the Restless . . . . Leslie Brooks
Lynde, Paul (1926-1982)
    The Hollywood Squares . . . . Himself

Majors, Lee (1940-)
The Big Valley . . . . Heath Barkley
The Six Million Dollar Man . . . . Col. Steve Austin
Mann, Colette
Prisoner: Cell Block H . . . . Doreen May Anderson
Mantooth, Randolph (1945-)
Emergency! . . . . paramedic John Gage
Marchand, Nancy (1928-)
Beacon Hill . . . . Mary Lassiter
Marie, Rose (1923-)
The Hollywood Squares . . . . Herself
Markham, Dewey "Pigmeat" (1904-1981)
Laugh-In . . . . Himself
Marshall, Don
Land of the Giants . . . . Dan Erikson
Marshall, E.G. (1910-)
The Bold Ones . . . . Dr. David Craig
The Defenders . . . . Lawrence Preston
Marshall, Penny (1942-)
Laverne and Shirley . . . . Laverne De Fazio
Marshall, Peter (1927-)
The Hollywood Squares . . . . Himself
Martin, Dick (1922-)
Laugh-In . . . . Himself
Martin, Pamela Sue (1953-)
Dynasty . . . . Fallon Carrington Colby
The Hardy Boys/Nancy Drew Mysteries . . . . Nancy Drew
Martindale, Wink (1934-)
Can You Top This? . . . . Himself
Marvin, Lee (1924-1987)
M Squad . . . . Lt. Frank Ballinger
Mase, Marino
Jericho . . . . Jean-Gaston Andre
Matheson, Don
Land of the Giants . . . . Mark Wilson
Mathers, Jerry (1948-)
Leave it to Beaver . . . . Theodore "Beaver" Cleaver
Mattingly, Hedley
Daktari . . . . Dist. Off. Hedley
Maunder, Wayne (1938-)
Lancer . . . . Scott Lancer
Mayer, Christopher
The Dukes of Hazzard . . . . Vance Duke
Mears, Deann
Beacon Hill . . . . Emily Bullock
Mellini, Scott
Father Murphy . . . . Ephriam Winkler
Melville, Sam (1940-)
The Rookies . . . . Off. Mike Danko
Meredith, Burgess (1908-)
Batman . . . . The Penguin

Meriwether, Lee (1935-)
Batman .... Catwoman
The Time Tunnel .... Dr. Ann MacGregor
Merrill, Gary (1914-1990)
Young Dr. Kildare .... Dr. Leonard Gillespie
Michael, George and Marjorie
The Michaels in Africa .... Themselves
Milland, Ray (1907-1986)
Markham .... Roy Markham
Miller, Cheryl (1943-)
Daktari .... Paula Tracy
Miller, Denise (1963-)
Fish .... Jilly Papalardo
Miller, Jeremy (1976-)
Growing Pains .... Ben Seaver
Miller, Mark
Guestward Ho! .... Bill Hooten
Mills, Alley
The Associates .... Leslie Dunn
Mills, Juliet (1941-)
Nanny and the Professor .... Phoebe Figalilly (Nanny)
Milner, Martin (1927-)
Adam-12 .... Off. Pete Malloy
Mimieux, Yvette (1939-)
The Most Deadly Game .... Vanessa Smith
Mitchell, Cameron (1918-1994)
The High Chaparral .... Buck Cannon
Mitchell, Don (1943-)
Ironside .... Mark Sanger
Moltke, Alexandra
Dark Shadows .... Victoria Winters
Montalban, Ricardo (1920-)
Fantasy Island .... Mr. Roarke
Montgomery, Elizabeth (1933-1995)
Bewitched .... Samantha Stephens
Moore, Candy
The Lucy Show .... Chris Carmichael
Moore, Mary Tyler (1936-)
The Mary Tyler Moore Show .... Mary Richards
Moore, Roger (1927-)
The Persuaders .... Lord Brett Sinclair
The Saint .... Simon Templar (The Saint)
Moorehead, Agnes (1906-1974)
Bewitched .... Endora
Moran, Erin (1961-)
Happy Days .... Joanie Cunningham
Joanie Loves Chachi .... Joanie Cunningham
Morgan, Harry (1915-)
Dragnet .... Off. Bill Gannon
M*A*S*H .... Col. Sherman Potter
Morris, Garrett (1937-)
Saturday Night Live .... Himself

Morris, Greg (1934-1996)
  Mission: Impossible . . . . Barney Collier
Morrison, Shelley (1937-)
  The Flying Nun . . . . Sister Sixto
Morrow, Vic (1932-1982)
  Combat . . . . Sgt. Chip Saunders
Morse, Barry (1919-)
  The Fugitive . . . . Lt. Philip Gerard
  Space: 1999 . . . . Prof. Victor Bergman
Moses, David
  The New People . . . . Gene Washington
Moses, William R. (1959-)
  Falcon Crest . . . . Cole Gioberti
Muldaur, Diana (1938-)
  Star Trek: The Next Generation . . . . Dr. Kate Pulaski
Mulhare, Edward (1923-)
  The Ghost and Mrs Muir . . . . Capt. Daniel Gregg
Mullavey, Greg (1939-)
  Mary Hartman, Mary Hartman . . . . Tom Hartman
Murphy, Ben (1941-)
  Alias Smith and Jones . . . . Jed "Kid" Curry (alias Thaddeus Jones)
Murray, Arthur (1895-1991)
  The Arthur Murray Party . . . . Himself
Murray, Bill (1950-)
  Saturday Night Live . . . . Himself
Murray, Don (1929-)
  The Outcasts . . . . Earl Corey
Murray, Jan (1917-)
  The Hollywood Squares . . . . Himself
Murray, Kathryn (1906-)
  The Arthur Murray Party . . . . Herself
Myers, Susan
  James at Fifteen . . . . Marlene Mahoney
Nabors, Jim (1932-)
  Gomer Pyle, U.S.M.C. . . . . Pvt. Gomer Pyle
Naish, J. Carrol (1900-1973)
  Guestward Ho! . . . . Hawkeye
Natoli, Sarah
  Fish . . . . Diane Pulaski
Naughton, James (1945-)
  Planet of the Apes . . . . Pete Burke
Needham, Connie (1962-)
  Eight is Enough . . . . Elizabeth Bradford
Nelson, Ed (1928-)
  The Silent Force . . . . Ward Fuller
Nesmith, Mike (1942-)
  The Monkees . . . . Himself
Newman, Laraine (1952-)
  Saturday Night Live . . . . Herself
Nicholas, Denise (1944-)
  Room 222 . . . . Liz McIntyre

Paul, Alexandra
    Paper Dolls . . . . Laurie Caswell (from the TV-movie)
Payne, John (1912-1989)
    The Restless Gun . . . . Vint Bonner
Pearlman, Michael (1974-)
    Charles in Charge . . . . Jason Pembroke
Pelikan, Lisa
    James at Fifteen . . . . Paisley
Peluce, Meeno (1970-)
    Voyagers! . . . . Jeffrey Jones
Peppard, George (1928-1994)
    The A-Team . . . . Col. John "Hannibal" Smith
    Banacek . . . . Thomas Banacek
    Doctor's Hospital . . . . Dr. Jake Goodwin
Perkins, Voltaire
    Divorce Court . . . . Judge Voltaire Perkins
Perlman, Rhea (1948-)
    Cheers . . . . Carla Tortelli
Perlman, Ron (1950-)
    Beauty and the Beast . . . . Vincent
Perry, Rod (1941-)
    S.W.A.T. . . . . Sgt. David "Deacon" Kay
Peters, Audrey
    Love of Life . . . . Vanessa Dale
Phillips, Mackenzie (1959-)
    The Hollywood Squares . . . . Herself
Philpott, John
    The Bugaloos . . . . Courage
Place, Mary Kay (1947-)
    Mary Hartman, Mary Hartman . . . . Loretta Haggers
Plumb, Eve (1957-)
    The Brady Bunch . . . . Jan Brady
Polinsky, Alexander
    Charles in Charge . . . . Adam Powell
Ponce, Poncie (1933-)
    Hawaiian Eye . . . . Kazuo Kim
Powers, Stefanie (1942-)
    The Girl From U.N.C.L.E. . . . . April Dancer
Price, Vincent (1911-1993)
    The Hollywood Squares . . . . Himself
Priest, Pat (1936-)
    The Munsters . . . . Marilyn Munster
Prince, Jonathan (1958-)
    Mr. Merlin . . . . Leo Samuels
Principal, Victoria (1945-)
    Dallas . . . . Pamela Barnes Ewing
Prinze, Freddie (1954-1977)
    Chico and the Man . . . . Chico Rodriguez
Pritchett, James
    The Doctors . . . . Dr. Matt Powers

Provine, Dorothy (1937-)
The Roaring 20's . . . . Pinky Pinkham
Provost, Jon (1950-)
Lassie . . . . Timmy Martin
Quayle, Anthony (1913-1989)
Strange Report . . . . Adam Strange
Radner, Gilda (1946-1989)
Saturday Night Live . . . . Herself
Randi, Justin (1967-)
Thunder . . . . Willie
Ratray, Peter
The New People . . . . George Potter
Ratzenberger, John (1947-)
Cheers . . . . Cliff Clavin
Raymond, Gary (1935-)
The Rat Patrol . . . . Sgt. Jack Moffitt
Redmond, Marge
The Flying Nun . . . . Sister Jacqueline
Reed, Donna (1921-1986)
Dallas . . . . Eleanor Southworth (Miss Ellie) Ewing
Reed, Lydia
The Real McCoys . . . . Aunt Hassie
Reed, Robert (1932-1992)
The Brady Bunch . . . . Mike Brady
The Defenders . . . . Kenneth Preston
Regalbuto, Joe
The Associates . . . . Eliot Streeter
Reiner, Rob (1945-)
All in the Family . . . . Mike Stivic
Reinholt, George (1940-)
Another World . . . . Steve Frame
Rey, Alejandro (1930-1987)
The Flying Nun . . . . Carlos Ramirez
Reynolds, Burt (1936-)
Hawk . . . . Lt. John Hawk
The Hollywood Squares . . . . Himself
Rhodes, Hari (1932-)
Daktari . . . . Mike
Rhue, Madlyn (1934-)
Executive Suite . . . . Hilary Madison
Rice, Howard
Room 222 . . . . Richie Lane
Rich, Adam (1968-)
Eight is Enough . . . . Nicholas Bradford
Richards, Kim (1964-)
James at Fifteen . . . . Sandy Hunter
Nanny and the Professor . . . . Prudence Everett
Richardson, Susan (1952-)
Eight is Enough . . . . Susan Bradford
Richman, Peter Mark (1927-)
Cain's Hundred . . . . Nicholas "Nick" Cain

Rigg, Diana (1938-)
   The Avengers .... Mrs. Emma Peel
Robbins, Peter
   Blondie .... Alexander Bumstead
Roberts, Pernell (1928-)
   Bonanza .... Adam Cartwright
Robertson, Dale (1923-)
   The Iron Horse .... Ben Calhoun
   Tales of Wells Fargo .... Jim Hardie
Rodriguez, Percy (1924-)
   Executive Suite .... Malcolm Gibson
   The Silent Force .... Jason Hart
Rogers, Roy (1912-)
   The Roy Rogers Show .... Himself
Roman, Greg
   The New Breed .... Off. Pete Garcia
Romero, Cesar (1907-1994)
   Batman .... The Joker
Rooney, Mickey (1920-)
   Playhouse 90 .... Sammy Hogarth
Rowan, Dan (1922-1987)
   Laugh-In .... Himself
Rowland, Jada (1943-)
   The Secret Storm .... Amy Ames
Russell, William
   Sir Lancelot .... Sir Lancelot
Ryan, Irene (1903-1973)
   The Beverly Hillbillies .... Daisy Moses ("Granny")
Ryan, Mitchell (1928-)
   Executive Suite .... Don Walling
Sajak, Pat (1947-)
   Wheel of Fortune .... Himself
Sargent, Dick (1933-1994)
   Bewitched .... Darrin Stephens
Savalas, Telly (1924-1994)
   Kojak .... Lt. Theo Kojak
Saxon, John (1935-)
   The Bold Ones .... Dr. Ted Stuart
Schell, Catherine
   Space: 1999 .... Maya
Schiegl, Kurt
   Strange Paradise .... Quito
Schneider, John (1954-)
   The Dukes of Hazzard .... Bo Duke
Schultz, Dwight (1947-)
   The A-Team .... Capt. H.M. "Howling Mad" Murdock
Scott, Eric (1958-)
   The Waltons .... Ben Walton
Scott, Kathryn Leigh
   Dark Shadows .... Maggie Evans/Josette DuPres

Stanley, Florence
Fish . . . . Bernice Fish
Stanwyck, Barbara (1907-1990)
The Big Valley . . . . Victoria Barkley
Stapleton, Jean (1923-)
All in the Family . . . . Edith Bunker
Stephens, James (1951-)
The Paper Chase . . . . James T. Hart
Stephens, Laraine
Bracken's World . . . . Diane Waring
Stern, Wes
Getting Together . . . . Lionel Poindexter
Stevens, Connie (1938-)
Hawaiian Eye . . . . Cricket Blake
Stevens, Craig (1918-)
Peter Gunn . . . . Peter Gunn
Stevenson, McLean (1929-)
The Hollywood Squares . . . . Himself
Stevenson, Parker (1952-)
The Hardy Boys/Nancy Drew Mysteries . . . . Frank Hardy
Stewart, Patrick (1940-)
Star Trek: The Next Generation . . . . Capt. Jean-Luc Picard
Stewart, Trish
The Young and the Restless . . . . Chris Brooks
Stollery, David
The Mickey Mouse Club . . . . Marty Markham
Storch, Larry (1923-)
F Troop . . . . Cpl. Randolph Agarn
Strangis, Judy
Room 222 . . . . Helen Loomis
Strickson, Mark
Doctor Who . . . . Turlough
Struthers, Sally (1947-)
All in the Family . . . . Gloria Bunker Stivic
Stuart, Mary (1926-)
Search for Tomorrow . . . . Joanne Gardner Barron
Sues, Alan
Laugh-In . . . . Himself
Sullivan, Susan (1944-)
Falcon Crest . . . . Maggie Gioberti
Summers, Yale
Daktari . . . . Jack Dane
Swit, Loretta (1937-)
M*A*S*H . . . . Maj. Margaret Houlihan
T, Mr. (1952-)
The A-Team . . . . Sgt. Bosco "B.A." Baracus
Takei, George (1940-)
Star Trek . . . . Mr. Sulu
Tarr, Justin (1934-)
The Rat Patrol . . . . Pvt. Tully Pettigrew

Tate, Nick
    Space: 1999 . . . . Capt. Alan Carter
Taylor, Robert (1911-1969)
    The Detectives . . . . Capt. Matt Holbrook
Tewes, Lauren (1953-)
    The Love Boat . . . . Cruise Director Julie McCoy
Thicke, Alan (1947-)
    Growing Pains . . . . Jason Seaver
Thinnes, Roy (1938-)
    The Invaders . . . . David Vincent
Thomas, Gareth
    Blake's 7 . . . . Roj Blake
Thomas, Marlo (1938-)
    That Girl . . . . Ann Marie
Thomas, Philip Michael (1949-)
    Miami Vice . . . . Det. Ricardo Tubbs
Thomas, Richard (1951-)
    The Waltons . . . . John-Boy Walton
Thomerson, Tim
    The Associates . . . . Johnny Danko
Thompson, Marshall (1925-)
    Daktari . . . . Dr. Marsh Tracy
Thompson, Sada (1929-)
    Family . . . . Kate Lawrence
Thorson, Linda (1947-)
    The Avengers . . . . Tara King
Throne, Malachi (1927-)
    It Takes a Thief . . . . Noah Bain
Tighe, Kevin (1944-)
    Emergency! . . . . paramedic Roy DeSoto
Tilton, Charlene (1958-)
    Dallas . . . . Lucy Ewing Cooper
Tomlin, Lily (1939-)
    The Hollywood Squares . . . . Herself
Tommano, Pieta
    Prisoner: Cell Block H . . . . Karen Travers
Tork, Peter (1944-)
    The Monkees . . . . Himself
Townsend, Jill
    Cimmaron Strip . . . . Dulcey Coopersmith
Travolta, John (1954-)
    Welcome Back, Kotter . . . . Vinnie Barbarino
Troup, Bobby (1918-)
    Emergency! . . . . Dr. Joe Early
Tucker, Forrest (1919-1986)
    F Troop . . . . Sgt. Morgan O'Rourke
Tully, Tom (1908-1982)
    The Lineup . . . . Insp. Matt Grebb
Urich, Robert (1946-)
    S.W.A.T. . . . . Off. Jim Street
    Vega$ . . . . Dan Tanna

Valentine, Karen (1947-)
    The Hollywood Squares .... Herself
    Room 222 .... Alice Johnson
Van Patten, Vincent (1957-)
    Apple's Way .... Paul Apple
Vaughn, Robert (1932-)
    The Man From U.N.C.L.E. .... Napoleon Solo
Vigoda, Abe (1921-)
    Fish .... Det. Phil Fish
Villechaize, Herve (1943-1993)
    Fantasy Island .... Tattoo
Vivyan, John (1916-1983)
    Mr. Lucky .... Mr. Lucky
Wagner, Lindsay (1949-)
    The Bionic Woman .... Jaime Sommers
Wagner, Robert (1930-)
    It Takes a Thief .... Alexander Mundy
    Switch .... Pete Ryan
Waite, Ralph (1928-)
    The Waltons .... John Walton
Walker, Clint (1927-)
    Cheyenne .... Cheyenne Bodie
Walker, Jimmie (1949-)
    Good Times .... James "J.J." Evans, Jr.
Walker, Kathryn
    Beacon Hill .... Fawn Lassiter
Walmsley, Jon (1956-)
    The Waltons .... Jason Walton
Walters, Laurie (1956-)
    Eight is Enough .... Joannie Bradford
Ward, Burt (1945-)
    Batman .... Dick Grayson (Robin)
Ward, Jonathan (1970-)
    Charles in Charge .... Douglas Pembroke
Warden, Jack (1920-)
    The Asphalt Jungle .... Matthew Gower
Weatherwax, Ken (1955-)
    The Addams Family .... Pugsley Addams
Weaver, Charley (see Cliff Arquette)
Weaver, Dennis (1924-)
    Gentle Ben .... Tom Wedloe
    Gunsmoke .... Chester Goode
    McCloud .... Dep. Marshal Sam McCloud
Webb, Jack (1920-1982)
    Dragnet .... Sgt. Joe Friday
Wells, Mary K.
    The Edge of Night .... Louise Grimsley Capice
Wendt, George (1948-)
    Cheers .... Norm Peterson

West, Adam (1928-)
    Batman . . . . Bruce Wayne (Batman)
    The Detectives . . . . Sgt. Steve Nelson
Wheaton, Wil (1972-)
    Star Trek: The Next Generation . . . . Ensign Wesley Crusher
Whelan, Jill (1966-)
    The Love Boat . . . . Vicki Stubing
Whitaker, Johnny (1959-)
    Family Affair . . . . Jody Davis
White, John Sylvester
    Welcome Back, Kotter . . . . Mr. Michael Woodman
White, Vanna (1957-)
    Wheel of Fortune . . . . Herself
Whitman, Stuart (1926-)
    Cimmaron Strip . . . . U.S. Marshal Jim Crown
Whitmore, James (1921-)
    My Friend Tony . . . . Prof. John Woodruff
Whittington, Dick
    Laugh-In . . . . Himself
Widdoes, James
    Charles in Charge . . . . Stan Pembroke
Williams, Anson (1949-)
    Happy Days . . . . Warren "Potsie" Weber
Williams, Barry (1954-)
    The Brady Bunch . . . . Greg Brady
Williams, Cindy (1947-)
    Laverne and Shirley . . . . Shirley Feeney
Williams, Clarence, III (1939-)
    The Mod Squad . . . . Linc Hayes
Williams, Grant (1930-1985)
    Hawaiian Eye . . . . Greg MacKenzie
Williams, Guy (1924-1989)
    Zorro . . . . Don Diego de la Vega (Zorro)
Williams, Robin (1952-)
    Mork & Mindy . . . . Mork
Williams, Van (1934-)
    The Green Hornet . . . . Britt Reid (the Green Hornet)
    SurfSide 6 . . . . Ken Madison
Wilson, Demond (1946-)
    The Hollywood Squares . . . . Himself
    Sanford and Son . . . . Lamont Sanford
Wilson, Flip (1933-)
    The Flip Wilson Show . . . . Himself
Winkleman, Michael (1946-)
    The Real McCoys . . . . Little Luke McCoy
Winkler, Henry (1945-)
    Happy Days . . . . Arthur "Fonzie" Fonzarelli
Winn, Kitty (1944-)
    Beacon Hill . . . . Rosamond Lassiter
Wixted, Michael-James (1961-)
    The Smith Family . . . . Brian Smith

EPISODES NOVELIZED LIST

This section provides a list of all the episodes novelized in the TV tie-ins. Episodes are sorted by show and listed either alphabetically, or in air-date order if indicated. The episodes' original air-dates are given in the second column. Notes concerning pilot episodes, two-part episodes, etc. are also given.

THE A-TEAM

"The A-Team"	Jan-23-1983	pilot episode
"Black Day at Bad Rock"	Feb-22-1983	
"Maltese Cow"	Dec-13-1983	
"The Only Church in Town"	Oct-11-1983	
"Recipe for Heavy Bread"	Sep-27-1983	
"A Small and Deadly War"	Feb-15-1983	
"Steel"	Nov-29-1983	
"When You Comin' Back, Range Rider?"	Oct-25-1983	

ALL IN THE FAMILY

"Archie is Jealous"	Mar-04-1972
"Archie's Aching Back"	Jan-26-1971
"Cousin Maude's Visit"	Dec-11-1971
"The Games Bunkers Play"	Nov-03-1972
"Second Honeymoon"	Dec-01-1973
"Women's Lib"	Mar-23-1971

AMAZING STORIES

"Alamo Jobe"	Oct-20-1985
"The Amazing Falsworth"	Nov-05-1985
"Boo"	Feb-16-1986
"Dorothy and Ben"	Mar-02-1986
"Fine Tuning"	Nov-10-1985
"Gather Ye Acorns"	Feb-02-1986
"Ghost Train"	Sep-29-1985
"Grandpa's Ghost"	May-25-1986
"Guilt Trip"	Dec-01-1985
"Hell Toupee"	Apr-13-1986
"The Main Attraction"	Oct-06-1985

"Mirror, Mirror"   Mar-09-1986
"The Mission"   Nov-03-1985
"Mr. Magic"   Nov-17-1985
"Mummy Daddy"   Oct-27-1985
"No Day at the Beach"   Jan-12-1986
"One for the Road"   Jan-19-1986
"Remote Control Man"   Dec-08-1985
"Santa '85"   Dec-15-1985
"The Secret Cinema"   Apr-06-1986
"The Sitter"   Jan-05-1986
"Vanessa in the Garden"   Dec-29-1985

BANACEK

"Let's Hear it for a Living Legend" Sep-13-1972

BANYON

"Banyon"   Mar-15-1971   TV-movie pilot

BATMAN

"Batman"   1966 companion film

BATTLESTAR GALACTICA

"Baltar's Escape"   Mar-11-1979
"Experiment in Terra"   Mar-18-1979
"Galactica Discovers Earth"   Jan-27-1980   3-part episode; Part II aired Feb-03, Part
                                                   III aired Feb-10
"Greetings from Earth"   Feb-25-1979
"Gun on Ice Planet Zero"   Oct-22-1978   2-part episode, concluded Oct-29
"The Living Legend"   Nov-26-1978   2-part episode, concluded Dec-03
"The Long Patrol"   Oct-15-1978
"Lost Planet of the Gods"   Sep-24-1978   2-part episode (aka "Tombs of Kobol")
                                                   concluded Oct-01
"Saga of a Starworld"   Sep-17-1978   3-hour pilot episode
"War of the Gods"   Jan-14-1979   2-part episode, concluded Jan-21
"The Young Lords"   Nov-19-1978

BEACON HILL

"Part I"   Aug-25-1975   pilot episode

BEWITCHED

Episodes novelized in the Dell book are listed
in air-date order.

"I, Darrin, Take This Witch,
    Samantha"   Sep-17-1964   pilot episode
"Mother Meet What's His Name"   Oct-01-1964
"It Shouldn't Happen to a Dog"   Oct-08-1964
"Help, Help, Don't Save Me"   Oct-15-1964
"Little Pitchers Have Big Fears"   Oct-22-1964
"The Witches Are Out"   Oct-29-1964
"The Girl Reporter"   Nov-05-1964

THE BIONIC WOMAN

"Canyon of Death"	Apr-14-1976	
"Claws"	Feb-25-1976	
"Welcome Home, Jaime"	Jan-11-1976	2-part pilot, started as *Six Million Dollar Man* episode Jan-11, concluded as *Bionic Woman* episode Jan-21

BLACK SHEEP SQUADRON

"Devil in the Slot"	Sep-28-1976
"Divine Wind"	Dec-14-1977
"The Fastest Gun"	Mar-22-1977
"The Hawk Flies on Sunday"	Dec-28-1977
"Hotshot"	Mar-15-1978

THE BOLD ONES

"A Quality of Fear"	Nov-14-1972
"A Standard for Manhood"	Oct-17-1972
"A Substitute Womb"	Oct-24-1972

BUCK ROGERS IN THE 25TH CENTURY

"The Awakening"	Sep-20-1979	pilot episode, first released as 1979 feature film *Buck Rogers in the 25th Century*

BURKE'S LAW

"Who Killed Beau Sparrow?"	Dec-27-1963

CAGNEY & LACEY

"Cagney & Lacey"	Oct-08-1981	TV-movie pilot

CHARLES IN CHARGE

"Charles in Charge"	Oct-03-1984	pilot episode
"Amityville"	Syndicated	

CHARLIE'S ANGELS

"Angels in Chains"	Oct-20-1976	
"Angels on a String"	Jan-19-1977	
"Angels on Ice"	Sep-21-1977	
"Charlie's Angels"	Mar-21-1976	TV-movie pilot
"The Killing Kind"	Nov-03-1976	

CHASE

"Chase"	Mar-24-1973	TV-movie pilot

COLUMBO

"Any Old Port in a Storm"	Oct-07-1973	
"By Dawn's Early Light"	Oct-27-1974	
"A Deadly State of Mind"	Apr-27-1975	
"Murder by the Book"	Sep-15-1971	pilot episode

DARK SHADOWS

"House of Dark Shadows"		1970 companion film

THE DEFENDERS

"All the Silent Voices"   Feb-01-1964
"Judgment Eve"   Apr-20-1963
"Ordeal"   Feb-02-1963

DOCTOR WHO

Show featured multi-episode serials, listed below. Air-dates given span serials'
first and last episodes, with numbers of episodes given. Only serial with named
episodes is "The Daleks." Its episodes are "The Dead Planet," "The Survivors," "The Escape,"
"The Ambush," "The Expedition," "The Ordeal," and "The Rescue."

"The Android Invasion"   Nov-22-1975 - Dec-13-1975   4 episodes
"Colony in Space"   Apr-10-1971 - May-15-1971   6 episodes
"The Daleks"   Dec-21-1963 - Feb-01-1964   7 episodes
"Day of the Daleks"   Jan-01-1972 - Jan-22-1972   4 episodes
"Genesis of the Daleks"   Mar-08-1975 - Apr-12-1975   6 episodes
"Invasion of the Dinosaurs" Jan-12-1974 - Feb-16-1974   6 episodes
"The Masque of Mandragora"   Sep-04-1976 - Sep-25-1976   4 episodes
"Revenge of the Cybermen"   Apr-19-1975 - May-10-1975   4 episodes
"The Seeds of Doom"   Jan-31-1976 - Mar-06-1976   6 episodes
"The Talons of Weng-Chiang" Feb-26-1977 - Apr-02-1977   6 episodes
"Terror of the Zygons"   Jul-30-1975 - Sep-20-1975   4 episodes

DOCTOR'S HOSPITAL

"One of Our Own"   May-05-1975   TV-movie pilot

FANTASY ISLAND

"The Beachcomber"   Sep-30-1978   in 2nd Ballantine
"The Devil and Mandy Bream" Oct-18-1980   in Weekly Reader book, novelized as
                                            "Mandy's Dream"
"Lady of the Evening"   Feb-25-1978   in 1st Ballantine
"The Last Whodunit"   Sep-30-1978   in 2nd Ballantine
"The Man From Yesterday"   Jan-31-1981   in Weekly Reader book
"Possessed"   Nov-22-1980   in Weekly Reader book, novelized as
                                            "Little Girl Lost"
"The Racer"   Feb-25-1978   in 1st Ballantine

FATHER MURPHY

"By the Bear That Bit Me"   Dec-01-1981   2-part episode, concluded Dec-08
"The First Miracle"   Apr-04-1982   2-part episode, concluded Apr-11

THE FUGITIVE

"Fear in a Desert City"   Sep-17-1963   pilot episode

GRIFF

"Man on the Outside"   Jun-29-1975   TV-movie pilot

GROWING PAINS

Episodes, adapted as chapters 1-5 in the Bantam book, are listed
in the order they appear. Air-dates unknown.

"Dirt Bike"
"Mike's Madonna Story"
"Springsteen"
"Standardized Test"
"Reputation"

GUNSMOKE

Short story novelizations from Ballantine's *Gunsmoke* are listed
in the order they appear.

"Reunion '78"	Mar-03-1956	TV episode
"Road Ranch"	Oct-31-1953	Radio episode adapted into Nov-30-1957 TV episode; aka "How to Kill a Woman"
"Grass"	Jul-11-1953	Radio episode adapted into Nov-29-1958 TV episode
"Gone Straight"	Aug-22-1953	Radio episode adapted into Feb-09-1957 TV episode
"Jayhawkers"	Apr-04-1953	Radio episode adapted into Jan-31-1959 TV episode
"Hot Spell"	Sep-17-1955	TV episode
"Overland Express"	Oct-31-1952	Radio episode adapted into May-31-1958 TV episode
"There Never Was a Horse"	Sep-19-1953	Radio episode adapted into May-16-1959 TV episode
"The Pesthole"	Apr-14-1956	TV episode
"Hickok"	Jul-25-1953	Radio episode

Episodes adapted in the Award series

"The Drummer"	Oct-09-1972	
"A Game of Death...An Act of Love"	Nov-05-1973	2-part episode, concluded Nov-12
"The Sodbusters"	Nov-20-1972	

HAPPY DAYS

"Fonzie Drops In"	Feb-26-1974

HEAD OF THE CLASS

Episodes, adapted as chapters 1-6 in the Bantam book, are listed
in the order they appear. Air-dates unknown.

"First Day"
"A Problem Like Maria"
"Crimes of the Heart"
"Cello Fever"
"Trouble in Perfectville"
"Parents Day"

HEC RAMSEY

"Hec Ramsey"   Oct-08-1972   pilot episode
"Mystery of the Yellow Rose"   Jan-28-1973

THE IMMORTAL

"The Immortal"   Sep-30-1969   TV-movie pilot

THE INCREDIBLE HULK

"The Incredible Hulk"   Nov-04-1977   TV-movie pilot

THE INVISIBLE MAN

"The Invisible Man"   May-06-1975   TV-movie pilot

JAMES AT 15

"Friends"   Oct-27-1977
"James at 15"   Sep-05-1977   TV-movie pilot

KNIGHT RIDER

"Hearts of Stone"   Jan-14-1983
"Knight Rider"   Sep-26-1982   pilot episode
"Trust Doesn't Rust"   Nov-19-1982

KOJAK

"The Chinatown Murders"   Sep-15-1974
"Death is Not a Passing Grade"   Jan-30-1974
"The Girl in the River"   Nov-21-1973
"Nursemaids"   Oct-20-1974
"Requiem for a Cop"   Nov-28-1973
"Siege of Terror"   Oct-24-1973
"Therapy in Dynamite"   Apr-10-1974
"The Trade-Off"   Mar-02-1975
"A Very Deadly Game"   Sep-29-1974

KRAFT TELEVISION THEATER

"Old MacDonald Had a Curve"   Aug-05-1953   TV-script
"Patterns"   Jan-12-1955   TV-script

KUNG FU

"Chains"   Mar-08-1973
"Kung Fu"   Feb-22-1972   TV-movie pilot
"A Praying Mantis Kills"   Mar-22-1973
"Superstition"   Apr-05-1973

LEAVE IT TO BEAVER

"Baby Picture"   Oct-31-1959   novelized as "Beaver's Baby Picture"
"Beaver and Henry"   Jun-18-1958   novelized as "Beaver's Big Game"
"Beaver and Violet"   May-07-1960
"Beaver Gets Adopted"   Feb-26-1959
"Beaver Makes a Loan"   Dec-12-1959
"Beaver the Athlete"   Jun-11-1959   novelized as "Beaver Plays Ball"

"Beaver the Magician"	Dec-19-1959	
"Beaver's Accordion"	Dec-24-1960	
"Beaver's Hero"	Apr-09-1959	
"Beaver's Pigeons"	Feb-12-1959	novelized as "Beaver and the Pigeons"
"Beaver's Short Pants"	Dec-13-1957	novelized as "Beaver Goes Shopping"
"Chuckie's New Shoes"	Dec-10-1960	
"The Horse Named Nick"	Apr-02-1959	novelized as two stories: "Beaver Goes to the Carnival" and "The Horse Named Nick"
"Lonesome Beaver"	Feb-28-1958	novelized as "Beaver and Wally"
"School Sweater"	Mar-05-1960	novelized as "Beaver and the School Sweater"
"Wally, the Businessman"	May-28-1960	novelized as "Wally Goes Into Business"
"Wally, the Lifeguard"	Oct-22-1960	
"Wally's Glamour Girl"	Dec-03-1960	
"Wally's Haircomb"	May-21-1959	
"Wally's Job"	May-28-1958	novelized as "Beaver and Wally"
"Wally's Play"	Jun-11-1960	

LUCAN

"Lucan"	May-22-1977	TV-movie pilot

LUCAS TANNER

"Lucas Tanner"	May-08-1974	TV-movie pilot
"A Matter of Love"	Sep-11-1974	
"Three Letter Word"	Oct-23-1974	

MAN FROM ATLANTIS

Show was piloted in four TV-movies, listed below in air-date order.

"Man From Atlantis"	Mar-04-1977	TV-movie pilot
"Death Scouts"	May-07-1977	sequel
"Killer Spores"	May-17-1977	sequel
"The Disappearances"	Jun-20-1977	sequel

MANNIX

"The Faces of Murder"	Feb-04-1973
"A Fine Day for Dying"	Oct-06-1974
"Round Trip to Nowhere"	Jan-02-1971
"A Walk on the Blind Side"	Oct-13-1974

MCCLOUD

"The Barefoot Stewardess Caper"	Dec-03-1972
"Butch Cassidy Rides Again"	Oct-14-1973
"The Disposal Man"	Dec-29-1971
"Lady on the Run"	Jan-26-1975
"The New Mexico Connection"	Oct-01-1972
"The Solid Gold Swingers"	Dec-02-1973

MCCOY

"The Big Ripoff"	Mar-11-1975	TV-movie pilot

MEDICAL STORY

| "Medical Story" | Sep-04-1975 | pilot episode |
| "The Right to Die" | Sep-11-1975 | |

MIAMI VICE

"Brother's Keeper"	Sep-16-1984	pilot episode, aka "Miami Vice"
"Calderone's Dream"	Oct-26-1984	
"Hit List"	Oct-19-1984	

MR. MERLIN

| "Mr. Merlin" | Oct-07-1981 | pilot episode, aka "The Cloning of the Green" |

MORK AND MINDY

| "Mork Moves In" | Sep-14-1978 | pilot episode, aka "Mork Hour Special" |
| "Mork Runs Away" | Sep-28-1978 | |

MURDER, SHE WROTE

"Deadly Lady"	Oct-07-1984	
"Horray for Homicide"	Oct-28-1984	
"It's a Dog's Life"	Nov-04-1984	
"Lovers and Other Killers"	Nov-18-1984	
"The Murder of Sherlock Holmes"	Sep-30-1984	pilot episode

THE NAKED CITY

"And a Merry Christmas to the Force on Patrol"	Dec-23-1958	
"Lady Bug, Lady Bug ..."	Dec-09-1958	
"Line of Duty"	Oct-14-1958	
"Meridian"	Sep-30-1958	pilot episode
"Nickel Ride"	Oct-07-1958	
"The Other Face of Goodness"	Dec-02-1958	
"Susquehanna 7-8367"	Dec-16-1958	
"The Violent Circle"	Oct-28-1958	

THE NAME OF THE GAME

| "Los Angeles: 2017" | Jan-15-1971 | |

THE NEW AVENGERS

"The Eagle's Nest"	Sep-05-1978	pilot episode
"House of Cards"	Oct-20-1978	
"To Catch a Rat"	Feb-16-1979	

THE NEW BREED

| "No Fat Cops" | Oct-03-1961 | pilot episode |

NIGHT GALLERY

"Clean Kills and Other Trophies"	Jan-06-1971	
"The Different Ones"	Dec-29-1971	
"Lindemann's Catch"	Jan-12-1972	

"Lone Survivor"	Jan-13-1971	novelized as "Soul Survivor"
"Make Me Laugh"	Jan-06-1971	
"The Messiah on Mott Street"	Dec-15-1971	
"Pamela's Voice"	Jan-13-1971	
"They're Tearing Down Tim Riley's Bar"	Jan-20-1971	

THE NIGHT STALKER

"The Night Strangler"	Jan-16-1973	TV-movie led to series

PAPER DOLLS

"Paper Dolls"	May-24-1982	TV-movie led to series

THE PERSUADERS

"Angie, Angie"	Mar-08-1972
"Five Miles to Midnight"	Feb-16-1972
"Overture"	Sep-18-1971
"Someone Like Me"	Nov-27-1971

THE PHIL SILVERS SHOW

Shooting scripts

"The Big Uranium Strike"	Mar-20-1956	
"Bilko in Wall Street"	May-15-1956	aka "Butterworth, Butterworth & Butterworth"
"Bilko's Battle With Hollywood"	Jan-03-1956	aka "Hollywood"
"The Bivouac"	Nov-29-1955	aka "Sick Call Ernie"
"The Case of Harry Speakup"	Mar-06-1956	aka "The Court Marshall"
"The Con Men"	May-01-1956	
"Dinner at Sowici's"	Feb-14-1956	
"The Millionaire"	Dec-27-1955	aka "Rich Kid" aka "The Platoon's Saloon"
"The Motor Pool Mardi Gras"	Nov-08-1955	aka "Mardi Gras"
"Personal Transportation Provided"	Oct-04-1955	aka "WAC"
"Rest Cure"	Feb-07-1956	
"The Singing Contest"	Dec-06-1955	aka "Singing Platoon"
"Transfer"	Jan-31-1956	
"The Visiting Congressman"	Jan-10-1956	aka "Investigation" aka "The Big Investigation"

PLANET OF THE APES

"The Cure"	Nov-29-1974
"The Deception"	Nov-01-1974
"The Gladiators"	Sep-20-1974
"The Good Seeds"	Oct-04-1974
"The Horse Race"	Nov-08-1974
"The Legacy"	Oct-11-1974
"The Surgeon"	Oct-25-1974
"The Tyrant"	Nov-22-1974

PLAYHOUSE 90

"Requiem for a Heavyweight"	Oct-11-1956	TV-script, found in *Kraft Television Theater* tie-in

POLICE WOMAN

"The Beautiful Die Young"	Sep-20-1974
"Warning: All Wives..."	Sep-27-1974

PRIVATE EYE

"Blue Movie"	Oct-02-1987	
"Flip Side"	Oct-16-1987	2-part episode, concluded Oct-23
"Nicky the Rose"	Sep-18-1987	
"Nobody Dies in Chinatown"	Nov-13-1987	
"Private Eye"	Sep-13-1987	pilot episode
"War Buddy"	Sep-25-1987	

QUINCY, M.E.

"Go Fight City Hall--To the Death"	Oct-03-1976	pilot episode
"The Thigh Bone's Connected to the Hip Bone"	Feb-11-1977	

RETURN TO THE PLANET OF THE APES

Episodes listed in air-date order

"Flames of Doom"	Sep-06-1975	pilot episode
"Escape from Ape City"	Sep-13-1975	
"A Date with Judy"	Sep-20-1975	aka "The Unearthly Prophecy"
"Tunnel of Fear"	Sep-27-1975	
"Lagoon of Peril"	Oct-04-1975	
"Terror on Ice Mountain"	Oct-11-1975	
"River of Flames"	Oct-18-1975	
"Screaming Wings"	Oct-25-1975	
"Trail to the Unknown"	Nov-01-1975	

THE ROCKFORD FILES

"The Kirkoff Case"	Sep-13-1974	
"The Rockford Files"	Mar-27-1974	TV-movie pilot
"This Case is Closed"	Oct-18-1974	

THE ROOKIES

"The Rookies"	Mar-07-1972	TV-movie pilot

S.W.A.T.

"Death Score"	Apr-07-1975	aka "Red September"

THE SAINT

"The Art Collectors"	Jul-30-1967
"The Death Game"	May-21-1967
"The Persistent Patriots"	Apr-27-1968
"The Power Artist"	Mar-09-1968

SAM BENEDICT

"Twenty Aching Years"	Oct-20-1962

SEARCH

| "Moonrock" | Oct-04-1972 | |
| "Probe" | Feb-21-1972 | TV-movie pilot |

THE SIX MILLION DOLLAR MAN

"The Deadly Test"	Oct-19-1975	
"Double Trouble"	Oct-03-1976	
"Love Song for Tanya"	Feb-15-1976	
"Pilot Error"	Sep-27-1974	
"The Rescue of Athena One"	Mar-15-1974	
"The Secret of Bigfoot Pass"	Feb-01-1976	2-part episode, concluded Feb-04
"Solid Gold Kidnapping"	Nov-17-1973	
"Straight On 'Til Morning"	Nov-08-1974	
"Wine, Women and War"	Oct-20-1973	

THE SIXTH SENSE

| "Witch, Witch Burning Bright" | Mar-11-1972 | shooting script |

SONS AND DAUGHTERS

| "Senior Year" | Mar-22-1974 | TV-movie pilot |

SPACE: 1999

Season One

All episodes in Season One but "Earthbound" were novelized in the Pocket series.

"Alpha Child"	Oct-14-1975
"Another Time, Another Place"	Sep-23-1975
"The Black Sun"	Nov-11-1975
"Breakaway"	Sep-09-1975
"Collision Course"	Sep-30-1975
"Death's Other Dominion"	Dec-30-1975
"Dragon's Domain"	Dec-16-1975
"Earthbound"	Jan-19-1976
"End of Eternity"	Nov-18-1975
"Force of Life"	Oct-07-1975
"The Full Circle"	Dec-23-1975
"Guardian of Piri"	Oct-21-1975
"The Infernal Machine"	Jan-26-1976
"The Last Enemy"	Dec-09-1975
"The Last Sunset"	Feb-09-1976
"Matter of Life and Death"	Sep-16-1975
"The Mission Link"	Feb-02-1976
"Mission of the Darians"	Nov-04-1975
"Ring Around the Moon"	Jan-06-1976
"Space Brain"	Feb-16-1976
"The Testament of Arkadia"	Dec-02-1975
"The Troubled Spirit"	Feb-23-1976
"Voyager's Return"	Nov-25-1975
"War Games"	Oct-28-1975

Season Two

All episodes in Season Two but "The Taybor" were novelized in the
Warner series.

"A B Chrysalis"	Nov-13-1976	
"All That Glisters"	Sep-25-1976	
"The Beta Cloud"	Jan-16-1977	
"Brian the Brain"	Oct-30-1976	
"The Bringers of Wonder"	Feb-20-1977	2-part episode, concluded Feb-27
"The Catacombs of the Moon"	Nov-20-1976	
"Devil's Planet"	Mar-20-1977	
"The Dorcons"	Mar-27-1977	
"Dorzak"	Mar-06-1977	
"The Exiles"	Dec-12-1976	
"The Immunity Syndrome"	Mar-13-1977	
"Journey to Where"	Oct-02-1976	
"The Lambda Factor"	Jan-23-1977	
"Mark of Archanon"	Oct-23-1976	
"A Matter of Balance"	Jan-09-1977	
"The Metamorph"	Sep-18-1976	
"New Adam, New Eve"	Oct-16-1976	
"One Moment of Humanity"	Jan-30-1977	
"The Rules of Luton"	Nov-06-1976	
"The Seance Spectre"	Feb-13-1977	
"Seed of Destruction"	Nov-27-1976	
"Space Warp"	Jan-02-1977	
"The Taybor"	Oct-09-1976	

STAR TREK

All 78 episodes are novelized in the Bantam series. Episodes are
listed alphabetically, with the book number in the Bantam series given.

"All Our Yesterdays"	Mar-14-1969	Book 4
"The Alternative Factor"	Mar-30-1967	Book 10
"Amok Time"	Sep-15-1967	Book 3
"And the Children Shall Lead"	Oct-11-1968	Book 12
"The Apple"	Oct-13-1967	Book 6
"Arena"	Jan-19-1967	Book 2
"Assignment: Earth"	Mar-29-1968	Book 3
"Balance of Terror"	Dec-15-1966	Book 1
"Bread and Circuses"	Mar-15-1968	Book 11
"By Any Other Name"	Feb-23-1968	Book 6
"The Carbomite Maneuver"	Nov-10-1966	Book 12
"Catspaw"	Oct-27-1967	Book 8
"The Changeling"	Sep-29-1967	Book 7
"Charlie X"	Sep-15-1966	Book 1
novelized as "Charlie's Law"		
"The City on the Edge of Forever"	Apr-06-1967	Book 2
"The Cloud Minders"	Feb-28-1969	Book 6
"The Conscience of the King"	Dec-08-1966	Book 1
"Court Martial"	Feb-02-1967	Book 2

"Dagger of the Mind"	Nov-03-1966	Book 1
"Day of the Dove"	Nov-01-1968	Book 11
"The Deadly Years"	Dec-08-1967	Book 7
"The Devil in the Dark"	Mar-09-1967	Book 4
"The Doomsday Machine"	Oct-20-1967	Book 3
"Elaan of Troyius"	Dec-20-1968	Book 7
"The Empath"	Dec-06-1968	Book 10
"The Enemy Within"	Oct-06-1966	Book 8
"The Enterprise Incident"	Sep-27-1968	Book 4
"Errand of Mercy"	Mar-23-1967	Book 2
"For the World is Hollow, And I Have Touched the Sky"	Nov-08-1968	Book 8
"Friday's Child"	Dec-01-1967	Book 3
"The Galileo Seven"	Jan-05-1967	Book 10
"The Gamesters of Triskelion"	Jan-05-1968	Book 12
"I, Mudd"	Nov-03-1967	Mudd's Angels
"The Immunity Syndrome"	Jan-19-1968	Book 9
"Is There in Truth No Beauty?"	Oct-18-1968	Book 10
"Journey to Babel"	Nov-17-1967	Book 4
"Let That Be Your Last Battlefield"	Jan-10-1969	Book 5
"The Lights of Zetar"	Jan-31-1969	Book 6
"The Man Trap" (pilot episode) novelized as "The Unreal McCoy"	Sep-08-1966	Book 1
"The Mark of Gideon"	Jan-17-1969	Book 6
"The Menagerie" - 2-part episode, concluded Nov-24	Nov-17-1966	Book 4
"Metamorphosis"	Nov-10-1967	Book 7
"Miri"	Oct-27-1966	Book 1
"Mirror, Mirror"	Oct-06-1967	Book 3
"Mudd's Women"	Oct-13-1966	Mudd's Angels
"The Naked Time"	Sep-29-1966	Book 1
"Obsession"	Dec-15-1967	Book 9
"The Omega Glory"	Mar-01-1968	Book 10
"Operation--Annihilate!"	Apr-13-1967	Book 2
"The Paradise Syndrome"	Oct-04-1968	Book 7
"Patterns of Force"	Feb-16-1968	Book 12
"A Piece of the Action"	Jan-12-1968	Book 4
"Plato's Stepchildren"	Nov-22-1968	Book 11
"A Private Little War"	Feb-02-1968	Book 10
"Requiem for Methuselah"	Feb-14-1969	Book 5
"The Return of the Archons"	Feb-09-1967	Book 9
"Return to Tomorrow"	Feb-09-1968	Book 9
"The Savage Curtain"	Mar-07-1969	Book 6
"Shore Leave"	Dec-29-1966	Book 12
"Space Seed"	Feb-16-1967	Book 2
"Spectre of the Gun" novelized as "The Last Gunfight"	Oct-25-1968	Book 3
"Spock's Brain"	Sep-20-1968	Book 8
"The Squire of Gothos"	Jan-12-1967	Book 11
"A Taste of Armageddon"	Feb-23-1967	Book 2
"That Which Survives"	Jan-24-1969	Book 9

"This Side of Paradise"	Mar-02-1967	Book 5
"The Tholian Web"	Nov-15-1968	Book 5
"Tomorrow Is Yesterday"	Jan-26-1967	Book 2
"The Trouble With Tribbles"	Dec-29-1967	Book 3
"Turnabout Intruder"	Mar-28-1969	Book 5
"The Ultimate Computer"	Mar-08-1968	Book 9
"The Way to Eden"	Feb-21-1969	Book 5
"What Are Little Girls Made of?"	Oct-20-1966	Book 11
"Where No Man Has Gone Before"	Sep-22-1966	Book 8
"Who Mourns for Adonais?"	Sep-22-1967	Book 7
"Whom Gods Destroy"	Jan-03-1969	Book 5
"Wink of an Eye"	Nov-29-1968	Book 11
"Wolf in the Fold"	Dec-22-1967	Book 8

STAR TREK ANIMATED SERIES

All 22 episodes are novelized in the Star Trek Log Book series.
Episodes are listed alphabetically, with the book number in
the Ballantine series given.

"Albatross"	Sep-28-1974	Book 6
"The Ambergris Element"	Dec-01-1973	Book 5
"Bem"	Sep-14-1974	Book 9
"Beyond the Farthest Star"	Dec-22-1973	Book 1
"The Counter-Clock Incident"	Oct-12-1974	Book 7
"The Eye of the Beholder"	Jan-05-1974	Book 8
"How Sharper Than a Serpent's Tooth"	Oct-05-1974	Book 6
"The Infinite Vulcan"	Oct-20-1973	Book 2
"Jihad"	Jan-13-1974	Book 5
"The Lorelei Signal"	Sep-29-1973	Book 2
"The Magicks of Megas-Tu"	Oct-27-1973	Book 3
"More Tribbles, More Troubles"	Oct-06-1973	Book 4
"Mudd's Passion"	Nov-10-1973	Book 3
"Once Upon a Planet"	Nov-03-1973	Book 3
"One of Our Planets is Missing"	Sep-23-1973	Book 1
"The Pirates of Orion"	Sep-09-1974	Book 5
"Practical Joker"	Sep-21-1974	Book 6
"Slaver Weapon"	Dec-15-1973	Book 10
"The Survivor"	Oct-13-1973	Book 2
"The Terratin Incident"	Nov-17-1973	Book 4
"Time Trap"	Nov-24-1973	Book 4
"Yesteryear" (pilot episode)	Sep-15-1973	Book 1

STAR TREK: THE NEXT GENERATION

"Encounter at Farpoint"	Sep-26-1987	pilot episode

THE STARLOST

"The Starlost"	Sep-22-1973	pilot episode, aka "Voyage of Discovery"

STARSKY AND HUTCH

"Bounty Hunter"	Apr-21-1976	
"Death Ride"	Sep-24-1975	
"Kill Huggy Bear"	Oct-29-1975	
"The Psychic"	Jan-15-1977	
"The Set-Up"	Jan-22-1977	2-part episode, concluded Jan-29
"Starsky and Hutch"	Apr-30-1975	TV-movie pilot
"Starsky and Hutch on Playboy Island"	Sep-17-1977	
"Terror on the Docks"	Nov-26-1975	

STOREFRONT LAWYERS

"A Man's Castle"	Sep-16-1970	pilot episode

SWITCH

"Round Up the Usual Suspects"	Mar-23-1976	
"Switch"	Mar-21-1975	TV-movie pilot

TALES FROM THE DARKSIDE

"The Devil's Advocate"	Syndicated
"Halloween Candy"	Syndicated
"In the Cards"	Syndicated
"Inside the Closet"	Syndicated
"The Odds"	Syndicated

TALES OF WELLS FARGO

"Alder Gulch"	Apr-08-1957	novelized as "The Vigilantes"
"The Auction"	Oct-28-1957	
"Belle Star"	Sep-09-1957	
"Billy the Kid"	Oct-21-1957	
"Doc Bell"	Jan-06-1958	
"John Wesley Hardin"	Sep-30-1957	
"Sam Bass"	Jun-10-1957	
"The Walking Mountain"	Feb-03-1958	novelized as "The Glory Hole"

THE TWILIGHT ZONE

"Back There"	Jan-13-1961	
"The Big, Tall Wish"	Apr-08-1960	
"Dust"	Jan-06-1961	
"Escape Clause"	Nov-06-1959	
"The Fever"	Jan-29-1960	
"A Hundred Yards Over the Rim"	Apr-07-1961	novelized as "Beyond the Rim"
"Judgment Night"	Dec-04-1959	
"The Lonely"	Nov-13-1959	
"The Man in the Bottle"	Oct-07-1960	
"The Midnight Sun"	Nov-17-1961	
"The Mighty Casey"	Jun-17-1960	
"The Mirror Image"	Feb-26-1960	
"Mr. Dingle, the Strong"	Mar-03-1961	
"The Monsters Are Due on Maple Street"	Mar-04-1960	
"The Night of the Meek"	Dec-23-1960	

"The Odyssey of Flight 33"	Feb-24-1961	
"The Purple Testament"	Feb-12-1960	
"The Rip Van Winkle Caper"	Apr-21-1961	
"The Shelter"	Sep-29-1961	
"Showdown with Rance McGrew"	Feb-02-1962	
"A Stop at Willoughby"	May-06-1960	
"A Thing About Machines"	Oct-28-1960	
"Walking Distance"	Oct-30-1959	
"Where is Everybody?"	Oct-02-1959	pilot episode
"The Whole Truth"	Jan-20-1961	

UFO

"Close-Up"	Syndicated	
"The Computer Affair"	Syndicated	
"Court Martial"	Syndicated	
"The Dalotek Affair"	Syndicated	
"Exposed"	Syndicated	
"Identified"	Syndicated	pilot episode
"Survival"	Syndicated	

U.S. STEEL HOUR

"The Rack"	Apr-12-1955	TV-script, found in *Kraft Television Theater* tie-in

V

"V"	May-01 - May-02-1983	2-part mini-series
"V: The Final Battle"	May-06 - May-08-1984	3-part sequel

VEGA$

"Vega$"	Apr-25-1978	TV-movie pilot

VOYAGERS!

"Voyagers!"	Oct-03-1982	pilot episode

THE WALTONS

"The Crisis"	Apr-19-1973	aka "An Easter Story"
"The Love Story"	Jan-18-1973	
"The Reunion"	Dec-14-1972	
"The Separation"	Sep-27-1973	
"The Typewriter"	Oct-12-1972	

TV SHOWS WITH TV TIE-INS

A FOR ANDROMEDA
THE A-TEAM
ADAM-12
THE ADDAMS FAMILY
THE ADVENTURES OF JIM BOWIE
  See JIM BOWIE
ALFRED HITCHCOCK PRESENTS
ALIAS SMITH AND JONES
ALL IN THE FAMILY
ALL MY CHILDREN
AMAZING STORIES
AMERICAN BANDSTAND
THE AMERICANS
ANDY BURNETT
  See WALT DISNEY
ANNA AND THE KING
ANNETTE
  See THE MICKEY MOUSE CLUB
ANNIE OAKLEY
ANOTHER WORLD
APPLE'S WAY
THE AQUANAUTS
ARREST AND TRIAL
ART LINKLETTER'S HOUSE
  PARTY
THE ARTHUR MURRAY PARTY
AS THE WORLD TURNS
THE ASPHALT JUNGLE
THE ASSOCIATES
THE AVENGERS
BAA BAA BLACK SHEEP
  See BLACK SHEEP SQUADRON
BANACEK
BANYON
BARETTA
BAT MASTERSON

BATMAN
BATTLESTAR GALACTICA
BEACON HILL
BEAUTY AND THE BEAST
BEN CASEY
THE BEVERLY HILLBILLIES
BEWITCHED
THE BIG VALLEY
THE BIONIC WOMAN
BLACK SHEEP SQUADRON
BLAKE'S 7
BLONDIE
THE BOLD ONES
BONANZA
BOOTS AND SADDLES
BRACKEN'S WORLD
THE BRADY BUNCH
THE BRIAN KEITH SHOW
  See THE LITTLE PEOPLE
BRIDGET LOVES BERNIE
THE BROTHERS BRANNAGAN
THE BUCCANEERS
BUCK ROGERS IN THE 25TH
  CENTURY
THE BUGALOOS
BURKE'S LAW
CHiPs
CADE'S COUNTY
CAGNEY & LACEY
CAIN'S HUNDRED
CAN YOU TOP THIS?
CANNON
CAPITOL
CAPTAIN DAVID GRIEF
CAPTAIN NICE
CHARLES IN CHARGE

CHARLIE'S ANGELS
CHASE
CHEERS
CHEYENNE
CHICO AND THE MAN
CIMMARON STRIP
CIRCUS BOY
COLUMBO
COMBAT
DAKTARI
DALLAS
DANGER MAN
DARK SHADOWS
DAVY CROCKETT
  See WALT DISNEY
DAYS OF OUR LIVES
THE DEFENDERS
THE DEPUTY
THE DETECTIVES
DIVORCE COURT
DOBIE GILLIS
  See THE MANY LOVES OF
  DOBIE GILLIS
DR. I.Q.
DR. KILDARE
DOCTOR WHO
THE DOCTORS
DOCTOR'S HOSPITAL
DRAGNET
THE DUKES OF HAZZARD
DYNASTY
THE EDGE OF NIGHT
EIGHT IS ENOUGH
87TH PRECINCT
ELLERY QUEEN
EMERGENCY!
EXECUTIVE SUITE
F TROOP
FALCON CREST
FAMILY
FAMILY AFFAIR
FAMILY FEUD
FAMILY TIES
FANTASY ISLAND
FATHER MURPHY
FATHER OF THE BRIDE
THE FELONY SQUAD
FISH
FLIGHT
THE FLIP WILSON SHOW
FLIPPER

THE FLYING NUN
FRONTIER
THE FUGITIVE
FURY
GADABOUT GADDIS
GALACTICA 1980
  See BATTLESTAR GALACTICA
THE GANGSTER CHRONICLES
GARRISON'S GORILLAS
THE GENE AUTRY SHOW
GENERAL HOSPITAL
GENTLE BEN
GET SMART
GETTING TOGETHER
THE GHOST AND MRS. MUIR
GIDGET
GILLIGAN'S ISLAND
THE GIRL FROM U.N.C.L.E.
THE GIRL WITH SOMETHING
  EXTRA
GOMER PYLE, U.S.M.C.
THE GONG SHOW
GOOD TIMES
THE GREEN HORNET
GRIFF
GRIZZLY ADAMS
  See THE LIFE AND TIMES OF
  GRIZZLY ADAMS
GROWING PAINS
GUESTWARD HO!
THE GUIDING LIGHT
GUNSMOKE
HAPPY DAYS
THE HARDY BOYS/NANCY DREW
  MYSTERIES
HARRY O
HAVE GUN, WILL TRAVEL
HAWAII FIVE-O
HAWAIIAN EYE
HAWK
HAZEL
HEAD OF THE CLASS
HEC RAMSEY
HERE COME THE BRIDES
HERE'S LUCY
THE HIGH CHAPARRAL
THE HOLLYWOOD SQUARES
HONEY WEST
HOTEL DE PAREE
HOUSE PARTY
  See ART LINKLETTER

HOW THE WEST WAS WON
I DREAM OF JEANNIE
I LOVE LUCY
I SPY
THE IMMORTAL
IN SEARCH OF ...
THE INCREDIBLE HULK
THE INVADERS
THE INVISIBLE MAN
THE IRON HORSE
IRONSIDE
IT TAKES A THIEF
IT'S YOUR MOVE
THE JACK PAAR TONIGHT SHOW
JAMES AT 15
JERICHO
JIM BOWIE
JOANIE LOVES CHACHI
JOHNNY STACCATO
JUDD FOR THE DEFENSE
KNIGHT RIDER
KNOTS LANDING
KOJAK
KRAFT TELEVISION THEATER
KUNG FU
LANCER
LAND OF THE GIANTS
LASSIE
LAUGH-IN
LAVERNE AND SHIRLEY
THE LAWRENCE WELK SHOW
LEAVE IT TO BEAVER
THE LENNON SISTERS
  See LAWRENCE WELK SHOW
LET'S MAKE A DEAL
THE LIFE AND TIMES OF GRIZZLY
  ADAMS
THE LINEUP
THE LINKLETTER SHOW
  See ART LINKLETTER'S HOUSE
  PARTY
LITTLE HOUSE ON THE PRAIRIE
THE LITTLE PEOPLE
LONGSTREET
LOST IN SPACE
LOVE, AMERICAN STYLE
THE LOVE BOAT
LOVE OF LIFE
LUCAN
LUCAS TANNER
THE LUCY SHOW
MCCLOUD

MCCOY
MACKENZIE'S RAIDERS
M SQUAD
M*A*S*H
MAGNUM, P.I.
MAMA
MAN FROM ATLANTIS
THE MAN FROM U.N.C.L.E.
MANNIX
THE MANY LOVES OF DOBIE
  GILLIS
MARCUS WELBY, M.D.
MARKHAM
MARY HARTMAN, MARY HARTMAN
THE MARY TYLER MOORE SHOW
MATT LINCOLN
MAVERICK
MAYA
MEDICAL CENTER
MEDICAL STORY
THE MEN FROM SHILOH
MEN INTO SPACE
MIAMI UNDERCOVER
MIAMI VICE
MICHAEL SHAYNE
THE MICHAELS IN AFRICA
THE MICKEY MOUSE CLUB
MISSION: IMPOSSIBLE
MR. ED
MR. LUCKY
MR. MERLIN
THE MOD SQUAD
THE MONKEES
MORK & MINDY
THE MOST DEADLY GAME
THE MUNSTERS
MURDER, SHE WROTE
MY FRIEND TONY
THE NAKED CITY
NAKIA
THE NAME OF THE GAME
NANCY
NANCY DREW
  See THE HARDY BOYS/NANCY
  DREW MYSTERIES
NANNY AND THE PROFESSOR
THE NEW AVENGERS
THE NEW BREED
THE NEW PEOPLE
THE NEWLYWED GAME
NIGHT GALLERY
THE NIGHT STALKER

THE NURSES
ONE LIFE TO LIVE
ONE STEP BEYOND
THE OUTCASTS
THE OUTSIDER
THE PAPER CHASE
PAPER DOLLS
PAPER MOON
THE PARTRIDGE FAMILY
THE PATTY DUKE SHOW
PEOPLE ARE FUNNY
PERRY MASON
THE PERSUADERS
PETER GUNN
PEYTON PLACE
THE PHIL SILVERS SHOW
PHYLLIS DILLER
PLANET OF THE APES
PLAYHOUSE 90
PLEASE DON'T EAT THE DAISIES
POLICE WOMAN
PRIMUS
THE PRISONER
PRISONER: CELL BLOCK H
PRIVATE EYE
QUINCY, M.E.
THE RAT PATROL
RAWHIDE
THE REAL MCCOYS
THE REBEL
THE RESTLESS GUN
RETURN TO THE PLANET OF THE
   APES
RHODA
THE RIFLEMAN
RIN TIN TIN
RIPCORD
RIPLEY'S BELIEVE IT OR NOT!
ROALD DAHL'S TALES OF THE
   UNEXPECTED
THE ROARING 20'S
THE ROCKFORD FILES
THE ROOKIES
ROOM 222
ROWAN & MARTIN'S LAUGH-IN
   See LAUGH-IN
THE ROY ROGERS SHOW
S.W.A.T.
THE SAINT
SAM BENEDICT
THE SANDY DUNCAN SHOW

SANFORD AND SON
SATURDAY NIGHT LIVE
SEA HUNT
SEARCH
SEARCH FOR TOMORROW
SECRET AGENT
THE SECRET STORM
SERGEANT BILKO
   See THE PHIL SILVERS SHOW
SERPICO
77 SUNSET STRIP
SHAFT
THE SHARI LEWIS SHOW
THE SILENT FORCE
THE SILENT SERVICE
SIR LANCELOT
THE SIX MILLION DOLLAR MAN
THE SIXTH SENSE
THE $64,000 QUESTION
THE SMITH FAMILY
SONS AND DAUGHTERS
SPACE: 1999
SPENSER: FOR HIRE
SPIN AND MARTY
   See THE MICKEY MOUSE CLUB
STAR TREK
STAR TREK ANIMATED SERIES
STAR TREK: THE NEXT
   GENERATION
THE STARLOST
STARSKY AND HUTCH
STOREFRONT LAWYERS
STRANGE PARADISE
STRANGE REPORT
SURFSIDE 6
SWITCH
TALES FROM THE DARKSIDE
TALES OF THE UNEXPECTED
   See ROALD DAHL'S TALES OF
   THE UNEXPECTED
TALES OF WELLS FARGO
TAMMY
TARZAN
THAT GIRL
THAT'S INCREDIBLE!
THEN CAME BRONSON
THE THIRD MAN
THIS MAN DAWSON
THUNDER
THE TIME TUNNEL
TOMA

THE TONIGHT SHOW STARRING
  JOHNNY CARSON
TRIALS OF O'BRIEN
TWELVE O'CLOCK HIGH
TWENTY-ONE
THE TWILIGHT ZONE
UFO
THE UGLIEST GIRL IN TOWN
THE UNTOUCHABLES
V
VEGA$
THE VIRGINIAN
VOYAGE TO THE BOTTOM OF
  THE SEA
VOYAGERS!
WACKIEST SHIP IN THE ARMY
WAGON TRAIN
WALT DISNEY

THE WALTONS
WANTED: DEAD OR ALIVE
WELCOME BACK, KOTTER
WELLS FARGO
  See TALES OF WELLS FARGO
WHAT ARE THE ODDS?
WHEEL OF FORTUNE
THE WILD WILD WEST
WYATT EARP
YOU'LL NEVER GET RICH
  See THE PHIL SILVERS SHOW
THE YOUNG AND THE RESTLESS
YOUNG DR. KILDARE
THE YOUNG LAWYERS
THE YOUNG REBELS
ZORRO

GRADING THE CONDITION OF TV TIE-INS

When viewed as items for collecting rather than for reading, the physical condition of the TV tie-ins becomes important. Square, tight spines and crisp, uncreased, blemish-free covers are the goal. Paperback books are graded on a scale which ranges from Mint to poor, and is the same grading scale used for other categories of antiques and paper collectibles. Each level of condition is described following, as an aid to the collector in the grading of the books in his or her own collection. Allowances are also made for variances between grades, such as Fine Minus (FN-), Very Fine Plus (VF+), etc.

Mint (M): A perfect book; just as clean and fresh and bright as the day it was issued; unopened; not a single blemish to be found; very rarely if ever is this grade used.

Near Mint (NM): A near perfect book; only a few very minor blemishes to be found upon close inspection; possibly unopened and almost certainly unread; spine square (sits at 90 degree angles from the covers); binding tight (covers unable to be opened far before resisting); cover and spine free from all but the smallest and fewest signs of wear; pages white; though quite uncommon this grade is sometimes found.

Very Fine (VF): A very high quality book; should be satisfying to even the most discriminating collector; a book showing minor flaws but whose overall condition is extremely sound; probably unread, or very carefully read; binding tight; spine square or nearly square (the faint beginnings of a spine role might be allowed); cover and spine fresh and bright, but a few minor impressions are allowed, such as creases, edge chips, or portions of rubbing or fading; no bends (severe creases); no spine tears (perpendicular rips across the spine); pages mostly white, though some slight yellowing might be detected along the edges; few if any interior flaws, such as writing; this grade is somewhat common.

Fine (FN): A sound, quality book; would be satisfying to many but not all collectors; a book with more noticeable flaws than the prior grade, perhaps a wider assortment of small flaws or one or two more serious flaws, but no severe flaws; no tape; binding likely less tight but cover likely not able to be fully opened; some spine role allowed; cover creases possible but few if any bends, and no serious bends; crease along the edge of the spine possible, from someone having read the book; spine tear possible; a respectable, if unsuperior, copy; this grade is fairly common.

Very Good (VG): An average quality book, flawed to the extent that many collectors would want to upgrade it; a well-worn book but not a bad book; this is the grade at which major flaws become present, if few in number, like cover bends, spine roles, spine tears, and significant interior wear; perhaps read by someone with no thought of preserving the book in mind; tightness likely gone; tape allowed; probably most books are in this condition.

Good (G): A definitely flawed copy but still intact and complete; a wide assortment of problems; a reading copy.

fair (f): A bad copy; a more severe or flawed example of the prior grade.

poor (p): A horrible copy; incomplete; pages or parts of the cover missing and many and great flaws present; the only reason to keep such a copy is for informational purposes.

NOTE: Some paperback book dealers use a different grading scale from the above, which instead ranges from Fine to poor. For comparative purposes, if using that scale, substitute the grades described above with the following grades: Mint (Fine), Near Mint (About Fine), Very Fine (Very Good/Fine), Fine (Very Good), Very Good (Good/Very Good), Good (Good), fair (poor).

SELECTED INDEX

BIBLIOGRAPHY

Alfred Hitchcock Presents, John McCarty and Brian Kelleher. St. Martin's Press (New York), 1985.

All My Afternoons: The Heart and Soul of the TV Soap Opera, Annie Gilbert. A & W Visual Library (New York), 1979.

Archie & Edith, Mike & Gloria: The Tumultuous History of All in the Family, Donna McCrohan. Workman Publishing (New York), 1987.

Bilko: The Fort Baxter Story, David Thomas and Ian Irvine. Vermilion (London), 1985.

Books in Print (Various Editions), R.R. Bowker Company (New York).

British Books in Print (Various Editions), J. Whitacre & Sons, Ltd. (London).

Captain's Logs: The Complete Trek Voyages, Edward Gross & Mark A. Altman. Image Publishing, 1993.

Children's Fiction Sourcebook, Margaret Hobson, Jennifer Madden, and Ray Prytherch. Ashgate Publishing Co. (Brookfield, Vermont), 1992.

Cinema Sequels and Remakes, 1903-1987, Robert A. Nowlan and Gwendolyn Wright Nowlan. McFarland & Company, Inc. (Jefferson, North Carolina), 1989.

Collectible Coloring Books, Dian Zillner. Schiffer Publishing, Ltd. (West Chester, Pennsylvania), 1992.

The Columbo Phile: A Casebook, Mark Dawidziak. The Mysterious Press (New York), 1989.

The Complete Actors' Television Credits, 1948-1988 (second edition), James Robert Parish and Vincent Terrace. The Scarecrow Press, Inc. (Metuchen, New Jersey), 1990.

The Complete Directory to Prime Time Network TV Shows, 1946-Present (Third Edition), Tim Brooks and Earle Marsh. Ballantine Books (New York), 1985.

The Complete Directory to Prime Time TV Stars, 1946-Present, Tim Brooks. Ballantine Books (New York), 1987.

The Complete Encyclopedia of Television Programs, 1947-1976 (Two Volume Set), Vincent Terrace. A.S. Barnes and Co., Inc. (New York), 1976.

Contemporary Authors (Various Editions), Thomas Wiloch, Index Coordinator. Gale Research Company (Detroit).

Contemporary Science Fiction Authors (First Edition), R. Reginald, Editor. Arno Press (New York), 1975.

Crime Fiction II: A Comprehensive Bibliography 1749-1990, Allen J. Hubin. Garland
   Publishing, Inc. (New York), 1994.
Cult TV: A Viewer's Guide to the Shows America Can't Live Without!!, John Javna. St.
   Martin's Press (New York), 1985.
Cumulative Paperback Index, 1939-1959, R. Reginald and M.R. Burgess.   Gale
   Research Company (Detroit), 1973.
Daytime Television Programming, Marilyn J. Matelski. Focal Press (Boston), 1991.
Dell Paperbacks, 1942 to Mid-1962: A Catalog-Index, William H. Lyles. Greenwood
   Press (Westport, Connecticut), 1983.
The Doctor Who Programme Guide, Volume 1, Jean-Marc Lofficier. Target Books
   (London), 1981.
The Emmys: Star Wars, Showdowns, and the Supreme Test of TV's Best, Thomas O'Neil.
   Penguin Books (New York), 1992.
The Encyclopedia of Animated Cartoons, Jeff Lenburg. Facts On File (New York),
   1991.
The Encyclopedia of Frontier and Western Fiction, Jon Tuska and Vicki Piekarski
   (Editors). McGraw Hill (New York), 1983.
The Encyclopedia of Science Fiction, John Clute and Peter McNicholls (Editors). Orbit
   (London), 1993.
The Encyclopedia of Science Fiction and Fantasy Through 1968, Donald H. Tuck.
   Advent: Publishers, Inc. (Chicago), 1978.
The Encyclopedia of Television Series, Pilots and Specials, 1937-1973, Vincent Terrace.
   New York Zoetrope (New York), 1986.
The Encyclopedia of Television Series, Pilots and Specials, 1974-1984, Vincent Terrace.
   New York Zoetrope (New York), 1985.
An Encyclopedia of Trekkie Memorabilia: Identification and Value Guide, Chris Gentry
   & Sally Gibson-Downs. Books Americana (Florence, Alabama), 1988.
Epi-Log Magazine (Various Issues), William E. Anchors, Jr.   Epi-Log Magazine
   (Dunlap, Tennessee).
The Famous Mister Ed: The Unbridled Truth About America's Favorite Talking Horse,
   Nancy Nalven. Warner Books (New York), 1991.
The Fugitive Recaptured: The 30th Anniversary Companion to a Television Classic, Ed
   Robertson. Pomegranate Press, Ltd. (Los Angeles), 1993.
The Great TV Sitcom Book (Expanded Edition), Rick Mitz. Perigree Books (New York),
   1988.
The Guide to Supernatural Fiction, Everett F. Bleiler. The Kent State University Press
   (Kent, Ohio), 1983.
Gunsmoke: A Complete History and Analysis of the Legendary Broadcast Series,
   SuzAnne Barabas and Gabor Barabas. McFarland & Company, Inc. (Jefferson,
   North Carolina), 1990.
Hake's Guide to TV Collectibles: An Illustrated Price Guide, Ted Hake.   Wallace-
   Homestead Book Company (Radnor, Pennsylvania), 1990.
Hancer's Price Guide to Paperback Books (Third Edition), Kevin Hancer. Wallace-
   Homestead Book Company (Radnor, Pennsylvania), 1990.
*Hawk's Authors' Pseudonyms II: A Comprehensive Reference of Modern Authors'
   Pseudonyms*, Pat Hawk (Southlake, Texas), 1995.

How Sweet It Was - Television: A Pictorial Commentary, Arthur Shulman and Roger Youman. Bonanza Books (New York), 1966.

International Authors and Writers Who's Who (various editions), Ernest Kay, Editor. Melrose Press (Cambridge, England).

Leonard Maltin's Movie and Video Guide 1995, Leonard Maltin. Signet Books (New York), 1994.

Les Brown's Encyclopedia of Television (3rd Edition), Lester L. Brown. Visible Ink Press (Detroit), 1992.

Lowery's The Collector's Guide to Big Little Books and Similar Books, Lawrence F. Lowery. Educational Research and Applications Corporation (Danville, California), 1981.

Magill's Survey of Cinema, English Language Films, Frank N. Magill, Editor. Salem Press (Englewood Cliffs, New Jersey), 1981.

The Man From U.N.C.L.E. Book, Jon Heitland. Titan Books (London), 1987.

The Motion Picture Guide, Jay Robert Nash and Stanley Ralph Ross, Editors. Cinebooks, Inc. (Chicago), 1985.

Motion Picture Series and Sequels: A Reference Guide, Bernard A. Drew. Garland Publishing, Inc. (New York), 1990.

Movies Made for Television, The Telefeature and the Mini-Series, 1964-1986, Alvin H. Marill. New York Zoetrope (New York), 1987.

The Nancy Drew Scrapbook, Karen Plunkett-Powell. St. Martin's Press (New York), 1993.

The Official Batman Batbook, Joel Eisner. Contemporary Books, Inc. (Chicago), 1986.

Official Price Guide Paperbacks (First Edition), Jon Warren. House of Collectibles (New York), 1991.

Official Price Guide Star Trek and Star Wars Collectibles (Third Edition), Sue Cornwell and Mike Kott. House of Collectibles (New York), 1991.

Official Price Guide to Paperbacks & Magazines, Charles and Donna Jordan. House of Collectibles (New York), 1986.

Paperback Parade: The Magazine For Paperback Readers and Collectors, Issue 18, Gryphon Publications (New York), May, 1990. "British TV Tie-Ins," Greg Goode and Grant Thiessen.

Paperbacks, U.S.A. - A Graphic History, 1939-1959, Piet Schreuders. Blue Dolphin Enterprises, Inc. (San Diego), 1981.

Prime-Time Television: A Pictorial History From Milton Berle to "Falcon Crest", Fred Goldstein & Stan Goldstein. Crown Publishers (New York), 1983.

Pseudonyms and Nicknames Dictionary (Third Edition), Jennifer Mossman. Gale Research Company (Detroit), 1987.

Putting Dell on the Map: A History of the Dell Paperbacks, William H. Lyles. Greenwood Press (Westport, Connecticut), 1983.

The Saint: A Complete History in Print, Radio, Film and Television of Leslie Charteris' Robin Hood of Modern Crime, Simon Templar, 1928-1991, Burl Barer. McFarland & Company, Inc. (Jefferson, North Carolina), 1993.

Science Fiction and Fantasy Literature, A Checklist 1700-1974, R. Reginald. Gale Research Company (Detroit), 1979.

Science Fiction and Fantasy Literature, 1975-1991, Robert Reginald. Gale Research Company (Detroit), 1992.

Serial Adventures, James Van Hise. Pioneer Books (Las Vegas), 1990.

The Soap Opera Encyclopedia, Christopher Schemering. Ballantine Books (New York), 1985.

Tarzan Of The Movies: A Pictorial History Of More Than Fifty Years Of Edgar Rice Burroughs' Legendary Hero, Gabe Essoe. The Citadel Press (Secaucus, New Jersey), 1968.

Television Comedy Series: An Episode Guide to 153 TV Sitcoms in Syndication, Joel Eisner & David Krinsky. McFarland & Company, Inc. (Jefferson, North Carolina), 1984.

Television Detective Shows of the 1970's: Credits, Storylines and Episode Guides for 109 Series, David Martindale. McFarland & Company, Inc. (Jefferson, North Carolina), 1991.

Television Drama Series Programming: A Comprehensive Chronicle, 1947-1959, Larry James Gianakos. The Scarecrow Press, Inc. (Metuchen, New Jersey & London), 1980.

Television Drama Series Programming: A Comprehensive Chronicle, 1959-1975, Larry James Gianakos. The Scarecrow Press, Inc. (Metuchen, New Jersey & London), 1978.

Television Drama Series Programming: A Comprehensive Chronicle, 1975-1980, Larry James Gianakos. The Scarecrow Press, Inc. (Metuchen, New Jersey & London), 1981.

Television Drama Series Programming: A Comprehensive Chronicle, 1980-1982, Larry James Gianakos. The Scarecrow Press, Inc. (Metuchen, New Jersey & London), 1987.

Television Drama Series Programming: A Comprehensive Chronicle, 1982-1984, Larry James Gianakos. The Scarecrow Press, Inc. (Metuchen, New Jersey & London), 1987.

Total Television: A Comprehensive Guide to Programming from 1948 to the Present (Third Edition), Alex McNeil. Penguin Books (New York), 1991.

TV Babylon, Jeff Rovin. Signet Books (New York), 1984.

TV Book: The Ultimate Television Book, Judy Fireman, Editor. Workman Publishing Company (New York), 1977.

The TV Collector Magazine (Various Issues), Diane L. Albert, Writer/Editor (Easton, Massachusetts).

The TV Encyclopedia, David Inman. Perigree Books (New York), 1991.

Twentieth-Century Crime and Mystery Writers (Third Edition), Lesley Henderson, Editor. St. James Press (Chicago and London), 1991.

Twentieth-Century Romance and Historical Writers (Second Edition), Lesley Henderson, Editor. St. James Press (Chicago and London), 1990.

Twentieth-Century Science-Fiction Writers (Third Edition), Noelle Watson & Paul E. Schellinger, Editors. St. James Press (Chicago and London), 1991.

Twentieth-Century Western Writers (Second Edition), Geoff Sadler, Editor. St. James Press (Chicago and London), 1991.

The Twilight Zone Companion, Marc Scott Zicree. Bantam Books (New York), 1982.

Two-Bit Culture: The Paperbacking of America, Kenneth C. Davis. Houghton Mifflin Company (Boston), 1984.

Video Movie Guide 1993, Nick Martin & Marsha Porter. Ballantine Books (New York), 1992.

The Video Sourcebook (16th Edition), Anjanelle M. Klisz, Editor. Gale Research Company (Detroit), 1995.

Who's Who (Various Series and Volumes), Marquis Who's Who, Inc. (Chicago).

Who's Who in Hollywood: The Largest Cast of International Film Personalities Ever Assembled, David Ragan. Facts On File (New York), 1992.

Who's Who in Television and Cable, Steven E. Scheuer, Editor. Facts On File (New York), 1983.

The World According to Beaver, Irwyn Applebaum. Bantam Books (New York), 1984.

The World Encyclopedia of Cartoons, Maurice Horn, Editor. Chelsea House Publishers (New York), 1983.

The World Encyclopedia of Comics, Maurice Horn, Editor. Chelsea House Publishers (New York), 1983.

and

The Author's Own TV Tie-In Collection

ABOUT THE AUTHOR

The author was born in France and grew up in the Pacific Northwest. He received a degree in Political Science from the University of Washington, and currently lives in Tucson, Arizona, where he appraises commercial real estate by profession. A movie and classic TV buff, he has collected TV tie-ins for many years, rarely reading, but carefully cataloguing each title for reasons even he doesn't fully understand. His unique literary odyssey has culminated in this work, which he hopes is both informative and fun.